THE ABOMINATION OF DESOLATION

A SERIES OF SEVEN
BOOK 1

CHARLES SCHIAVO

WHITE PINE
PUBLISHING
Consultants

CONTENTS

Foreword	ix

PART I

1. INTELLIGENT DESIGN	3
2. THE EVERLASTING GOSPEL	21
Interesting Information	22
The Message For This Time Part One	24
The Message Continues - The Sacrificial Offerings Symbolizing Christ's Death Upon Calvary's Cross Is Not The Atonement!	31
3. A BRIEF INTRODUCTION TO – THE BORN AGAIN EXPERIENCE	36
4. THAT SHALL SAVE HIS PEOPLE FROM THEIR SINS	39
They shall Call Evil Good and Good Evil – Justification by Faith Is Not God's Completed Work for Our Salvation	41
5. SANCTIFICATION IS GOD'S PREDETERMINED PLAN FOR OUR SALVATION	55
God Has Predestined All to be Saved Through the Sanctification of Their Characters	55
Sanctification is a Bible Doctrine	62
6. WHOSOEVER COMMITS SIN TRANSGRESSES – ALSO GOD'S HOLY TEN COMMANDMENT LAW	79
7. RESPECTING CASE AGREEMENT	88
Opening Statement	
The Retranslation of Romans 6:12-13	100
The Retranslation of Romans 6:15	103
The Retranslation of Romans 6:15-16	107
The Retranslation of Romans 6:17-19	110
The Retranslation of Romans 6:20-23	111
8. IN ROMANS 7:4-6 THE APOSTLE SAYS WE HAVE DIED TO THE LAW	113

9. THE APOSTLE PAUL SAYS - CHRIST IS THE END OF THE LAW FOR ALL WHO BELIEVE	125
10. THE APOSTLE PAUL SAYS – IF YOU ARE LED BY THE SPIRIT, YOU ARE NOT UNDER THE LAW	137
The Retranslation of Galatians 5:16-18	144
The retranslation of Galatians 5:19-21	146
Conclusion	147
11. THE PROTESTANT AND EVANGELICAL CHURCHES SAY – GOD'S HOLY LAW WAS NAILED TO THE CROSS	149
Opening Statement	149
The Retranslation of Colossians 2:8-14	152
The Retranslation of Colossians 2:15-17	155
12. THE PROTESTANT AND EVANGELICAL CHURCHES CLAIM – GOD'S HOLY LAW HAS BEEN ABOLISHED	165
Closing Thoughts	172
13. THE PARABLE OF THE WEDDING FEAST	179
14. SPIRITUAL INFLATION – THE ILLUSION OF SALVATION, NOW AND IN THE JUDGMENT	188
15. FIGHT THE GOOD FIGHT OF FAITH	200
16. LEGALISM IS MANMADE SALVATION	210
Legalism! Legalism!	213
17. THE MYSTERY HIDDEN FOR AGES	224
18. EVERY IDLE WORD MEN SHALL SPEAK – THEY SHALL GIVE ACCOUNT IN THE JUDGMENT	245
19. THE "TRUE WITNESS" SAYS "I KNOW YOUR WORKS"	259

PART II
A MESSAGE FOR THIS TIME!

20. THE SECOND WOE HAS PASSED –	269
Behold The Third Woe Will Come Quickly	
21. THIS IS OUR ASSURANCE – "THE LAODICEAN MESSAGE"	306
22. THE HEALTH MESSAGE IS THE RIGHT ARM OF THE THREE ANGEL'S MESSAGE	317
23. LET THE READER UNDERSTAND	348

Conclusion	353
Coming Soon...	371

The Abomination of Desolation, Volume 1

© 2025 by Charles Schiavo

All rights reserved. No part of this book may be reproduced, stored in a retrieval system, or transmitted in any form or by any means—electronic, mechanical, photocopying, recording, or otherwise—without the prior written permission of the publisher, except for brief quotations used in reviews or articles.

Published by
White Pine Publishing
P.O. Box 112
Posen, MI 49776
info@whitepinepublishing.com
989-464-9499 (call or text)

First Edition: 2025

ISBN:
978-1-77443-113-9 Hardcover book
978-1-77443-112-2 Electronic book
978-1-77443-111-5 Paperback

Printed in the United States of America.

For permissions or inquiries, contact:
White Pine Publishing
P.O. Box 112
Posen, MI 49776
info@whitepinepublishing.com
989-464-9499 (call or text)

To the family I never knew I had and everything that make me whole.

FOREWORD

As someone who assisted in publishing this book, I had the pleasure of engaging deeply with Charles's ideas. His work is not just a study of biblical prophecy; it is a challenge—to read scripture with precision, to test its claims, and to consider its implications for the past, present, and future. Throughout this book, Charles urges readers to pay close attention to key passages, particularly in *Daniel 11* and *Revelation 17*, as they provide a prophetic lens through which history and destiny converge.

A central influence on Charles's work is *The Great Controversy* by Ellen G. White. In that text, White presents history as the unfolding of a cosmic struggle between truth and deception, between God's law and human rebellion. Charles expands on this framework, refining its implications and applying them to our time. Like White, he sees prophecy not as a collection of vague or mystical predictions, but as a structured, historical account of God's interaction with humanity.

To approach this book as a philosopher, particularly a Platonist, is to recognize its search for an underlying order beneath the surface of religious history. Plato taught that beyond the world of appearances lies a realm of Forms—unchanging, eternal truths that shape the transient realities we experience. In a similar way, *The Great Contro-*

versy and *The Abomination of Desolation* suggest that history is not a series of random events but the unfolding of a divine pattern. Charles's method is rigorous and exacting; he asks not only what the scriptures say, but how they align with historical developments and eschatological truth.

Both *The Great Controversy* and this book argue that we are living in a climactic moment of history. As in Plato's *Allegory of the Cave*, where the philosopher struggles to bring light to those in darkness, Charles's work is an attempt to illuminate the forces at play in the world—forces that many do not recognize. He challenges readers to examine not just their beliefs but their assumptions about reality itself. The battle over truth, as both White and Charles argue, is not merely a theological debate; it is the foundation of history's final conflict.

This book is not an easy read, nor is it meant to be. It demands careful thought, rigorous examination, and a willingness to question comfortable narratives. Whether you are a believer, a seeker, or a skeptic, Charles's approach insists on intellectual engagement. He does not ask for passive acceptance but for critical reflection.

In that spirit, I encourage you to read this book with an open but discerning mind. Consider its claims, weigh its arguments, and above all, seek the deeper reality beneath the surface of the text.

Daniel Sanderson

PART I

1

INTELLIGENT DESIGN

It was during the final editing of this book that I made a business trip to Denver, Colorado, to provide financing for a sporting complex in Virginia Beach, Virginia. During that trip, I did a little sightseeing to mix business with a minute of pleasure. Some of the tourist attractions I visited during the trip to Colorado were the Rocky Mountain National Park, the Garden of the Gods, and Pikes Peak, just to name a few. However, Pikes Peak was my favorite. This majestic monument stands 14,183 feet above sea level and has both a road and a railroad train capable of taking visitors to the summit of the mountain. The temperature at the bottom of the mountain was a comfortable 55 degrees and very calm. However, by the time I got to the top of Pikes Peak, the temperature was radically different; 23 degrees below zero with winds gusting between 30 to 50 miles per hour. Those at the top of the mountain managing the visitor's center said these types of weather conditions were quite normal. On the way to the top, at around 11,500 feet above sea level, I observed the trees had stopped growing. At around 13,500 feet, I stopped to read a sign on the side of the road the park officials had provided for those driving to the top in their cars.

After getting out of the car with the wind whipping around 35 miles per hour, producing a wind-chill factor low enough to make even breathing a chore, I was able to scratch off some of the frost that had accumulated on the surface of the sign I was attempting to read. During this brief moment, I read something that had a tremendous impact on my mind regarding the theory of evolution versus creation. The little bit of information I was able to read on the sign stated, "past this point in elevation no life can exist for any length of time" because of the severity of the elements and being considerably higher than the tree line, no vegetation could grow to sustain life. Notwithstanding my desire to read on, the harsh weather conditions forced me back into my car, however, while curiously thinking about the content of the message I continued to the top of the mountain. When finally reaching the top, I asked one of the workers inside the visitor center what the information on the sign meant. She stated that past 13,500 feet no life could exist for any length of time due to the lack of vegetation, and the weather conditions were too extreme to sustain life. This information inspired me to write the first chapter of this book, and I decided to title it, "Intelligent Design."

I have talked to people for years, who claim they are agnostics, atheists, and/or professed Christians who deny the biblical accounts of creation and believe in some theory blending evolution and creation. All three groups similarly believe humans evolved from some lower forms of life into what we are today. The very foundation of this theory must acknowledge that matter has always existed because every scientist has admitted life could not possibly evolve out of something that does not exist. Consequently, to be an agnostic, atheist, and/or a professed Christian who believes in a theory blending evolution with creation, all three groups have either knowingly or unknowingly accepted the assumption that matter has always existed because life cannot evolve out of something that simply does not exist. With this understanding already firmly established in my mind, the question I asked myself while at the top of Pikes Peak was very simple. Addressing the illogical conclusion reached by the agnostics, atheists, and/or professed Christians who deny the biblical account of creation while subliminally accepting the idea that matter has always existed, the question that must be asked is how could life evolve out of the lifeless environment of open space, which is set at three degrees Kelvin above absolute zero, if nothing can exist at the top of Pikes Peak, past 13,500 feet above sea-level, because of the extreme weather conditions and the absence of vegetation?

In the year 1905, Albert Einstein introduced the theory of relativity in a paper entitled "The Electrodynamics of Moving Bodies." Einstein's theory of relativity addresses the structure of space-time travel. However, if looked at more closely, using the foundation of Einstein's theory one can mathematically compute the effect moving objects have on the space-time continuum when traveling at any speed in the vacuum of open space. With the following small adjustments made to Einstein's equation $E = mc^2$, [energy [E] is equal to the mass [M] of an object times the speed of light [C] squared] someone could conclude that angels traveling in the vacuum of open space would use no time to arrive at their destination unlike those objects subjected to gravitational fields. This concept is based upon the idea that everything travels at a predetermined speed with time travel set at the speed of light, $E = mc^2$; thus, if the speed of time were exceeded then angels traveling faster than light would arrive at their destination instantly, while those subjected to gravitational fields would take millions of years to arrive at the same location.

Accepting Einstein's conclusion that mass creates gravitational fields, then gravitational fields affect the time it takes for someone to travel from point A to point B, which is essentially Einstein's "theory of relativity." Accepting Einstein's equation that $E = mc^2$ correctly calculates the speed of light, then Einstein's "theory of relativity" states if the speed of light is exceeded traveling from point A to point B is reached instantaneously, without affecting the relativity of the space-time continuum. According to Einstein's theory of relativity, when the speed of light is exceeded, which requires negative mass, those traveling faster than time through the vacuum of open space will not affect their relativity to those subjected to the bonds of gravitational fields. However, Einstein's "theory of relativity" breaks down if point B is endless. If point B is the end of the universe, then point B is infinite, which must be represented by the constant X in the proposed mathematical equation, and the entire equation must be reversed-divided by the exponent D, representing the final destination which is also an infinite number. When traveling at 60 miles per hour calculating the exponent is very simple. Spead equals distance divided by time. Consequently, time equals distance divided by speed, and when you substitute this time value into this formula, time equals 1/60 of the distance traveled, which is the exponent in the mathematical equation when calculating the time it takes to get to your destination when traveling at 60 miles an hour. Consequently, after making the mathematical adjustments to Einstein's equation, $E = mc^2$, if you travel faster than the speed of light from point A to point B, with point B representing the end of the universe, which is endless, you will instantly arrive at point A, with all things remaining relative. Those traveling faster than the speed of light simply get to their destination instantly; consequently, the proposed mathematical equation just presented establishes that the universe is endless. Albert Einstein also stated that the temperature in the nothingness of open space was for some unknown reason set at about 3 degrees (Kelvin) above absolute zero, which is much colder than the 23 degrees Fahrenheit below zero I experienced while at the top of Pikes Peak. This idea (the temperature of open space) has been universally accepted by the scientific world and presents a real problem for agnostics and atheists who believe in some form of evolution outside of the biblical accounts of creation to establish the origin of life.

The Milky Way galaxy is home to approximately 400 billion stars and our own sun and solar system. Scientists believe it would take a spaceship traveling at the speed of light 200,000 years to cross the entire Milky Way galaxy. It is estimated that there are between 200 billion (2×10^{11}) to two trillion galaxies in the observable universe. Most galaxies are 1,000 to 100,000 parsecs in diameter (approximately 3,000 to 300,000 light years) and are separated by distances on the order of millions of parsecs (hereafter megaparsecs). The parsec symbol is (PC) representing the length used to measure the distances between astronomical objects outside the Solar System. One Parsec is equal to the distance light travels in one year, which is 3.26 light-years. Since one Parsec represents the distance light travels in one year, one (PC) would equal 206,265 astronomical units (AU) or (19.2 trillion miles). In the classic film Star Wars, Han Solo claimed that his Millennium Falcon "made the Kessel Run in less than twelve parsecs." The Kessel Run was one of the most heavily used smuggling routes in the Galactic Empire; however, it's interesting to note that a parsec represents the distance between astronomical objects outside our Solar System, not the speed it takes to reach those astronomical objects. In addition, to emphasize how ridiculously inaccurate Han Solo's claim was "that his Millennium Falcon made the Kessel Run in less than twelve parsecs," the only way anyone could travel twelve parsecs in less than one hundred thousand trillion lifetimes is if they were traveling faster than the speed of light. As established in the preceding paragraphs, if you travel faster than the speed of light you arrive at your destination instantaneously, however, all things remain relative to each other, and you don't affect the space-time continuum.

The cosmological horizon consists of the observable universe, which is made up of the galaxies where their light has already reached Earth, which excludes the galaxies and/or celestial bodies where powerful telescopes have not yet observed the light from these objects. Scientists believe that the cosmological horizon, consisting of the observable universe, makes up about 10% of the galaxies that actually exist in the observable universe. The fact is the universe is endless, which means there are an infinite number of galaxies existing in the unobservable universe. Astronomers have calculated that the present telescopes employed to observe the cosmological horizon, consisting of the observable universe, are about 13 billion years old. Regarding how old is the universe, the Bible doesn't give any expressed representations as to its exact age, however, many uninformed Christians erroneously believe the Earth and the Universe are only six thousand years old. They give evidence of the same by quoting Genesis 1:1; "In the beginning, God created the heavens and the earth." The Hebrew word בָּרָא translated as "created," appears in the perfect tense, and when retranslated by the 70 elders into the Greek language it appears in the Septuagint as a verb, in the indicative aorist, active, 3rd person singular. The aorist dictates the inspired writer is not designating any specific time when the creation of the heavens of the Earth took place, just that at some point in time God created the planet Earth with its atmosphere. It's also important that when researching (AU), the cosmological horizon, consisting of the observable universe, is about 13 billion years old, which is much older than the six thousand years most Christians believe the Earth and the universe are; however, the Hebrew word הַשָּׁמַיִם translated as "heavens" appears in the absolute construction, which means "the heavens" that were at some point in time created belong to the Earth, and have nothing to do with how old is the universe. Therefore, the cosmological horizon, consisting of the observable universe, represents a small fraction of several trillion galaxies and/or celestial bodies whose light has not yet been observed by powerful telescopes.

The solar system that planet Earth exists as the third planet consists of an extremely small star with several other planets revolving around the sun in a very specific order. It's important to understand that the cosmological horizon, which is the observable universe, has trillions of stars that are sometimes billions of times larger than our sun, which is extremely important to consider when contemplating the theory of creation vs evolution. If our sun was 10% larger, its gravitational pull would eventually suck all the planets that make up our solar system into its mass thereby increasing its size and the results of its mass increasing the sun's gravitational pull becoming much stronger. This phenomenon has resulted in stars existing in the universe that are billions of times larger than our sun, with their gravitational pull becoming so strong it results in a supernova explosion or the gravitational pull becoming so strong that it crushes the molecular construction of the atoms making up the molecules that form all matter, resulting in a black hole in the space-time continuum. In addition, if our sun was ten percent smaller the planets in the solar system would eventually drift off into outer space creating arctic winters that would eradicate all life as we know it today. Therefore, our existence on planet Earth is the direct result of several factors that have been perfectly calculated to sustain life as we observe it today, establishing there is without question an intelligent design to the universe.

Albert Einstein stated that the temperature in the observable universe was for some unknown reason set at about 3 degrees (Kelvin) above absolute zero. This idea (the temperature of open space) has been confirmed by the scientific world and presents a real problem for agnostics and atheists who believe in some form of evolution outside of the biblical accounts of creation to establish the origin of life. Using the thermodynamic temperature scale Kelvin, absolute zero is the point where no more heat can be removed "or extracted" from any object. According to the three thermodynamic temperature scales, absolute zero is equal to 0 degrees Kelvin, or -273.15 degrees Celsius, or -459.67 degrees Fahrenheit. In classic kinetic theory, there should be no movement of individual molecules at absolute zero; however, recent experiments have shown that this is not the case, which we will soon find out exposes a real problem with the theory of evolution. There are three temperature scales used to represent how hot or cold any object is at any given point in time. The temperature of any object depends on how fast the atoms inside the molecules are oscillating. At absolute zero, the oscillations of these atoms are the slowest they can possibly be however, recent studies have established that even at absolute zero the motion of these atoms, which make up the molecules that form the 100-plus elements found in the periodic table, do not completely stop.

Molecules are small particles that make up all living and non-living things. Molecules are made up of even smaller particles called atoms. Atoms are made up of even smaller particles called protons, neutrons, and electrons. The protons and neutrons that make up the core of every atom are made up of even smaller particles called quarks. In the basic construction of every atom, electrons rotate around its core, which is made up of protons and neutrons. The electrons are about 2,000 times smaller than the protons, which are just slightly smaller than neutrons. If a hydrogen atom were drawn to scale, the electrons are so small if the core of an atom were the size of a golf ball the electrons rotating around its core would be about 2,500 miles apart at their furthest point. The following information is extremely important as it stands at the foundation of the controversy between creation and evolution. The specific number of protons and neutrons that make up the core of every atom, along with the electrons rotating around its core, determines the difference between the 100-plus elements found in the periodic table. Of the 100-plus different elements that make up the periodic table, 75% exist in all living things.

All matter, living or non-living, exists in five states: solid, liquid, gas, plasmas, and something referred to as a condensate, with the latter called, the "Bose-Einstein Condensate," which can only be unnaturally achieved in scientific laboratories. When matter is unnaturally cooled to temperatures approaching "absolute zero," the "intelligent design" that governs the interworking of the atom stops functioning. As a result, matter collapses into something called a quantum state. When matter is unnaturally cooled to "absolute zero," the disorganization this cooling has on the molecules becomes apparent when viewed at a microscopic scale. In this unnatural quantum state, when light is passed through matter its speed is slowed to less than 15 miles per hour. Einstein demonstrated that cooling matter to very low temperatures caused the programming [the intelligent design] of that atom to become disorganized and collapse (or "condense") into an abnormal quantum state, which resulted in a new fifth state of matter. In this disorganized fifth state of matter, it would be impossible to differentiate between any of the 100-plus elements on the periodic table because the "intelligent design" of the molecules, which make up all matter, has stopped functioning correctly. With molecular motion almost stopped, the atoms simply collapse (falls) into a quantum state, and the 100-plus elements that make up all matter on the periodic table no longer retain their identity. All matter becomes the same when unnaturally cooled to temperatures approaching absolute zero, the atoms collapse into an unnatural quantum state resulting from the lack of molecular motion. Therefore, by expounding upon Einstein's discovery, the fraud indigenous to evolution will be clearly exposed, because the conditions existing in the lifeless environment of open space are for some unknown reason uniformly fixed by some intelligent designer at about three (3) degrees Kelvin above absolute zero, where the disorganized fifth state of matter, the "Bose-Einstein Condensate," doesn't naturally exist.

The controversy can now be made very clear, the Apostle Paul speaking of Christ says, "He is the image of the invisible God, the first-born of all creation; for by Him all things were created in heaven and on earth, visible and invisible whether thrones or dominions or principalities or authorities-all things were created through Him and by Him all things hold together." Colossians 1:15-16. Conversely, according to the positions held by agnostics, atheists, and/or professed Christians who deny the biblical accounts of creation, all three groups believe that intelligent life evolved from matter that has always existed, first as a solid, then as a liquid, a gas, and then in its plasma form. The agnostics, atheists, and/or the professed Christians who deny the biblical accounts of creation do not believe that matter existed in the Bose-Einstein condensate, because this state of matter completely undermines the theory of evolution.

As stated before, the Bose-Einstein condensate creates a real problem for the evolutionist by clearly establishing there is an intelligent designer of the universe, which settles the controversy between creation and evolution. Why? Because the facts will reveal that some "intelligent designer" set the temperature of the lifeless environment of open space at three (3) degrees Kelvin above absolute zero, by which all things hold together. Our scientists have already stated that the liquid, gas, and/or plasma forms of matter came into existence after the solid state of matter. They believe the solid state of matter evolved into these higher forms of matter, and then life as we know it evolved from that point in time. This conclusion also causes some real problems for evolutionists. The theory of evolution, which has been universally accepted by the scientific world, has at its very foundation the belief that pre-existing solid dust particles floating around in the vacuum of open space, held together because the temperature was set at three (3) degrees Kelvin above absolute zero, bonded together and eventually form the liquid, gas, and plasma forms of matter seen in our world today. This theory is predicated upon the preexisting fact that any moving object produces kinetic energy resulting from the motion of that object bouncing off other solid objects producing even more kinetic energy. The belief that life emerged from this theory is better known today as evolution.

According to evolutionists, after trillions of years, life evolved from the results of kinetic energy created from the motion of preexisting dust particles that were held together because the temperature of outer space was set no lower than three degrees Kelvin above absolute zero. These preexisting dust particles somehow bonded together to form one large body of matter that superheated and then exploded forming billions of galaxies. This is called "The Big Bang Theory." When properly considered, the basis of "The Big Bang Theory" also denies the very foundation of evolution. Why? Because the theory of evolution is based upon an intelligent designer of the universe establishing the pre-existing law of kinetic energy and the preexisting law holding all things together. Since "The Big Bang Theory" is based upon these two preexisting laws, then evolution is flawed, why, because there must have been an intelligent designer of the universe who established these two preexisting laws. Therefore, since matter cannot hold together at temperatures less than three (3) degrees Kelvin above absolute zero and the Big Bang Theory is predicated upon the belief that moving objects produce kinetic energy, then whoever established these two preexisting laws is the intelligent designer of the universe; and it's my intention to prove that the intelligent designer of the universe is Jesus Christ who holds all things together by the power of His might. Colossians 1:15-16.

A perfect vacuum is created when the gaseous pressure of absolute zero is obtained. At one time, this was only a philosophical concept. However, the effects of cooling matter to "absolute zero" have now been observed not just in theory but also in practical application by those scientists who advocate that life evolved from kinetic energy, which is produced from the motion of pre-existing dust particles rubbing together and exploding after trillions of years. They believe this theory over the biblical accounts of creation. As stated earlier the reaction of atoms existing in the unnatural fifth state of matter called the "Bose-Einstein Condensate," creates some real problems for those who believe in "The Big Bang Theory." The Big Bang Theory not only relies upon the preexisting law holding these pre-existing dust particles together in the vacuum of open space but also subliminally relies upon the belief in the law dictating that these pre-existing dust particles produce kinetic energy when colliding with pre-existing dust particles in addition to the pre-existing laws of molecular structure.

The controversy can now be clearly exposed; the evolutionists believe that life resulted from the production of kinetic energy which is produced from the motion of pre-existing dust particles that are made up of molecules that form the basic structure of all matter. This means [which is obvious] that the "intelligent design" of the molecules also pre-existed these alleged pre-existing dust particles. The idea that life came into existence after trillions of years resulting from the pre-existing law of kinetic energy which is produced from the motion of these pre-existing dust particles [also held together by pre-existing laws] establishes there must be a pre-existing "intelligent designer" of the universe and where there is intelligence there is a living thinking being. Consequently, according to the evolutionists "The Big Bang Theory" is based upon the pre-existing law of kinetic energy producing heat resulting from the motion of pre-existing dust particles bonding together which caused them to eventually superheat and then explode into separate galaxies. In conjunction with this idea, "The Big Bang Theory" also concludes that during the cooling process, the pre-existing matter that was held together because the temperature of the universe was set at three degrees Kelvin above absolute zero eventually transformed into the higher forms of matter and evolved into the complex living organisms seen in our world today _**and all this took place in the frigid environment of open space**_.

The question that must be posed to the evolutionists, who so illogically believe in their beloved "Big Bang Theory," is this, did the law that determines kinetic energy is produced from the motion of pre-existing objects colliding together also pre-exist the law holding all these preexisting dust particles together? Think about what I'm saying right now, in addition, the programming that holds all things together must have also pre-existed the preexisting dust particles. In addition, the intelligent design of the molecule[s] themselves [that makes up the preexisting dust particles] must have also pre-existed the actual preexisting dust particles themselves, why, because its identity is dictated by how many electrons rotate around the core of its atom, along with the specific number of protons and neutrons that make up its core, which in turn defines the difference between these preexisting dust particle[s] and the other 100 plus elements found in the periodic table? This means the intelligent design of the molecule[s] must have also pre-existed all pre-existing matter, not just the pre-existing dust particles themselves. If the pre-existing intelligent design of the molecule[s] along with the pre-existing law of kinetic energy and the pre-existing law holding all things together did not pre-exist all matter, there is no scientific platform for the evolutionists to conclude these pre-existing dust particles rubbed together and after trillions of years formed life as we know it today. Think about how destructive this argument is to the theory of evolution.

If the intelligent design of the universe is not set by a higher power, why does matter return to its original state after it's interrupted by the unnatural cooling of matter called the "Bose-Einstein Condensate?" Consequently then, and even more conclusive, is that the set programming reorganizes the same matter that's become disorganized when cooled to temperatures approaching absolute zero. The biblical accounts state God destroyed the antediluvian world by a flood because of their wickedness and all but Noah and his family were spared. Genesis 6:13-22. God gave Noah the exact dimensions of the ark and explicit directions regarding its construction. Consequently, I ask you which came first, the ark or the designer of the ark. Therefore, the question the evolutionists must answer is this, if the law that determines kinetic energy is produced from the motion of objects colliding, along with the law governing the design of the molecules themselves, and the law holding the same preexisting dust particles together, did these laws pre-exist the formation of all pre-existing matter; if the answer is yes then there is without question overpowering evidence clearly dictating there exists an "intelligent designer' of the universe.

Computers have always fascinated me, in fact, every time I go by a computer store, I experience a strong desire to go in and observe the latest and greatest technology. On one occasion, I attended a computer show where hundreds of merchants were gathered inside the Bob Carpenter Center located on the campus of the University of Delaware. After paying my admission fee, I wandered around the exhibits like a kid in a candy store. After becoming so completely intoxicated by all this technology, for some unknown reason I decided to build a computer with components I purchased from the vendors operating at the exhibits. Notwithstanding the fact that I simply did not have a clue how to build a computer, this served as no deterrent to curb my enthusiasm for building my own computer. I promptly spent twice the amount of money I normally would have if I simply purchased the computer from any computer store. At the end of my shopping extravaganza, what I had was a bunch of components floating around my office, and to make matters worse, when my computer was finally assembled, I discovered the components simply did not match. Consequently, without an operating system controlling the components I assembled into a working computer (even if I had purchased components that matched), with no operating system preordained by an "intelligent designer" giving life to the computer, at the end of the day all I had was a lifeless computer.

The computer parts floating around my office are like the dust particles the evolutionists' state have always existed that were floating around in the frigid environment of lifeless open space. Even if these dust particles, which allegedly pre-existed, were correctly assembled to form the 100 plus elements that make up the periodic table, without an operating system governing their behavior all you would have is a bunch of lifeless matter, "components" floating around in the frigid environment of lifeless open space that is held together because the temperature was set at 3 degrees Kelvin above absolute zero. Now think about the sign I read on the way to the top of Pikes Peak. Even if my computer was assembled correctly, with components that actually matched, if an operating system is not installed, and preordained by an "intelligent designer," all I would have is a lifeless computer. Albert Einstein said the temperature in the vacuum of open space is for some unknown reason fixed at 3 degrees Kelvin above absolute zero, thus excluding the fifth state of matter called the "Bose-Einstein Condensate;" conclusion [FACT] the only way all matter holds together is if it's preordained by an intelligent designer. This is the same intelligent designer Albert Einstein said must have "correctly" matched the exact number of protons, neutrons, and electrons establishing the difference between the 100-plus elements that make up the periodic table, which is interrupted when matter is cooled to temperatures approaching absolute zero. Therefore, the facts are clear there must be an "intelligent designer" of the universe, which the Bible says is Jesus Christ who holds all things together" by the power of his might. Colossians 1:15-16.

It takes more faith to conclude that life could evolve from pre-existing dust particles floating around in the lifeless environment of open space, which are held together because the temperature is set at three degrees Kelvin above absolute zero than it does for the Christian to believe in the biblical accounts of creation. The odds that at some point in time these allegedly "pre-existing" dust particles, existing in the lifeless environment of open space set at 3 degrees Kelvin above absolute zero, just happened to rub together to produce enough heat to correctly form the complex proteins and amino acids necessary to sustain life, (without "pre-existing programming) is beyond our mathematical capabilities to accurately compute. However, let us speculate on these odds through an example. The likelihood that life could evolve in the lifeless environment of open space, even with the pre-existing law setting the temperature of outer space at 3 degrees Kelvin above absolute zero holding these pre-existing dust particles together, [without a preexisting operating system governing molecular construction or the preexisting law governing kinetic energy] it would be greater than the odds of a tornado blowing through a local salvage yard and assembling a Boeing 767 Jetliner. Evolution requires blind faith in the pre-existence of all matter, yet more importantly, evolution requires a subliminal blind faith in the pre-existence of laws that govern the behavior of all this allegedly pre-existing matter. However, for the Christian, the fact that Christ, the Creator of the universe holds all things together by the power of His might, clearly established that this intelligent design is not conjecture, it is a reality!

At what point does any individual say, "Why am I here," as they ponder with amazement the magnificence of the intelligent design of the universe?" Every day people die, yet for others, life goes on. If you think about how small our earth is in relation to the enormity of the universe, with its complex solar systems, planets, suns, and galaxies, what other conclusion can you possibly make regarding the origin of the universe, except for the "Most High" is the intelligent designer of all things and accept the biblical accounts of creation? Think for a moment and imagine that you were the creator of all things and the only being that existed in the universe. As the creator, you knew the exact date and time each item was created, because you made everything that existed in the universe. Then, one day, you came upon something that you did not create. Let's say you found a Rolex Presidential Timepiece, a real marvel of engineering. What is the only logical conclusion you could make? That another being of equal creative ability also existed in the universe. Now look to the sky; admire the grandeur of the universe how much more magnificent is it than the Rolex Presidential Timepiece? This is why the prophet exclaims, "A fool in his heart says that there is no God." Psalms 14:1, and Psalms 53:1. Look to the heavens and count the stars if you can, and then ask yourself this question, who made these things? How could these things exist without the intelligent designer Albert Einstein said fixed the temperature of open space at 3 degrees Kelvin above absolute zero and not at "absolute zero" where no movement of individual molecules exists prohibiting all matter from holding together? Therefore, there is no other logical conclusion that can be reached; they exist and hold together because the intelligent designer of the universe is the "Most High" Who holds authority over eternity.

Except for creation, what could science or logic possibly offer anyone regarding the origin of the universe? There are only two positions that can account for the source of life. The first is obvious, the biblical account of creation. While this position has received criticism because it requires faith in a pre-existing Creator, the theory of evolution requires even more blind faith than does that of the creationists. Evolutionists are forced to accept the position that matter has always existed, which is ridiculous. They believe that matter has always pre-existed because life cannot be created out of matter that simply does not presently exist. In addition, they also unknowingly believe the complex operating system that governs the behavior of all living and non-living things must have also pre-existed all matter. These same scientists ridicule Christians who believe in a pre-existing Creator, who has no end or beginning, and while they vigorously claim everything must have a beginning, they inconsistently claim dust particles pre-existed all things. Evolutionists make this statement without applying the same criticism to their own theories regarding the origin of the universe.

The Christian believes the intelligent designer of the universe is Jesus Christ, the God of creation who has existed as long as time itself. Just as time has no beginning, so does He who is before all things; the God of creation is older than time itself. Imagine for a moment that nothing existed in the entire universe; it was completely void of all living and non-living things. The universe itself [emptied of all matter] is still something; so please try to eliminate "the empty universe itself" and think about what you would have left, now try and get rid of it; please think about what I'm saying. Think about trying to eliminate "the empty universe itself," it's impossible, and actually mind-boggling to a certain extent. If you ask the evolutionists how the universe came into existence; they will probably say it's as old as time itself; both have no beginning. The scientific community arrogantly maintains matter has always existed, while they deny the God of creation has always existed. Consequently, what takes more faith, to believe in the God of creation who has always existed or that matter has always existed along with its complex operating system governing the behavior of all living and non-living things? Therefore, the entire theory of evolution is based upon unfounded conjecture because it's based upon the theory that all matter has always existed along with the law holding all matter together, in addition to the pre-existing law of kinetic energy, and the law differentiating these pre-existing dust particles from the other 100 plus elements listed on the periodic table!

This chapter in this series of books has presented powerful arguments supporting the fact that the intelligent designer of the universe is the God of the Bible prophecies who holds all things together by the power of His might. Colossians 1:16-18. In an attempt to convince the reader, that the intelligent designer of the universe is the author of the Bible, great lengths have been taken to prove the extreme accuracy of the Bible prophecies. Once the prophecies are shown to be accurate, the gospel invitation advocated by the prophets and apostles can be accepted, comprehended, and the plan of salvation can be intelligently followed; thus, believers can be freed from "that which causes sin" in their lives thereby making them immune to Satan's temptations. The words of the prophets clearly detail the rise and fall of nations with such precision that it denies being a mere coincidence. However, some in their misguided logic take the position that the prophets wrote after the events foretold in the scriptures had actually taken place. With the discovery of the Dead Sea Scrolls, archeologists have unearthed every book of the Bible, except for the book of Ruth, and all these books have been verified and authenticated by experts on both sides of the creation question. The discovery of the Dead Sea Scrolls has not only confirmed the grammatical accuracy of the Bible but also the exactness of the chronological progression of the prophecies. As a result of the discovery of the Dead Sea Scrolls, no scoffer can say the prophets wrote after the historical events had taken place. The discovery of the Dead Sea

Scrolls has put these critics to rest. However, it doesn't matter what starting point in history the atheist and agnostic pick, I will prove the accuracy of Bible prophecy using any specific point in history. The precision and accuracy of the prophecies point to the Divine origin of the Bible; <u>**this fact, like creation, can only be ignored, it cannot be denied**</u>. 2 Peter 1:19. The reader's faith in the Bible and its Author can be firmly established because of the Bible's ability to predict future events before they have actually taken place. Therefore, this seven-book series of books titled "The Abomination of Desolation" is designed to introduce the reader to the "Most High" as the intelligent designer of the universe, who inspired the prophets and apostles to write of the everlasting gospel by which the fallen sons of Adam can be "born again" and subsequently freed from "that which causes sin" in their lives, and; as a result, obey and live. John 3:36.

2

THE EVERLASTING GOSPEL

Throughout history, humanity has been plagued by various deadly diseases, including the black plague, malaria, smallpox, and "HIV" human immunodeficiency virus, the virus that causes AIDS. These are just a few deadly diseases humanity has been forced to encounter. The alleged deadly virus COVID-19 is the latest killer disease humanity has encountered, and according to the U.S. Center for Disease Control, COVID-19 has been declared a pandemic. The U.S. Center for Disease Control and Prevention (CDC) is a privately owned company masquerading as a government agency. The CDC first recognized COVID-19 as a pandemic on March 11th, 2020; however, the following information represents suspicious activity! "The 6.2 trillion-dollar stimulus package" [HR 748] was introduced to Congress in January 2019, almost one year before even one Covid-19 case was reported in the World. The "6.2 trillion-dollar stimulus package" was allegedly passed to offset the negative effects of 60 million people dying worldwide of COVID-19; however, our government gave the U.S. banks almost $5 trillion dollars of the $6.2 trillion dollar stimulus package. The real reason the $6.2 trillion dollar stimulus package was introduced to Congress was the U.S. Banks were bankrupt and the U.S. economy was going to crash, evidenced by the

Repo rates spiking to 10% on 9-17-2019. However, prophetically speaking, it's obvious the pandemic was totally satanic and designed to serve as another 5 trillion-dollar government bailout of the U.S. banks, in addition to crashing the economy, killing the U.S. dollar, and replacing it with a one-world cashless fiat currency system thereby giving government[s] total control over who can buy or sell anything without the approval of the central banksters. Therefore, this sequence of events just described will give the governments total control over who can buy or sell anything without their approval, which is in harmony with Bible prophecy. Revelation 13:15-17.

Interesting Information

The CDC owns the patents to the coronavirus; (see Federal Case Number 120-CV-01384 LPS) consequently, it's a man-made pathogen; you can't patent something that occurs naturally in nature. In addition, the CDC has been involved in the "gain of function research" GOFR for at least the last 20 years. (see Federal Case Number 120-CV-01384 LPS). The GOFR is designed to mutate animal viruses [that cannot infect humans] into deadly pathogens capable of killing millions of people. Genetic research has indicated that COVID-19 was created in a laboratory, and (Federal Case Number 120-CV-01384 LPS) has provided overpowering information establishing that the CDC along with several other prominent U.S. universities, Harvard University and North Carolina Chapel Hill were involved in the GOFR, which is mutating animal viruses [that cannot infect humans] into deadly pathogens capable of killing millions of people, which is completely illegal. Consequently, in 2014-15 when world-renowned virologists started complaining about the CDC's involvement in the GOFR, the NIH [National Health Institute] was forced to cut the CDC's funding. After the NIH cut the CDC's funding, the GOFR was subcontracted to a company named Eco-Health Alliance, which the United States Government through the Obama and Trump administrations subsequently funded to continue with the GOFR, which represents criminal behavior. Interesting information, Peter Daszak is the president of Eco-Health Alliance and a board member of the WHO, the World Health Organization. When the same world-renowned virologists continued complaining about the United States funding the GOFR because it violates the Nuremberg Ten laws and treaties, the GOFR was moved to the Wuhan Institute of Virology (WIV), so they could finish mutating SARS Covid-2 into Covid-19 essentially creating a bio-weapon capable of killing millions of people.

The owners of the Federal Reserve Bank, here in the United States, hereafter the central banksters, subsequently instructed the WIV to release Covid-19 into society. Once this new killer disease (COVID-19) appeared in the United States, there was a mad rush to find a cure, so government mandates were issued to mass vaccinate the entire population allegedly to protect them from this man-made planned demic. The planned demic produced enormous profits for "the merchants and the great men of the earth" who are deceiving the unsuspecting multitudes with their sorcery. Revelation 18:23. The Greek word φαρμακεία, translated as "sorcery" in Revelation 18:23, is pronounced "pharmakeia," with its first definition being injecting poisons, toxic prescription medications into your system. When researching any killer disease, investigators first attempt to establish its origin. They try to come up with patient zero, the first person who contracted the killer disease. This discovery can be a long and laborious process. Therefore, notwithstanding that, after a cursory examination was performed establishing the CDC owns the patents to the coronavirus, and they have been involved in the GOFR for the last 20 years, (see Federal Case Number 120-CV-01384 LPS) humanity has encountered one killer disease that's far more onerous to implement its cure; however, we know the sin virus originated in Eden when Adam first transgressed God's holy requirements and its cure is not the Greek word φαρμακεία, translated as "sorcery" in Revelation 18:23, which is pronounced "pharmakeia," the cure for the sin virus is the everlasting gospel.

The Message For This Time Part One

It will be firmly established in this first book, spearheading a series of seven books, titled "The Abomination of Desolation" that the everlasting gospel was designed to "bring about the obedience of [our] faith" in all of God's holy requirements. Romans 1:5, Romans 16:25-26, 1 Corinthians 3:16, 1 Corinthians 11:29. With this thought in mind, these Bible verses (Hebrews 10:26-27, John 3:36) more clearly represent the message for this time (Revelation 14:6-13) than does the peace and safety message currently being presented from the pulpits of Christendom today. The Apostle Paul says if you sin deliberately after receiving the knowledge of the truth, there no longer remains a sacrifice for sin but only a fearful prospect of judgment pointing to the lake of fire that will consume the transgressors of God's holy law shortly after the conclusion of the investigative judgment. Hebrews 10:26-27, Daniel 7:9-10. In harmony with this understanding, the Apostle John says, "He who believes in the Son has life; however, he who does not obey the Son shall not see life, but the wrath of God rests upon him." John 3:36.

The scriptures do not recognize the idea that belief represents anything other than noncompromising obedience to all of God's holy requirements. James 2:19-26, John 14:15. The compromised state of existence, that all of humanity has been born into, required the introduction of the everlasting gospel to successfully counteract humanity naturally joining Satan in his rebellion against the authority of the government of Heaven. Romans 3:23, Romans 8:1-4. However, the introduction of the everlasting gospel doesn't make void our responsibility to obey God's holy requirements (Romans 3:31); on the contrary, it establishes our acknowledgment that the wages of sin should require the death of the transgressor and that man as God created him could obey all of God's holy requirements. In support of this understanding, the Bible emphatically states that after the gospel invitation closes, sinners will be destroyed in the lake of fire with the Devil and his evil angels, which is the second death, (Revelation 20:15) and this destruction of the Devil, his evil angels, in the lake of fire, along with all of humanity that have joined Satan's rebellion will be condoned by the fallen and unfallen worlds. Consequently, the Bible says sin shall not arise a second time.

The everlasting gospel was introduced to correct the sin problem in fallen humanity, not the exact opposite as subliminally advocated by the majority of the Christian churches today. In order to eliminate any confusion on this subject, the Bible clearly defines sin as the transgression of God's holy law (Romans 3:19-20, Romans 7:7-12) and specifically states that God's holy law will be the standard of righteousness used by Christ to evaluate our characters during His final work of mediation, which is the investigative judgment. James 2:8-12. Therefore, the message for this time points believers to the soon close of Christ's final work of mediation, which is the investigative judgment and the spiritual preparation necessary to "endure the day of His coming," for the prophet says, "Who can stand when He appears." Malachi 3:1-5, Revelation 14:6-7, Daniel 7:9-20.

THE MESSAGE FOR THIS TIME PART ONE CONTINUED
THE FALLEN NATURE IS "THAT WHICH CAUSES SIN" IN OUR LIVES

The Bible is very clear on this extremely important subject; researching the origin of the sin problem in humanity is very simple, while the application is very difficult, with its cure being made extremely complex by our religious leaders. In the pandemic called the sin virus, Adam is patient zero; he and his wife were the first humans to contract the sin virus when they first disobeyed their Creator's requirements. When Adam transgressed, his nature fell, and to make matters worse, he passed his fallen defective nature onto his offspring from generation to generation. The result of being born with a fallen defective human nature (Romans 3:23) [the virus that causes sin in our lives] is that if it's not put to death (Romans 8:12-13), the infected humans will inevitably commit the unpardonable sin [after probation closes] and will be rightfully destroyed by the holy angels at the Lord's second coming. Matthew 13:41. Therefore, to cure the sin problem in fallen humanity, the "Most High" introduced the "everlasting gospel" so that all those who desired to put to death the fallen nature they received at birth from their earthly parents [without their consent] may choose to obey and live. John 3:36, Romans 16:25-27.

In every age of earth's history, there has been witnessed the results of the power of good and the power of evil working upon the hearts and minds of fallen humanity. The results of this conflict can be easily observed by comparing the actions of those possessing the Spirit of God's nature with the actions of those controlled by the fallen nature they inherited at birth from their earthly parents. In the beginning, our first parents were created in perfect harmony with the nature of God; their nature was unfallen, producing no internal conflict with their desires to obey the laws of the government of heaven. However, after yielding to one temptation, their nature became defective, which produced an unnatural and overpowering sinful propensity to transgress. These unnatural propensities were not in harmony with God's nature (Genesis 5:1); consequently, being naturally rebellious, they had no defense against Satan's temptations. Romans 8:5-8. Therefore, the scriptures make it perfectly clear why all of humanity has sinned.

The scriptures make it perfectly clear that all have sinned, having been born into this world through no fault of their own, possessing an overpowering propensity to transgress God's holy law, which they inherited at birth without their consent from their earthly parents. Romans 3:23, Psalms 14:1-3. The results of Adam's one transgression created an unnatural and overpowering propensity to disobey God's authority, (Romans 7:14-24), and this unnatural overpowering propensity to disobey God's authority _**was passed on to**_ his descendants from generation to generation. Genesis 5:3, Romans 6:14-16. The consequences of Adam's one transgression had serious and long-lasting side effects for the entire human race; because of Adam's one transgression, all his descendants _**without exception**_ inherited an unnatural and overpowering propensity to transgress; and to make matters even more complicated they received this defect without their consent at birth. 1 Peter 1:17-18. This unnatural **and** overpowering propensity to transgress God's holy law is defined in the Bible as the carnal nature (Romans 7:14), which the apostle calls "the body of sin and death" (Romans 7:25) and says it must be put to death (Romans 8:12-13) if we are to receive eternal life. The carnal nature, more often referred to as the fallen nature, which all of humanity inherited without their consent at birth from our earthly parents, is the reason why all of Adam's descendants have transgressed God's Holy Ten Commandment Law; therefore, our fallen nature is referred to in the scriptures as "that which causes sin" in our lives, (Romans 5:12-19, Romans 3:23) and the Bible is clear, it must be put to death if we are to receive eternal life. Matthew 13:41.

When Christ appeared as a lowly babe in Bethlehem, His nature was distinctly stamped with a seal of devotion leading Him to naturally obey His Father's law. This natural obedience resulted from the same unfallen nature Adam and Eve possessed before their first transgression. 1 John 3:9, Hebrews 1:3. The scriptures make it perfectly clear why Christ did not sin (Romans 5:12-14, Romans 1:4). At birth, Christ received His Father's unfallen nature, (Matthew 1:20) being "conceived of the Holy Spirit" He had no propensity to transgress. The Bible is very clear on this point; Christ was born holy, "full of grace and truth." John 1:14, Luke 1:35. Conversely, the fallen sons of Adam were not born holy, "full of grace and truth," they were born defective, possessing at birth their parents' unnatural propensity to transgress God's holy requirements. The result of inheriting Adam's fallen defective nature has caused all his descendants to transgress God's holy law. Romans 3:23, Ephesians 4:22-24. The gospel clearly states the defective nature producing our sinful propensities to transgress God's holy law must be put to death (Romans 7:4-6), our fallen nature must be killed (Ephesians 4:22-24), **_we must be born again_** (1 John 5:18), receiving a new life from above (John 3:3-9) or we will continue in transgression clearly dictating we are unworthy to receive eternal life, which takes place after the conclusion of Christ's final work of mediation, hereafter referred to as the investigative judgment. Daniel 7:9-10, Revelation 14:6-7, 2 Corinthians 5:10 and 1 Corinthians 6:10-11. Therefore, this is why the Bible says if we, by the Spirit, "put to death" the fallen defective nature we inherited at birth [without our consent] from our earthly parents, we will receive eternal life. Galatians 5:24, Romans 8:12-13.

The fallen defective human nature we inherited at birth from our earthly parents [without our consent] is "that which causes sin" in our lives. The Bible is clear on this subject, our fallen nature must be put to death, or we will continue to transgress and inevitably commit the unpardonable sin sometime after human probation closes. Notwithstanding the unfairness of being born into this world with a fallen nature, the Bible explicitly states, "that the wages of sin is [still] death" in this dispensation (Romans 7:14-25, Romans 6:23, John 8:34, and 2 Peter 3:11-12). Consequently, God mercifully introduced the everlasting gospel through the merits of Calvary's Cross. Accordingly, when believers claim Christ's blood paid the penalty they rightfully deserve for their transgressions of God's holy law, the Bible says they are "justified by faith," and that this "justified" state of existence gives them free access to Christ's "daily mediation" so they can by the Spirit put to death "that which causes sin" in their lives. Romans 8:12-13. In Romans 6:16, the apostle clearly defines the problem with fallen humanity by stating sinners are actually slaves to their sinful propensities, by emphatically declaring the following, "Do you not know that if you yield yourself to anyone as obedient slaves, you are slaves of the one whom you obey, either of sin, which leads to death, or of obedience, which leads to righteousness." In the following chapter, the same apostle says (Romans 7:21-25) that this unnatural propensity to transgress God's holy law is "the law of sin," working death in our lives. Immediately after the fall of our first parents, God, speaking through His servant Moses (Genesis 4:6-7), defines the sin problem in the same way, ***plainly stating***, that "the law of sin working death in our lives" remains close at hand, trying to control our actions and Christ says the very same thing in John 8:34-45, everyone who commits sin is a slave to sin, and a slave to sin shall not inherit eternal life. Therefore, your everyday actions will confirm whose nature you possess

(Romans 8:5-7, Colossians 3:5-13), and because faith without corresponding works does not exist (James 2:17), our actions will confirm if we have developed a saving relationship with Jesus Christ; consequently, the real "born again" believers will be seen naturally keeping God's holy law because they are no longer controlled by "that which causes sin" in their lives. Revelation 14:12, John 14:15, 1 John 5:4, and Galatians 5:24.

The apostle says he found it "to be a law that when [he] wanted to do right evil lies close at hand," trying to control his actions. Romans 7:21. Again, the Bible is extremely clear on these points, 1) all of Adam's descendants have been born with an unnatural and overpowering propensity to transgress God's law. Romans 5:12-14. 2) Inheriting this defect was one of the reasons why the everlasting gospel was offered to fallen humanity. 3) Inheriting this defective nature is the reason why all of humanity requires redemption from the power of sin working death in our lives. Romans 7:4-6. 4) The scriptures teach that the fallen nature we inherited at birth from our earthly parents is the direct result of Adam's first transgression. Romans 3:23. 5) As a result of Adam's one transgression, "all have sinned," having been born defective. 6) Again, the everlasting gospel was introduced because there can be no compromise on this decree, "that the wages of sin [requires] the death" of the transgressor. Romans 6:23. 7) consequently, it's because of God's great mercy that this death sentence has been [temporarily stayed] postponed; nevertheless, the message for this time clearly states that the death sentence God's holy law demands will be imposed upon transgressors sometime after human probation closes. Matthew 13:24-43, Romans 5:12-19, John 3:36. Accordingly, the gospel invitation teaches that God's mercy will not endure forever; therefore, regardless of your acknowledgment that Christ's blood paid the penalty you rightfully deserve for your transgressions of the law if you expect to receive a positive verdict in the judgment, the fallen nature you inherited at birth [without your consent] from your earthly parents must be put to death, or you will inevitably commit the unpardonable sin after human probation closes and be rightfully destroyed for the good of the universe with the devil and his evil angels in the lake of fire; which is the second death. Revelation 20:1-15.

The everlasting gospel was specifically designed so that the fallen sons of Adam, born into this sin-sick world, through no fault of their own, possessing an unnatural propensity to transgress God's holy law, would not remain permanently enslaved to their sinful propensities. After the fall of our first parents, God's ***plan of salvation***, established before the foundation of the world, was mercifully introduced, in order to establish, that man, as God created him, could obey the law. This provision represents the good news of the Bible, establishing that God mercifully provided a way of escape for all of Adam's descendants so they could choose to obey and live if they complied with the conditions established by God for their deliverance from the power of sin in their lives. The plan of salvation states that after the fall of our first parents, a Redeemer ***would pay*** the penalty sinners rightfully deserve for their transgressions of the law. This provision was introduced so that all of Adam's descendants, after claiming by faith that the promised Redeemer ***would pay*** the penalty they rightfully deserve for their transgressions, could enjoy free access to Christ's "daily mediation" so they could obtain the real forgiveness of their sins in preparation for His final work of mediation, which is the investigative judgment. The scriptures are very clear on this point, the standard of righteousness used by Christ to evaluate our characters during His final work of mediation, which is the investigative judgment, will be God's Holy Ten Commandment Law as originally proclaimed by God Himself amid the thunders of Mt. Sinai. James 2:8-12, Daniel 7:9-10. Therefore, the message for this time states that justified believers must become naturally obedient to the laws of the government of heaven if they expect to be deemed worthy to receive eternal life at the conclusion of Christ's final work of mediation, which is the investigative judgment. **Revelation 14:6-7.**

The Message Continues - The Sacrificial Offerings Symbolizing Christ's Death Upon Calvary's Cross Is Not The Atonement!

In harmony with the title of **this section**, it's important to understand that throughout the entire Old Covenant dispensation, the sacrificial offerings symbolized Christ's death upon Calvary's Cross, representing the forfeited life of the promised [Redeemer] who <u>*would pay*</u> the penalty sinners rightfully deserve for their transgressions of the law. The terms and conditions of salvation under the Old Covenant dispensation were confirmed between the parties through faith that "the sacrificial offerings" represented the forfeited life of the promised Redeemer who would pay the penalty sinners rightfully deserve for their transgressions of the law. **However, it's essential for the reader to understand what the apostle is trying to communicate in Hebrews 10:4 when he says it's impossible that the blood of these animals could take away sins. Isaiah 1:12-18.** The sacrificial offerings were performed in the outer court of the earthly sanctuary; consequently, they were not the atonement for transgressions, and since they were only in effect until Christ, the promised Redeemer, <u>*paid*</u> the penalty sinners rightfully deserved for their transgressions of the law these animal sacrifices were obviously symbolic of Christ's death upon Calvary's Cross paying the price for the sins of the world. Therefore, throughout the Old Covenant dispensation, God's plan of salvation was confirmed between the parties through animal sacrifices; however, the message for this time clearly brings to view that these animal sacrifices were performed in the outer court of the earthly sanctuary; consequently, the justification received after claiming these animal sacrifices represented the forfeited life of the promised redeemer could not possibly represent the atonement for transgressions. Hebrews 10:4, James 2:8-12, and Revelation 14:6-7.

The animal sacrifices of the Old Covenant dispensation symbolized Christ's death upon Calvary's Cross; however, the message for this time clearly states that <u>*the justification believers received after claiming by faith that these animal sacrifices represented the forfeited life*</u>

of the promised Redeemer were not the atonement for their transgressions. The atonement is very specific, it's the blotting out of sins truly forgiven from the Book of Records at the conclusion of Christ's final work of mediation, which is the investigative judgment. Without question, the Old Covenant believers could stand before God _justified by faith_ because they believed that the animal sacrifices represented the forfeited life of the promised Redeemer who _would pay_ the price they rightfully deserved for their transgressions of the law. However, the important truths concerning the atonement are taught by the earthly sanctuary and its services. These animal sacrifices were performed in the outer court of the earthly sanctuary and could not possibly be the atonement for transgressions; the atonement for the sins was performed in the second apartment of the earthly sanctuary during the Day of Atonement specifically for the cleansing of sins transferred there through the animal sacrifices, which concluded the sacrificial service of atoning for transgressions. Leviticus 16:6-30. Consequently, to preach the gospel of Jesus Christ in its fullness, the patriarchs and prophets of the Old Covenant dispensation were admonished to present (Christ) the promised Redeemer not only as a substitute for the death penalty sinners rightfully deserve for their transgressions of God's holy law but also as humanity's Great High Priest who could, through His daily mediation forgive their sins permanently delivering justified believers from **the power of sin** and Satan's temptations. This permanent deliverance from **the power of sin** and Satan's temptations must be obtained in preparation for Christ's final work of mediation, which is to make atonement for the sins truly forgiven at the conclusion of the investigative judgment. Isaiah 53:1-12, Revelation 11:15-19. The message for this time specifically states that Christ has provided a sacrifice for the sins of the world, and that by faith in His perfect sacrifice, believers must access His daily mediation to receive the real forgiveness of their sins in preparation for His final work of mediation, which is the investigative judgment. Therefore, the message for this time declares that all those who expect to receive a positive verdict from Christ, during His final work of mediation, will by faith claim justification and subsequently access His "daily mediation" to receive the real forgiveness of their sins in preparation for His final work of atonement, which is the blotting out of sins truly forgiven from the Book of Records at the conclusion of the investigative judgment.

The scriptures are extremely clear on this point, the animal sacrifices **_themselves_** were not the atonement for transgressions, the final atonement takes place during Christ's final work of mediation, specifically for the blotting out of sins truly forgiven from the Book of Records at the conclusion of the investigative judgment. The message for this time declares that the hour of His judgment has come, (Revelation 14:6-7), representing the soon close of human probation, (Revelation 10:7), when the prophet says the dead are to be judged by those things which are written in the Book of Records <u>according to their works</u> and **_not_** by what they profess to believe; (Revelation 11:15-19). Consequently, only those who have received **_<u>the real forgiveness of their sins</u>_** will obtain a positive verdict during Christ's final work of mediation, which is the investigative judgment. Daniel 7:9-10. **_<u>The real forgiveness of sins</u>_** is particularly evidenced by believers keeping God's Holy Ten Commandment Law as originally proclaimed amid the thunders of Mt. Sinai. Revelation 14:12. The prophet sees this great multitude of believers keeping the commandments because they have (while human probation lingers) previously put to death, by the Spirit, their fallen nature, qualifying these justified [born-again] believers as the great multitude (Revelation 7:9) who have received the seal of the living God upon their forehead; consequently, they receive a positive verdict from their Great High Priest in the judgment; **thereby** avoiding the death sentence sinners rightfully deserve for their transgressions of God's holy law. John 3:36, Hebrews 10:26, Revelation 14:6-7, Revelation 20:15.

After Calvary, the Old Covenant dispensation with its sacrificial services passed away, and we are now living under the New Covenant dispensation. In this dispensation, God's plan of salvation is confirmed between the parties when believers by faith accept Christ's death upon Calvary's Cross "**_<u>has paid</u>_**" the penalty sinners rightfully deserve for their transgressions of the law. In the New Covenant dispensation, believers can stand justified before God when they claim by faith, that Christ's death upon Calvary's Cross "*has paid*" the penalty they rightfully deserve for their transgressions of the law. However, in both dispensations, claiming Christ's death has paid the penalty sinners rightfully deserve for their transgressions of the law is not the atonement, to preach the gospel of Jesus Christ in its fullness, God's plan of salvation must deliver believers so completely from the power of sin in their lives that resistance to sin and Satan's temptations becomes as natural for them as it was for Adam before his first transgression in Eden. John 8:31-36, Romans 8:12-14. The Bible is clear that this type of obedience can only be exercised if there has been a change in nature. Ephesians 4:22-24. This change in nature occurs through the new birth evidenced by the believers' desire to comply with all the conditions of God's "covenant" of salvation, which has been freely offered to humanity immediately after the fall of our first parents. Therefore, according to God's covenant of salvation, freely offered to Adam's descendants in both dispensations, eternal life can be granted to those who, by faith in the merits of Calvary's Cross, access Christ's daily mediation and develop characters in harmony with God's holy law. Jeremiah 31:31-34, Hebrews 10:16-18.

Through faith in the sacrifice provided for humanity's transgressions, believers living in both dispensations can, through Christ's daily mediation, be empowered by the Holy Spirit to resist sin and Satan's temptations and naturally do what is right in the eyes of the Lord. John 1:12, Romans 8:1-4. Through the new birth, believers become empowered by the Holy Spirit to naturally resist sin and Satan's temptations (Ephesians 4:22-24), consequently, the born-again experience makes them eternally secure against Satan's temptations. The Bible says we must be born again so that obedience becomes as natural for the born-again believer as it was for Adam before his fall. The born-again experience establishes that man, as God created him, could keep the law. 1 John 5:4. After Calvary's Cross, the Old Covenant dispensation, with its sacrificial services, passed away. Accordingly, we are now living in the New Covenant dispensation. However, the plan of salvation is the same in both dispensations, consequently, it's impossible that repeated claims made upon justification can take away sins. Hebrews 10:4. After believers claim Christ's blood *paid* the penalty they rightfully deserve for their transgressions of God's holy law, they must access His daily mediation seeking the power of the Holy Spirit to put to death "that which causes sin" in their lives before human probation closes, those who receive the real forgiveness of their sins will receive a positive verdict from Christ during His final work of mediation, which is to make final atonement for the sins truly forgiven at the conclusion of the investigative judgment. Revelation 14:6-7. Therefore, this specific understanding of the atonement represents the message for this time and not the peace and safety message sounding from the pulpits of Christendom today.

3

A BRIEF INTRODUCTION TO – THE BORN AGAIN EXPERIENCE

The Bible is specific about what represents the born-again experience, and it's those who understand the malignant nature of sin who would rather die than transgress God's holy law are the true born-again believers. Jesus Christ told Nicodemus we **_must_** be born again if we are to receive eternal life (John 3:7); the reason for this command is not that complex, whoever sins (transgresses the law) becomes a slave to their sinful propensities and a slave to sin shall not (cannot) inherit eternal life. John 8:33-34. This understanding is why the apostle says "born again" believers will not transgress God's holy law. 1 John 5:18. The reason for their noncompromising commitment to obedience, is through the new birth, their nature has become changed, consequently, death is far more desirable than becoming a slave to sin and Satan's temptations. Through the power of the Holy Spirit, they can now choose to do what is right in the eyes of the Lord because they're no longer controlled by their old, fallen, and defective nature. 1 John 3:9. The Apostle Paul says when this change occurs, "born again" believers will aggressively seek the real forgiveness of their sins from their all-powerful High Priest, in preparation for the judgment. Hebrews 10:16-18. Therefore, the real "born again" believer walks not after their old fallen nature, but by faith their actions are motivated by their new, "born again" nature. Ephesians 4:22-24, 2 Corinthians 7:1.

Simply put, the born-again experience means the sinners' nature has changed. This change in nature is what "bring[s] about the obedience of [their] faith" (Romans 16:25-26), and it's because of this change that the true "born again" believer will be seen naturally obeying God's Holy Ten Commandment Law. 1 John 5:3, Hebrews 8:10. In the last days of Earth's history, the prophet sees these "born again" believers "keeping the commandments," while the entire Christian world has declared God's holy law changed and/or abrogated, while maintaining that any gospel demanding obedience to the same is a yoke of bondage. These satanic claims are made because almost the entire Christian world believes God's holy requirements cannot be obeyed, which occupies the very foundation of Satan's rebellion. Conversely, in this dispensation, born-again believers will be seen "keeping the commandments of God" because they have accessed Christ's "daily mediation" to obtain the real forgiveness of their sins. Therefore, the real "born again" believer will be seen naturally keeping the commandments of God because the righteousness of the law has been written upon their hearts and minds, which just happens to be the new covenant promise of salvation. Revelation 14:12, and Hebrews 10:16-18.

The obedience directly linked to the "born again" experience is what modern-day Christianity has rejected as legalism. 1 John 5:18, John 17:22-23, Ephesians 4:12-14. The scriptures teach that Christ came to save His people "from" their sins (Matthew 1:21) and that Christ is the mediator of the new covenant promise of salvation, which is designed to write God's holy law upon the hearts and minds of believers. Hebrews 9:15, Hebrews 12:24. It is only by accessing Christ's "daily mediation" can our overpowering propensity to transgress God's holy law be put to death (Romans 7:4-6) so we can, by the power of the Holy Spirit, choose to obey and live. John 3:36. The promise of salvation (Hebrews 8:10) involves changing the believers' nature (Ephesians 4:22-24) so that they can naturally obey God's law. John 14:15, 1 John 2:3-6. The born-again experience is different from sanctification, which is continual and ongoing; as believers become aware of their defects, they access Christ, the mediator of the new covenant promise of salvation, to receive the real forgiveness of their sins. Consequently, born-again believers move on from victory over sin to new victories over recently discovered sins. Hebrews 10:16-25, Hebrews 9:15, Hebrews 12:24, Hebrews 8:1-5, Luke 1:77, 1 John 1:9. This understanding represents "the keys to the kingdom of heaven," spoken of by Christ in Matthew 16:19, which commands justified believers to access His "daily mediation" in the new covenant heavenly sanctuary so they can obtain the real forgiveness of their sins, representing the ongoing sanctification of their character that must be obtained in preparation for Christ's final work of mediation, which is the investigative judgment. Hebrews 9:8-9, Hebrews 10:16-25.

Through the everlasting gospel, fallen humanity can choose to obey and live if they, by faith in Christ's substitutional sacrifice, access His "daily mediation" in the new covenant heavenly sanctuary and by the power of the Spirit put to death their unnatural propensity to transgress God's holy law. Romans 8:12-13. In both dispensations, the promise of salvation freely offered to the fallen sons of Adam is very simple and direct; believers can, by faith, claim Christ's death paid the penalty they rightfully deserve for their transgressions. This is called justification by faith, which will be further defined in the next chapters. After claiming justification by faith, believers can, with joyful anticipation, access Christ's "daily mediation" to obtain the real forgiveness of their sins, leading to the ongoing sanctification of their character. This concept will also be further defined in the next chapters, along with an extremely detailed explanation of the born-again experience. Therefore, if you are born again, you will desire true forgiveness of your sins; consequently, you will have, by the Spirit, put to death "that which causes sin" in your life, resulting in you obeying God's holy law as naturally as Adam did before his first transgression and receive a positive verdict in the judgment. 1 John 2:4-5, Romans 16:25-26, Romans 7:4-6, Hebrews 10:16-18, Romans 8:12-13.

4

THAT SHALL SAVE HIS PEOPLE FROM THEIR SINS

In Matthew 1:21, Christ, He who was symbolized throughout the entire Old Covenant dispensation as the _**promised**_ Redeemer, is presented to the fallen sons of Adam in the New Covenant dispensation as the Redeemer _**who has come**_ to deliver His people _**from**_ the power of sin working death in their lives. After claiming justification by faith, those who comply with the conditions of God's "covenant" *of salvation* will access Christ's daily mediation and, by the Spirit, put to death their sinful propensities so they can naturally obey and live. Ezekiel 20:11; Leviticus 18:5; Deuteronomy 27:26. This "covenant," and no other, is the _**promise of salvation**_ freely offered to fallen humanity in both dispensations. John 3:16, Deuteronomy 10:12. If anyone complies with the specific terms of salvation, they will claim Christ died for their transgressions and subsequently access His daily mediation to receive the real forgiveness of their sins. The plan of salvation imparts to believers the power of the Holy Spirit for the deliverance _**from**_ their sinful propensities. John 8:34. In Matthew 1:21, the apostle writes, "For it is written, "She will bear a son, and you shall call his name Jesus, for He will save His people _**from**_ their sins." The Bible teaches that the promise of salvation taught in the Old

Covenant dispensation is the same as the promise of salvation taught in the New Covenant dispensation. In the first book of the New Testament, meticulous Matthew writes that Christ was born as the promised Redeemer, who would save His people *from* their sins. The Greek word ἀπὸ, translated as "*from*" in Matthew 1:21, means separation from or motion away from something, denoting separation from a particular person or place or a specific set of circumstances. The Greek word ἀπὸ has a Strong's Concordance call number of 575; Thayer's Bible Dictionary defines the meaning of the Greek word ἀπὸ, as separation, meaning "any kind of separation of one thing from another by which the union or fellowship of the two is destroyed." Therefore, with the definition of the Greek word ἀπὸ clearly defined as "separation," what the apostle is trying to communicate in Matthew 1:21, is that Christ's mission was to separate His people "*from*" their sins, not just provide a sacrifice for their transgressions.

It was Christ's mission to save His people "*from*" their sins. This separation would be made possible by providing a sacrifice for sins, so those claiming His blood paid the penalty they rightfully deserve for their transgressions of the law could be justified by faith, giving them the right to access His daily mediation so they could by the Spirit put to death their **fallen nature**, defined as (**that**) in the phrase, "**that** which causes sin" in their lives. This is how the everlasting gospel was designed to fix the sin problem in fallen humanity. The fallen sons of Adam who claim Christ's substitutional sacrifice paid the penalty they rightfully deserve for their transgressions of the law may come boldly to the throne of grace accessing Christ's "daily mediation" so they could by the Spirit separate themselves *from* "that which causes sin" in their lives. Romans 7:4, Genesis 5:3.

The scriptures explain why the "Most High" mercifully offered fallen humanity redemption from their sinful propensity to transgress His laws. As stated earlier, without their consent, the entire human race has been born with a fallen defective human nature, which has caused all of Adam's descendants to transgress God's holy law. Romans 3:23. The theologians refer to this unnatural propensity to transgress God's holy law as the fallen nature. The **fallen nature** we inherited at birth from our earthly parents is "**that** which causes sin" in our lives. Christ's mission was to save His people *__from__* their sins by imparting to believers the Holy Spirit so they could put to death their **fallen nature,** which is their unnatural propensity to transgress His laws. Romans 7:21-25, Romans 8:12-13. Therefore, the *__everlasting gospel__* was designed to bring about the obedience of our faith by providing those who have transgressed God's holy law with justification giving them the right to claim by faith Christ's death paid the penalty they rightfully deserve for their transgressions so *__they could access__* His "daily mediation" and *__by the Spirit__* put to death "**that** which causes sin' in their lives. Romans 1:5, Romans 16:25-26.

They shall Call Evil Good and Good Evil – Justification by Faith Is Not God's Completed Work for Our Salvation

The rejection of light leaves men captives of Satan's malignant temptations and subjects of his kingdom having no ability to control their sinful propensities. The rejection of light causes professed believers to call the everlasting gospel "*__evil__*" (and a yoke of bondage) and Satan's counterfeit gospel "*__good__*," while creating the illusion of salvation. The peace and safety message sounding from the pulpits of Christendom today is causing professed believers to arrogantly maintain they are saved the very moment justification by faith is claimed, regardless of their unsanctified characters. The scriptures do not support this arrogant assumption of salvation. Consequently, before moving on from this point, some theological terms must be identified and defined so they can be clearly understood to avoid the confusion existing in Christendom today regarding the everlasting gospel, which believers are being called out of by God's last-day remnant people. Revelation 14:8. These specific terms are "justification by faith," and the "born-again" experience, which will both be defined in this chapter. The next chapter will define "sanctification," however, defining what it means to be truly forgiven of your sins will be explained in the next book in this series of books titled "The Abomination of Desolation." This chapter will define the meaning of *justification by faith* along with *the born-again* experience; determining what constitutes receiving the **_real forgiveness of your sins_** will be defined in the second book in this series of books; after "the antichrist of Bible prophecy" has been identified and "the mark of the beast" has been clearly defined. However, for clarification purposes, when the actual desire to commit a specific sin no longer exists believers can be considered truly forgiven of that specific sin. However, only truly born-again believers can actually be forgiven of their sins, which is why the born-again experience makes them eternally secure against all of Satan's future temptations. 1 John 3:9. Therefore, it will be established in this chapter that the rejection of light leaves professed believers captive of Satan's malignant temptations and subjects of his kingdom because they will have no ability to control their sinful propensities resulting in them inevitably committing the unpardonable sin sometime after human probation closes; consequently, they will be justly destroyed with the Devil and his evil angels in the lake of fire, which is the second death.

It's essential to understand the plan devised for our salvation is not that difficult to comprehend; if it were, then sinners would have a legitimate objection if they were condemned to their eternal destruction during Christ's final work of mediation, which is the investigative judgment. To further define the plan of salvation, certain concepts must be repeated to adequately explain that the born-again experience is a prerequisite for receiving eternal life. The reason the everlasting gospel was offered to fallen humanity occupies the very foundation of why all of Adam's descendants have transgressed God's holy requirements. The cure to the sin problem is the born-again experience resulting in believers claiming justification by faith which means they have acknowledged that they deserve to die because they are transgressors of God's holy law. Romans 3:31. As justified believers, they are commanded to access Christ's daily mediation to obtain the real forgiveness of their sins resulting in the ongoing sanctification of their character and a positive verdict in the judgment. The fact that God's holy law is the standard of righteousness used by Christ to evaluate our characters during the investigative judgment is why Christ told Nicodemus the born-again experience is essential to receive eternal life because the born-again believer would rather die than transgress God's holy law since death is far more desirable than becoming a slave to Satan and his malignant temptations. Therefore, it's critical to understand that the plan of salvation is not that difficult to comprehend; unfortunately, our religious leaders have distorted the everlasting gospel into a license to sin.

The Holy Spirit is to convict the world of **sin**, of **righteousness**, and of the coming **judgment**. The Bible teaches "that the wages of sin is [still] death" in this dispensation, (Galatians 2:17-18, Romans 6:23) with **sin** being just as clearly defined as the transgressions of God's Holy Law, which will be the standard of **righteousness** used by Christ to evaluate our characters in the **judgment**. To avoid the death sentence sinners rightfully deserve for their transgressions of the law, the "Most High" introduced the "everlasting gospel." The everlasting gospel is designed to impart believers with the Holy Spirit so they can naturally obey the **law** and live **righteous** lives in preparation for the **judgment**. When the Holy Spirit convicts someone of **sin**, they will clearly understand they deserve to die "eternally" because they have transgressed God's holy law, which will be the standard of **righteousness** employed by Christ to evaluate our characters during His final work of mediation, which is the **investigative judgment**. Those convicted of **sin** will subsequently claim Christ died for their transgressions of the law so they can form sanctified **righteous** characters in preparation for the **judgment**. Therefore, those claiming Christ died for their transgressions of the law can stand "justified by faith" before God because Christ's death upon Calvary's Cross has paid the penalty they rightfully deserve for their **transgressions**, with **sin** being just as clearly defined in the Bible as the transgressions of

God's holy law, so they are properly motivated to form sanctified **righteous** characters in preparation for Christ's final work of mediation, which is the **investigative judgment.**

The everlasting gospel teaches believers are not saved simply because they have claimed justification by faith; those claiming justification by faith must form **righteous** characters in harmony with God's holy law if they expect to receive a positive verdict from Christ during His final work of mediation, which is the **investigative judgment.** Romans 6:20-22. The scriptures are clear **on this point, the Holy Spirit is to convict the world of sin,** because "the wages of sin is still death in this dispensation." Those claiming "justification by faith" are commanded to come boldly to the throne of grace demanding access to Christ's daily mediation for the deliverance from "that which causes **sin**" in their lives for the specific purposes of forming **righteous** characters in harmony with the law in preparation for Christ's final work of mediation, which is the **investigative judgment.** If they make this spiritual preparation, by forming sanctified [**righteous**] characters, in harmony with God's holy law God's promise is they will not be destroyed in the lake of fire with the Devil and his evil angels, which is the second death. The Bible writers clearly state when "justification by faith" is claimed, believers should rejoice in the hope of receiving the glory of God (Romans 5:1-2), which is clearly defined in these Bible verses as the **sanctification** of their character. 2 Corinthians 3:17-18, Romans 8:28-30. Nevertheless, when Satan's malignant nature maintains control of the human mind, light becomes darkness, and professed believers call the "everlasting gospel," designed to save God's people *from* their sins, "*evil*" and a yoke of bondage, while calling Satan's counterfeit gospel that tolerates continued transgressions, "*good*" because it creates "the illusion of salvation now and in the judgment." Isaiah 5:20, Revelation 3:1, Revelation 3:15-17.

There is no ambiguity on the following points being established, evidenced by Christ's words to Nicodemus when He commanded him that we must be "born again" if we are to receive eternal life. John 3:1-9. Consequently, if justified believers want to receive eternal life, according to Christ's own words, they must be "born again," which will be demonstrated by the ongoing sanctification of their character resulting in them reflecting Christ's unfallen nature [possessing] "true righteousness and holiness." 2 Corinthians 7:1. In referencing the accuracy of the above statements, the Apostle Paul commands believers to "put off your old nature that belongs to your former manner of life, which is corrupted through the deceitfulness of lust, and be renewed in the spirit of your mind, by putting on the new nature created after the likeness of God in true righteousness and holiness." Ephesians 4:22-24. **Therefore, those who have been truly born again have put to death their fallen nature evidenced by them forming sanctified characters in harmony with God's holy law in preparation for Christ's final work of mediation, which is the investigative judgment.** Romans 5:1-2, 2 Corinthians 3:17-18, Galatians 5:16-24.

The scriptures are clear; notwithstanding the accuracy of the above-highlighted statement, our claims made upon justification must lead to the ongoing sanctification of our nature, or we will be found unworthy of receiving eternal life during **Christ's final work of mediation, which is the investigative judgment.** Romans 6:20-22. The everlasting gospel proffering "justification by faith" to fallen humanity specifically says "born again" believers will naturally obey the law resulting in the ongoing sanctification of their characters. 1 Thessalonians 4:3. The same apostle introducing justification by faith (Romans 5:1-2) prays, "The God of peace sanctify you wholly; and may your spirit and soul and body be kept blameless at the coming of our Lord Jesus Christ." 1 Thessalonians 5:23. The "Most High" has predestined fallen humanity to be saved through the ongoing sanctification of their characters; consequently, the true born-again believers will use "justification by faith" to access Christ's "daily mediation" to be "cleansed from all unrighteousness" in the hope of receiving a positive verdict in the judgment. 2 Thessalonians 2:13, 1 John 1:9. The Bible is clear on this point, no one is saved simply by claiming justification by faith; unless justified believers are truly "born again" they will not have a burning desire to form sanctified characters in harmony with

God's holy law in preparation for **Christ's final work of mediation, which is the investigative judgment**. Therefore, the Bible is very clear, hypocrites will be destroyed by the holy angels at the Lord's second coming. Matthew 13:41-42.

The actual facts are most Christians are hypocrites, they do not believe the born-again experience is evidenced by the ongoing sanctification of their character, with the end of this maturation process being eternal life. The majority are deceived on this point, maintaining they have the "assurance of salvation now and in the judgment" immediately after claiming "justification by faith," while they legalistically employ their claims that Christ's substitutional sacrifice has paid the penalty they rightfully deserve for their transgressions of the law thereby creating the illusion of salvation while they continue to transgress. **This is called hypocrisy!** Without question, Christ died for the sins of the world; consequently, all may claim "justification by faith," subsequently pointing to His blood paying the penalty they rightfully deserve for their transgressions of the law. However, it's a false gospel that provides alleged believers with "the assurance of salvation now and in the judgment" simply by claiming Christ's death paid the penalty they rightfully deserve for their transgressions of the law. This false doctrine distorts the gospel into a license to sin, evidenced by alleged believers disregarding the requirement to form sanctified characters in this life. The false doctrines that produce the illusion of salvation now and in the judgment immediately after claiming justification by faith represent a false gospel that the scriptures do not recognize. It is a counterfeit, false, cheap grace gospel that saves professed believers simply by claiming justification by faith, the biblical facts are clear, the alleged believers' claim made upon justification must produce sanctified characters or these hypocritical believers will be condemned in the judgment to their eternal destruction with the Devil and his evil angels in the lake of fire, which is the second death. Therefore, the everlasting gospel demands justified believers to put to death the fallen defective nature they inherited at birth from their earthly parents if they expect to be awarded eternal life during Christ's final work of mediation, which is the investigative judgment. Matthew 22:11-13, Romans 6:20-22.

The confusion existing on the subject of "justification by faith" has caused many to accept the false gospel that abounds in Christendom today; however, it is easy to differentiate between Satan's "_evil_" counterfeit gospel that allegedly saves professed believers in their sins, and God's "_good_" true "everlasting gospel" that saves believers "from" their sins. Two byproducts distinguish Satan's efforts to distort God's "_good_" everlasting gospel into a license to sin. The "_evil_" counterfeit gospel advocated by Satan always makes an excuse for continued transgressions while demonstrating a perfect hatred for God's Holy Ten Commandment Law. The prophet says woe unto them that call God's true everlasting gospel _evil_ and Satan's counterfeit gospel _good_; that puts _darkness_ for _light_, and _light_ for _darkness_; that puts _bitter_ for _sweet_, and _sweet_ for _bitter_. Isaiah 5:20. The counterfeit faith linked to the justification indigenous to Satan's false gospel encourages the continued transgressions of God's holy law while creating the illusion of salvation now and in the judgment for those making a mere profession of faith in Christ's atoning blood. The true plan of salvation requires justified believers to form sanctified characters in this life. The question believers must ask themselves is this; am I following the true gospel that requires justified believers to separate themselves "from" their sins, or am I following Satan's counterfeit gospel that provides believers with only the illusion of salvation immediately after making a profession of faith in Christ's atoning blood? Isaiah 30:1.

The confusion existing in Christendom today is the result of the counterfeit gospel being presented to the sin-loving multitudes of this generation from the pulpits of Christendom today. This counterfeit gospel assures professed believers of their salvation now and in the judgment immediately after claiming Christ's blood paid the penalty they rightfully deserve for their transgressions of the law, regardless of their true spiritual condition. This concept will be expounded upon more fully in the next chapter of this book; however, this chapter is specifically designed to teach you that the gospel of Jesus Christ is designed to save you from your sins, the extent of which will not be completely comprehended until you understand what it means to be truly forgiven of a sin! Luke 1:77. Therefore, the confusion existing in Christendom today on the subject of "justification by faith" has caused many to accept Satan's "*evil*" legalistic gospel; however, it is easy to identify because it always saves professed believers in their sins.

The scriptures clearly outline the specific terms of "the new covenant promise of salvation." Hebrews 8:10, Hebrews 10:16-18. The question, "What must I do to be saved" has been answered in God's word. Matthew 19:16-22. No one should be confused about how to obtain eternal life. John 3:16. The everlasting gospel clearly states after the "born again" experience, believers will, through faith in the merits of Christ's death upon Calvary's Cross, access Christ's "daily mediation" to obtain the real forgiveness of sins in preparation for His final work of mediation which is the investigative judgment. The "born again" believer will not be destroyed with Satan and his evil angels in the final eradication of sin and sinners in the lake of fire, which is the second death. Revelation 19:19-21, Revelation 20:12-15. The Bible clearly states that rebellion against the authority of God must be eradicated for the good of the universe. The judgment message of Revelation the 14th chapter plainly states God is giving the guilty inhabitants of the earth one last opportunity to form sanctified characters in harmony with His holy law before human probation closes. After probation closes, rebellion against the authority of God can be effectively eradicated with the approval of the universe. The parable of the wedding feast plainly teaches that our character will be investigated to determine if we are worthy to receive eternal life. Matthew 22:11-14, Romans 8:30. The proclamation of the everlasting gospel in harmony with the commencement of the judgment message, makes up the first part of the threefold warning message contained in Revelation the 14th chapter, emphatically demanding justified believers to form sanctified characters in this life now while human probation lingers. Revelation 7:1-4. This is the message for this time. Therefore, the "everlasting gospel" categorically states justified believers must form sanctified characters in harmony with God's Holy Ten Commandment Law now while probation lingers, or they will be destroyed with the Devil and his evil angels in the lake of fire, which is the second death. Hebrews 8:10, Hebrews 10:16-18.

The plan of salvation, established before the foundation of the universe, was designed to save humanity from their unnatural propensity to transgress God's holy law. The unnatural propensity to sin is defined in the Bible as our fallen nature, which has caused all of Adam's descendants to transgress God's holy law. The Apostle Paul clearly illustrates this point in his discourse in the book of Romans; "When you were slaves of sin, you were free regarding righteousness. But what return did you get from the things you are now ashamed? The end of those things is death. But now that you have been set free from sin and have become servants of God, the return you get is sanctification and its end, eternal life." Romans 6:20-22.

The born-again experience is different from the deliverance of specific individual sins. The deliverance from specific sins is called in the Bible sanctification. The Apostle Paul says God has chosen all to be "saved through the sanctification of the spirit by the belief in the truth." 2 Thessalonians 2:13. The Bible does not recognize "belief in the truth" outside of obedience to all of God's holy requirements. John 3:36, John 14:15, and 1 John 2:3-5. The "born again" experience, which results in claims being made upon justification, will naturally lead to the ongoing sanctification of our characters, representing the believer's desire to be truly forgiven of specific individual sins. Again, the desire to be truly forgiven from specific sins is called Bible sanctification, and it's God's predetermined plan, established before the foundation of the world, which was designed to [permanently] save His people *from* their sins. Ephesians 1:4.

This is why claiming justification by faith cannot assure anyone of their salvation now and in the judgment (Matthew 7:21, Romans 8:24) because claiming "justification by faith" has clearly acknowledged their understanding that the wages of sin still demands the death of the transgressor, (Galatians 1:17-18) and unless their born again experience is genuine (1 John 3:9), their transgressions will inevitably continue after human probation closes. As a result, when these alleged justified believers transgress God's holy requirements after human probation closes, they will be justly destroyed with the Devil and his evil angels in the lake of fire regardless of the number of times they have claimed justification by faith before and after human probation closes. Therefore, the plan devised for our salvation, established before the foundation of the universe, [it] was predetermined that humanity must be given an opportunity to put to death their unnatural propensity to sin, [defined in the Bible as <u>*the fallen nature*</u>] because <u>*this defect*</u> has caused all of Adam's descendants to transgress God's holy law; inevitably causing, [if] <u>*the fallen nature*</u> has *not been put to death*, these unsanctified alleged believers to transgress God's holy requirements after human probation closes, which is the unpardonable sin, resulting in God justly destroying these unsanctified hypocrites in the lake of fire with the Devil and his evil angels, which is the second death.

The Bible says we must be born again before human probation closes. John 3:7. When a believer makes a firm commitment to obey God's holy law, this is the byproduct of the born-again experience. Even though it doesn't always happen in this exact order, after the born-again experience is realized, justification by faith is claimed. The born-again believer realizes that the fallen nature we inherited at birth from our earthly parents [without our consent] must be put to death for them to obey God's holy law, naturally and willfully in this life. Colossians 3:5-10. If justified believers are to stand in the presence of God without a mediator after human probation closes, they must have already, by the Spirit, put to death "that which causes sin" in their lives while human probation lingers. 1 Peter 2:8, Romans 8:5-13. The desire to put to death "that which causes sin" in our lives is the direct result of the "born again" experience. In John 3:3-9, while speaking to Nicodemus, Christ says all the fallen sons of Adam must be "born again" if they are to receive eternal life. However, the born-again experience is not the completed work of sanctification; the apostle makes it very clear that sanctification is the work of a lifetime.

In 1 John 3:1-9, the prophet says the "born again" believer chooses not to _sin_; with _sin_ being clearly defined in the Bible as the transgression of God's holy law. Romans 3:19-20, Romans 4:15, Romans 7:7-12, 1 John 3:4. The new covenant promise of salvation was designed to write God's holy law upon the hearts and minds of justified believers, so obedience becomes as natural for them as it was for Adam before his first transgression in Eden. Hebrews 10:16-18. Again, the "born again" experience is not sanctification; it is the beginning of sanctification, with the end of this sanctifying process leading to eternal life. After the real born-again believer claims justification by faith, they will rejoice in the hope of becoming sanctified by the truth; and the Psalmist says God's holy law is the truth (Psalms 119:142). The Bible is clear, the real born-again believer desires to obey all of God's requirements naturally, willfully, and as perfectly as possible. Psalms 119:1-4. Therefore, as new truths are continually revealed, the real born-again believer will immediately begin obeying these new truths, representing the continual [ongoing] sanctification of their character, which is the work of a lifetime. 1 John 5:3.

In both dispensations, the fallen sons of Adam have been given two options. They can die in their sins or claim justification by faith while rejoicing in the hope of being delivered "from" the power of sin in their lives. This deliverance from the power of sin is made possible only by claiming justification by faith and subsequently accessing Christ's "daily mediation" to receive real forgiveness of their sins in preparation for His final work of mediation, which is the investigative judgment. Those who have received the real forgiveness of their sins [are having] God's holy law written upon their hearts and minds so they can obey the law naturally, representing the ongoing sanctification of their character. The firm commitment to obey all of God's requirements represents the "born again" experience leading justified believers to form ongoing sanctified characters in this life, and the truly born-again believer realizes the end of this ongoing sanctifying process [and not the beginning] is eternal life. Hebrews 8:10, Jeremiah 31:31-34. Therefore, this is the correct understanding of justification by faith and the everlasting gospel!

The Christian churches of this generation [are representing] the correct understanding of justification by faith and the everlasting gospel as "legalism" and something "evil," while Satan's counterfeit gospel is presented to the sin-loving multitudes as something "good" and desirable. The present-day distortion of God's plan of salvation creates "the illusion of salvation now and in the judgment" <u>*simply by making a profession of faith in Christ's atoning blood*</u>. The sin-loving multitudes of this generation have become drunk with the wine of the fornicated doctrines taught them by their religious leaders. As a result, they do not recognize that "their claims made upon justification" are not God's completed work for their salvation. This distortion of the everlasting gospel is an "abomination" unto the Lord because it removes Christ as the believers' only mediator and judge. The removal of Christ as the believers' only mediator and judge [is] the abomination that's making a "host" of professed believers spiritually "desolate" <u>*while they feel saved and forgiven of their sins*</u>. In their spiritually drunken and confused condition, these professedly *justified* believers feel no need to form sanctified characters in this life. Therefore, in their drunken spiritual condition, the sin-loving multitudes of this generation are calling Satan's counterfeit gospel "**good**" while they call the true everlasting gospel "**evil**" and legalistic.

The deception in Christendom today revolves around the believer's distorted understanding of *justification,* sanctification, the born-again experience, and what it really means to be truly forgiven of their sins. This is why the prophet refers to the Catholic, mainline Protestant, and Evangelical churches of this dispensation as Babylon, literally representing the confusion existing in Christendom today. As a result of this confusion, the sin-loving multitudes of this generation feel saved and forgiven of their sins immediately after claiming justification by faith. Consequently, they simply do not access Christ, their only mediator and judge, demanding from their all-powerful Mediator the real "let-go-ness" of their sins. The real forgiveness of sins results [represents] the sanctification of the believer's character producing a positive verdict in the judgment. Revelation 17:1-5, Revelation 3:17-18. The majority rely upon their religious leaders to teach them the great truths of salvation while neglecting the careful study of the scriptures for themselves. Therefore, we are instructed to investigate the scriptures individually because our salvation depends on how we view and implement these saving truths in our lives.

Those who claim to be *__justified__* by faith must clearly understand what their claims mean; by claiming Christ's blood paid the penalty you rightfully deserve for your transgressions, you are establishing your acknowledgment that God's holy law exists, which defines sin in your life. Romans 3:31, Galatians 2:17-18. The Bible clearly states where there is no law, there is no transgression (Romans 4:15), and that through the law comes knowledge of sin. Romans 3:19-20. In addition, the wages of sin is [still] death in this dispensation, and Christ emphatically states that a slave to sin will not receive eternal life. Romans 6:23, John 8:34-36, 2 Peter 2:19-21, Hebrews 10:26-27. Therefore, the alleged Christian churches of this generation are representing Satan's open rebellion against the authority of God as the pure religion of the Bible; consequently, God's plan of salvation, designed to save believers "from" their sins, is called "evil" while Satan's counterfeit gospel, is called "good."

The professed Christian churches of this dispensation are misrepresenting the gospel to gain popularity with the sin-loving multitudes of this generation. They advocate Satan's counterfeit gospel, satanically designed to create only the illusion of salvation, while professed believers remain slaves to their sinful propensities. Throughout the ages, the great truth of *__justification__* by faith has stood as a mighty beacon guiding repentant sinners to the ways of life; conversely, the Christian churches of this generation are representing justification by faith as a license to sin. The reader must understand that sanctification stops when the truth is rejected, and there no longer remains a sacrifice [justification] for your transgressions of God's holy law. Hebrews 10:26-27. In addition, the distorted understanding of "justification by faith" is further exasperated by the misunderstanding of what it means to be truly forgiven of sin. This combination distorts the believer's comprehension of what constitutes salvation representing the confusion existing in Christendom today. Therefore, the confusion existing in Christendom today is a direct result of our religious leaders distorting the everlasting gospel into a license to sin by removing Christ as our only mediator and judge, which is the abomination of the intentional action of making a host of believers spiritually desolate while creating the illusion of salvation now and in the judgment simply by claiming Christ died for your transgressions of the law.

5

SANCTIFICATION IS GOD'S PREDETERMINED PLAN FOR OUR SALVATION

God Has Predestined All to be Saved Through the Sanctification of Their Characters

The "Most High" has predestined all of mankind to be saved through the sanctification of the character resulting from the new birth, which naturally leads them to access Christ's mediation to obtain the real forgiveness of their sins. The born-again believer will rejoice in the hope of developing a sanctified character in harmony with God's Holy Ten Commandment Law. 2 Thessalonians 2:13-14, Romans 5:1-2, John 3:3-9. The strength and nobility of character lost in the consequences of sin are recreated through the new birth resulting in believers receiving a new unfallen human nature. Ephesians 1:3-14, Ephesians 4:22-24. This process of letting go of sin[s] through Christ's mediation is called Bible sanctification. Titus 2:11-14, 2 Corinthians 3:17-18, 2 Corinthians 7:1, Revelation 22:11. In the beginning, Adam was created in the image and likeness of his Creator. Genesis 5:1. Adam was created as a free moral agent, possessing the ability to distinguish between right and wrong, and, if he so desired, obey his Creator's laws. However, after Adam's fall, he was no longer a free moral agent; consequently, his ability to naturally obey God's laws was forfeited by yielding to his first transgression. As a result, he no longer had a defense against Satan's temptations; his nature had fallen; consequently, his desires were at war with the principles of God's government. Genesis 5:3, Romans 8:5-7. After Adam committed his first transgression, he could no longer render willing obedience to the laws of the government of heaven; he now possessed an unnatural and overpowering propensity to transgress. Genesis 4:6-7, Romans 7:21-24. Adam's defective character was passed to all his descendants from generation to generation. The fallen nature passed on to all of Adam's descendants from generation to generation is what produces the overpowering propensity to transgress God's holy law previously defined as "that which causes sin" in our lives. The Bible says that unless this defective fallen nature is put to death (Romans 7:4-6), we will remain slaves of sin and controlled by Satan's temptations, consequently, we will inevitably commit the unpardonable sin after the close of human probation and be rightfully destroyed with the Devil and his evil angels in the lake of fire, which is the second death. Matthew 13:41-42, Matthew 25:41. Therefore, if justified believers aren't "born again," they will possess no desire to form sanctified characters in this life, consequently, they cannot justly receive a positive verdict in the judgment. John 3:3-9, 1 John 3:9.

The Bible says after Adam's first transgression, his nature became defective, and this fallen defective nature was passed on to all succeeding generations. Romans 3:23. As a result of Adam's fallen defective nature being passed on to all succeeding generations, when Adam's descendants begot sons and daughters, they were born in their parents' image, possessing a fallen defective human nature just like their parents. Genesis 5:3. The Bible is very specific on this point; the second coming of Christ doesn't change the character of anyone; all are given sufficient probationary time to form sanctified characters in harmony with God's holy law now while human probation lingers. The actual change that takes place at the second coming, "in a moment, in the twinkling of an eye, at the last trump," is strictly physical, "For this mortality must put on immortality," only the righteous will receive eternal life. If you are truly "born again," you will possess a burning desire to form a sanctified character in harmony with God's holy law before human probation closes. If you are not constantly moving forward from victory to victory, in your battle against sin and Satan's temptations, you are not born again, consequently, you will suffer the second death in the lake of fire originally prepared for the Devil and his evil angels regardless of how many times you have claimed justification by faith. This message completely contradicts the peace and safety message presently being proclaimed from the pulpits of Christendom today. Therefore, the peace and safety message presently being proclaimed from the pulpits of Christendom today allegedly saves professed believers in their sins, and not from that which causes sin in their lives.

The deceptive message presently being proclaimed from the pulpits of Christendom today creates only the illusion of salvation simply by claiming justification by faith. As a result of the illusion of salvation being created by the false gospel presently being proclaimed from the pulpits of Christendom today, the unsuspecting multitudes feel no need to overcome every sin; consequently, they neglect the sanctification of character the Bible demands all must possess in preparation for the investigative judgment; consequently, they will inevitably commit the unpardonable sin after human probation closes. John 1:12-13. The message for this time is very simple, the sanctification of our character is not an option like air-conditioning on an automobile that we can accept or reject; it's a prerequisite for receiving eternal life. In the beginning, humanity was created in the image and likeness of the Creator, and God's plan of salvation is designed to impart the strength and nobility of character lost in the consequences of sin (1 John 3:1-3); therefore, this is called Bible sanctification, with its end being eternal life. John 17:17-19, 2 Corinthians 7:1.

The Apostle Paul says God has predestined everyone to be saved through the "born again" experience producing a sanctified character (2 Thessalonians 2:13), and because the wages of sin is still death, the continued sanctification of our character is obviously a predetermined requirement if we expect to receive a positive verdict in the judgment. The "grace of God has appeared for the salvation of all men, training us to renounce irreligion and worldly passion and to live sober, upright, and godly lives in this world, awaiting our blessed hope, the appearing of the glory of our great God and Savior Jesus Christ, who gave Himself for us to redeem us from all iniquity and to purify for Himself a people of His own who are zealous for good deeds." Titus 1:11-14. Therefore, the scriptures make it clear that the sacrifice provided for our transgressions has been deemed full and complete; as a result, [all of fallen humanity] who claim "justification by faith" may obtain eternal life if they simply comply with the conditions specifically designed for their salvation. Hebrews 10:16-18.

Notwithstanding that eternal life has been offered to all of Adam's descendants, according to God's word, after claims are made that Christ's death paid the penalty you rightfully deserve for your transgressions of the law, there still remain conditions that must be complied with before eternal life can be granted you in the judgment. The condition that must be complied with after justification by faith is claimed, is the ongoing sanctification of your character. The Bible specifically says God has "chosen us in Him before the foundation of the world that we should be holy and blameless before Him." Ephesians 1:4. According to the plainest statements found in the scriptures, after the "born again" experience, believers will naturally desire to be delivered from the power of sin in their lives in preparation for the investigative judgment. This is done so they don't commit the unpardonable sin after human probation closes. Again, the ongoing deliverance from the power of sin in our lives is called Bible sanctification, which has been established as the prerequisite for receiving eternal life. Romans 6:20-22, 2 Thessalonians 2:13. The evidence found in the scriptures dictates the everlasting gospel was designed to bring about the obedience of our faith in God's holy laws. Romans 16:25-26. Those who claim Christ's blood paid the penalty they rightfully deserve for their transgressions are admitting that they deserve to die because they are transgressors of the law. Therefore, because the wages of sin is [still] death in this dispensation, notwithstanding your claims made upon justification, only those who have become "born again" and are [continually] becoming "sanctified by the truth" will be awarded eternal life after the conclusion of Christ's final work of mediation, which is the investigative judgment.

The Old Testament prophets and the New Testament apostles have established that after claiming justification by faith, there will be no stopping point in the development of our Christian experience. Romans 5:1-2, Philippians 3:10-15. After justification by faith is claimed, our response should be, "Yes, Lord, please cleanse me from all unrighteousness." 1 Peter 2:9, 1 John 1:9. The "Most High" demands perfect obedience to His holy law. Matthew 5:48, John 17:20-23. The word of God commands us to become sanctified by the truth (Hebrews 12:14, Genesis 17:1); consequently, no sin can be tolerated in those who shall walk with Christ in white. John 8:34-36. Through faith in Christ's substitutional sacrifice, justified believers are to receive the real forgiveness of their sins from their Great High Priest in preparation for the investigative judgment. If truly forgiven, believers will obey the law as naturally as Adam did before his first transgression in Eden. Hebrews 10:1-2. The scriptures teach that after claiming Christ's sacrifice paid the penalty you rightfully deserve for your transgressions of the law; you are commanded to boldly access Christ's "***daily mediation***" so you can become empowered by the Holy Spirit and put to death "that which causes sin" in your life. Romans 8:12-13. Therefore, this cleansing from all unrighteousness is called Bible sanctification.

Those who understand that claims made upon justification give believers free access to Christ's "***daily mediation***" so they can put to death "that which causes sin" in their lives have been given the keys to the kingdom of heaven. Matthew 16:9. Those who have the keys to the kingdom of heaven will come boldly to the throne of grace (Hebrews 4:16), demanding from their all-powerful Mediator cleansing from all unrighteousness. 1 John 1:9. This deliverance from the power of sin in our lives is the good news of the Bible, resulting in the sanctification of your character; consequently, true born-again believers clearly understand that God has predestined all of humanity to be made eternally secure against Satan's temptations by obtaining victory over "that which causes sin" in their lives. This victory over our fallen nature is the result of the "born again" experience, evidenced by the numerous commands found in the Bible that born-again believers must form sanctified characters in harmony with God's holy law while human probation lingers. Hebrews 10:16-25. The Bible is extremely clear on this point, claiming justification by faith is not salvation (Romans 5:1-2); if you expect to be awarded eternal life at the conclusion of the investigative judgment (Revelation 14:6-7), you must come boldly to the throne of grace rejoicing in the hope of being cleansed from all unrighteousness, this is called Bible sanctification and its end is eternal life. Romans 3:2-22. Therefore, the process of being cleansed from all unrighteousness is called Bible sanctification, which the Old Testament prophets and the New Testament apostles have established as a prerequisite for receiving eternal life. Hebrews 12:14, Hebrews 10:26.

In this dispensation, our claims made upon justification create free access to Christ's daily mediation so we can obtain the real forgiveness of our sins. Through Christ's "daily mediation," justified believers can be truly forgiven of their sins representing the ongoing sanctification of their characters, and if successful, they will be awarded eternal life at the conclusion of Christ's final work of mediation, which is the investigative judgment. Romans 6:20-22. After claiming justification by faith, our conscience is placed where it can be purged from our propensity to transgress God's holy law. This cleansing takes place by accessing Christ's daily mediation to receive the real forgiveness of our sins. The real forgiveness of sins represents the sanctification of our character, and through this process, believers are being prepared for eternal life. The Apostle Paul expounds upon this concept in Romans 8:28, "We know that in everything God works for good with those who love Him, who are called according to His purpose. For those whom He foreknew, He also predestined _**to be conformed to the image of the Son**_, so that He might be the firstborn among many brethren." In 2 Corinthians 7:1, the Apostle Paul emphasizes its essential to form sanctified characters in this life. The Apostle Paul commands believers to obtain the "holiness [of character] without which no one will see the Lord." Hebrews 12:14. Consequently, the goal of the new covenant promise of salvation is made extremely clear, God's holy law must be written upon the hearts and minds of believers, so obedience becomes as natural for them as it was for Adam before his first transgression. Hebrews 8:10, Hebrews 10:16-18.

The Apostle Paul says "Therefore, having these promises, beloved, let us cleanse ourselves [by accessing Christ's daily mediation to deliver us] from the defilement of the flesh and by the spirit perfect holiness in fear of God." This cleansing "from the defilement of the flesh" is done so that we do not commit the unpardonable sin after the close of human probation. All the prophets and apostles refer to this "holiness" of character as Bible sanctification, which is the predetermined way God has chosen all of humanity to receive eternal life. 2 Thessalonians 2:13. In this generation, our religious leaders are robbing the unsuspecting multitudes of the "born again" experience. Revelation 14:8. Salvation is not awarded to anyone simply because they find themselves in the unique position of claiming Christ died for their transgressions. According to the Apostle Paul, the keys to the kingdom of heaven represent our understanding that through Christ's daily mediation, we can receive the real forgiveness of our sins (Luke 1:77) resulting in the ongoing sanctification of our characters in the hope of receiving a positive verdict in the judgment. Accessing the daily mediation of Christ in the heavenly sanctuary to obtain the real forgiveness of our sins is as essential to the plan devised for our salvation as was His death upon Calvary's Cross. Therefore, this is the correct understanding of the everlasting gospel, which was established before the foundation of the universe, it was predetermined that Christ's death would give Him the right to mediate for the real forgiveness of our sins and make the final determination of who is worthy to receive eternal life at the conclusion of His final work of mediation, which is the investigative judgment. Revelation 14:6-7, Daniel 9-10, Daniel 8:14, Revelation 11:15-19.

Sanctification is a Bible Doctrine

When translating Greek (the original language of the New Testament) into English, words have attached codes that must be considered if a proper understanding of the Bible verse is to be obtained. For instance, if a Greek word appears with a participle attached to the root of the word, the translator should add either the suffix "ing" or "ed" when translating the Greek word into English. If a Greek word has a perfect tense attached, this indicates an event has taken place in the past, which has a definite application in the present. If a word appears in the passive voice, the subject of the sentence is performing the action or is the recipient of the action of the Bible verse, depending on the verbal construction. Therefore, the point is this, the moods and tenses attached to the Greek words appearing in the Bible verse have a dramatic effect on the way they should be translated into the English language.

In John 17:19, Acts 20:32, and Acts 26:18, the Greek word ἡγιασμένοις [translated as sanctified] appears in the participle perfect passive. This grammatical nuance gives the Greek word ἡγιασμένοις [translated as sanctified in the previously referenced Bible verses] the same force and effect as the Greek word ἁγιασμόν translated as sanctified appearing as a noun in Romans 6:19 and Romans 6:22, [why] because the Greek word ἡγιασμένοις translated as sanctified in John 17:19, Acts 20:32 and Acts 26:18 all appear in the perfect tense. In John 17:19, Acts 20:32, and Acts 26:18, because the Greek word ἡγιασμένοις [translated as sanctified] appears in the perfect tense, this represents an already accomplished action in the past that has a specific application to the present. The subject of the sentence is sanctified and/or has already developed a sanctified character. In Ephesians 5:26 and Hebrews 13:12, the Greek word ἁγιάσῃ [translated as sanctification] appears in the subjunctive, which represents the mood of possibility. The believer *may* become sanctified or *may not* develop a sanctified character before human probation closes. In 1 Thessalonians 5:23, the Greek word ἁγιάσαι [translated as sanctification] appears in the optative; consequently, when properly translated into the English language, the proper translational equivalent would be, "I wish sanctification would take place" to the subject of the sentence. Therefore, the way words are translated from the original language is important, particularly "sanctification," because it describes God's predetermined way fallen humanity is to receive eternal life, "For this is the will of God, even your sanctification." 1 Thessalonians 4:3.

There is much more to the plan of salvation than simply acknowledging that a man named Jesus Christ lived and died two thousand years ago and presumptuously declaring yourself saved and forgiven of your sins. Those who claim justification (Romans 5:1-2) should rejoice in the hope of sharing the glory of God, and the Apostle Paul says, "sharing the *glory* of God" represents the sanctification of our character. It's essential to understand the believer's nature must be changed "from one degree of glory to another" (2 Corinthians 3:17-18) if they expect to be awarded eternal life after the conclusion of the investigative judgment. The Apostle Paul teaches true sanctification is a Bible doctrine; as a result, since sanctification is God's predetermined way anyone is to receive eternal life, your claims made upon justification must lead to the sanctification of your character if you expect to receive a positive verdict in the judgment. Romans 6:20-22. Therefore, the reader should understand our English Bibles are translated from Greek words that have specific definitions and attached stems, which must be investigated if a proper understanding of the plan devised for our salvation is to be obtained.

The Greek word translated as "sanctification" appears many times in the New Testament and is translated in various ways, "consecrate" (John 17:17-19), "holiness" (Hebrews 12:14), and/or "holy," Revelation 22:11. However, on many occasions, because the moods and tenses attached to the Greek word that should be translated as "sanctification," are misapplied, the word itself is mistranslated; as a result, the reader comes away with an entirely different understanding of what the inspired writer was trying to communicate. The translation of Revelation 22:11 represents a perfect example of how misapplying the moods and tenses attached to the Greek words appearing in the Bible verse cause mistranslations, creating confusion regarding the readers' understanding of the Bible verse. Conversely, if properly translated, the proclamation found in Revelation 22:11 should be very clear. In our modern Bibles, the end of Revelation 22:11 reads like this; "he who is holy, let him be holy still." The second Greek word ἁγιασθήτω, translated as "<u>holy</u>," should be translated as **sanctified** in the Bible verse. This information confirms what the Apostle Paul has already established; justified believers must form sanctified characters before human probation closes if they expect to receive a positive verdict in the judgment. Romans 6:20-22. In Revelation 22:11, the second Greek word ἁγιασθήτω, translated as "holy," has the same definition as the Greek word ἁγιασμόν, translated as sanctification in these Bible verses, Romans 6:19-22. In Revelation 22:11, the Greek word ἁγιασθήτω, translated the second time as "holy," has the same meaning as the Greek word ἁγιασμῷ, translated as sanctification in 2 Thessalonians 2:13. In 2 Thessalonians 2:13, the apostle says God has predestined everyone to be saved through the sanctification of their characters. The Strong's call number for the Greek word ἁγιασμόν, translated as "sanctification" in these Bible verses, Romans 6:19-22, and translated as "sanctified" in 2 Thessalonians 2:13, is (38); however, because the Greek word ἁγιασθήτω, translated the second time as "holy," in Revelation 22:11, is a verb and not a noun, the Strong's call number is (37) and not (38), as it is in Romans 6:19, Romans 6:22 and 2 Thessalonians 2:13. Therefore, in all of these Bible verses, Romans 6:19, Romans 6:22, 2 Thessalonians 2:13, and Revelation 22:11, the same information is being communicated, "we must become sanctified by the truth," before human probation closes, if we expect to receive eternal life, because the Greek word being employed in all of these Bible verses has the exact same definition.

In Revelation 22:11, the prophet's statement, "he who is holy, let him be holy still," announces the close of human probation. Consequently, before human probation closes (Revelation 22:11), your claims made upon justification must have separated you from your sins, representing Bible sanctification. If you are not sanctified, notwithstanding your claims made upon justification, you will be destroyed with the Devil and his evil angels in the lake of fire, which is the second death. In John 17:17, Christ says sanctify them by the truth thy word is truth, and because the Greek word ἁγίασον, translated as sanctified, is a verb and not a noun, the Strong's call number is 37, which appears as a command issued by Christ; consequently, the best possible translation of the Bible verse should be, "believers must become sanctified by the truth" if they are going to receive eternal life. Therefore, in John 17:17, the Greek word ἁγίασον, translated as sanctified, has the same meaning as the Greek word ἁγιασθήτω, translated the second time in Revelation 22:11, as **holy**, "he that is holy let him be **holy** still, or better translated as "he that is holy let him be **sanctified** (37) still."

The above-referenced information establishes that only those who have formed sanctified characters before human probation closes will receive a positive verdict in the judgment. These Bible verses, very clearly establish that, *<u>at some point in time</u>*, those claiming justification by faith *<u>must</u>* become "sanctified" by the truth if they expect to be awarded eternal life after the conclusion of Christ's final work of mediation, which is the investigative judgment. Revelation 22:11, John 17:17. In 1 Peter 3:15, the same Greek word ἁγιάσατε [translated as sanctified] is also being employed by the inspired writer, which also appears as a command, stating that you *<u>must</u>* sanctify (37) the Lord Jesus Christ daily in your hearts. The command to form sanctified characters in this life is not a suggestion; it comes to us as a command; if you are to receive eternal life, justified believers must form sanctified characters, with the end of this maturation process being eternal life. The statement, "he who is holy let him be [**sanctified**] (37) still" (Revelation 22:11) is very important because this proclamation marks the close of human probation and describes the sanctified character of the saved who have employed their claims made upon justification to cleanse themselves from all unrighteousness. 2 Thessalonians 2:13, Titus 2:11-14, and 1 John 1:9. Therefore, those who have keys to the kingdom of heaven clearly understand, after claiming justification by faith, they *<u>must</u>* form sanctified characters in this life (John 17:17), or they will be destroyed with the Devil and his evil angels in the lake of fire, which is the second death. Romans 5:1-2, 2 Thessalonians 3:17, Revelation 20:15, and Matthew 25:41.

In his letter to the Thessalonian Church, the Apostle Paul declares, "This is the will of God, even your sanctification," and he goes on to pray, "may the very God of peace sanctify you wholly." 1 Thessalonians 4:3, and 1 Thessalonians 5:23. The apostle teaches the true meaning of Bible sanctification, which is righteousness, and states it must be obtained if believers are going to be deemed worthy to receive eternal life in the judgment. The Savior prayed for His disciples, "Sanctify them through thy truth; and specifically says, **_thy word is truth_**" (John: 17:17, John 17:19), and the Apostle Paul says believers are to be "sanctified by the Holy Spirit," Who is to lead believers into all truth. Romans 15:16. Obviously then, it's the work of the Holy Spirit to sanctify believers, which takes place by convicting the world of sin and of righteousness and of the judgment to come. John 16:8-11. The judgment to come is the message for this time, commanding all believers claiming justification by faith to form sanctified characters in preparation for Christ's final work of mediation, which is the investigative judgment. Revelation 14:6-7. Jesus told His disciples, "When the Spirit of truth comes, he will guide you into all truth" (John 16:13), and the Psalmist says, "**_Thy law is the truth_**." Psalm 119:142. The plan of salvation is being made very clear; through the Spirit of God, the great principles of righteousness embodied in His law are to be written upon the hearts and minds of believers in both dispensations. Hebrews 8:10, Jeremiah 31:31-34. The apostle says having God's holy law written upon our hearts and minds is the New Covenant promise of salvation. Therefore, having God's holy law written upon our hearts and minds clearly defines the plan devised for our salvation in both dispensations, (Hebrews 8:10, Jeremiah 31:31) specifically because God's holy law will be the standard of righteousness used by Christ to evaluate our characters during His final work of mediation, which is the investigative judgment. James 2:8-12, Revelation 14:6-7, Revelation 20:12.

The Apostle Paul says God's law is "holy, and just, and good"

(Romans 7:12), and it's a transcript of the Divine perfection. Psalms 119:1. It stands to reason that a character formed in harmony with God's law will also be holy (Titus 2:11-14), and this "holiness" of character should be translated as sanctification in the following Bible verses. Revelation 22:11, Hebrews 12:14, Genesis 17:1, 1 Peter 3:15. The sanctification of our character is a command given to fallen defective humanity by God as a prerequisite for receiving eternal life. The Greek word ἁγιασμόν, translated as "holiness" in Hebrews 12:14, is the same Greek word ἁγιασμόν, translated as "sanctification" in Romans 6:19 and Romans 6:22. It is God's predetermined plan (2 Thessalonians 2:13) to write His holy law upon the hearts and minds of believers so they can obey His law naturally, willingly, and perfectly just as Adam did before his first transgression. Again, this is called Bible sanctification; and Christ is a perfect example of such a "holy" and sanctified character. It was Christ who uttered words that for anyone else would have been blasphemy, "I have kept my Father's commandments" and "I do always those things that please Him." John 15:10, John 8:29, John 17:17-19. The possibility of forming sanctified characters in preparation for the judgment is the good news of the Bible; the followers of Christ can become like Him in character by forming sanctified characters in harmony with the principles of His holy law. John 14:15, and 1 Corinthians 7:1. Again, this is called Bible sanctification, which is a prerequisite for receiving a positive verdict in the judgment. Therefore, salvation is not obtained simply by claiming that Christ died for your transgressions of the law; it's made extremely clear justification must lead to the sanctification of your character, with its end being eternal life. Romans 6:20-22.

The rich young ruler came to Christ, asking, "What must I do to be saved," and His response was, "If you would enter life, keep the commandments." The rich young ruler then asked, "Which commandment," Christ's response was, "You shall not kill, you shall not commit adultery, you shall not steal, you shall not bear false witness, honor your father and mother, and you shall love your neighbor as yourself." Matthew 19:17-20. After hearing this, the young man responded that he had vigorously kept all these commandments since his childhood and wanted to know what he lacked. Christ said, "If you would be _perfect_" sell all you have and come and follow me." Matthew 19:21. This was not an empty invitation. It's obvious Christ was trying to make the young man aware of a flaw in his character, that's why He said, "if you would be perfect _sell_ what you have and _come and follow me_." In Matthew 19:21, the word Christ employed, translated as "_perfect_" has a Strong's Concordance call number of (5046), which means "complete and/or perfect" and looks like this τέλειος in the original language. The Friberg's Greek Lexicon defines the Greek word τέλειος as, "complete, perfect, undivided, entire (Romans 12:2, and 1 Corinthians 13:10); of persons, *complete, perfect* (Matthew 5:48) with its chief component meaning, fully developed, of persons, being *fully grown, and mature* (1 Corinthians 14:20) of things *fully developed, and or complete,* with its chief component meaning, fully prepared or readiness, *complete, perfect.* Colossians 1:28, James 3:2. Therefore, in all its meanings, τέλειος carries the component of "a purpose that has been achieved."

The _perfection of character_ referred to by Christ in Matthew 19:21 is the _same perfection of character_ referred to by the Apostle Paul in Philippians 3:12-15. This is not sinless perfection; it represents the born-again experience, a perfect attitude toward obeying God's laws. When _the perfection of character_ is developed, rendering willing obedience to all of God's requirements, the very moment truth is revealed becomes the most important thing in the justified believer's life. The thief on the Cross was born again; he had developed this perfect attitude; he was not ignorant of the justifying power the promised Redeemer could provide believers. In the last moments of life, the thief saw in Christ, dying upon Calvary's Cross, the Messiah of Bible prophecy, He who was to save His people from their sins. Matthew 1:21. The thief was familiar with Christ's words (Matthew 13:36-43) and that the manner of His first advent was not in accordance with the expectations held by the ignorant multitudes. Now in his dying hour, the thief understood Christ's mission was to deliver believers "from" their sins; and said with hopeful anticipation, "Lord could you remember me when you come into your kingdom." Luke 23:42.

The thief was saved at the last hour for one reason and one reason only, because he was born again, perfectly convinced that death would be far better than transgression, and he was determined to obey all of God's requirements. Matthew 20:1-16. This attitude represents the "born again" experience when believers come to understand that it would be far better to die rather than knowingly transgress even one of God's requirements. The One who gives life says, "Walk before Me and be ye perfect" (Genesis 17:1), and the Apostle Peter says, "He who called you is holy, so be yourselves holy in all your conduct." 1 Peter 1:15. The apostle says, if you would be perfect, "Put off your old nature, which belongs to your former manner of life and is corrupt through deceitful lust, and be renewed in the spirit of your mind, and put on the new nature created after the likeness of God in true righteousness and holiness." Ephesians 4:22-24. The rich young ruler asked Christ, "What must I do to be saved," and His response was, "If you would enter life, keep the commandments." Matthew 19:17. Therefore if Christ was asked the same question today, why would you assume His response would be anything different than "if you would enter life keep the commandments." Revelation 12:17, Revelation 14:12.

The Apostle Paul's attitude towards his own personal salvation is made very clear, "Not that I have already obtained this [salvation] or am already **_perfect_**, but I press on to make it my own because Christ Jesus has made me His own." Philippians 3:11-15. The apostle emphasizes that "the perfection of character" is the goal justified believers are to obtain if they are going to successfully resist sin and Satan's temptations. The perfection of character is evidenced when believers would rather die than knowingly transgress any of God's laws, His moral law, (the Ten Commandments), or His health laws. John 14:15, 1 John 3:9, 1 Corinthians 11:29, and 1 Corinthians 3:16-17. The Bible clearly teaches that the violation of God's moral law and His laws of health is sin, and since the wages of sin leads to the second death, the everlasting gospel is *"good news"* for those looking to avoid the promise of God's unmingled wrath being poured out upon the willful transgressors of His laws, that takes place shortly after the conclusion of Christ's final work of mediation, which is the investigative judgment. Revelation 14:6-7, Revelation 16:1-21. After the conclusion of the investigative judgment, the opportunity to form sanctified characters in harmony with God's holy law has been finally and irrevocably withdrawn; why, because human probation closes after the conclusion of the investigative judgment. The plan devised for our salvation is not about a profession of faith (Matthew 7:21) God's plan of salvation was designed to give believers the opportunity of developing the strength and nobility of character lost in the consequence of sin. The perfection of character referred to by Christ when addressing the rich young ruler is the born-again experience, leading to the real forgiveness of sins, resulting in the ongoing sanctification of the believer's character. Matthew 19:21. The Apostle Paul says when believers understand the everlasting gospel in this light, they have the "keys to the kingdom of heaven" and a correct understanding of the plan devised for their salvation. Philippians 3:11-15.

In Ephesians 4:13, the apostle represents salvation as a maturing process. In this process, justification by faith is claimed *until we* "all attain" (these two words appear in the subjunctive), so a better translation would be "until we *may attain* to the unity of the faith and the knowledge of the Son of God, to mature manhood to the measure of the stature of the fullness of Christ." The "unity of the faith" referred to in Ephesians 4:13 is not the fellowship with one another many people claim it means. The Greek word "unity" should be translated as oneness, which represents the same relationship Christ had with His Father, which He refers to when praying for His disciples. John 17:17-23. Through faith in Christ's atoning sacrifice, believers can access His "daily mediation" to have their sins truly forgiven. The "oneness of the faith" results from an ongoing relationship with Christ, resulting from the Holy Spirit being imparted to believers, empowering them with the strength and nobility of character lost in the consequence of sin. The "oneness of the faith" results from the born-again experience, stemming from the believers' willingness to render perfect obedience to the laws of the government of heaven. Revelation 14:12.

In Ephesians 4:13, the "oneness of the faith" is what Christ was referring to in John 17:23 because the same Greek word is employed in both Bible verses. In John 17:23, the Greek word translated as "oneness" appears in the perfect tense; consequently, it refers to an already accomplished action that has a continuing and ongoing application in the present. Therefore, the "unity of the faith," appearing in Ephesians 4:13 and John 17:23 represents a completed work, and yet an ongoing process at the same time, of receiving the actual forgiveness of all your sins, promised to believers in both dispensations, which is the good news; it's the goal of the everlasting gospel to cleanse believers from all their unrighteousness. John 1:9-13.

The Apostle Paul continually emphasizes redemption means the ongoing "deliverance" from the power of sin in the believer's life. Luke 2:77. In Ephesians 4:13, "The knowledge of the Son of God" is the knowledge that all must have if they are to receive eternal life. John 17:3, 1 Corinthians 1:30. Accordingly, eternal life is given "to a mature [sanctified] man" who would rather die than knowingly transgress any one of God's requirements. Here, the Greek word translated as mature (Strong's call number 5046) is the same Greek word τέλειον, translated as perfect in Philippians 3:15. Consequently, it should be translated as "perfect" in Ephesians 4:13 to obtain the best understanding of the Bible verse. The best translation of the Greek word τέλειον, translated as mature in Ephesians 4:13 would be "to a perfect man," representing then the completed yet ongoing work of the sanctification of the believer's character as predetermined by God for our salvation through the "everlasting gospel," which represents the good news of the Bible. The everlasting gospel is to "bring about the [present and ongoing] obedience of our faith," which will be joyfully performed by the sanctified "born again" believer[s]. Romans 16:25-26. Moving on with the retranslation of Ephesians 4:13, the rest of the Bible verse should read like this: "To the measure" (better translated as to the extent) "of the stature" (better translated as the maturity) "which belongs to the fullness of Christ." In Ephesians 4:11-12, after referencing why the gifts of the Spirit were given to the church, if Ephesians 4:13 was translated correctly, it would read like this, "Until we may possibly attain to the oneness of the faith and the knowledge of the Son of God into a perfect man to the extent of the maturity, which belongs to the fullness of Christ," and this the apostle says is called Bible sanctification.

The unsuspecting multitudes of this generation believe in a counterfeit gospel taught them by their church leaders. This counterfeit gospel is perfectly calculated to deceive the unsuspecting multitudes with pleasing doctrines designed to create the illusion of salvation by removing Christ as their only mediator and judge. This distortion of the everlasting gospel is an "abomination" unto the Lord because it makes believers who are actually spiritually "desolate" feel "assured of their salvation now and in the judgment" simply by claiming justification by faith. In this dispensation, the illusion of salvation is created immediately after professed believers claim Christ's death paid the penalty they rightfully deserve for their transgressions of the law. Revelation 3:17-18. This subliminal distortion of the everlasting gospel occurs when eternal life is promised the very moment believers make a profession of faith in Christ's atoning blood; consequently, the unsuspecting multitudes believe in a counterfeit gospel that's quite different from the everlasting gospel advanced in the scriptures. Romans 6:20-22. The scriptures are clear; if you are to receive eternal life, you must be "born again," which results in the sanctification of your character (John 3:7), producing an attitude that you would rather die than knowingly commit one sin. 1 John 3:9, 1 John 5:18.

In the judgment, a mere profession of faith in Christ's atoning blood means absolutely nothing. Matthew 7:21. The knowledge of Christ's daily mediation to forgive sins in conjunction with His final work of mediation to make atonement for sin, which is the blotting out of sins truly forgiven from the books at the conclusion of the investigative judgment, is the key that unlocks the door of your salvation. The "keys to the kingdom of heaven" is the understanding that a channel of communication has been opened between God the Father and fallen sinful humanity through the merits of Calvary's Cross so that believers who claim justification by faith can access Christ's "daily mediation" to receive the real "let-go-ness" of their sins leading to the sanctification of their character and a positive verdict in the judgment. Conversely, the counterfeit gospel taught believers by their church leaders today removes Christ as the believer's only mediator and judge; this results in the sin-loving multitudes pronouncing themselves saved and forgiven immediately after they claim "justification by faith" regardless of their unsanctified spiritual condition. Daniel 8:11-12.

The Apostle Paul clearly states if we expect to receive eternal life, we must put off the old nature and "put on the new nature created after the likeness of God in true righteousness and holiness." Ephesians 4:23. The plan of salvation, established before the foundation of the world, presents the believer with the wonderful opportunity of forming a Christ-like character in this life so they can naturally obey the laws of the government of heaven. However, left to ourselves, we cannot obtain the holiness of character God's word declares we must have before salvation can be granted to anyone in the judgment. In the judgment, "No value is attached to a mere profession of faith in Christ; only the love which is shown by works is counted genuine." The Great Controversy, by, E.G., White, Page 487. "Jesus died to save his people from their sins, and redemption in Christ means to cease the transgression of the law of God and to be free from every sin; no heart that is stirred with enmity against the law of God, is in harmony with Christ, who suffered upon Calvary's Cross, to vindicate and exalt the law before the universe." The Signs of the Times, Article by, E.G., White, July 21, 1890, Part # 5. If the gospel message is correctly understood, claims made upon Christ's blood require those making these claims to form sanctified characters while the gospel invitation lingers. The everlasting gospel demands those claiming justification by faith must be "cleansed from all unrighteousness." 1 John 1:9. In direct opposition to this understanding, the sin-loving multitudes of this generation profess to have "the assurance of salvation now and in the judgment" immediately after claiming Christ's blood paid the penalty they rightfully deserve for their transgressions of God's Holy Ten Commandment law.

If the fallen nature we inherited at birth from our earthly parents has not been put to death, pronouncing yourself saved and forgiven after claiming justification is nothing more than an illusion. Galatians 5:24. The everlasting gospel is "good news" for those born into this world possessing the defective nature they inherited at birth without their consent from their earthly parents. The fallen nature we inherited at birth without our consent from our earthly parents creates an overpowering propensity to transgress God's requirements. The "good news" was designed to save Adam's descendants from their sins by making them eternally secure against Satan's temptations. The "good news" points to the deliverance from the power of sin in our lives, which takes place when the fallen nature we inherited at birth without our consent has been put to death. Ephesians 4:22-24. According to the gospel message, through the merits of Christ's death and His subsequent mediation, Adam's descendants can, by the Spirit, put to death the overpowering sinful propensities that caused them to transgress. Romans 7:4-6, Romans 8:12-13. Those who have rejected the "good news" will neglect to put to death "that which causes sin" in their lives while human probation lingers. Therefore, notwithstanding your spiritual association, **_liberal_** or **_conservative_**, if you have accepted a counterfeit gospel that creates the **_illusion_** of salvation outside of putting to death the fallen defective nature you inherited at birth without your consent from your earthly parents, you will surely transgress after probation closes and suffer the second death with Satan and his evil angels in the lake of fire. Revelation 20:1-15.

The good news of the Bible is translated as the everlasting gospel. The everlasting gospel points to God's mercy while establishing that justice makes up the foundation of the law and the government of heaven. The introduction of the everlasting gospel explicitly addresses the circumstances surrounding our transgressions. Romans 5:12-14. The fallen defective nature we received at birth has caused all of Adam's descendants to transgress God's holy law. As a result, it was preordained before the foundation of the world that fallen humanity would be given another opportunity to form sanctified characters in harmony with the law and the government of heaven. This is good news for Adam's descendants who have been born into this world "through no fault of their own," possessing a fallen defective nature. The everlasting gospel clearly states that Christ, one equal to the law, would pay the penalty sinners rightfully deserve for their transgressions of God's holy law and subsequently mediate for the forgiveness of their sins. However, God's mercy in offering His Son as a sacrifice for the sins of the world does not nullify the fact that "the wages of sin is [still] death" in this dispensation. This death sentence will be executed upon transgressors shortly after human probation closes. The price of offering the everlasting gospel to our fallen race establishes God's mercy while vindicating the death sentence the transgressions of His holy law demands. Therefore, the good news of the Bible establishes that justice and mercy stand at the foundation of the law and the government of heaven.

    The Bible clearly states all of Adam's descendants have been predestined to be saved; (Romans 8:29-30, Ephesians 1:3-14) the lake of fire was originally prepared for the Devil and his evil angels. Matthew 25:41, Revelation 20:12-15. In spite of the fact that all have been predestined to be saved by the sanctification of their characters, few will actually comply with the conditions of eternal life, which is putting to death "that which causes sin" in their lives. Matthew 7:13-14. In Romans 8:1-4, the Apostle Paul says, God has done what the law weakened through the flesh could not do; sending His own Son in the likeness of sinful flesh and for sin, He condemned sin in the flesh. The term "in the flesh" appears as the indirect object in the Bible verse, so it would be better translated as He condemned sin "by the flesh," meaning the flesh is the moving agent. The term "by the flesh" represents those who have transgressed the law because they were born into this world through no fault of their own, possessing **_a fallen nature_** previously defined as "that which causes sin" in our lives. In

Romans 8:3, when the term "by the flesh" is correctly understood, it's addressing the reasons why the everlasting gospel was mercifully introduced to our fallen race. In Romans 8:4, the apostle is contrasting the fallen nature with the unfallen nature by saying Christ came so that the just requirements of the law might be fulfilled in those who walk not **_by the flesh_** (as the moving agent in their lives causing them to transgress the law) but **_by the Spirit_** as the moving agent enabling them to willingly obey the law. In addition, the justice of God makes available the Holy Spirit, Who stands RWA, ready, willing, and able, to empower justified believers to obey the law by forming righteous, sanctified, "born again" characters in preparation for the investigative judgment. Romans 8:12-13, Galatians 5:16-24. Therefore, the Bible clearly states that all of Adam's descendants have been predestined to be saved; (Romans 8:29-30, Ephesians 1:3-14) if they simply comply with the conditions of receiving eternal life, which states only born-again believers can receive eternal life. John 3:7.

The everlasting gospel was offered to fallen humanity on specific conditions, and simply claiming justification by faith does not satisfy these conditions; we must be born again, our fallen nature must be put to death, and we must become sanctified by the truth if we are going to receive a positive verdict in the judgment. In the judgment, a mere profession of faith means absolutely nothing; we are not saved by our works, but we are definitely judged by what we say and do in this life. Romans 2:6-13, Revelation 20:12, 2 Corinthians 5:10, Matthew 16:27, and Matthew 12:36. In Romans 8:12-13, the two natures are being contrasted by the apostle who says if you live **_by the flesh_** (as the moving agent causing you to transgress), you will die, but if you **_by the Spirit_** put to death the deeds of the flesh, [representing the death of your fallen nature] you will live. Galatians 5:24. The Bible clearly says all of Adam's descendants have sinned, having been born "controlled **_by the flesh_**" meaning they were born with a fallen human nature. Romans 3:23, Romans 7:21. In Romans 8:1-4, the term "**_by the flesh_**" represents those who have transgressed the law because they were born [without their consent] possessing **_a fallen defective nature_**.

Therefore, in Romans 8:1-4, the apostle says God has done what the law weakened by the flesh could not do; sending His own Son in the likeness of sinful flesh, and for sin, He could now justly condemn those who have sinned even though they were born controlled *by the flesh*, meaning they are controlled by their fallen defective human nature.

In harmony with this understanding, Christ died so that the just requirements of the law could be fulfilled in those who walk not according to the flesh but by the power of the Holy Spirit working righteousness in their lives. Therefore, the Bible says all have been predestined to be saved through the sanctification of their characters, no one is saved simply by acknowledging Christ died for their transgressions of the law. The Bible is extremely clear, the entirety of fallen humanity has been predestined to be saved through the sanctification of their character. Romans 8:29-30, Ephesians 1:3-14. The introduction of the everlasting gospel allows the Godhead to justly condemn all those to their eternal destruction who have sinned even though they were born controlled *by the flesh* specifically because they have refused to repent. After acknowledging Christ's death paid the penalty you rightfully deserve for your transgressions of the law, accessing His "daily mediation" to receive the real forgiveness of your sin in preparation for the investigative judgment is essential to the plan devised for our salvation. The good news of the Bible represents the offer to receive eternal life if believers, *by the Spirit*, put to death the deeds of the flesh in preparation for Christ's final work of mediation, which is the investigative judgment. Therefore, these born-again, sanctified believers will not be destroyed in the lake of fire with the Devil and his evil angels, which is the second death. Matthew 25:41, Revelation 20:12-15.

In Romans 8:28-34, the Apostle Paul specifically addresses the need for *justified* believers to form *sanctified* characters in preparation for Christ's final work of mediation, which is the investigative judgment. In Romans 8:28-30, the apostle addresses the idea of predestination by stating, "we know that in everything God works for good with those who love Him, who are called according to His purpose.

For those whom He foreknew, He also predestined <u>*to be conformed to the image of His son*</u> so that He may be the first-born among many brethren. In Romans 8:33-34, after saying believers are to reflect the image of their Savior, the Apostle Paul asked this fundamental question, "<u>*Who shall bring any charge against God's people*</u>? The answer to this question is obvious and direct, it is God, the Justifier, who will condemn those living by the flesh, [more specifically] it is Jesus Christ who died and was raised from the dead, who is [in possession] of the right hand of the power [of the universe] and intercedes for our transgressions, that will preside in the judgment.

The answer to the question, "<u>*Who shall bring any charge against God's people*</u> is made very clear; it is <u>*Jesus Christ*</u> grammatically linked to [**the Justifier**] who will condemn all those who have refused to put to death "that which causes sin" in their lives. It is <u>*Jesus Christ*</u> "who shall bring charges against those" who have claimed <u>*justification by faith*</u> and refused to <u>*form sanctified characters in this life*</u>. The justifying power of Calvary's Cross gives all the fallen sons of Adam, born into this world through no fault of their own possessing an overpowering propensity to transgress, the right to freely access Christ's daily mediation and by the Spirit put to death "that which causes sin" in their lives. Those who refuse to comply with the conditions of eternal life will be condemned by Christ, "the Justifier," because they have refused to form sanctified characters in this life. Those who see themselves as helpless sinners, condemned to death because they have transgressed God's holy law, may receive a positive verdict in the judgment if they comply with the conditions of eternal life, which is to obey and live. John 3:36. Therefore, at the final execution of the judgment, which is the lake of fire, Satan, his evil angels, and all those who have refused to form sanctified characters in this life, will unanimously proclaim, "that justice and mercy stand at the foundation of the law and the government of heaven."

6

WHOSOEVER COMMITS SIN TRANSGRESSES – ALSO GOD'S HOLY TEN COMMANDMENT LAW

Notwithstanding the character flaws indigenous to fallen humanity, which have caused all of Adam's descendants to transgress God's laws, the everlasting gospel was introduced and clearly states that God will not force salvation upon anyone if they choose to continually transgress His holy Law[s]. The Bible defines sin as the transgression of God's laws, both His Ten Commandment Law, and His health laws. Romans 3:19-20, 1 John 3:4, 1 Corinthians 3:16-17 and 1 Corinthians 11:29. It was God himself who proclaimed His Holy Ten Commandment Law amid the thunders of Mt. Sinai and wrote them upon two tables of stone, so none need err regarding their understanding of sin along with the penalty associated with its violations. The gospel was introduced because the penalty linked to sin demands the eternal destruction of the transgressor, regardless of the circumstances surrounding the transgression or if the sin took place in either dispensation. Romans 6:23, Romans 5:12-14. The Bible emphatically states all have sinned, which is defined in the Bible as the transgressions of the law. In the executive judgment, during the 1,000-year millennium (Revelation 20:4-6), when the saved of all ages review the Book of Records (Revelation 20:13) it will be categorically settled in the minds of the unfallen worlds that the Holy Spirit was sent to lead all of humanity to repentance, yet the majority rejected this gracious offer of eternal life. Revelation 20:7-10. The Bible is clear on the following points: (John 16:8) [1] that the Holy Spirit was sent to convict the world of **sin**, which is defined as the transgression of God's holy law. 1 John 3:4 KJV. [2] The Holy Spirit was sent to convict the world of **righteousness**, Romans 8:4, which is defined as obedience to God's holy law. [3] The Holy Spirit was sent to convict the world that God's holy law, will be the standard of **righteousness** used by Christ to evaluate our characters during His final work of mediation, which is the investigative **judgment**. James 2:12-16, Daniel 7:9-10.

The Holy Spirit will convict the world of the coming **judgment**, (Revelation 14:6-7, Daniel 7:9-10) which specifically takes place during the sealing time. Revelation 7:1-4, Revelation 14:1-7. The Bible says it's during the sealing time that the dead will be judged by those things which are written in the books according to their works, and not by what they profess to believe. Consequently, starting with the commencement of Christ's final work of mediation, "for the cleansing of sins truly forgiven from the heavenly sanctuary," (Daniel 8:14) the "wise" (Daniel 10:1) will wash their robes and make them white by the blood of the Lamb in preparation for the time when they must stand in the presence of God without a mediator after human probation closes. Revelation 10:5-7, Revelation 11:15-19, Daniel 8:14, Revelation 14:6-7, and 2 Corinthians 5:10. Therefore, due to the character flaws indigenous to fallen humanity, the prophets of the past dispensation and the apostles of this dispensation have established that the everlasting gospel was introduced because the wages of sin requires the death of the transgressor in both dispensations; consequently, after Calvary's Cross, Christ ascended into the heavenly sanctuary, (Hebrews 9:12-15) to mediate for the real forgiveness of our sins, (Hebrews 9:23-24) in preparation for His final work of mediation, (Daniel 8:14) which is the investigative judgment (Revelation 11:15-19) and the Holy Spirit was dispatched to the Earth to convict the world of **sin**, of **righteousness**, and of the coming **judgment**. John 16:7-11, Revelation 14:6-7, Daniel 7:9-10, Revelation 11:15-19.

When Christ was asked, which is the greatest commandment in

the law, His response was not that the law is a yoke of bondage specifically because it can't be kept or that His sacrifice for the sins of the world would free humanity from their obligation of rendering strict obedience to the law as advocated by the mainline Protestant and Evangelical Churches of this dispensation. To the contrary, Christ's response was, "Thou shall love the Lord thy God with all thy heart, and with all thy soul, and with all thy mind. This [Christ said] is the first and the greatest commandment in God's Holy Ten Commandment Law, and the second is like unto it, 'Thou shall love thy neighbor as thyself.' This is why Christ declared that on these two commandments, "hangs all the law and the prophets." Matthew 22:37-40. In harmony with this understanding, the Apostle Paul says that we should love our neighbor as ourselves (Romans 13:8-10), and Christ specifically defines love as obedience to the law. Christ said, "If you love Me, you will keep my commandments, (John 3:36, John 14:15) while explicitly advising us that "if you keep my commandments, you shall abide in my love; even as I have kept my Father's commandments, and I'm abiding in His love." John 15:10. It is not enough to profess love for God while continuing to transgress His laws; Christ emphatically states that this is hypocrisy, (Matthew 23:1-7), which is why the evidence of our love must be evaluated in the judgment, (Revelation 20:11-15) the biblical facts are clear, a profession of faith means absolutely nothing, only those that are strictly obeying God's laws will be accounted worthy to receive eternal life in the judgment. Therefore, this understanding is in harmony with the parable of the wedding garment, (Matthew 22:11-14) those clothed with the wedding garment have the Holy Spirit, (Revelation 19:7-9) which abides only in those that are keeping God's holy law. John 14:15-17, Revelation 14:12.

The everlasting gospel clearly states that eternal life is not awarded to alleged believers in the judgment based on their professions, believers must have the Holy Spirit evidenced by their obedience to God's laws if they are to receive eternal life. See the parable of the ten virgins. In John 16:7-15, and John 15:26, Christ says the Holy Spirit [the Counselor] will convict the world that God's holy law, will be the standard of **righteousness** used by Christ to evaluate our characters during His final work of mediation, which is the investigative **judgment**. James 2:12-16. In John 14:21, Christ says, "He who has my commandments and keeps them, this is he that loves me and will be loved by My Father," and the Trinity will be manifested in them, John 14:21-26, this is why the prophet declares that, "this is the love of God that we keep His commandments." 1 John 5:3. Therefore, it should be noted that the same prophet declares our willing obedience to God's holy law gives evidence of our love, <u>*for he who says I love God and disobeys His commandments is a liar*</u> and the truth is not in him, but whoever <u>**keeps His words**</u> in him truly love for God is perfected. 1 John 2:3-4, John 17:3, 1 John 4:7-8.

There are virtually hundreds of references where Christ defines love as obedience to His laws. John 14:21. The reader needs to understand that when Christ was asked, which is the greatest commandment in the law, His response was, "Thou shall love the Lord thy God with all thy heart, and with all thy soul, and with all thy mind. This [Christ said] is the first and the greatest commandment in God's Holy Ten Commandment Law, and the second is like unto it, 'Thou shall love thy neighbor as thyself.' Therefore, when asked, which is the greatest commandment in the law, Christ took this opportunity to define the importance of keeping the law, not that His death would free humanity from their obligation of rendering strict obedience to His Holy Ten Commandment Law; conversely, Christ's response was in harmony with the New Covenant promise of salvation: (Hebrews 8:10), those who have God's holy law written upon their hearts and minds, will love God with all their heart and their neighbor as themselves, and Christ, along with all of the prophets and apostles, have clearly stated that this love will be evidenced by believers keeping the law, and on these two commandments "hangs all the law and the prophets." Matthew 22:37-40.

Notwithstanding the powerful arguments already presented establishing that our faith doesn't make void God's holy law, from the pulpits of Christendom today, our religious leaders are declaring that God's holy law, as originally proclaimed by "the Most High" amid the thunders of Mt. Sinai, is no longer binding upon believers of this generation. While the Catholic Church claims to have the power to change God's holy law, the mainline Protestant and Evangelical Churches are both claiming that the law has been abrogated because it's a yoke of bondage, primarily because it can't be kept, evidenced by the fact that all have sinned. Therefore, according to the scriptures, nothing could be further from the truth; just because all have sinned doesn't mean that the law is no longer binding thereby justifying continued transgressions. Romans 5:12-14, Romans 3:19-21.

The Apostle Paul says, "If it had not been for the law, [he] should not have known what sin is" (Romans 7:7) and that our faith does not make void God's holy law; on the contrary, it establishes the existence of God's holy law. Romans 3:31. In fact, the very moment believers claim, "justification by faith," they are admitting they deserve to die because they are transgressors of the law. Galatians 2:17-18. The Bible says you cannot transgress something that does not exist (Romans 4:15), and the same apostle that declared, "the wages of sin is death," emphatically affirms that God's law is holy, just, and good, (Romans 7:12) consequently, it cannot be a yoke of bondage as advocated by the mainline Protestant and Evangelical Churches of this dispensation. The Bible teaches that the transgressors of God's Holy Ten Commandment Law will be condemned in the judgment and specific instructions are coming from the apostles and prophets warning us not to turn "justification by faith" into a license to transgress God's holy law. **Romans 6:1-2**. Therefore, this chapter is designed to establish **that sin** is the "transgression of God's Holy Ten Commandment Law" (1 John 3:4), which includes the Seventh Day Sabbath, that love is defined as obedience to the law, 1 John 5:3, John 14:15 and that the law as originally proclaimed by God himself amid the thunder of Mt. Sinai will be the standard of **righteousness** used to evaluate our characters in the **judgment.** James 2:8-12.

The correct understanding of the gospel and its relationship to God's holy law is specifically defined by the Apostle Paul in the Book of Romans. In Romans 3:19-20, the Apostle Paul says, "Now we know, [meaning everyone should know this information], that whatever the law says it speaks to those who are under the law so that ***every mouth*** *may be stopped* and the whole world may be held accountable to God; for no human being will be justified in his sight by works of the law *since through the law comes the knowledge of sin*." As stated earlier the Apostle John says the Holy Spirit will convict the world of **sin** and of **righteousness** and of the coming **judgment**. Consequently, after being convicted of *sin*, believers will fully comprehend their need for a Savior because they are transgressors of the law and since the penalty associated with their transgressions is death they will claim "justification by faith" and rejoice in the hope of forming **sanctified characters** in harmony with God's holy law (Romans 5:1-2) knowing the **sanctification of our characters** must be obtained in preparation for Christ's final work of mediation, which is the **investigative judgment**.

The new covenant promise of salvation is designed to write God's holy law upon the hearts and minds of believers so that obedience becomes as natural for them as it was for Adam and Eve before their first transgression. Hebrews 8:10. The law defines *sin* and our need for a Savior to pay the price for our *transgressions of the law*. 1 John 3:4, Hebrews 9:15, Hebrews 10:16-24. The same gospel that justifies sinners includes a **judgment** message promising death to those who refuse to overcome "that which causes *sin*" in their lives. Matthew 13:41. The gospel writers collectively say Christ was manifested to take away our sins, and in him, there was no sin. 1 John 3:4-9. Conversely, the professed Christian churches of this generation are claiming God's holy law was abolished at Calvary's Cross; if this were true, sinners would not need Christ to die for their transgressions, take away their sins, or mediate for the forgiveness of their sins. The scriptures emphatically state, "Where there is no *law*, there is no *transgression*" (Romans 4:15), and if the law was made void by Christ's death upon Calvary's Cross, [after Christ died for the sins of the world] why do the apostles clearly define **sin** *as the transgression of the law* (Romans 7:7), and why does the apostle state God's Holy law will be the standard of righteousness used by Christ to evaluate our characters in the judgment. James 2:10-12, Matthew 19:16-21, 1 John 3:4.

In the last two chapters, it was established those claiming justification by faith must put to death "that which causes _sin_" in their lives. The Bible is clear on this point, if any of the fallen sons of Adam are going to receive eternal life, crucifying the flesh with its sinful desires must be done in preparation for the coming **judgment;** why, because the **law** will be the standard of **righteousness** used by Christ to evaluate our characters. James 2:8-12. In harmony with this line of thinking, the Bible calls the process of forming characters in harmony with God's holy law, sanctification, **with its end** leading to a positive verdict in the judgment. Romans 6:20-22. This is why the Apostle Paul says, "Now we know, [meaning everyone should know this information] that whatever the law says, it speaks to those who are under the law so that _**every mouth may be stopped**_ and the whole world may be held accountable to God, for no human being will be justified in his sight by works of the law _**since through the law comes the knowledge of sin**_." Since God's holy law will be the standard of righteousness in the judgment, it cannot be a yoke of bondage, as alleged by the mainline Protestant and Evangelical churches of this dispensation; the Bible is extremely clear on this subject, where there is no law there can be no transgression, obviously then, God's laws, both His Holy Ten Commandment law and His health laws are still binding upon believers today, specifically because _**through the law comes the knowledge of sin**_."

There is No Biblical Support that God's Holy Law Has Been Changed or Abrogated

As advocated by the Catholic, mainline Protestant, and Evangelical Churches of this generation there is no biblical support that God's Holy Law has been changed by the Catholic Church or abrogated by our faith in Jesus Christ as advocated by the Mainline Protestant, and Evangelical Churches of this generation. The following Bible verses, Romans 6:14, Romans 7:4-6, Romans 10:4, Galatians 5:16-18, Colossians 2:13-14, and Ephesians 2:14-15 do not even remotely support the idea that God's holy law can be changed and/or has been made void after believers claim by faith Christ's death paid the penalty sinners rightfully deserve for their transgressions of the law. However, this is exactly what is being taught by the Catholic, mainline Protestant, and Evangelical Churches of this generation. The reason they have gotten away with this abomination, that's making a host of unsuspecting believers spiritually desolate, is the sin-loving multitudes of this generation do not investigate Bible truths for themselves. The majority prefer to rely upon their religious leaders to guide them to the Promised Land. As a result, false doctrines abound regarding the important truths concerning our salvation, particularly the perpetuity and the unchangeable nature of God's Holy Ten Commandment Law, which defines sin in both dispensations and will be the standard of righteousness used to evaluate our characters during Christ's final work of mediation, which is the investigative judgment.

I Charge You in the Presence of God and of Christ Jesus!

The Apostle Paul says, "I charge you [meaning the pastors] in the presence of God and of Christ Jesus who is to judge the living and the dead, and by the appearing of His kingdom: preach the word, be urgent in season, convince, rebuke, and exhort, be unfailing in patience and teaching. For a time is coming when people will not endure sound teaching but having itching ears, they will accumulate for themselves teachers to suit their own liking and will turn away from listening to the truth and wander into myths. 2 Timothy 4:1-4. As professed believers, we must diligently study the scriptures for ourselves, or we will be deceived by those promising us the very gates of paradise. The apostle admonishes believers to research the definitions of words and become familiar with their mandatory case agreement while correctly applying the moods and tenses attached to the words appearing in any Bible verse. This is so important because our religious leaders are misrepresenting the meaning of these Bible verses (Romans 6:14, Romans 7:4-6, Romans 10:4, Galatians 5:16-18, Ephesians 2:14-15, and Colossians 2:13-14) to gain popularity with the sin-loving multitudes of this generation. The professed Christian churches of this generation are using these Bible verses to deceive the unsuspecting multitudes with the idea that God's holy law has been done away with, consequently, it will not be the standard of righteousness used to evaluate our characters during Christ's final work of mediation, which is the investigative judgment. In the next chapters the following Bible verses, Romans 6:14, Romans 7:4-6, Romans 10:4, Galatians 5:16-18, Colossians 2:13-14, and Ephesians 2:14-15 will be meticulously investigated making it obvious that believers are being deceived by their church leaders and that they should separate themselves immediately from these religious organizations less they partake of their sins and receive the outpouring of God's unmingled wrath after human probation closes.

7
RESPECTING CASE AGREEMENT
OPENING STATEMENT

When studying scripture, understanding the meaning of words appearing in any Bible verse (is) [without question] extremely important. However, understanding the importance of properly applying the case agreement of the words appearing in the original language, while correctly amplifying the moods and tenses attached to these words is just as important, if a correct understanding of any Bible verse is to be obtained. The written communication in God's word breaks down when the translators ignore the meaning of the words appearing in any Bible verse. However, when the case agreement of the Greek words appearing in the original language is disregarded, while the moods and tenses attached are misapplied and/or completely ignored, it becomes a total disaster. This unconscionable behavior has resulted in poor translations of many Bible verses, which distorts the readers' understanding of what the inspired writer was trying to communicate. Without question, the biblical principles the inspired writers are trying to communicate cannot be properly understood if the definitions of words appearing in the original language are intentionally distorted, while their mandatory case agreement is completely disregarded and the moods & tenses attached to the Greek words appearing in the Bible verse are ignored by the translators, this outrageous behavior has produced the total confusion existing in Christendom today regarding the everlasting gospel and the perpetuity of God's Holy Ten Commandment Law.

This chapter is designed to establish that the intentional distortion of the following Bible verses [by the translators] (is) the main reason why many professed believers have a distorted understanding of the everlasting gospel and the perpetuity of God's Holy Ten Commandment Law. Romans 6:14, Romans 7:4-6, Romans 10:4, Galatians 5:16-18, Colossians 2:13-14, and Ephesians 2:14-15. The Churches of Babylon, identified by the second angel of Revelation the fourteenth chapter as the Catholic, mainline Protestant, and Evangelical churches, use these poorly translated Bible verses to deceive the unsuspecting multitudes of this dispensation regarding the perpetuity of God's Holy Ten Commandment Law and the plan devised for our salvation. Revelation 14:8. The unsuspecting multitudes have accepted false doctrinal beliefs, which are being advanced by the Churches of Babylon, specifically by the Catholic Church declaring that they have the authority to change God's holy law (Daniel 7:25) while her daughter harlots, the mainline Protestant and Evangelical Churches, who have become drunk by the wine of the Papacy's abominations are asserting that God's holy law is no longer binding upon the justified believers living in this dispensation. Revelation 17:1-6. The reason why the Papacy's daughter harlots are claiming God's Holy Ten Commandment Law is no longer binding upon the justified believers living in this dispensation is that after believers claim Christ's death paid the penalty they rightfully deserve for their transgressions of God's holy law, as justified believers they are assured of their salvation and subsequently released from rendering strict obedience to the same because any gospel demanding strict obedience to God's holy law represents a yoke of bondage primarily because it can't be kept and that rendering strict obedience to God's Holy Ten Commandment Law is no longer a requirement to obtain eternal life for those living in this failed dispensation, which according to the dispensational churches will soon be replaced with a dispensation of righteousness during the 1,000 year millennium. Revelation 20:1-15.

To clearly understand any Bible verse, you must first become familiar with biblical Greek grammar. When translating biblical Greek into the English language, the first literal definition of a word, according to the context established by the inspired writer, must be employed except if it's being superseded by the "case agreement" of the words appearing in the preceding and proceeding Bible verses. If the "case agreement" of the words is not respected, it will be virtually impossible to obtain a correct understanding of the Bible verse. The reason for this emphatic statement must be clearly understood; case agreement <u>*overrules*</u> the first literal definition of the words appearing in any Bible verse. However, the only way case agreement can overrule the first literal definition of the words appearing in any Bible verse, is if case agreement condones the conversion of the word into its secondary morphological meaning; otherwise, the first, or the appropriate literal meaning of the word must be employed in every circumstance to protect the integrity of the Bible verse. Therefore, in biblical Greek, words having the same case agreement define and/or amplify the same ideas introduced in the preceding and proceeding Bible verse[s].

It must be understood that <u>*without exception*</u>, the case agreement established by the inspired writer in the preceding and proceeding Bible verse[s] will overrule the first literal definition of the words appearing in any Bible verse. The relationship between the words grammatically linked together by their case agreement <u>*cannot be broken under any set of grammatical circumstances*</u>. In biblical Greek, this is called respecting case agreement, and the Catholic, mainline Protestant, and Evangelical church theologians should understand that the case agreement of the words appearing in these Bible verses, Romans 6:14, Romans 7:4-6, Romans 10:4, Galatians 5:16-18, Colossians 2:13-14, and Ephesians 2:14-15, <u>*cannot be broken under any set of grammatical circumstances*</u>. In order to clearly understand these Bible verses, Romans 6:14, Romans 7:4-6, Romans 10:4, Galatians 5:16-18, Colossians 2:13-14, and Ephesians 2:14-15 you must first become familiar with the definitions of the words, along with the moods and the tenses attached to these same words while respecting their mandatory case agreement and then compare this information to the definitions, the moods, and tenses along with the case agreement of the words appearing in the preceding and proceeding Bible verse[s]. Therefore, respecting these grammatical principles is the only way to obtain a correct understanding of what the inspired writer is trying to communicate in any Bible verse, which is something that the Catholic, mainline Protestant, and Evangelical church theologians should have clearly understood.

In biblical Greek, there are five separate and distinct cases, and they are as follows, 1) the (**nominative**), 2) the vocative, 3) the genitive, 4) (the dative), and 5) the (*accusative*). In the following examples, the **nominative** identifying the **subject** will appear in **bold letters**, the vocative identifying the speaker, and the genitive identifying possession, will be referenced but not specifically identified, the dative identifying the indirect object, will be underlined, and the *accusative* identifying the *direct object* will appear in *italics*, in the retranslated Bible verses. Around one hundred and forty-four thousand words appear in the New Testament, with 65% of them having assigned cases. This includes nouns, adjectives, participles, pronouns, and articles. The vast number of nouns, adjectives, participles, pronouns, and articles having assigned cases, coupled with a wide variety of potential uses controlled by the stems attached to the words, demands that the relationship of these words to the words appearing in the **nominative case**, the *accusative case* and the dative case, must be identified when translating the Greek into the English language, or a proper understanding of any Bible verse will be impossible.

This chapter will emphasize that the relationship of the Greek words grammatically linked together by their case agreement, *cannot be violated or broken under any set of grammatical circumstances* if a proper understanding of the following Bible verses is to be obtained. Romans 6:14, Romans 7:4-6, Romans 10:4, Galatians 5:16-18, Colossians 2:13-14, and Ephesians 2:14-15. Therefore, investigating the definitions of the words appearing in the Bible verse is extremely important, while becoming familiar with their moods and tenses is absolutely essential; however, respecting case agreement becomes paramount because the ideas introduced by the inspired writer in the following Bible verses, Romans 6:14, Romans 7:4-6, Romans 10:4, Galatians 5:16-18, Colossians 2:13-14, and Ephesians 2:14-15 are defined and amplified by the case agreement of the words appearing in the preceding and proceeding Bible verses, otherwise, a correct understanding of any Bible verse cannot be obtained; and this understanding of case agreement is in harmony with Biblical hermeneutics, as taught by every Biblical Greek scholar.

In Romans 6:14 the Apostle Says We Are Not Under the Law but Under Grace

It will be clearly established in this chapter that *the law* we are not under is *our fallen nature,* which the Apostle Paul says must be put to death if we are to receive a positive verdict in the judgment. Romans 8:12-13, Galatians 5:24. In Romans 6:14, if the Bible verse was retranslated from the original language with the **subject** appearing in **bold** letters, the *direct object* appearing in italics, and the indirect object, underlined, the retranslated Bible verse would read like this; "For in the future **sin** will have no power over you because you are not presently *under the law*, you are presently *under grace*. In Romans 6:14, the subject of the Bible verse is **sin**, and the biblical definition of **sin** is the transgression of God's Holy Ten Commandment Law. The term *"under the law"* appears as the *direct object* in the Bible verse, while *under grace* appears as *the second direct object* in the Bible verse. In Biblical Greek to respect case agreement sometimes *two direct objects* appear in the same Bible verse, when this takes place, the correct English translation demands that *the second direct object* acts [grammatically] like the indirect object in the English translation of the Bible verse. Therefore, to obtain the clearest understanding of what the apostle is trying to communicate when he says that "you are not *under the law,* but [you are] presently *under grace,"* we will retranslate Romans 6:12-23 from the Greek, the original language of the New Testament.

In the retranslation of these Bible verses Romans 6:12-23 into the English language, the **subject** will appear in **bold** letters, the *direct object* will appear in *italics*, and the <u>indirect object will appear, underlined</u>, for clarification purposes. This designation will make it easy for the reader to identify the "case agreement" of the words, so the information communicated can be correctly applied according to the context established by the inspired writer in the preceding and proceeding Bible verses, which makes for extremely strong written communication. Identifying the "case agreement" of the words makes it easy for the reader to understand there is a specific relationship between the words grammatically linked together appearing in the Bible verses. After this retranslation is completed, it will become clear what the Apostle Paul is trying to communicate in Romans 6:14 when he says, "*You are not under the law* but *under grace.*" Therefore, after the retranslation of Romans 6:12-23 is completed, it will become clear that *the law* we are not under if we are *under the grace* of Christ's justifying power, is *our fallen nature*. Romans 7:21. This is why the Apostle Paul says that our fallen nature, which all of humanity has inherited without their consent at birth from our earthly parents, must be put to death if we are to receive eternal life, (Romans 7:21-25, Romans 7:14-20, Romans 8:12-13) primarily because it's been identified as "*that which causes sin*" in our lives.

In Romans 6:14, the only way to understand what the apostle Paul is trying to communicate when he says, "<u>**You are not under the law but under grace**</u>," is to identify the case agreement of the words appearing in the Bible verse and then compare this information with the case of the words appearing in the preceding and proceeding Bible verses. In Romans 6:14, the Apostle Paul says that you are not *under the law*, which appears in *the accusative case*; as a result, it is grammatically linked, by its mandatory case agreement, to the command made by the Apostle Paul appearing in Romans 6:12-13, admonishing believers not to *yield themselves* to their <u>sinful propensities</u>. In the preceding and proceeding Bible verses, the Apostle Paul establishes that *our* *fallen nature* produces our <u>sinful propensities</u> and says that this defect has caused all of Adam's descendants to transgress God's holy law, Romans 3:10-18, Romans 3:23, Romans 5:12-14, and then he continues to establish the same thing in Romans 7:1-28, and Romans 8:1-39. Therefore, the Apostle Paul admonishing believers not to *yield themselves* to their <u>sinful propensities</u> represents an ongoing theme employed by the apostle in several other books of the Bible. Galatians 2:17-21, Galatians 3:19-29, Galatians 5:16-24, Ephesians 2:14-15, Ephesians 4:22-24, and Colossians 2:13-14.

The phrase *<u>you are not under the law but under grace</u>* can only be understood if the ideas advanced in the Bible verse are grammatically linked by their case agreement to the phrases employed by the apostle in the preceding and proceeding Bible verses. In Romans 6:12-13, the apostle admonishes believers not to *yield themselves* to their **<u>sinful propensities</u>,** which is referred to several times in the book of Romans, specifically in the sixth, seventh, and eighth chapters. Romans 6:14-22, Romans 7:1-6, Romans 7:14-25, Romans 8:1-13. In Romans 6:12-13, the apostle commands believers not to *yield themselves* to their <u>sinful propensities</u>, and this is the accentuating principle the Apostle Paul is trying to establish when he says, that "all have **sinned**" having been born defective. Romans 3:23. The defect that all of humanity has inherited at birth is our parents' *fallen nature*, which has caused all of Adam's descendants to transgress God's holy law due to inheriting their parents' <u>sinful propensities</u>. This is why the Apostle Paul says that <u>the carnal nature</u> has "caused him to do the very things that he hates." Romans 7:15. Consequently, "<u>the carnal nature</u>," introduced by the Apostle Paul in Romans 7:14, which he says acts like a law in Romans 7:21 "causing him to do the very things that he hates," is specifically represented by the apostle as [the moving agent] in Romans 7:22-24, establishing that <u>the carnal nature</u> is controlling his actions. This slavery to the law of sin results in the Apostle Paul exclaiming, "Who can deliver me from this body of death." Romans 7:24. The Apostle Paul subsequently answers this rhetorical question by stating, "Thanks be to God through our Lord Jesus Christ." Romans 7:25. Therefore, the overpowering <u>sinful propensity to transgress God's holy law, (referred to by the Apostle Paul in Romans 7:14 as the carnal nature, which he specifically says acts like a law in Romans 7:21) is what the same apostle is representing in Romans 6:14 as *the law* that justified believers are not *under* if they are *under the grace* of Jesus Christ's justifying power.

The reader must understand the following twelve (12) points before delving into the grammatical arguments establishing that the overpowering sinful propensity to transgress God's holy law, (referred to by the Apostle Paul, in Romans 7:14, as the carnal nature, which he says (acts like a law in Romans 7:21), is what the same apostle is representing in Romans 6:14 as *the law* that believers are not *under* if they are *under the grace* of Jesus Christ's justifying power. This conclusion is further evidenced by the Apostle Paul in Romans 8:2 when he emphatically states that "the law of the Spirit of life in Jesus Christ has sent me free from the law of sin and death." Therefore, before getting deep into the ***technical grammatical arguments*** establishing that the overpowering sinful propensity to transgress God's holy law, (referred to by the Apostle Paul in Romans 7:14 as the carnal nature, which he says acts like a law in Romans 7:21 causing him to do the very things that he hates) that he emphatically states must be put to death in Romans 8:12-13, is what the Apostle Paul is representing in Romans 6:14 as *the law* that believers are not *under* if they are *under the grace* of Jesus Christ's justifying power; consequently, for the reader to properly understand these ***technical grammatical arguments***, the information being communicated in the following twelve (12) points must be understood.

(1st point) The apostle begins the book of Romans with the idea "that *the grace of Christ* justifying power was introduced to fallen humanity so that all may receive eternal life, which is "good news" for the fallen descendants of Adam, translated in the Bible as the everlasting gospel, which is designed to bring about the obedience of our faith" in God's holy law, (Romans 1:5) and just happens to be the New Covenant promise of salvation. Hebrews 8:10.

(2nd point) In Romans 6:14, the phrase "you are *under* the *grace*" of Jesus Christ's justifying power is linked, by its case agreement, to the

Apostle Paul's statement commanding us to yield *our bodies as instruments* of righteousness as those who have been raised from the dead and by the power of God we are to presently walk in newness of life. Romans 6:1-4.

(3rd point) In Romans 6:15-16, the apostle specifically says the *grace* of Christ was not introduced to free believers from their obligation of rendering perfect obedience to God's Holy Ten Commandment Law. Romans 3:31, Romans 6:1-2, John 14:15, and 1 John 2:4.

(4th point) In Romans 6:1, the apostle asks the question shall we continue to sin so that grace abounds, his response is "by no means." How can we who have died to sin still live in it any longer," with sin being clearly defined in the scriptures as the transgressions of God's Holy Ten Commandment Law as originally proclaimed by God Himself amid the thunders of Mt. Sinai?

(5th point) In Romans 3:31, the apostle says our faith in Jesus Christ's justifying power doesn't make void our obligation to strictly obey God's holy law, on the contrary, when believers claim "justification by faith" they are admitting they clearly understand that God's law exists and that the penalties linked to its transgressions requires the death of the transgressor. Romans 6:23.

(6th point) In Romans 6:15-16; the apostle says, "What shall we say then, that are we to continue to sin because we are not under the law but under grace? By no means! Do you not know that if you yield yourselves to anyone as obedient slaves, you are slaves to the one you obey; **either sin, which leads to death**, or obedience, which leads to righteousness."

(7th point) In Romans 6:15-16, the apostle specifically says **sin**, which is defined in the Bible as the transgression of the law, (Romans 3:19-20) **leads to the second death**; because everyone who commits sin is a slave to sin and a slave to sin shall not inherit eternal life. John 8:34. The reader must stay focused; sin is clearly defined in the scriptures as the transgressions of God's Holy Ten Commandment Law as originally proclaimed by God Himself amid the thunders of Mt. Sinai, (Romans 7:1-7, James 2:8-12) and the apostle emphatically says that the wages of sin is still death in this dispensation. Romans 6:23.

(8th point) The Apostle Paul says in Romans 7:7, "if it had not been for the law, he would not know what sin is; declaring that "I would not know what it is to covet if the law didn't say you shall not covet." Romans 7:7. In addition, the Apostle James says that God's Holy Ten Commandment Law will be the standard of righteousness employed by Jesus Christ to evaluate our characters during His final work of mediation, which is the investigative judgment. James 2:8-12.

(9th point) In Romans 8:2 the apostle says God's grace is **the law** of the Spirit of life, which has set him free from **the law** of sin and death; consequently, to set your mind on the deeds of the flesh is death; and the phrase, "the deeds of the flesh," is grammatically linked by its case agreement to our fallen nature. Romans 8:6. In Romans 8:12-13, the Apostle Paul goes on to say that if you are controlled by the flesh, meaning your fallen nature, you will die, but if you by the power of the Holy Spirit put to death your fallen nature you will be awarded eternal life in the judgment.

(10th point) The apostle ends the Book of Romans by reconfirming the same point he started the Book of Romans with, (Romans 1:5), by declaring that the everlasting gospel was introduced to "<u>**bring about the obedience of our faith**</u>" in God's holy law (Romans 16:25-26) and not the exact opposite as advocated by the mainline Protestant and Evangelical Churches of this generation.

(11th point) As stated earlier, the only way to understand what the Apostle Paul is trying to communicate when he says <u>**you are not under the law but under grace**</u> is to identify the case agreement of the words appearing in Romans 6:14 and then make sure the information agrees with the concepts meticulously developed by the inspired writer in the previous and the following Bible verses. Romans 6:12-13, Romans 6:15-23. As stated earlier, case agreement allows the inspired writer to define and then amplify ideas introduced in the Bible verse by the information introduced in the preceding or proceeding Bible verses. Consequently, the only way to obtain the clearest understanding of what the apostle is trying to communicate in Romans 6:14 is by superseding the definitions of the words appearing in the Bible verse by the concepts developed in the proceeding and proceeding Bible verses, which are all welded together by their case agreement. This is called respecting case agreement, which the mainline Protestant and Evangelical Church theologians should have clearly understood <u>**cannot be broken under any set of grammatical circumstances**</u>. Therefore, in Romans 6:14, the apostle emphatically states "for **sin** will have no dominion over you since you are not *under the law* but *under grace*," the apostle's comment should be very clear if you are respecting the case agreement of the words appearing in the preceding and proceeding Bible verses; consequently, the very idea that the grace of Christ has freed those claiming "justification by faith" from rendering strict obedience to God's Holy Ten Commandment Law is without <u>*grammatical*</u> foundation, primarily because the same apostle clearly states that the grace of Christ was introduced to bring about the obedience of our faith in God's holy law and not the exact opposite. Romans 1:5 and Romans 16:25-27.

(12th point) continued, The erroneous theological beliefs advocated by the mainline Protestant and Evangelical Churches, advancing inaccurate ideas claiming that the Apostle Paul, in Romans 6:14, is declaring that God's Holy Ten Commandment Law is no longer binding upon believers of this dispensation, is emphatically and categorically denied by the same apostle in Romans 3:31; where the Apostle Paul employs a double negative with a subjunctive kicker to deny the idea of the possibility of the fact existing that faith in Christ's sacrifice upon Calvary's Cross makes void the believers' responsibility of keeping God's Holy Ten Commandment Law, particularly when the same apostle begins and ends the book of Romans with the idea that the everlasting gospel was introduced to bring about the obedience of our faith, Romans 1:5 and Romans 16:25-27. Therefore, the only way to understand what the Apostle Paul is trying to communicate when he says <u>**you are not under the law but under grace**</u> is to identify the case agreement of the words appearing in Romans 6:14 and then make sure the information agrees with the information introduced in the previous and the following Bible verses. Romans 6:12-13, Romans 6:15-23.

(13th point) In Romans 6:14, the term *"you are not under the law"* appears as the first direct object in the Bible verse, while the term *under grace* appears as the second direct object in the Bible verse. When two direct objects appear in the same Bible verse, the second direct object acts like the indirect object in English grammar to produce the best possible translation of the Bible verse. In Romans 6:14, this application makes *the grace* of Christ perform grammatically like the indirect object in the English translation of the Bible verse. In biblical Greek, when an indirect object is employed, this designates "the person to whom or for whom something is done," either **positively** or **negatively**. The phrase *"under the grace"* of Christ's justifying power is the moving agent, by which believers can **positively** put to death *their fallen sinful nature,* thereby setting them free from <u>their sinful propensities</u>, which the Apostle Paul says acts like a law. Romans 8:1-4, Ephesians 4:22-24. As a result, **sin** in the future will no longer have dominion over those who are *under the grace* of Christ justifying power; because they are no longer controlled by <u>their sinful propensities,</u> (Romans 8:2) which the apostle specifically says acts like a law in these Bible verses, Romans 7:21, and Romans 8:2; consequently, the apostle says our fallen nature must be put to death if we are to receive a positive verdict during Christ's final work of mediation, which is the investigative judgment. Romans 8:12-13, Genesis 4:6-7, Colossians 2:11, Daniel 7:9-10, Revelation 14:6-7.

The Summary of the Opening Statements

The Apostle Paul has established that the fallen nature we inherited, without our consent, at birth from our earthly parents is the law of **sin** working death in our lives. Romans 6:18-19. The fallen nature we inherited at birth from our earthly parents is referred to by the apostle in Romans 7:14 as *"the carnal nature,"* grammatically linked by its case agreement to *"the desires"* of the flesh, which the Apostle Paul says must be put to death if we are going to receive eternal life.

Romans 7:14-25, Romans 8:12-13. In Romans 6:14, when the Apostle Paul says you are not *under the law* but *under grace,* he is simply drawing upon the information previously established in Romans 6:12-13, which he reconfirms in Romans 6:15-16 and further expounds upon in Romans 6:17-22, Romans 7:1-6, Romans 7:14-25, and Romans 8:1-13 along with several other books of the Bible. Galatians, 5:16-24 and Colossians 3:7-11. The apostle says those *under the grace* of Christ's justifying power are not *under* the law, meaning the controlling power of their *fallen* sinful *nature.* 1 Peter 1:13-19. The *fallen nature,* which all have received at birth, creates these overpowering sinful desires of the flesh; and the Apostle Paul says this defect has caused all of Adam's descendants to transgress God's Holy Ten Commandment Law. Romans 3:23.

In Romans 7:21, the Apostle Paul calls "the carnal nature" (Romans 7:14) a law that makes him a slave to sin, causing him to perform the deeds of the flesh, which the Apostle Paul emphatically says he hates. Romans 7:18-20. In Romans chapter eight, the Apostle Paul says, "If you by the Spirit put to death the deeds of the flesh [the flesh being grammatically linked to our carnal nature] you will live." Romans 7:14-15, Romans 8:12-13. Therefore, in Romans 6:14 when the case agreement of the words appearing in the Bible verse is respected, the point the Apostle Paul is making becomes very clear; "for **sin** in the future will no longer have any power over you because you are not presently *under the law* of sin and death, you are now as justified believers, presently *under the grace* of Jesus Christ; consequently, you can freely access His daily mediation to receive the real forgiveness of your sinful propensities in preparation for Christ's final work of mediation, which is the investigative judgment.

The Retranslation of Romans 6:12-13

This is how Romans 6:12-13 would read when retranslated from the original language, with the **nominative case, which is the subject** appearing in **bold** letters, the *accusative case, which is the direct object* appearing in *italics,* and the <u>dative case</u>, which is <u>underlined</u>, identifying <u>the indirect object</u> in the Bible verse. The designation of the **subject,** *the direct object,* and <u>the indirect object</u> enables the reader to easily follow the case agreement of the words appearing in the Bible verse. Again, the relationship between these words, welded together by their case agreement, ***<u>cannot be broken under any set of grammatical circumstances</u>***.

In Romans 6:14, the words identified by their case are grammatically linked together; consequently, they define and/or amplify the same ideas introduced in the preceding or proceeding Bible verses. Romans 6:12-13, Romans 6:15-23. In Romans 6:12 the apostle says, "Therefore, you must not let **sin** <u>control</u> you <u>by</u> *obeying* <u>its desires;</u> we will look at this phrase first. In this Bible verse, the Greek word βασιλευέτω, translated as "you must not let," **sin** <u>control</u> you <u>by</u> *obeying* <u>its evil desires</u>, appears in the imperative mood, which means it's not a suggestion, it's a command, that "you must not let "**sin** <u>control</u> you <u>by</u> *surrendering to* <u>its</u> <u>evil</u> <u>desires.</u>" In Romans 6:13, the Apostle Paul is simply communicating the same information established in the previous Bible verse, that *the fallen nature,* which all have inherited at birth from their earthly parents, creates *these overpowering sinful desires, consequently, he's admonishing believers not to allow these evil desires to control their actions.* The apostle repeatedly says this *defect,* [*the fallen nature*], has caused all of Adam's descendants <u>to transgress</u> God's holy laws (Romans 3:23), accordingly, the apostle says [*it*] must be put to death if we are to receive eternal life. Romans 8:12-13, Galatians 5:24.

The Bible is extremely clear on this point, the everlasting gospel was introduced to fix the **sin** problem in fallen humanity, conversely, the everlasting gospel was not introduced to provide eternal life to transgressors who simply admit that Christ died for their transgressions of God's holy law. Romans 1:5, Romans 16:25-27. In Romans 6:12-13, the **subject** is identified as **sin**; and since these Bible verses are connected by a conjunction, the **subject** remains the same in both Bible verses, and since **the subject** of Romans 6:12-13 is grammatically linked by its case agreement to the **subject** appearing in Romans 6:14, the subject is **sin** in all three of these Bible verses. In Romans 6:14, the apostle is commanding believers not to let **sin** control their actions by surrendering to <u>its sinful desires</u>, because in the future, as justified believers, they "are not presently under *the law* [**of sin and death**] but they are presently *under the grace of Christ's justifying power as the moving agent working righteousness in their lives*; therefore, the claims made by the mainline Protestant and Evangelical Churches of this dispensation, that in Romans 6:14, the apostle is stating God's holy law has been made void by the believers' faith, is without any biblical support whatsoever because it violates the case agreement of the words appearing in the preceding and proceeding Bible verses.

This is how Romans 6:13 would read when retranslated from the original language, with the *direct object* appearing in *italics* and the <u>indirect object underlined</u>. In the retranslation of Romans 6:13, the identification of the *direct object* and <u>indirect objects</u> enables the reader to easily recognize the case agreement of the words appearing in the Bible verse. In the retranslation of Romans 6:13, no attempt is being made to make the Bible verse conform to English grammatical standards simply to provide a smoother reading. There is no **subject** in the Bible verse, and the <u>indirect object</u> will appear at the end of two prepositional phrases, to produce a literal word-for-word translation of the Bible verse. The key to understanding any Bible verse is to link the ideas collectively communicated *<u>together</u>* through their case agreement with the information presented in the preceding and proceeding Bible verses.

The following is a word-for-word retranslation of Romans 6:13, "Neither you must not yield your *bodies as weapons* of wrongdoing <u>through transgressions</u> rather you must yield *yourselves as those* having been raised from the dead <u>by God</u> and your *bodies as instruments* of righteousness <u>to God</u>." Again, the reader needs to understand the effects the imperative mood is having on the Greek word παριστάνετε, translated as you must not yield. Consequently, this statement comes to us as a command, so resisting your sinful propensities is not a suggestion or an option, the communication is made emphatically clear, that *we must not yield our bodies as weapons of wrongdoing* <u>through transgression</u> *but rather as those* having been raised from the dead <u>by God</u> and *your bodies as instruments* of righteousness <u>to God</u>. As established earlier, in Romans 6:12-13, the **subject** is the power of **sin**, which the apostle emphatically states in Romans 6:14 that believers are not *under* if they are *under the grace* of Christ's justifying authority. When Romans 6:12-13, is retranslated from the original language, the **subject is sin**, which is grammatically linked by its mandatory case agreement to the **subject** appearing in Romans 6:14, which is also **sin**, consequently, the apostles' statement, in Romans 6:14, becomes very clear. Therefore, in Romans 6:12-13, after commanding believers not to *yield their bodies as weapons* of wrongdoing <u>through transgression</u>, but rather they must yield *themselves as those* having been raised from the dead <u>by God</u> and *their bodies as instruments* of righteousness <u>to God</u>; in Romans 6:14, the apostle goes on to say, that **sin** in the future will have no dominion over you because you are not presently *under the law* but, as justified believers, you are presently *under the grace* of Christ's redeeming power.

The Retranslation of Romans 6:15

In Romans 6:14, the only way to find out what you are not *under* is to identify the **subject**, the *direct object,* and the <u>indirect object</u> in the Bible verse and then according to their case agreement apply this information to the ideas developed in the preceding and proceeding Bible verses. Romans 6:12-13, and Romans 6:15-23. In Romans 6:12, the **subject** is **sin**, and the *direct object* appears as a command not to allow *ourselves to be controlled* by **sin's** <u>evil desires</u>. In Romans 6:12, **sin's** *<u>evil desires</u>* have been identified as the <u>indirect object</u>, representing [**the negative effect**] the moving agent is having upon our lives. **The negative effects** of those controlled by the power of **sin** in their lives will be the **continual** transgressions of God's holy law. Romans 7:14-25, Romans 8:2. As a result, these slaves <u>to their sinful propensities</u> will inevitably commit the unpardonable **sin** sometime after human probation closes. Therefore, the [**negative effects**] of this slavery to **sin's** *<u>evil desires</u>* leads to the second death in the Lake of Fire, originally prepared for the Devil and his evil angels. Romans 6:23, Revelation 20:1-15.

In all three Bible verses, the **subject** is **sin.** Romans 6:12-14. In Romans 6:12-13, the *direct object* is the command not to yield *ourselves to* sin's <u>evil desires</u>, with sin's <u>evil desires</u> being clearly identified as the <u>indirect object</u> in the Bible verse. In Romans 6:13, the same command is repeated, not to yield our *bodies as instruments* of wrongdoing <u>through the power</u> of sin working death in our lives, with death representing the [**negative effects**] <u>the moving agent</u> is having in our lives. In both Bible verses (Romans 6:12-13), the controlling power of **sin's** <u>evil desires</u>, working death in our lives, is being contrasted <u>with the</u> [**positive effects**] <u>the power</u> of God's grace is having upon our lives, working *righteousness and eternal life*. This deliverance from the power of **sin** in our lives is only made possible <u>*by the justifying power of Christ's grace*</u> resulting from His death upon Calvary's Cross [and] His subsequent "daily mediation" in the heavenly sanctuary to forgive the sins of justified believers.

In Romans 6:12-14, the apostle is using the <u>indirect object</u> to develop two contrasting moving agents. In these Bible verses, there are two commands. The first command is not to yield *ourselves* <u>to the power</u> of **sin** working death in our lives. The first command is being contrasted with the second command, that we must yield our *bodies as instruments* of righteousness <u>through the power</u> of God's grace working righteousness in our lives. In Romans 6:14, the only way to find out what you are not under is to identify the **subject** of the Bible verse and then, according to case agreement, apply this information to what's being communicated in the preceding and proceeding Bible verses, Romans 6:12-13, and Romans 6:15-16, since these concepts are welded together by their case agreement. Therefore, if you follow the case agreement of the words appearing in Romans 6:12-23 what the apostle is saying in Romans 6:14, becomes extremely clear, for **sin** in the future will have no dominion over you since you are not presently *under the law* of sin and death, as justified believers you are presently *under the grace of Christ redeeming power*.

In Romans 6:12, the apostle is representing that the *law* we are not under *is grammatically welded by its mandatory case agreement* to the command that believers must not *obey* their sinful propensities. Romans 7:14, Romans 7:21. In Romans 6:13, the same command is being repeated, demanding that, by the grace of Christ's justifying power, we no longer have to yield our *bodies as instruments* of wrongdoing by the power of **sin** working death in our lives. The power of sin is caused by *our fallen nature* (Romans 7:14) which according to the Apostle Paul acts like a law. Romans 7:21. In Romans 6:12-13, the command clearly states "not to yield *ourselves* to our sinful desires, which is being contrasted with the second command that believers must "yield their bodies *as instruments* of righteousness to God as *those who* have been raised from the dead by His justifying grace working righteousness in their lives. In Romans 6:12-13, these two commands, are grammatically linked respectively "through their mandatory case agreement," to *the law* that we are *not under* if we are *under the grace* of Christ, as a result, when case agreement is respected, it's easy to understand what the apostle is communicating in Romans 6:14, as justified believers we "are not *under the law [of sin and death] if we are under* [the] *grace* of Christ's justifying power working righteousness in our lives.

In Romans 6:14, what the apostle is actually saying should be extremely clear, if you are truly justified by faith, you can't be controlled by your *fallen nature*, which, in Romans 6:14, the apostle represents this concept as believers **not** being "*under the law*, but under grace." The Apostle Paul's statement, appearing in Romans 6:14, "that you are under the law" [*is grammatically welded by its mandatory case agreement*] to the commands appearing in Romans 6:12-13, admonishing believers not to *obey their* sinful propensities evidenced by them yielding *their bodies as instruments* of wrongdoing resulting from the power of **sin** working death in their lives. In Romans 6:14, the term "*you are under the law*" appears as the first *direct object* in the Bible verse. The term "*you are under grace*" appears as the second direct object in the Bible verse and this phrase "*you are under grace*" is *grammatically welded by its mandatory case agreement* to the apostle's command appearing in Romans 6:13, that believers are to yield their *bodies as instruments* of righteousness <u>to God</u> *as those who* have been raised from the dead <u>by His</u> grace working righteousness in their lives. However, to avoid any confusion, the apostle summarizes the statement that he made in Romans 6:14, "that you are not *under the law, but <u>you are under grace</u>*," specifically by asking the following rhetorical question [appearing in Romans 6:15-16], which he makes emphatically clear, "Therefore *then, may* we continue to sin because we are not under the law but <u>*under grace*</u>?" The apostle's response is impossible to misunderstand, "Do not at any time wish for this, for you already know <u>to whom</u> you are presently yielding *yourselves* <u>to</u> as *obedient servants,* you are **slaves** <u>to whom</u> you obey; either of sin, <u>which leads to death</u>, or *obedience, which leads to righteousness.*"

In Romans 6:15-16, the Apostle Paul asks the following rhetorical question to clarify what he was saying in Romans 6:14, "Therefore *then, may* we continue to sin because we are not *under the law* but <u>*under grace*</u>?" The apostle emphatically says, "Do not at any time wish for this, for you already know <u>to whom</u> you are presently yielding *yourselves* as *obedient servants,* you are **slaves**<u> to whom </u>you obey; either of sin, <u>which leads to death</u>, or obedience, *which leads to righteousness.*" It's important to understand that sin is defined in the Bible as the transgressions of God's holy law, so obviously, the apostle is not stating God's holy law is no longer binding upon believers living in this dispensation since he is clearly stating that the wages of sin "leads to slavery to our sinful propensities and death." In Romans 6:14, the apostle's statement "for sin will have no dominion over *you because you are not under the law,* but <u>*you are under grace*</u>" is not condoning continued transgressions; however, to avoid any confusion, the apostle repeats the same idea in Romans 6:15-16, by asking a rhetorical question, "shall we continue to sin because we are not under the law but under grace." The answer to this question is made extremely clear, "do not wish for that," because you already know that if you yield yourselves to sin you become slaves to your sinful propensities, and Christ says that a slave to sin shall not inherit eternal life. John 8:34-35.

So obviously, according to the Apostle Paul, God's holy law is still binding upon believers living in this dispensation, because you can't transgress something that doesn't exist; (Romans 4:15) or that's no longer binding upon the justified believers living in this dispensation. Galatians 2:17-19. **If the law was no longer binding upon the believers living in this dispensation, why would the apostle warn believers about the ramifications directly linked to their continued transgressions?** Therefore, if the case agreement of the words appearing in the preceding and proceeding Bible verses is respected, what the apostle is saying in Romans 6:14, becomes extremely clear, if you do not put to death your fallen nature (Romans 8:12-13) you will eventually commit the unpardonable sin after human probation closes and you will be destroyed in the lake of fire with the Devil and his evil angels, which is the second death, this understanding is in perfect harmony with Christ's statements appearing in John 8:34-35 that a **slave** to **sin** shall not inherit eternal life.

The Retranslation of Romans 6:15-16

After reading Bible verses like Romans 3:19-21, Romans 3:31, and Romans 5:1-2 what the apostle is saying in Romans 6:14 should be extremely clear, for **sin** in the future will have no **dominion** *over you because as a justified believer,* you are not presently *under the law* of **sin** and controlled by your sinful desires. The apostle says justified believers are *under the grace* of Christ, operating as the moving agent producing righteous behavior in their lives. Romans 7:1-6, Romans 7:14-24, Romans 8:1-24. When Romans 6:15-16 is retranslated from the original language, with the **subject** appearing in **bold** letters, the *direct object* appearing in *italics,* and the indirect object underlined, the retranslation of these Bible verses establishes that claiming justification by faith doesn't make void our obligation to obey God's holy law. Romans 7:7, Romans 3:19-21, and Romans 3:31. After stating that **sin** in the future will have no more power over justified believers because they are not under the law of sin, they are now presently *under the grace of Christ;* to make his point even clearer the apostle asks the following rhetorical question, "Therefore *then* after claiming justification by faith *may* we possibly continue to sin because we are not *under the law* but *under grace*; [his response could not be made any clearer]; you should not be found at any time wishing for this, for you already know that <u>the power</u> you are presently yielding *yourselves to as obedient slaves* you are **slaves** <u>to that power</u> you are presently obeying, either of sin, *which leads to death* or obedience *that leads to righteousness.*" In these two Bible verses, Romans 6:15-16 we have the same two contrasting powers identified in the previous three Bible verses (Romans 6:12-14) the apostle is contrasting the *law* of **sin** and death with *the redeeming grace* of Christ's justifying power. With this information in hand, the question that must be repeatedly asked the mainline Protestant and Evangelical church theologians is this: do we then make void God's holy law after claiming justification by faith? The answer couldn't be made any clearer, the apostle exclaims, "To the contrary, we establish the existence of God's holy law," which defines sin in our lives, while establishing the need for justified believers to access Christ's "daily mediation" to obtain the real forgiveness of their sinful propensities in preparation for His final work of mediation, which is the investigative judgment. Romans 3:31, Galatians 2:17-19, Revelation 14:6-7.

In Romans 6:16, the Greek word οἴδατε, translated as "you already know," appears in the indicative perfect active. This means the apostle feels the Bible verse hardly needs any further explanation[s]. The apostle feels that you should "already know that <u>the power</u> you are presently yielding *yourselves to as obedient slaves,* you are **slaves** <u>to that power</u> you are choosing to obey," either of sin, which leads to death, or righteousness, which leads to eternal life. The Greek word translated as **slave** appears as the **subject** in the Bible verses. The Greek words translated as, yielding *yourselves as the slave of sin,* appears as *the direct object* in the Bible verse, while yielding *yourselves* as obedient servants *into righteousness* appears as *the second direct object* in the Bible verses. As already established the second direct object acts like <u>the indirect object</u> in the English translation of the Bible verse. The <u>indirect object</u> is the moving agent in the Bible verses, which is identified <u>as the power</u> of Christ's *grace enabling* justified believers to live righteous lives. Consequently, when the case agreement of the words is respected, understanding what the Apostle Paul is saying in Romans 6:14 becomes obvious, if you yield *yourselves to sin you are still under the law* of sin and death, and you will eventually commit the unpardonable sin and die in the lake of fire; however, if *by the grace* of Christ, you, <u>by the power</u> of the Spirit, put to death the defective fallen nature you inherited at birth from your earthly parents, you will naturally obey and live. Romans 8:12-13. This is what the apostle is communicating in Romans 6:14, "for **sin** [in the future] will have no dominion over you because you are not *presently* under *the law* [of sin and death] but [you are, as justified believers, presently] *under* [the] *grace of Jesus Christ*. Romans 8:1-4.

In Romans 6:14, the Greek word κυριεύσει, translated as "dominion," appears in the future tense, and the Greek word ἐστε, translated as "you are," appears in the indicative present active. In Romans 6:14, the apostle is simply expounding upon the principles indigenous to the everlasting gospel, "that in the future [as justified believers] sin will have no dominion over you because you are *presently* [not] *under the law* of sin [as the moving agent working death in your lives], you are *presently under the grace* of Christ, as the moving agent, *working righteousness in your lives*. After making this statement, the apostle, in the following Bible verses says, "Therefore *then,* as justified believers *can* we possibly continue to sin because we are not *under the law* but *under grace*; [you should not be found at any time wishing for this], for you should already know that <u>the power</u> you are presently yielding *yourselves to as obedient slaves,* you are **slaves** <u>to that power</u> you are obeying, either of sin, *which leads to death* or obedience *that leads to righteousness.*" Romans 6:15-16. In Romans 6:16, the apostle employs the Greek word οἴδατε, translated as "you already know," [appearing in the indicative perfect active], this grammatical nuance is employed to emphasize something that the apostle feels you, meaning, the Catholic, mainline Protestant and Evangelical church theologians should already know that **sin** in the future will have no power over justified believers, because [as] justified believers, they are not *under the law* of **sin** but they are <u>under the grace</u> of Christ's justifying power working righteousness in their lives.

The Retranslation of Romans 6:17-19

In Romans 6:17-19, the apostle continues to expound upon the contrasting powers working life or death in our lives, which he defined in Romans 6:14 as being under the law of sin which leads to death or being under the grace of Christ leading to obedience and eternal life. John 3:36. In Romans 6:17-18, the apostle says, "But **thanks** be <u>to God</u> that you who were continually **slaves** of sin you now understand, that at some point in time, you can *become obedient* from the inner heart having been delivered *a pattern* of teaching establishing that **you can be set free** from sin, so you can, at some point in time, be made <u>servants of righteousness</u>. After stating he has established this *pattern* of teaching, that **you can be set free** from sin, so you can, at some point in time, be made <u>servants of righteousness</u>, the apostle goes on to address *the natural inadequacies* of our fallen sinful defective nature. In Romans 6:19, the apostle says, for just as you, at some point in time, yielded *yourselves as servants* <u>to impurity, caused by lawlessness,</u> *existing in that great state of lawlessness,* in the same way, at some point in time, you must now submit yourselves as *servants* <u>of righteousness</u> *leading to your sanctification with its end eternal life.* In the above retranslation of Romans 6:19 the believers *existing in that great state of lawlessness are grammatically linked to their fallen nature*. There is nothing that I can add to the retranslation of Romans 6:19 to make it any clearer, except for this; while the apostle recognizes *the natural inadequacies* of our fallen defective sinful human nature, he reemphasizes that our deliverance from the power of sin is not a suggestion; it's a command. If we expect to receive eternal life, we must, by the Spirit, put to death *our fallen nature* and form *sanctified righteous characters* in this life, so that we can naturally obey God's holy law and live. After the close of human probation, all those still controlled by their *fallen nature*, defined as "that which causes sin in our lives" will inevitably commit the unpardonable sin after human probation closes and will be destroyed by His holy angels at the Lord's second coming. Matthew 13:41-42.

The Retranslation of Romans 6:20-23

In Romans 6:20-23, the apostle sums up his powerful discourse by stating, "for when you were **slaves** of sin you were not <u>led by righteousness</u>; but *what return* did you receive <u>from what</u> you are now ashamed, for **the end** of those things is **death**. But now that you recognize, **at some point in time, you can be set free** from sin; you **understand, at some point in time, you can be made servants** <u>of God</u>, *leading to your sanctification and its end eternal life*. As a result of this last statement, in Romans 6:23, the Apostle Paul states his position as clearly as he can, "for **the wages** of sin **is death**, but **the free gift** of God **is eternal life** <u>through [the grace] of Christ Jesus</u> working righteousness in our lives; again, contrasting the two moving agents. Consequently, by following the mandatory case agreement of the words appearing in these Bible verses, Romans 6:12-23, it's easy to understand what the apostle is trying to communicate in Romans 6:14; those who are *under the grace* of Christ [as the moving agent working righteousness in their lives] are not *under the law* of sin and death, representing the controlling power of their fallen nature causing them to transgress God's holy laws. Therefore, the "wise" who understand the vision of Daniel 8:14, clearly comprehend that *existing in that great state of lawlessness* [representing our fallen nature] is completely unacceptable, the everlasting gospel demands believers put to death their fallen sinful nature if they expect to receive a positive verdict from Christ during His final work of mediation, which is the investigative judgment. Romans 8:12-13, Galatians 5:24, Daniel 7:9-10, and Revelation 14:6-7.

When retranslating Romans 6:12-23 from the original language, with the **subject** appearing in **bold** letters, the *direct object* appearing in *italics,* and the <u>indirect object underlined</u>, it's been established that claiming justification by faith doesn't make void our obligation to obey God's holy law. In Romans 6:16, the apostle employs the Greek word οἴδατε, translated as "you already know," [appearing in the indicative perfect active], this grammatical nuance is employed by the apostle to emphasize something that he feels you, meaning, the Catholic, mainline Protestant and Evangelical church theologians should already know that **sin** in the future will have no power over justified believers, because [as] justified believers, they are not *under the law* of **sin** but they are <u>under the grace</u> of Christ's justifying power working righteousness in their lives. Therefore, the very idea advanced by the mainline Protestant and Evangelical Churches that the Apostle Paul in Romans 6:14 is stating that God's Holy Ten Commandment Law is no longer binding upon believers living in this dispensation is not even remotely supported by the scriptures. Romans 3:31, Romans 3:19-20, Romans 7:7-14, Galatians 2:17-19, Romans 8:1-13 and James 2:8-12.

8

IN ROMANS 7:4-6 THE APOSTLE SAYS WE HAVE DIED TO THE LAW

In Romans 7:4-6, to obtain the clearest understanding of the statement made by the apostle Paul, "You have died to the law through the body of Christ," we will employ the same format used in retranslating Romans 6:12-23. The **subject** will appear in **bold** letters, the *direct object* will appear in *italics*, and the <u>indirect object will be underlined</u>. This will be done to obtain the clearest understanding of these Bible verses. In the retranslation of the following Bible verses, the definitions of the words, along with their moods and tenses, are being properly defined and amplified, which is the only way to obtain the clearest insight into these Bible verses. Romans 7:1-6. Therefore, the following explanations will establish the very idea that our faith in Christ's death paid the penalty we rightfully deserve for our transgressions has made void our obligation to obey God's holy law is [satanic] and by no means supported by the scriptures.

In Romans 7:1-3, the Apostle Paul makes a comparison; and the symbolism employed needs no explanation. Those who have claimed justification have agreed to put on the wedding garment. They have been married to Christ, and the robe of His righteousness is clothing them while they seek the sanctification of their character. The church is the bride of Christ, and her members are yoked to their Leader by holy matrimony. However, the apostle warns us not to defile our garments by indulging in unlawful practices. In Romans 7:1-6, the apostle is saying professed believers, who claim Christ's blood paid the penalty they rightfully deserve for their transgressions of the law, are committing adultery when they allow themselves to be controlled by their sinful propensities causing them to transgress God's holy law. They are acting like harlots when they allow themselves to be controlled by Satan's temptations. In Romans 7:1-3, the Apostle Paul makes a comparison, which is designed to illustrate how those claiming justification by faith, while remaining under the control of their fallen defective human nature, are committing adultery because they are giving themselves over to the controlling power of Satan and his temptations. They are hypocrites when claiming to be Christians, having previously pledged themselves to follow Christ's commands, while they are acting like harlots by allowing themselves to be controlled by their fallen, sinful nature. These alleged justified believers are acting like adulterers because they are still under *the law* of sin. Romans 6:12-16, Romans 7:14-24. Therefore, in Romans 7:1-6, while the definitions along with the moods and tenses attached to the words appearing in the original language have been properly defined and amplified, the case agreement of these words must be followed to obtain the clearest understanding of the following Bible verses.

After introducing the idea that unfaithful Christians are committing adultery when they allow themselves to remain under the control of their carnal nature, [defined by the apostle in Romans 6:12-23 as being controlled by *the law* of sin], the Apostle Paul starts his discourse in Romans the seventh chapter by comparing unfaithful believers to adulterers. Romans 7:1-3. However, in Romans 7:4-6, after making the comparison of unfaithful believers to adulterers, the apostle says, "Likewise, my brethren, when **you** are, at some point in time, made dead <u>to the law</u> through the body of Christ *you can belong* <u>to another</u>, <u>*to him who*</u> *was raised* from the dead, so that you may possibly bear fruit <u>to God</u>." Romans 7:5. "For while you were continually living <u>by the flesh</u>, **the misfortunes** of sin, **this** through the law, they were continually at work in your bodies eventually leading you to bear fruits to death." Romans 7:6. However, now, at the time you have been delivered from this law; **at the time you have died** to that which continually held *you captive, you* can now render service by the newness of the Spirit and not by observing written codes. In Romans 6:12-23, after introducing the idea that believers are not *under the law* of sin if they are *under the grace* of Christ, in Romans 7:1-3, the apostle creates an example, by comparing adultery to the unholy union of those claiming to be married to Christ while they are still under the controlling power of their fallen sinful nature, evidenced by them yielding to their sinful propensities. In Romans 7:1-3, the apostle calls this unholy union adultery, like a woman who lives with another man while her husband is still alive. In Romans 7:1-3, the apostle uses the example of adultery to further define what he means to be *"under the law,"* previously introduced in these Bible verses. Romans 6:12-22. This is why the apostle starts his discourse in Romans 7:4, with "**likewise** my brethren you have died to this law through the body of Christ so you can belong to another to Him who was raised from the dead" so that you may walk in newness of life. Romans 7:4. Therefore, the apostle says, "If you by the Spirit put to death the deeds of the flesh, you will live." Romans 8:12-13. Therefore, the apostle is seen continually emphasizing the goal of the everlasting gospel is to create, by His Spirit, true righteousness in our lives, not just an outward adherence to written codes. Romans 7:6.

In Romans 7:1-3, the Apostle Paul starts his discourse by asking a rhetorical question. The apostle inquires, are you ignorant of the term *"under the law,"* which was clearly defined in the previous chapter? In Romans 6:12-22, the term *"under the law"* was clearly defined as being controlled by our sinful propensities, *"that great state of lawlessness"* representing our fallen nature, which all have inherited at birth from their earthly parents. As previously introduced in the last chapter, the term *"under the law"* appears as the first *direct object* in the retranslation of Romans 6:14, "For **sin**, in the future, will have no power over you because you are not presently [*under the law*] but presently *under grace*. In Romans 7:1-3, the apostle expects you to understand the previously defined term, "*under the law,*" representing "*that great state of lawlessness,*" which was introduced in Romans 6:12-22, and is grammatically linked to the *italicized phrases* appearing in the following retranslated Bible verse. "<u>Whatever</u> you are presently yielding yourselves to as obedient slaves, you are **slaves** to that power which you are obeying either of sin *that leads to death* or obedience which leads to righteousness." The term "*under the law*" means you are still controlled <u>**by the flesh**</u>, representing your sinful passions are still controlling your actions; you are not your own, because you are controlled by "*that great state of lawlessness,*" which is grammatically linked to the fallen sinful nature, you inherited at birth from your earthly parents. Therefore, in Romans 7:1, the apostle says I am speaking <u>to those who understand</u> what it means to be *under the law,*" which means you are still controlled <u>**by the flesh**</u>, representing your sinful passions are still controlling your actions; you are not your own, because you are still controlled by "*that great state of lawlessness,*" which is the fallen sinful nature you inherited, at birth, from your earthly parents.

In Romans 7:1, the apostle says, "Do you not know brethren for I'm speaking to those that know *the law*, that **the law** is binding on a person only during his life." It's important to understand the second time the Greek word translated as "**the law**" appears in the Bible verse, it's [**the subject**] representing God's Ten Commandments. In Romans 7:1, the **law** appearing as the **subject** is referring to God's moral law, demanding that a woman stay married to her husband as long as he's alive. In Romans 7:1-3, after introducing the idea that unfaithful Christians are committing adultery when they are controlled by their fallen nature, the apostle's statement, "You have died <u>to the law</u>," can only be understood by respecting the case agreement of the words employed in the preceding Bible verses and further expounded upon in the proceeding Bible verses. This is why the apostle starts his discourse in Romans 7:1-3 by asking a rhetorical question, are you ignorant brethren, for I am speaking <u>to those who know</u> the *law*? The apostle is trying to expound upon the point he established in Romans 6:12-23. This is why the first time the Greek word, translated as *"the law"* in Romans 7:1, appears in the accusative case. Consequently, it's grammatically impossible to interpret the Greek word translated as *"the law,"* the first time it appears in Romans 7:1, that it's talking about God's Holy Ten Commandment Law. This understanding is grammatically impossible.

In Romans 7:1, the Greek word translated the first time as *"the law,"* is grammatically linked to those who are still controlled **by the flesh**, meaning their sinful passions are still controlling their actions. The apostle is drawing a comparison between those who are still controlled by their sinful passions to a married woman who is committing adultery. In this example, *the law* appearing as [*the direct object*] is linked by its mandatory case agreement to the sinful propensities every person has inherited at birth from their earthly parents; it's *the law* of sin (Romans 7:21) *"that great state of lawlessness,"* which still controls your actions *if your fallen nature has not been put to death.* Romans 8:12-13. Therefore, if you are still controlled by your sinful propensities, the apostle is comparing you to an unfaithful wife; consequently, in Romans 7:4, it's grammatically impossible to interpret the apostle's statement, "likewise my brethren you have died to the law through the body of Christ," to mean that God's holy law is no longer binding upon justified believers today as advocated by the confused pastors of the mainline Protestant and Evangelical churches of this dispensation.

It's important to recognize that the apostle says that I am speaking to those who understand *"the law."* The phrase *"the law"* appears in *the accusive case* and has been grammatically linked to those still under the control of their sinful passions, so *it* can't be referencing the Holy Law of God, which appears in **the nominative case**. In Romans 7:1, the Greek word translated as *"the law"* is linked by its case agreement to our *sinful propensities*. This concept was previously established in Romans the sixth chapter. In Romans 6:12-22, the phrase *"under the law"* represents those controlled by their *fallen nature*, *"that great state of lawlessness"* producing the uncontrollable sinful passions, causing all of Adam's descendants to transgress God's holy requirements. Romans 7:21. The fallen nature all have received at birth, creates uncontrollable sinful passions, which the apostle says has caused all of Adam's descendants to transgress God's holy law. Romans 3:23.

If the Bible were a legal brief, the phrase *"under the law"* would be considered a previously defined term, which must be understood in its proper context if any instructional value can be derived from Romans the seventh and eighth chapters. The phrase *"under the law"* represents the power of sin working death in the lives of those born into this world through no fault of their own possessing their parents' fallen defective nature. With the term *"under the law,"* having been previously defined in Romans the sixth chapter, as *"that great state of lawlessness,"* it's completely unimaginable why any church organization would interpret Romans 7:1-6 to mean that God's holy law has been made void by our faith, and, as a result, it's no longer binding upon believers today. Romans 3:31.

To counteract this idea that God's holy law has been made void by our faith, and it's no longer binding upon believers today the Apostle Paul starts his discourse in Romans the seventh chapter by asking a rhetorical question, "Are you ignorant brethren for I am speaking <u>to those who know</u> *the law*, that **the law** has dominion over a man *as long as he lives.*" In Romans 7:1, because *the law* [representing our fallen nature] appears in the *accusative case,* and **the law** [representing God's Holy Ten Commandment Law] appears in the **nominative case**, it's grammatically impossible they are referring to the same law since these two words have different case agreement; consequently, only those churches trying to deceive you would take the position that *the law, we are not under* is **God's Holy Ten Commandment law.**

In Romans 7:1, the holy **law** of God [**the subject**] demands that a **woman** stay married to her **husband** as long as he lives, and if she violates the 7th commandment, she will be called an **adulteress**. In the example in Romans 7:1, *the law* appearing as [*the direct object*] is grammatically linked by its case agreement to our sinful propensities, representing *"that great state of lawlessness"* every person has inherited at birth from their earthly parents. It's *the law* of sin and death that controls your actions, assuming *your fallen nature has not been put to death.* Romans 8:12-13. In Romans 7:1-3, two separate and distinct laws are introduced, previously established as opposing moving agents in these Bible verses. Romans 6:12-23. In Romans 7:1, *the first law* appears as the *direct object,* and **the second law** appears as the **subject** of the Bible verse; consequently, these two laws cannot be referring to the same law, it's grammatically impossible, which is something that the Catholic, mainline Protestant and Evangelical theologians should clearly understand. In any Bible verse, the **subject** cannot be the *direct object* of the Bible verse; this is not only grammatically impossible but also completely and intentionally deceptive. This is why the apostle starts his discourse with the statement, "I am speaking to those who *know the law;* because he has already established that **sin** in the future will have no dominion over a person if they are *under* the *grace of Christ* operating as the moving agent working *righteousness* in their lives. Romans 6:12-22.

In Romans 7:1, if the case agreement of the words is respected, what the apostle is saying becomes very clear. The apostle is speaking to those who understand the following defined terms, *"under the law,"* along with the term *"under grace,"* both of which were previously introduced in Romans 6:12-23. Those under *the grace* of Christ, [as the moving agent working righteousness in their lives], are not *"under the law"* of sin and death, representing, *"that great state of lawlessness,"* which is grammatically linked to *their sinful propensities.* Romans 7:21. It's been established that the fallen nature is what's causing humanity to **sin**, yielding **death** in their lives. In Romans 7:4, this is why the apostle says, likewise, [*in the same way*] my brothers, **you** will, at some point in time, be made dead to the law through the body of Christ *so that you can belong* to another, to Him who has been raised from the dead, so you can, at that point in time, possibly bear fruits to God by developing a righteous character.

In Romans 7:2, the apostle references **the second law** appearing in Romans 7:1 [**which is the subject**] and says **that the married woman** is bound by law to her husband as long as he is alive. In Romans 7:3, the apostle goes on to say, "Consequently, if she becomes <u>married to another man</u>, she will be called **an adulteress**. However, if her **husband dies,** she will be **freed** from the law demanding [she stay married], and *she will not be called an adulteress if she becomes* <u>married to another man</u>. In Romans 7:1, the holy **law** of God [**the subject**] demands that a **woman** stays married to her **husband** as long as he lives, and if she violates the 7th commandment, she will be called an **adulteress;** however, in the example given in (Romans 7:1-3) the first *law* [*the direct object*] is grammatically linked by its case agreement to the binding relationship every person has to their fallen nature, representing, *"that great state of lawlessness,"* which creates the overpowering sinful propensities to transgress God's holy law, yielding death in our lives. Therefore, any other interpretation of this Bible verse represents a complete prevarication [meaning a deliberate and intentional attempt to deceive] because it violates the mandatory case agreement of the Greek words appearing in the Bible verses.

In Romans 7:1, *the law,* [*the direct object*], is grammatically linked by its case agreement to the already defined term, *"under the law,"* previously introduced in Romans 6:14-23, and defined as *"that great state of lawlessness"* and *the law* of sin and death. In Romans 7:1, the apostle represents unfaithful Christians, who are still *"under the law,"* meaning their fallen nature still controls their actions, as committing adultery. In Romans 7:1-3, the apostle is comparing those who claim to be married to Christ while *still under the control of the law of sin,* as adulterers, because they have given themselves to another power, thereby violating **the binding relationship of the marriage vows as commanded by the moral law.** The apostle is grammatically linking the first *"law"* to *the binding relationship all of Adam's descendants have to their fallen defective nature, producing sinful propensities, which have caused all of them to transgress.* The Bible teaches all will continue to sin unless counteracted by *the grace* of Christ working righteousness in their lives. In Romans 7:1-3, the apostle introduces the idea <u>to those who understand</u> the previously defined term *"under the law,"* by plainly stating the only way *this great state of lawlessness* can be broken is if you, <u>by the Spirit,</u> put to death the fallen defective nature you inherited at birth, without your consent, from your earthly parents. Romans 8:12-13.

In Romans 7:1-3, after comparing the adulterous actions of a woman who is breaking her marriage vows to unfaithful believers who are still controlled by their fallen sinful nature, the apostle, in Romans 7:4, starts his discourse by saying, "Likewise my brethren **you**, at some point in time, must be made dead <u>to the law</u> through the body of Christ *so that you can belong* <u>to another</u>, <u>*to him who* was raised</u> from the dead so that you may possibly bear fruit *<u>for God</u>*, and through His *grace* live righteous lives. According to the example given in Romans 7:1-3, the only way you can bear fruit to God is if you, by the Spirit, put to ***death*** the fallen nature you inherited at birth from your earthly parents. Romans 8:12-13. Otherwise, you are committing adultery if you claim justification by faith while allowing yourselves to be controlled by your sinful passions. This is the reason why the apostle says, "I am speaking to those who know *the law*." Therefore, those who know *the law* understand claiming "justification by faith" must **set them free** from *the law* of sin and death; as a result, **they can be made servants** <u>of God</u>, *leading to their sanctification and its end, eternal life*. Romans 6:22.

In Romans 5:1-2, the Apostle Paul says, **having been justified** by faith we have *peace with God* through our Lord Jesus Christ, by Him we have obtained *access* <u>through faith</u> into this *grace and <u>by</u> this* we can be <u>empowered</u> to stand while rejoicing <u>in the hope</u> of sharing the glory of God." As established earlier, "sharing the glory of God" represents the sanctification of our characters. 2 Corinthians 3:17-18, Romans 6:20-22, 2 Thessalonians 2:13-14. In Romans 5:1-2, the Apostle Paul establishes, "faith" in the saving grace of Christ is our only hope, those who by a living active faith are overcoming sin because they are *under the grace* of Christ are not *"under the law"* of sin working death in their lives. Romans 6:12-16. In Romans 7:1, the apostle goes on to say unless you are ignorant of the saving grace of Christ you will by the Spirit put to death "that which causes sin" in your lives. If you do ***not*** "by the Spirit" put to death your fallen nature, the apostle says you are committing adultery. Consequently, if you follow the case agreement of the words appearing in Romans 7:4, it's easy to understand what the apostle is saying, "likewise," [meaning in the same way], if you claim to be Christian while remaining under the controlling power of your fallen nature you are still (*under the law*) and are committing adultery. In Romans 7:4, when the apostle says, "We have died to the law through the body of Christ," this statement can only be understood by those who comprehend the previously defined terms, "*under the law*" is being contrasted with the phrase "*under the grace*" of Christ. The only way justified believers can bear fruit to God is if *the law* of sin, [which is grammatically linked to our fallen carnal nature], is being daily put to death. Romans 8:1-25. Therefore, after claiming justification by faith, those who understand the gospel will rejoice <u>in the hope</u> of sharing [possessing] the glory of God," which represents the ongoing sanctification of their characters. Romans 6:20-22.

In Romans 7:5, the apostle says, "For when we were controlled <u>by the flesh</u>, **the misfortunes** of sin, **this** through the law, were continually at work <u>in your bodies</u> *leading you, at some point in time, to bear fruits to death*. This Bible verse establishes that those born with a fallen nature are destined to transgress God's holy law *at some point in their lives*. Romans 3:9-18, Psalms 14:1-3, Romans 3:23. <u>The flesh</u>, the <u>indirect object</u> of the Bible verse, represents *that great state of lawlessness,* working as the moving agent in the lives of those born into this world, without their consent, possessing a fallen nature. The flesh causes **the misfortunes** of sin, evidenced by the Greek word translated as **this** (being directly linked by its case agreement) to the Greek word translated as **the misfortunes** of sin. The phrase through the law, [the law appearing in the possession], is continually at work <u>in your bodies</u>, *leading you to, at some point in time,* **sin,** **bearing** *fruits* <u>to death</u>. The **flesh** <u>causes</u> **the misfortunes** of sin, and the **flesh** is grammatically linked to the fallen defective nature we inherited at birth from our earthly parents. This is the law referred to by the apostle in Romans 7:21, which is continually at work <u>in all the fallen sons of Adam</u>, *causing them to eventually, at some point in time, transgress God's holy law.*

At the conclusion of chapter seven, the apostle declares, so I find it to be a **_law_** that when I want to do good, evil stands close at hand trying to control my actions, and in desperate exaltation, he exclaims, "Who can deliver me from this body of death." Romans 7:24. The apostle then proclaims thanks be to God through our Lord Jesus Christ, so then, I of myself serve the law of God with my mind, but with my flesh, I serve the law of sin. Romans 7:25. The information presented in chapters five through eight of the Book of Romans is why God is justified in saying the gospel of Jesus Christ is to obey and live for eternity or disobey and die in the lake of fire, which is the second death. John 3:36. In Romans 7:5, the apostle says, "For when we were controlled <u>by the flesh</u> **the misfortunes** of sin, **this** through the law, were continually at work <u>in your bodies</u> *leading you to, at some point in time, bear fruits of death, however, after claiming justification by faith (Romans 5:1) you can put to death the deeds of the flesh (Romans 8:12-13) so you can bear fruits to God (Romans 7:4) resulting from you not being "under the law [of sin] but under the grace" of Christ.* Romans 6:14.

In Romans 7:6, the apostle concludes his example by saying, "But now we have, at some point in time, been delivered from this law; **we have died, then,** <u>to that which</u> held us continually captive, so that *we* can render service <u>by the newness</u> of the Spirit and not <u>by obeying</u> a set of written ceremonial requirements. At the time of Christ's first advent, the bigoted Jews rejected Christ's message of salvation through His sacrifice and subsequent daily mediation to forgive sins; why, because they already felt saved and forgiven after performing the rigorous exactions of the ceremonial laws. Isaiah 1:10-18. In Romans 7:6, the apostle says; that after believers claim justification by faith, they can be delivered "**_from_**" the law of sin by which they were continually held captive so they can serve God <u>by the newness</u> of the Spirit and not <u>by rigorously keeping a list of ceremonial duties</u> that once performed created the illusion of salvation.

The Greek word translated as "**_from_**" in Romans 7:6, has a Strong's call number of 575; in Thayer's Greek Lexicon, it means any form of separation by which the union of the two is destroyed. In Romans 7:4, when the apostle says, "We have died to the law," the grammatical evidence is overpowering; he is not declaring that God's holy law is void and no longer binding upon the believers living in this dispensation. This interpretation violates the case agreement of the words appearing in the Bible verse; in addition, it's simply not biblical (Romans 4:15) and contradicts the direct testimony of the same apostle. Romans 7:7, Romans 3:19-21, and Romans 3:31. Conversely, when case agreement is respected, what the apostle is communicating becomes extremely clear; those claiming justification by faith must separate themselves "from" *the law* of sin because existing in "*that great state of lawlessness*" they will continue to transgress **God's holy law** and are likened to a **woman committing adultery**. Therefore, in Romans 7:1-6, what the apostle is saying becomes extremely clear; the fallen nature we received at birth, without our consent, must be put to death, or we will continually transgress God's Holy Ten Commandment Law and be destroyed in the lake of fire with the Devil and his evil angels, which is the second death. Romans 8:12-13.

9

THE APOSTLE PAUL SAYS - CHRIST IS THE END OF THE LAW FOR ALL WHO BELIEVE

There is not one Bible verse where the incorrect interpretation more clearly defines the confusion existing in Christendom today than does the erroneous understanding of Romans 10:4 that states faith in Christ's death upon Calvary's Cross has made void our responsibility to keep God's Holy Ten Commandment Law. The scriptures clearly state God's Holy Ten Commandment Law will be the standard of righteousness used to evaluate our characters during Christ's final work of mediation, which is the investigative judgment. Romans 2:12-16. James 2:8-13, Revelation 14:6-7, Daniel 7:9-10. Here is how Romans 10:4 reads in the (KJV) King James Bible, "For Christ is the end of the law for righteousness to everyone that believeth." Here is how Romans 10:4 reads in the (RSV) Revised Standard Version; "For Christ is the end of the law for everyone who has faith may be justified." Here is how Romans 10:4 reads in the (CSB) The Catholic Study Bible; "For Christ is the end of the law for the justification of everyone who has faith." Here is how Romans 10:4 reads in the (NASB) The New American Standard Bible; "For Christ is the end of the law for righteousness to everyone who believes." Here is how Romans 10:4 reads in the (NIV) The New International Version; "Christ is the culmination of the law so that there may be righteousness for everyone who believes." Here is how Romans 10:4 would read if correctly translated from the original language with the **subject** appearing in **bold** letters, the *direct object* appearing in *italics*, and the indirect object underlined, "For **Christ is the fulfillment** of the law *leading to true righteousness* for those who believe." In the scriptures, true righteousness is defined by obedience to God's holy requirements. Romans 2:25-29, 1 John 2:28-29, 1 John 3:7, Revelation 20:12. Therefore, it is inconceivable to believe the mainline Protestant and Evangelical Churches of this generation can be so ignorant of the scriptures to support their erroneous interpretation of Romans 10:4, which states that claiming justification by faith has made void our responsibility to keep God's Holy Ten Commandment Law. Romans 3:31, Romans 4:15, Romans 7:7-12.

At the time of Christ's first advent, the counterfeit gospel advanced by the Pharisees subliminally introduced ideas that salvation was based upon how perfectly they kept a manmade list of ritualistic requirements. Romans 7:6, Romans 9:30-33. The Jews, the professed people of God at the time of Christ's first advent, considered themselves righteous because they had rigorously followed a list of ceremonial requirements that, once performed, created the illusion of salvation now and in the judgment. Hebrews 10:1-6, Isaiah1:10-18. In addition, the religious leaders of that generation erroneously applied the prophecies describing the glory of Christ's Second Advent to the prophecies describing the Messiah's humble first advent. As a result, the religious leaders of that generation rejected Christ as the Messiah because He did not come in the manner they had expected and, most importantly, had predicted. They were not looking for the Messiah to save them from their sins (Matthew 1:21); they taught the Messiah of Bible prophecy would deliver Israel from the yoke of Roman oppression. Consequently, they failed to obtain true righteousness defined by God's holy law. They rejected and killed Christ, whose character was the very "fulfillment" of the law defining true righteousness in their lives. Romans 10:4.

The people who claimed to be looking forward to the Messiah's first advent had Christ killed for the blasphemy they themselves were committing. The Jews stumbled over Christ, the true cornerstone of their salvation because they were spiritually blinded by their own self-righteousness. "They stumbled because they disobeyed the word as they were destined to do" (1 Peter 2:8, RSV) consequently, they made no effort, by the Spirit, to put to death "that which causes sin" in their lives. Romans 8:12-13. There is no one Bible verse where its incorrect interpretation more clearly defines the confusion existing in the Christian world today than does the erroneous belief that faith in Christ's substitutional sacrifice has made void our responsibility to keep God's Holy Ten Commandment Law. Therefore, to counter-act this type of thinking, the Apostle Paul says, "do we then make void the law through faith; by no means, on the contrary, we establish the law." Romans 3:31.

This is how Romans 10:4 would read when retranslated from the original language with the **subject** appearing in **bold** letters, the *direct object* appearing in *italics* and the <u>indirect object underlined</u>; "For **Christ is the fulfillment** of the law *leading to true righteousness for* <u>those</u> <u>who</u> <u>believe</u>." In Romans 10:4, the Greek word translated as "end" of the law in the KJV, CSB, NASB, RSV, and as the "culmination" of the law in the NIV, has a Strong's call number of (5056) and looks like this τέλος, in the original language. In its exact form, the Greek word τέλος appears in the New Testament thirty-two times. The KJV translates the Greek word τέλος, as "end" 27 times, "continually" 1 time, "custom" 2 times, "uttermost" 1 time, and "finally" 1 time. The RSV translates the Greek word τέλος as end 23 times, continually 1 time, fulfillment 1 time, revenue 2 times, last 1 time, aim 1 time, purpose 1 time, outcome 1 time, and finally 1 time. The NIV translates the Greek word τέλος, as end 18 times, outcome 1 time, keeps 1 time, fulfillment 1 time, result 2 times, culmination 1 time, revenue 2 times, destiny 1 time, last 1 time, goal 1 time, finally 2 times and end-result 1 time. In Friberg's Greek lexicon, the definitions of the Greek word τέλος is defined as 1) "termination, end, 2) forever, continually, 3) outcome, goal, aim, fulfillment, as an action, achieved, carried out, and/or the fulfillment" of something, 4) as a tax, tribute, custom, duty, or revenue.

In Luke 22:37, (KJV) the same Greek word τέλος, is employed, "For I say unto you that what is written must yet be accomplished in me, and he was reckoned among the transgressors: for the things concerning me have an end. (5056) The same Bible verse reads like this in the RSV, "For I tell you that this scripture must be fulfilled in me, and he was reckoned with the transgressors; for what is written about me has its fulfillment." (5056) In Luke 22:37, the KJV translates the Greek word τέλος, as "end" while the RSV translates the same Greek word τέλος, as "fulfillment" in harmony with the definition assigned by Friberg's Greek Lexicon, obviously, in Luke 22:37 Doctor Luke is not stating the things concerning Christ have been terminated [ended] and are no longer binding upon the believers living in this dispensation.

In 1 Timothy 1:5, (KJV) the same Greek word τέλος, is employed, "Now the end (5056) of the commandments is charity out of a pure heart and of a good conscience and of faith unfeigned." To interpret 1 Timothy 1:5, as meaning God's holy law terminates charity, a good conscience, and genuine faith, is crazy and irresponsible. The RSV translates 1 Timothy 1:5 like this, "Whereas the aim (5056) of our charge is love that issues from a pure heart and a good conscience and sincere faith." The translators of the RSV recognize the context of the Greek word τέλος, must be considered if a proper representation of the action taking place in the Bible verse is to be correctly represented. The great truth concerning the perpetuity of God's holy law in conjunction with the proclamation of the judgment message (Revelation 14:6-7) as it relates to the final withdrawal of the "everlasting gospel," (Revelation 10:5-7) will distinguish God's true church as we near the close of human probation. Revelation 7:1-4, Daniel 11:40-45, Revelation 14:12. Therefore, after a brief investigation of the Greek word τέλος, appearing in Romans 10:4 and translated by the KJV, CSB, NASB, RSV as "Christ is the end of the law" and by the NIV as "Christ is the culmination of the law," the erroneous belief held by the mainline Protestant and Evangelical Churches that Christ's substitutional sacrifice has made void our responsibility to keep God's Holy Ten Commandment Law must be questioned because it's obviously inconsistent with the new covenant promise of salvation Hebrews 8:10, and what the Bible teaches that God's Holy Ten Commandment law will be the standard of righteousness used by Christ to evaluate our characters during His final work of mediation, which is the investigative judgment.

In Romans 10:4, the same Greek word τέλος, translated as [Christ is the "end" of the law] by the KJV, CSB, NASB, and the RSV appears in James 5:11, and is translated by the KJV as; "you have heard of the patience of Job and have seen the "end" (5056) of the Lord; that the Lord is very pitiful and of tender mercy." In James 5:11, the same Greek word τέλος is translated by the RSV as; "You have heard of the steadfastness of Job and you have seen the purpose (5056) of the Lord, how the Lord is compassionate and merciful." The translation of James 5:11, by the RSV is a better representation of the action taking place in the Bible verse. Job's faith did not terminate the Lord's existence and/or make void the Lord's authority. In James 5:11, the same Greek word τέλος, translated by the KJV as "you have seen the end of the Lord," is translated by the Phillips Bible as; "You have heard of Job's patient endurance and how God dealt with him at the "end" (5056) and therefore you have seen that the Lord is merciful and full of understanding pity for us men." It's obvious the Greek word τέλος, does not always mean termination. The context of the Bible verse must be considered if a correct understanding of the action taking place is to be obtained.

In Romans 10:4, the same Greek word τέλος, translated by the (KJV) as "Christ is the end of the law," is employed by the inspired writer in 1 Peter 1:9, and it's translated by (KJV) as; "receiving the end (5065) of your faith, even the salvation of your souls." Our faith does not terminate and/or make void our salvation. The RSV and the NIV translate (1 Peter 1:9) markedly different, "The outcome (5056) of your faith you obtain the salvation of your souls." The mainline Protestant and Evangelical Church theologians who interpret Romans 10:4 as meaning "Christ is the "end" of the law, [meaning the termination of the law], could not have investigated the subject very carefully to arrive at such an erroneous conclusion. Therefore, by laboring to make void our responsibility to keep God's holy law, to get around the obligation of the Seventh-day Sabbath, these blind guides are doing Satan's work of misleading the unsuspecting multitudes of this generation by calling evil good and good evil (Isaiah 5:20) thereby creating a careless, indifferent attitude, that excuses sin and encourages continued transgressions, worldliness, and backsliding.

The same Greek word τέλος, translated in Romans 10:4 (KJV) as "Christ is the end of the law," also appears in Revelation 21:6 and Revelation 22:13. In these two Bible verses, Christ says, "He is the Alpha and the Omega, the Beginning and the (5056) End." Christ is not referring to the terminating and/or the "end" of His existence. In Matthew 10:22, the same Greek word τέλος is translated by almost every modern Bible as; "you will be hated by all for my name's sake, but he who endures into the end (5056) the same will be saved." Again, we are not talking about the termination of all the saved or some other crazy interpretation. The apostle is referring to believers who endure into the fulfillment of all things, "the same shall be saved." In Romans 13:7, the same Greek word τέλος is translated two times as a duty or custom. If we are to understand Romans 10:4 to mean Christ is [the "termination" (5056) of the law], then the same understanding must also be applied to James 5:11, which states Job's faith terminated (5056) the existence of the Lord. In addition, the same understanding must also be applied to 1 Peter 1:9, which states the "end" (5056) of our faith terminates our salvation. In the thirty-two times, the exact form of the Greek word τέλος appears in the New Testament, the context must be considered and compared to what the Bible teaches on the subject to obtain the best possible translation of the Greek word τέλος, as it appears in any Bible verse. As a result of this brief examination, it can be confidently stated that there is not one Bible verse where its incorrect interpretation more clearly exposes the confusion existing in the Christian world today than does the erroneous doctrine advanced by the mainline Protestant and Evangelical Churches that our faith in Christ's death upon Calvary's Cross has made void our responsibility to keep God's Holy Ten Commandment Law.

In Romans 9:1, the Apostle Paul speaks of the sorrow he felt for his fellow countrymen who had rejected the righteousness of Christ and had Him killed for the blasphemy that they themselves were committing. This dialog continues for the entire chapter and concludes in Romans 11:36 with the idea that all glory belongs to our Creator forever and ever. However, in Romans 9:30-33, the Apostle Paul specifically outlines the real problems associated with Pharisaical Legalism, the prevailing religion of the day. The apostle, quoting the Prophet Isaiah says, "Though the number of the sons of Israel are like the sands of the sea, only a remnant of them will be saved." In Romans 9:30-33, he gives the reasons why "only a remnant of them will be saved." The Israelites equated righteousness based upon their performance of the ceremonial law, while they continually violated the requirements of the moral law. Isaiah 1:12-18. They believed strict adherence to the ceremonial law represented true righteousness, which created the illusion of salvation now and in the judgment.

The Jewish people were under the mistaken impression that their rigorous adherence to the exactions of the ceremonial law justified them in God's sight and thereby "assured them of their salvation now and in the judgment." However, they were no different from the misguided Christians of this generation. The Jews sacrificed lambs and goats, rigorously performed the exactions of the ceremonial law, and then declared themselves saved and forgiven of their sins. They were completely devoid of the righteousness that comes from genuine faith in Christ's substitutional sacrifice and the real forgiveness of sins that could only be received from accessing Christ's daily mediation in the heavenly sanctuary. The love of the truth, which would conform their lives and character to the image of their Creator, was replaced by self-righteousness created by strict observance of the sacrificial system. Isaiah 28:14-29, Isaiah 29:9-16, Isaiah 30:1. The sacrificial system was designed to point believers to Christ as the Lamb of God who died for our transgressions giving Him the right to mediate for the real forgiveness of our sins. The misguided Jews of that generation rejected the righteousness offered them through faith in

Christ's substitutional sacrifice giving Him the right to mediate for the real forgiveness of their sins. The bigoted Jews of that generation preferred the "self-righteousness" created by performing the exactions of the ceremonial law rather than accessing Christ's daily mediation to obtain the real forgiveness of their sins; therefore, they had Christ killed for the blasphemy that they themselves were committing.

The Jews, like so many professed Christians today had a distorted understanding of the everlasting gospel. The alleged justification they received after sacrificing animals, along with their rigorous exactions to the ceremonial law, created only the illusion of salvation. This misunderstanding distorted the gospel invitation into a license to sin. As a result of transforming the everlasting gospel into a license to sin, the Apostle Paul says the Jews stumbled over Christ, the cornerstone of their salvation. They did not claim justification by faith to access Christ's "daily mediation" to receive the real forgiveness of their sins for the sanctification of their characters. They considered themselves saved and forgiven immediately after performing the rigorous exactions of the ceremonial law. As a result, they were made self-righteous in their own eyes and killed anyone who disagreed with their self-serving interpretation of the gospel invitation.

The same self-righteousness exists in the Christian world today; after believers claim "justification by faith" they declare themselves saved and forgiven of their sins. This self-righteousness creates the illusion of salvation. This illusion of salvation is based totally upon the believers of this generation rigorously claiming justification by faith, which removes Christ as their only mediator and judge. The so-called Christians of this generation stumble for the same reasons the bigoted Jews stumbled during Christ's first advent. Romans 9:30-33, 1 Peter 2:7-8. The Jews rejected and killed Christ during His first advent because they were not looking for the Messiah of Bible prophecy to save them from their sins. They considered themselves saved and forgiven after participating in the sacrificial system. In like manner, the so-called Christians of this generation stumble because they are not looking to be saved from their sins. The confused multitudes of this generation are seen declaring themselves saved and forgiven immediately after ritualistically claiming justification by faith, while they, like the bigoted Jews of Christ's day, continue to transgress God's holy law.

The self-righteous Christians of this generation condemn the Jews as legalists while they refuse to form sanctified characters in preparation for the investigative judgment, which is the message for this time. Revelation 14:6-7. They have declared God's holy law <u>void</u> and/or a yoke of bondage while they reject Christ as their only mediator and judge, in the same way, the Jews did during His first advent. Romans 4:15. Their declaration God's holy law is no longer binding upon believers today creates a careless, indifferent spirit that excuses sin and encourages continued transgressions, worldliness, and backsliding. The alleged Christians of this generation have stumbled because they have rejected Christ as their only mediator and judge by declaring themselves saved and forgiven immediately after ritualistically claiming justification by faith like the Jews did in the past dispensation. The alleged Christians of this generation, who believe they are assured of their salvation now and in the judgment immediately after claiming Christ's death paid the penalty they rightfully deserve for their transgressions of the law, are bigger legalists than the Jews who killed Christ for the blasphemy that they themselves were committing. Therefore, the prophecies predict the professed Christians of this generation, will, just like the Jews did in the past dispensation, reject and kill anyone for the blasphemy that they themselves are committing. Revelation 13:11-18.

In Romans 2:25-29, the Apostle Paul describes the problems created by the misunderstanding of the gospel invitation held by his fellow countrymen. The Apostle Paul says, "keeping the ceremonial law" is of value if you obey the Ten Commandment Law; but if you break God's Holy Ten Commandment Law "keeping the ceremonial law" and circumcision becomes uncircumcision. The apostle is very specific regarding the existence of God's holy law in this dispensation. The believers living in this generation must understand their obedience to God's Holy Ten Commandment Law is essential if they are to receive eternal life. Romans 2:26-29, 1 John 2:4. The Prophet Isaiah condemned the Jews who believed their sacrifices and offerings, along with their rigorous exactions to the ceremonial law, had secured for them righteousness and eternal life while they continued to transgress God's holy law. Isaiah 1:10-15. In Romans 9:27-33, after clearly outlining the problem with the understanding of the gospel held by his fellow countrymen, the apostle goes on to say, that the stumbling block for believers living in this generation is the same as it was for the unbelieving Jews in the past dispensation. The true believer is being admonished to "wash yourself and make yourself clean; remove the evil of your doings from before my eyes, cease from doing wickedness, learn to do good, seek justice, correct oppression, defend the fatherless, plead for the widow." Isaiah 1:16. The prophets of the past dispensation and the apostles of this generation are saying this is the real religion of the Bible and true righteousness. James 2:14-26. Therefore, the Jews were completely ignorant of this one fact, the everlasting gospel was introduced to bring about the obedience of our faith; not to sacrifice animals and then declare themselves saved and forgiven while they continue to transgress God's holy law.

The apostle says God's holy law will be the standard of righteousness used to evaluate our characters during Christ's final work of mediation, which is the investigative judgment. The ignorance of this one fact produced the illusions of salvation, resulting in the Jews confusing true righteousness for their rigorous exactions to the ceremonial law. The apostle says they were incapable of being put into subjection <u>to the righteousness</u> of God due to their misguided understanding of the everlasting gospel. In their blind zeal, they replaced the requirement of genuine obedience to the moral law, with a false gospel creating the illusion of salvation based upon an outward display of forms and ceremonies. Isaiah 28:14-22. In Romans 10:4, to help believers avoid this same type of self-righteousness, gripping his fellow countrymen, the Apostle Paul admonishes the believers of this generation to meditate upon Christ's sanctified character. It is only by doing this will believers be properly motivated to access Christ's "daily mediation" to receive the fulfillment of the new covenant promise of salvation. Romans 1:1-6, Titus 2:11-14, 2 Corinthians 7:1. Therefore, the apostle says the everlasting gospel was introduced so that God's Holy Ten Commandment law can be written upon the hearts and minds of believers; this he says is the fulfillment of the new covenant promise of salvation. Hebrews 8:10, Hebrews 10:16-18.

In Romans 10:2, the apostle says the Jews had great *zeal* for God but not *according to true knowledge*. In Romans 10:2, the Greek words translated as *zeal* and *true knowledge* appear respectively as the *direct object* and the *modifier* of the *direct object*. The point being made by the apostle is this; the Jews had great *zeal* but lacked *true knowledge* of the everlasting gospel. In Romans 10:3, the apostle goes on to say the **Jews being ignorant (the subject)** *of true knowledge (the direct object)* **they established (the modifier of the subject)** *their own righteousness (a modifier of the direct object)* and [as a result] they were incapable of being put into subjection <u>to true righteousness</u> (<u>the indirect object</u>) of God. The Apostle said the Jews believed in and had great "*zeal*" for a plan, but they had no "*true knowledge*" of God's true plan of salvation. Isaiah 30:1. In like manner, the distorted "*knowledge*" of the everlasting gospel existing in the Christian world today produces a blind "*zeal*" for a false gospel that tolerates continued transgressions.

The false gospel advanced by the mainline Protestant and Evangelical Churches teaches believers that they are eternally secure in their salvation immediately after claiming justification by faith while they continue to transgress God's holy law. In addition, the mainline Protestant and Evangelical Churches are teaching believers that God's holy law has been made void by our faith primarily because it's a yoke of bondage. These blind guides are teaching that God's laws, both His moral law and His health laws cannot or do not need to be obeyed by the believers living in this dispensation. 1 John 5:3, John 14:15, 1 Corinthians 11:19, and Philippians 3:9, 1 Corinthians 3:16-17. Addressing the professed Christian Churches of this generation who teach "Christ is the end of the law for all who believe" (Romans 10:4) if the Apostle Paul were alive today he would say they have great *zeal* but they lack *true knowledge* of the everlasting gospel, which is designed to write God's Holy Ten Commandment Law upon the hearts and minds of believers living in both dispensations. Jeremiah 31:31-33, Hebrews 8:10, Hebrews 10:16-25. Therefore, after a brief investigation of the Greek word τέλος, appearing in Romans 10:4 that's translated, by the KJV, CSB, NASB, and RSV as "Christ is the end of the law" and translated in the NIV as "Christ is the culmination of the law," the erroneous belief held by the mainline Protestant and Evangelical Churches that Christ's substitutional sacrifice has made void our responsibility to keep God's Holy Ten Commandment Law must be questioned because it's obviously inconsistent with the new covenant promise of salvation Hebrews 8:10, and what the Bible teaches on the perpetuity of God's Holy Ten Commandment law. Romans 2:12-16. Romans 3:19-20, Romans 3:31, Romans 7:7-12, John 14:15, 1 John 5:3.

10

THE APOSTLE PAUL SAYS – IF YOU ARE LED BY THE SPIRIT, YOU ARE NOT UNDER THE LAW

The Apostle Paul is emphatic about the fact that the believer's faith in Christ's atoning blood does not make void the obligation of keeping God's Holy Ten Commandment Law as originally proclaimed amid the thunders of Mt. Sinai. Romans 3:31, Romans 4:15, Galatians 2:17-18, Romans 3:19-21, Romans 7:7-12. There should be no misunderstanding among the mainline Protestant and Evangelical church theologians about what the apostle means in Galatians 5:18 when he says, "If you are led <u>by the Spirit</u>, you are not *"under the law."* Grammatically speaking, it's virtually impossible to misunderstand what the apostle means when he says "If you are led <u>by the Spirit</u>, you are not *"under the law,* primarily because the phrase *"under the law"* is welded by its mandatory case agreement to *the deeds* of the flesh appearing in Galatians 5:16 which the same apostle says in Romans 8:12-13 must be put to death is we are to receive a positive verdict in the judgment. Galatians 5:24.

Consequently, it's grammatically impossible to apply the apostle's comment appearing in Galatians 5:18, "if you are led <u>by the Spirit</u>, you are not *"under the law,"* to God's Holy Ten Commandment Law, primarily because this interpretation violates the case agreement of the words appearing in the Bible verse. Accordingly, any interpretation contradicting that the phrase *"under the law"* refers to "the fallen nature" all of humanity has received at birth [without their consent] from their earthly parents is a distortion of the Bible verse. The correct interpretation of the Bible verse should be obvious, "If you are led <u>by the Spirit</u>, you are not *"under the law,"* of sin and death, this concept is welded by its mandatory case agreement to *the carnal nature* the Apostle Paul says must be put to death if we are to receive eternal life. Romans 7:14, Romans 7:21, Romans 8:12-13, and Galatians 5:24. Therefore, for the mainline Protestant and Evangelical Church theologians to take the position that the Apostle Paul is saying God's Holy Ten Commandment Law, as originally proclaimed amid the thunders of Mt. Sinai, is no longer binding upon believers living in this dispensation is not supported by the scriptures and is consequently, a complete prevarication, meaning it's a deliberate attempt to deceive.

In Galatians 5:18, the Apostle Paul says, "If you are led <u>by the Spirit</u>, you are not *"under the law."* To correctly understand this phrase, we will look at Galatians 5:16-24 in the original language. However, before retranslating Galatians 5:16-24 from the original language, it's important to reference some already defined terms relevant to what the apostle is trying to communicate in Galatians 5:16-24 because the correct understanding of the same is specifically germane to the plan devised for our salvation. These already defined terms are "that which causes sin" in our lives, representing the fallen human nature all of Adam's descendants have inherited at birth, without their consent, from their earthly parents. The phrase "you are under the law," represents those who are still controlled by their fallen nature evidenced by them yielding to their sinful propensities, and the phrase "you are under the grace" of Christ representing believers who understand that they must by the Spirit [at some point in time] crucified their fallen nature, representing the death of "that which causes sin" in their lives. In addition, the reader must understand that "the carnal nature," produces the "desires of the flesh," which means the adulterous believer who has not put to death their fallen nature is still under "the law of sin and death," consequently, they cannot be "assured of their salvation now and in the judgment" immediately after claiming justification by faith, because they obviously have not been born again, consequently, they cannot receive a positive verdict in the judgment.

These specifically defined terms have been introduced in Romans the sixth and seventh chapters and are referenced repeatedly in Romans the eighth chapter along with other books in the Bible. Therefore, these previously defined terms are repeatedly employed by the apostle to establish the everlasting gospel was designed to provide justified believers with free access to Christ's daily mediation so they can put to death their fallen nature, which has caused all of Adam's descendants to transgress God's Holy Ten Commandment Law by yielding to their overpowering sinful propensities. Romans 8:12-13, Galatians 5:24.

In Romans, the seventh chapter, the apostle references the "carnal nature." Romans 7:14. The apostle clearly states that the carnal nature produces the overpowering sinful "*desires* of the flesh," which made him captive to "*the law* of sin and death" dwelling in his members. Romans 7:21-24. Those under the control of "*the law* of sin and death" are **slaves** to their sinful passions. They are controlled by the "*fallen defective nature*" they inherited at birth [without their consent] from their earthly parents. The "*law* of sin and death" is grammatically linked to our "fallen defective human nature," which has caused all of Adam's descendants to transgress God's holy law. Romans 3:23. It is only through *the grace* of Christ can believers claim, "justification by faith" and be delivered from "*the law* of sin" working "death" in their lives. The "*law* of sin," represents "the body of death," that the Apostle Paul longed to be delivered from, as referenced in Romans 7:24; it's the "carnal nature" (Romans 7:14); it's the law of sin and death, (Romans 7:21) that all of humanity has been sold under resulting from Adam's first transgression. Romans 5:12-14. Consequently, as previously established the "carnal nature" is without question "that which causes sin" in our lives and must be put to death if we are to see eternal life. Romans 8:12-13, Galatians 5:24.

Those who are "*under the grace*" of Christ are those believers who have claimed "justification by faith" and come boldly to the throne of grace accessing His "daily mediation" so they can, by the Spirit, put to death "*that which causes sin*" in their lives. As stated earlier to correctly understand what the apostle means when he says, "If you are led by the Spirit you are not "*under the law*," (Galatians 5:18), these previously defined terms must be understood, (1) the "carnal nature," Romans 7:14, (2) the "desires of the flesh" (Galatians 5:16) and (3) "the law of sin and death" (Romans 7:21-23) all of which are grammatically linked to the "fallen nature" that produces the "*overpowering sinful desires*" of the flesh, representing *that great state of lawlessness*, which has caused all of Adam's descendants to transgress God's Holy Ten Commandment Law. Romans 6:12-23. Therefore, after retranslating Galatians 5:16-24 from the original language, it will be easily established that those who are led by the Spirit are not "*under the law*" of sin working death in their lives. Romans 7:21-25, Romans 8:1-4.

The term "*under the law*," originally introduced in Romans 6:14-16, references those who have transgressed God's holy law, because they are still controlled by the desires of the "flesh," meaning their fallen nature is still controlling their actions causing them to transgress God's holy law. Romans 7:21-24. Consequently, the apostle says the alleged believers, who, after claiming "justification by faith," are committing adultery when yielding to their fallen nature. Romans 7:1-6. The Apostle Paul continually emphasizes that the weakness of our flesh, which he represents as our fallen nature (Romans 8:1-4) has caused [is causing] all of Adam's descendants to transgress God's holy law due to their inability to control their sinful desires. Romans 6:12-22, Romans 7:14-25. In Romans the seventh chapter, the apostle says, "the carnal nature" produces "the sinful desires of the flesh," which he defines in Romans 7:21-23 as "the law of sin and death" and the same phrase is linked by its mandatory case agreement to the carnal nature. Romans 7:14. Therefore, the Apostle Paul says the carnal nature produces the desires of the "flesh," which he defines in Romans 7:14-25 as "the law of sin and death" dwelling in our members and emphatically says that it must be put to death if we are to receive eternal life in Galatians 5:24 and Romans 8:12-13.

In Romans 8:5-13, the Apostle Paul says, "the carnal nature," producing the sinful desires of the "flesh," must be put to death if a positive verdict in the judgment is to be received. This is why the apostle says those controlled by the fallen defective nature, they received at birth without their consent from their earthly parents, cannot receive eternal life. They are still *"under the law"* of sin and consequently, controlled by the fallen nature working death in their lives. Conversely, the term *"under the grace"* of Christ (Romans 6:14) becomes specifically applicable to those who, after claiming justification by faith, (Romans 5:1-2) realize they no longer are slaves to their sinful passions. Romans 7:24-25. As justified believers they are no longer *"under the law"* of sin working death in their lives; they *are under the grace of Christ's redeeming power, and* they rejoice in the hope of forming [sanctified] characters knowing that its end is eternal life. Romans 6:12-22. These "born again' believers understand God's Holy Ten Commandment Law will be the standard of righteousness used by Christ to evaluate their characters during His final work of mediation, which is the investigative judgment. As a result, the truly born-again believer will rejoice in the hope of forming "sanctified" characters in perfect harmony with God's holy law in preparation for Christ's final work of mediation, which is the investigative judgment. Romans 6:20-22, and 2 Thessalonians 2:13. Therefore, after claiming "justification by faith" they understand eternal life is predicated upon believers forming sanctified characters in harmony with God's holy law in preparation for the time when they must stand in the presence of God without a mediator in the heavenly sanctuary after human probation closes when Christ concludes His final work of mediation, which is the investigative judgment. Romans 2:12-16, Daniel 7:9-10.

After looking at Galatians 5:16-24 in the original language, it will be established that "the carnal nature" producing the sinful desires of the flesh must be put to death if justified believers are to receive eternal life. Romans 8:12-13. It is only *by the grace* of Christ can justified believers access Christ's daily mediation and by the Spirit put to death, *"that which causes sin"* in their lives. Romans 7:21-25. Consequently, by following the case agreement of the Greek words appearing in Galatians 5:15-24, it is virtually impossible to misunderstand what the Apostle Paul is trying to communicate. In Galatians 5:18 the apostle says, "If you are led <u>by the Spirit</u>, you are not *under the law*." In Galatians 5:18, the apostle is referring to the truly born-again believers who are not controlled by their carnal nature, meaning the overpowering sinful desires of the "flesh" are no longer causing them to transgress God's holy law. Therefore, for the mainline Protestant and Evangelical Churches to teach that God's Holy Ten Commandment Law has been done away with by our faith is 100% grammatically inaccurate, satanically motivated, and cannot be supported by the scriptures, and is exemplifying the confusion existing in Christendom today, which the guilty inhabitants of the earth are being called out of by the second angel of Revelation the 14th chapters which represents "the message for this time." Revelation 14:6-13, Revelation 18:1-4.

In these Bible verses, Romans 7:5, Romans 7:18, and Romans 7:25, the Apostle Paul employs the Greek word σαρκί, translated as "in the flesh," which has a Strong's call number of 4561, its morphological meaning represents the fallen nature that must be put to death if believers are to receive eternal life. In its exact form (noun dative feminine singular), the Greek word σαρκί, appears in the New Testament (39) thirty-nine times. The same Greek word σαρκίm, (4561) appears approximately (147) one hundred and forty-seven times, in a variety of different forms. It's a well-traveled word; consequently, there should be no ambiguity associated with its interpretation. Therefore, the best possible translation of the Greek word σαρκί, when it appears as a noun in the dative case would be "by the flesh," clearly representing that our fallen nature is the moving agent in our lives causing us to perform the action identified in the Bible verses. Romans 8:3.

In Romans 6:19, the same Greek word σαρκί, (4561) appears, only this time as a noun in the genitive case, feminine, singular. The best possible translation of the Greek word σαρκί, (4561) appearing as a noun in the genitive case, feminine, singular, would be "of the flesh." The reason for this translation is the apostle says our fallen human nature possesses *the inadequacies* of the flesh, representing the overpowering sinful propensities that all have inherited at birth from their earthly parents. The *inadequacy of the flesh* (4561) is grammatically linked, by its case agreement, to *that great state of lawlessness* existing *in fallen humanity,* which the apostle says acts like a law in Romans 7:21, and goes on to say that it's the "law of sin" which has caused all of Adam's descendants to transgress God's holy law and must be put to death if justified believers are to receive eternal life.

In Romans 7:14, the Apostle Paul says we already know this, [meaning nothing new being introduced] **that the law** is **spiritual, but I am carnal sold** *under the control of sin.* Consequently, for the mainline Protestant and Evangelical Churches to misunderstand this concept represents absolute total unadulterated confusion. The apostle goes on to say because of the weakness "of the flesh," he cannot control his actions, which he says is caused by **his fallen carnal nature.** Romans 7:14-20. The fallen **carnal nature** produces the overpowering desires of the flesh (4561) and is repeatedly represented by the apostle as "the law of sin and death," causing all of humanity infected with the sin virus to transgress God's holy requirements.

In Romans 7:5, Romans 7:18, and Romans 7:25, the Greek word σαρκί, translated as "in the flesh" (4561), is represented as the carnal nature, which is grammatically linked by its case agreement to "the law of sin" (Romans 7:23), which controls the actions of all those who are not "under the grace" of Christ's justifying power. The apostle emphatically says the carnal nature, producing the deeds of the flesh (4561), is "the law of sin," controlling the lives of Adam's descendants who are not under the grace of Jesus Christ after claiming justification by faith. This is why the Apostle Paul admonishes believers that the carnal nature must be put to death if they are to receive a positive verdict in the judgment. Romans 8:12-13, Daniel 7:9-10. In Galatians 5:18, the Apostle Paul emphatically states that those who have by the Spirit put to death their fallen carnal nature are not under the law of sin and death. There should be absolutely no confusion on this very important subject; justified believers are not under the law, [of sin and death] if they are under the justifying grace of Jesus Christ. Romans 5:1-2, Romans 6:14. Therefore, for the mainline Protestant and Evangelical church theologians to misrepresent and/or misunderstand this concept, represents the total confusion (Babylon) existing in Christendom today, which all are being presently called out of by the second angel, (Revelation 14:8) and represents the message for this time that will be re-proclaimed by those who still believe in the original Advent Message just before the close of human probation. Revelation 18:1-4.

The Retranslation of Galatians 5:16-18

If Galatians 5:16-18, were retranslated from the original language, with the **subject** appearing in **bold** letters, the *direct object* appearing in *italics,* and the indirect object, underlined, the Bible verses would read like this; remember the only way to understand what the apostle is trying to communicate is by following the case agreement of the words appearing in the retranslated Bible verses. In Galatians 5:16, the apostle is commanding believers to walk by the spirit and unequivocally says if they do there is absolutely no possibility of them performing *the desires* of the flesh. In Galatians 5:17, the apostle gives the reasons for this emphatic statement, "For **the flesh,** its desires are against the Spirit and **the Spirit** are against the flesh, for **these,** they are opposed to each other to possibly prevent *these desires* and keep you from doing *these things*." In Galatians 5:17, these two phrases, [to possibly prevent *"these desires" and* keep you from doing *"these things"*] are both grammatically welded by their mandatory case agreement to the phrase *"the desires* of the flesh" in Galatians 5:16, which the apostle emphatically states you can't possibly perform if you are led by the Spirit. This is why, after making the emphatic comment in Galatians 5:16 (if you "walk by the spirit you cannot possibly perform *the desires* of the flesh,) the apostle goes on to say, in Galatians 5:18, "if you are led by the Spirit, you are not *under the law.*" The *phrase* "you are not *under the law"* is welded by its mandatory case agreement to the two phrases employed by the apostle in Galatians 5:17, to possibly prevent *"these desires" and* to possibly keep you from doing *"these things."* These two phrases "to possibly prevent *"these desires"* and to possibly keep you from doing *"these things"* are both grammatically welded by their mandatory case agreement to *"the desires"* of the flesh employed by the apostle in Galatians 5:16. Therefore, it's extremely important to understand that in Galatians 5:16 the Apostle Paul is employing a double negative with a subjunctive kicker to deny the idea of the possibility of the fact existing that if you walk <u>by the Spirit</u> you will perform *"the desires"* of the flesh. Galatians 5:16.

It's important to understand that the phrase "<u>by the Spirit</u>" employed by the apostle in Galatians 5:16 represents the moving agent in the Bible verse. In Galatians 5:17, the apostle says the Holy Spirit will keep believers from performing *"these things"* and the phrase *"these things"* is welded by its mandatory case agreement to *"the desires"* of the flesh employed by the apostle in Galatians 5:16 representing the moving agent in the Bible verse. This is why the apostle, in Galatians 5:16, is commanding believers to "walk by the Spirit" because if they do, he says they cannot "possibly perform *the desires* of the flesh. The reader needs to understand that a born-again believer would rather die than knowingly transgress God's holy law. 1 John 3:9, and 1 John 5:18-20. The reason the apostle emphatically states that if you "walk by the Spirit" you cannot "possibly perform *the desires* of the flesh, stands at the foundation of the plan devised for our salvation. As established earlier the term employed by the Apostle Paul in Galatians 5:18 *"under the law"* is grammatically linked, by its mandatory case agreement, to *the desires* of the flesh employed by the apostle in Galatians 5:16, which the apostle says you cannot possibly perform because the <u>Spirit</u> "keeps you from doing *these things."* Galatians 5:17. There is no other interpretation available. Therefore, when you follow case agreement of the words appearing in Galatians 5:16-18 understanding what the apostle is saying becomes so clear that no one can misunderstand his communication in Galatians 5:16, the Apostle Paul is commanding believers to walk <u>by the</u>

<u>Spirit</u>, and says if they do he's denying the idea of the possibility of the fact existing that they will perform "the desires of the flesh."

When the definitions of the words appearing in the original language are properly translated, with the moods and tenses correctly amplified, understanding what the apostle is communicating is not that difficult. The reason why the apostle says, "If you are led <u>by the Spirit</u>, you are not *under the law*" is not that difficult to understand, born again believers who walk <u>by the Spirit</u> [as the moving agent working righteousness in their lives] are not controlled by *the desires* of the flesh; as a result, they "are not *under the law*" of sin working death in their lives. The term *"under the law"* has already been clearly defined many times; consequently, for the mainline Protestant and Evangelical Churches to misunderstand this fact is simply inexcusable and satanic at its very foundation. The apostle is so emphatic about our ability to resist sin, that the overpowering communication coming from him in Galatians 5:16 comes across as a command to walk <u>by the Spirit.</u> In this command, the apostle is employing the strongest language at his disposal, a double negative with a subjunctive kicker, to deny the idea of the possibility of the fact existing that if you walk by the Spirit, you will perform the desires of the flesh. The reason why you will not perform *the desires* of the flesh is that you are not under the controlling power of your *fallen nature*; as a result, the apostle says you are not *under the law*, which is grammatically linked to *our fallen nature,* which produces *(the desires of the flesh)* causing all of Adam's descendants to transgress God's Holy Ten Commandment Law. Romans 7:14, Romans 7:21, Romans 8:12-13, Galatians 5:24.

The retranslation of Galatians 5:19-21

In Galatians 5:19-21, the apostle identifies the works of the flesh, so there is no confusion regarding the true nature of your alleged conversion experience. If Galatians 5:19-21, were retranslated from the original language with the **subject** appearing in **bold** letters, the *direct object* appearing in *italics,* and the <u>indirect object underlined</u>, the Bible verses would read like this; remember the only way to understand what the apostle is trying to communicate is to follow the case agreement of the words appearing in the Bible verse[s]. However, before looking at the retranslation of Galatians 5:19-21 please recall what the apostle emphatically states in Galatians 5:16; the Apostle Paul commands believers to walk by the spirit, so there is no possibility of them performing the desires of the flesh. In Galatians 5:19-21, the apostle identifies the deeds of the flesh so believers can recognize who is controlling their actions. The apostle says, "Here is the **evidence of the works** of the flesh, whoever is **sexually immoral, impure, licentious,** [practicing] **idolatry,** [practicing] **sorcery,** which should be translated as taking pharmaceutical medications or using illegal drugs, [demonstrating] **hostility,** [creating] **strife, jealousy,** experiencing fits of **rage, selfishness, dissension,** [whoever is] **teachings false doctrines,** [experiencing] **envy, drunkenness,** and **those likeminded** to those who I warned before just as I have previously mentioned to them that those **practicing these** such things they shall not gain possession of the kingdom of God. The apostle had previously said, "**The flesh,** its desires are against the Spirit, and **the Spirit** are against the flesh, for **these** they are opposed to each other." Consequently, in order to contrast these two opposing authorities, the flesh and the Spirit, the apostle in Galatians 5:22-24 identifies **the fruits** of the Spirit, and says they are **love, joy, peace, patience, kindness, generosity, faith, humility,** and **self-control,** against these, there exists no such **law**. The apostle concludes his powerful dissertation on the supremacy of Christ's grace, working the deliverance of those born "under the law" of sin, by clearly stating "**those who** belong to Jesus Christ will have, at some point in time, crucified the flesh that causes these desires and those lustful passions.

Conclusion

When the definitions of the words appearing in the original language are properly translated, with the moods and tenses correctly amplified, and if the mandatory case agreement of the words is respected, understanding what the apostle is saying in Galatians 5:18 becomes so obvious it cannot possibly be misunderstood. "If you are led <u>by the Spirit</u>, you are not *under the law*" of sin, meaning your sinful passions aroused by your fallen nature are not controlling your actions. It's just not that difficult to understand, those who walk <u>by the Spirit</u> are not governed by *the desires* of the flesh; (Galatians 5:16) they are *under the grace* of Christ (Romans 6:14) so they have crucified[ing] *the flesh* that <u>causes these desires and lustful passions</u>. Galatians 5:16-24. Those who have crucified *the flesh* that <u>causes these desires, and lustful passions</u> are not under the law of sin; as a result, they must be born again and will not be destroyed with the Devil and his evil angels in the lake of fire, which is the second death. Revelation 20:12-15. Therefore, for the Catholic, mainline Protestant, and Evangelical church theologians to state that if you are led by the Spirit you no longer have to keep God's Holy Ten Commandment Law, not only violates the mandatory case agreement of the words employed by the inspired writer in the Bible verses, at its very foundation is satanic, representing a lawlessness attitude that stands at the foundation of Satan's rebellion against the authority of the Government of Heaven.

11

THE PROTESTANT AND EVANGELICAL CHURCHES SAY – GOD'S HOLY LAW WAS NAILED TO THE CROSS

Opening Statement

In the Sermon on the Mount, Christ declared, "Think not that I have come to destroy the law or the prophets: I have not come to destroy but to fulfill. For verily I say unto you, till heaven and earth pass, not one jot or one tittle shall in no wise pass from the law, till all be fulfilled." Matthew 5:17. In direct opposition to what Christ is requesting, "Think not that I am come to abolish the law," the mainline Protestant and Evangelical Churches of this generation are teaching the exact opposite. These blind guides claim that God's holy law has been abolished, having been nailed to Calvary's Cross. They claim Christ "fulfilled" the law (Matthew 5:17), inaugurating salvation exclusively by acknowledging that Christ's death paid the penalty sinners rightfully deserve for their transgression of the law. This conclusion is inconsistent with the plan devised for our salvation. The mainline Protestant and Evangelical Churches are saying Christ fulfilled the law. As a result, He subsequently abolished the law of the Old Covenant dispensation by "nailing it to Calvary's Cross." It will be established [that this interpretation] is not supported by the scriptures, because it violates the case agreement of the words employed by the inspired writer.

In direct opposition to this line of thinking, that Christ "fulfilled" the law inaugurating salvation exclusively by claiming justification by faith, the apostle says where there is no law, there is no transgression. Romans 4:15. Since you can't transgress something that doesn't exist why does the apostle specifically declare that God's holy law will be the standard of righteousness used by Christ to evaluate our characters during His final work of mediation, which is the investigative judgment? Revelation 14:6-7, James 2:8-12. Obviously, since you can't transgress something that doesn't exist; consequently, if the law has been made void by our faith, why does the apostle say that the wages of sin is still death in this dispensation? Romans 6:23. How can the mainline Protestant and Evangelical Churches claim God's holy law is no longer binding upon believers after claiming "justification by faith" when the apostle emphatically states that our faith does not make void God's holy law? Romans 3:31. How can the mainline Protestant and Evangelical Churches claim God's holy law is no longer binding upon believers after claiming "justification by faith" when the Bible specifically defines sin as the transgressions of the law in this dispensation? Romans 3:19-20. How can the mainline Protestant and Evangelical Churches claim God's holy law is no longer binding upon believers after they claim "justification by faith since "we are not under the law" during the New Covenant dispensation even though the Bible expressly says everyone is under the law? Romans 3:19-20, Galatians 4:4-5. How can the mainline Protestant and Evangelical Churches claim God's holy law is no longer binding upon believers after claiming "justification by faith when the Bible specifically says that the new covenant promise of salvation is designed to write God's holy law upon the hearts and minds of believers? Hebrews 8:10. Therefore, in direct contrast to what Christ is requesting, "Think not that I have come to abolish the law," the mainline Protestant and Evangelical Churches of this generation are teaching the exact opposite.

The Greek word πληρῶσαι translated as "fulfilled" in Matthew

5:17, has a Strong's call number of (4137) and appears (4) four times in its exact form and an additional (90) ninety times in various forms throughout the New Testament. The (3) three other times the exact form of the Greek word πληρῶσαι appears in the New Testament are found in Matthew 3:15, Romans 15:13, and Colossians 1:25. The mainline Protestant and Evangelical Churches claim Christ came to "fulfill" the law and by fulfilling it, He "abolished" the law, which just happens to be the very thing Christ asked us not to even consider. However, interpreting the Greek word πληρῶσαι, to mean "abolish" [translated as "fulfilled" in Matthew 5:17], the same interpretation should apply to the other (3) three times the same Greek word πληρῶσαι appears in the following Bible verses. Matthew 3:15, Romans 15:13, and Colossians 1:25.

In Matthew 3:15, Christ addresses John's refusal to baptize Him in the Jordan by saying, "Let it be so; for thus it is fitting for us to "fulfill" all righteousness." If we use the same self-serving interpretation for the Greek word πληρῶσαι, to mean "abolished," [meaning do away with the law or to terminate the law] this interpretation should mean that all righteousness would have been "abolished" at Christ's baptism. This is a ridiculous interpretation considering the exact form of the Greek word πληρῶσαι, is employed by meticulous Matthew, who received this designation because of his precise use of grammar. If the same self-serving contradictory interpretation employed by the mainline Protestant and Evangelical Churches regarding Christ's statement appearing in Matthew 5:17 was also employed to interpret Romans 15:13 and Colossians 1:25, the results would become so entirely convoluted that it's not even worth explaining how completely disjointed these Bible verses would become when interpreting "fulfill" to mean "abolished" and or "terminated." These apostate churches take the position that because Christ said, "Think not that I have come to abolish the law but to fulfill the law," this means that by "fulfilling" the law, He was "abolishing" the law. This same self-serving contradictory interpretation of the Greek word πληρῶσαι is precisely what the mainline Protestant and Evangelical Churches are teaching today. They claim Christ "fulfilled" the law (Matthew 5:17), inaugurating salvation in the New Covenant dispensation exclusively by faith alone and, by doing so, abolished the Ten Commandment Law of the Old Covenant dispensation by "nailing it to the cross." Colossians 2:14.

If Colossians 2:13-14 were retranslated from the original language with the **subject** appearing in **bold** letters, the *direct object* appearing in *italics,* and the indirect object underlined, the retranslation of the Bible verses will establish that what was nailed to Calvary's Cross was the record of our debt; and not God's Holy Ten Commandment Law; remember, the only way to understand what the apostle is trying to communicate in Colossians 2:13-14 is by following the case agreement of the words appearing in the retranslated Bible verse[s]. After Colossians 2:13-14 has been retranslated from the original language, with the definitions of the words properly represented, with the moods and tenses attached to the words correctly amplified, and the case agreement of the words respected, understanding what the apostle is trying to communicate becomes so apparent that any other interpretation must be considered a deliberate attempt to deceive. Therefore, this chapter will establish what was nailed to Calvary's Cross was the record of our debt created by our transgressions of God's Holy Ten Commandment Law and not the law itself, which is completely unjustified considering Christ asked us not to even consider that He came to abolish one dot of the law.

The Retranslation of Colossians 2:8-14

To get the most precise understanding of Colossians 2:13-14, we will first look at Colossians 2:8-12 in the original language, so please follow the case agreement of the words appearing in the Bible verses. This will help you understand what is being communicated by the apostle in the following Bible verse[s]. In Colossians 2:8-10, the apostle says, "You must not let, **for whatever reason,** these things exist **making** *you* **captive** utilizing philosophy and empty *deception according to the tradition* of human standards *in harmony with the elementary principles* of the world and not *according to*

Christ because <u>in Him</u> dwells **all the fullness** of the Godhead in human form and <u>by Him</u>, you **having already been made complete,** He exists as **the one at the head** of all beginnings and authority. In Colossians 2:11-12, the apostle goes on to say "<u>by Him</u> you were at some point in time circumcised <u>with the circumcision not made with human hands by the putting off</u> the body of flesh <u>by the circumcision</u> of Christ, you having **been made at that time buried with** <u>him through baptism by whom</u> you were also at the same time raised together by means of the same faith by the power of God that raised *Him* from the dead." The apostle's statements in Colossians 2:11-12 are connected to Colossians 2:13 by the means of a conjunction so please continue to follow the case agreement; "and *you who were presently dead* <u>by your transgressions</u> and <u>the un-circumcision</u> of your flesh He at some time made *you* alive <u>through Himself</u> **having at the same time canceled the debt** that stood against you *because of all your transgressions.*" In Colossians 2:14, the apostle goes on to say; "**having at that time canceled** *the record of one's debt* **which** continually stood **against** <u>us because of its legal demands</u> *this* He has taken away from our midst **nailing** *it* <u>to Calvary's Cross</u>." In Colossians 2:13-14, by following the case agreement of the words employed by the Apostle Paul in these Bible verses, it's obvious what was nailed to Calvary's Cross was the legal demands of death created by your transgressions of God's holy law and not the Ten Commandments that defines sin in both dispensations. In the following retranslation of Colossians 2:14, please pay close attention to the words appearing with bracketed Strong's call numbers because they all appear in *the accusative case*, consequently, they all have the same assigned case agreement. The following is Colossians 2:14 retranslated from the original language, with the **subject** appearing in **bold** letters, the *direct object* appearing in *italics with* bracketed Strong's call numbers, and the <u>indirect object, underlined</u>. In Colossians 2:14, the apostle says; "**having at that time canceled,** *the record of one's debt,* [Strong's number (5498)] **which** continually stood **against** <u>us because of its legal demands</u> *this* [Strong's number (846)] He has taken away from our midst **nailing** *it* [Strong's number (846)] <u>to Calvary's Cross</u>."

In the retranslation of Colossians 2:14, the Greek word χειρόγραφοναὐτὸ, [Strong's number (5498)] is translated as *the record of one's debt*. The Greek word χειρόγραφοναὐτὸ, [Strong's number (5498)] translated (as *the record of one's debt*) is welded by its case agreement to the Greek word translated as "this," in the phrase translated as, "*this* He has taken away," **nailing** it to Calvary's Cross. In the retranslation of Colossians 2:14, the Greek word αὐτὸ [Strong's number (846)] translated as "*it,*" in the phrase "**nailing** it to Calvary's Cross" is also welded by its case agreement to the Greek words χειρόγραφοναὐτὸ, [Strong's number (5488)] translated as *the record of one's debt,* along with the Greek word αὐτὸ [Strong's number (846)] translated as "*it,*" in the retranslated phrase "**nailing** it to Calvary's Cross."

In the retranslation of Colossians 2:14, the Greek word αὐτὸ [Strong's number (846)] translated the first time in Colossians 2:14 as "*this,*" and translated the second time in Colossians 2:14 as "it," are both grammatically linked through their mandatory case agreement to the Greek word χειρόγραφοναὐτὸ, translated as, *the record of one's debt,* [Strong's number (5498)]. Consequently, what the apostle is saying in Colossians 2:14 becomes very easy to understand [if] you simply follow the case agreement of these three Greek words, designated by their Strong's call numbers, [1] χειρόγραφοναὐτὸ, [Strong's number (5498)], [2] αὐτὸ [Strong's number (846)] and [3] αὐτὸ [Strong's number (846)]. In Colossians 2:14, the apostle says; "**having at that time canceled** *the record of one's debt* (5498), **which** continually stood against us because of its legal demands *this* (846) He has taken away from our midst, **nailing** it (846) to Calvary's Cross."

In Colossians 2:13, the phrase "*all your transgressions*" is grammatically linked through case agreement to the phrase "*the record of one's debt*" appearing in Colossians 2:14, [Strong's number (5498)]. Consequently, what the prophet is saying becomes very clear when you follow the case agreement. The apostle is saying "*this*" [Strong's number (846)] (meaning) [*the record of your debt*] [Strong's number (5488)] was set aside nailing "*it*" [the record of our debt] to Calvary's

Cross. The apostle is saying your violations of God's holy law created a legal demand requiring your death, and *"this"* [legal demand] has been set aside **nailing** *"it"* [Strong's number (846)] to Calvary's Cross." It becomes easy to determine what was nailed to the cross when you follow the case agreement of the words. *"The record of your debt"* represents the legal demands created by *"your transgressions"* of God's holy law, *"this,"* the apostle says, has been set aside, nailing *"it"* to Calvary's Cross. Colossians 2:12-14. Consequently, by following the case agreement of the words appearing in Colossians 2:12-14, it becomes easy to determine that God's moral law was not nailed to Calvary's Cross as erroneously claimed by the mainline Protestant and Evangelical Churches. God's holy law defines sin (Romans 3:19-20), and the wages of sin still demand the death of the transgressor in this dispensation. Romans 6:23. The everlasting gospel has been established upon the justifying power of Calvary's Cross because the wages of sin is still death in this dispensation. The Bible says you can't transgress something that doesn't exist, (Romans 4:15), and the very moment you claim justification by faith you are admitting that you are a transgressor of God's holy law. Galatians 2:17-19. Therefore, in Colossians 2:12-14, what the apostle is saying becomes very clear, after claiming justification by faith *"the record of your debt,"* that has been created by *"all of your transgressions,"* of God's holy law, the Apostle Paul says in Colossians 2:14, *"this, record of your debt,"* was at that specific time set aside nailing *"it"* to Calvary's Cross.

The Retranslation of Colossians 2:15-17

In Colossians 2:13, the phrase *"all your transgressions"* is grammatically linked through case agreement to the phrase *"the record of one's debt"* appearing in Colossians 2:14, [Strong's number (5498)]. The everlasting gospel was founded upon the justifying power of Christ's death upon Calvary's Cross. Consequently, when "justification by faith" is claimed it temporally sets aside *"the record of your debt,"* which was created because of *"all your transgressions"* of God's holy law subsequently nailing *it* to Calvary's Cross. Colossians 2:13-14. After making this comment, the apostle says in Colossians 2:15-17 that this action **disarmed** *"the principalities and supernatural powers"* <u>by making known to all</u> His **triumph**, creating a public spectacle **of** *them* <u>by this</u>," meaning [<u>through His sinless life and substitutional sacrifice upon Calvary's Cross</u>]. (Colossians 2:16) Consequently, **for whatever reason,** *you* cannot pass judgment upon them <u>by eating</u> and <u>drinking or by taking part</u> in a festival or a new moon or the Sabbaths (Verse 17); these are **only a shadow** of the future coming of **the physical body** of Christ. Therefore, it's important to pay **close** attention to the Greek word translated as "you" in Colossians 2:16 to get the best possible understanding of what the apostle is trying to communicate.

In Colossians 2:16, the Greek word Μὴ [translated] as "cannot," denies the "idea" there could exist any justifiable reason for condemning anyone for refusing to keep the ceremonial laws. The Greek word σῶμα translated as "**the physical body,**" appears (70) seventy times in the New Testament, and every time the Greek word σῶμα appears, it represents the **physical body** of someone. In Colossians 2:16, the direct object is *"you,"* which is grammatically linked by its case agreement to *"the principalities and supernatural powers"* appearing in Colossians 2:15. The *"principalities and supernatural powers"* in Colossians 2:15 were trying to deceive new believers with their false "ideas," empty talk, and *human traditions* <u>by</u> demanding new believers keep the ceremonial laws. The Greek words translated as "festivals" and "new moons," and the "Sabbaths" all appear in the genitive case. The fact that these Greek words all appear in the genitive case means they are collectively welded by their mandatory case agreement to <u>the indirect object</u> identified in Colossians 2:16-17, which is the <u>eating and drinking and by taking part in</u> the "festivals" and the "new moons" and the "Sabbaths." Consequently, because the "festivals," the "new moons," and the "Sabbaths" are grammatically linked to <u>the indirect object in the same Bible verse</u>, the apostle is explicitly stating that they are all collectively "**only a shadow**" pointing to "**the physical**" coming of Christ's first advent. Colossians 2:17.

In Colossians 2:16, the phrase translated as "**for whatever reason" is grammatically linked by case agreement to the phrase "they are **only a shadow** of the future coming of **the physical body** of Christ." Colossians 2:16-17. The term "**for whatever reasons**" addresses the condemnation of *those* trying to pass judgment upon believers for not keeping the ceremonial laws. Consequently, because the Greek words translated as "festivals," the "new moons" and the "Sabbaths" are grammatically linked by case agreement to the Greek words translated as "<u>eating and drinking, and by taking part in</u>" the ceremonial laws, they are all collectively **only a shadow** of the future coming of **the physical body** of Christ.

The <u>ceremonial laws</u> foreshadowed Christ's first advent and His subsequent daily and final work of mediation in the antitypical heavenly sanctuary. Hebrews 8:1-5. This is the point the Apostle Paul is making in Hebrews 10:1 "for the law was but a shadow" of Christ, the true reality of the entire sacrificial system of the Old Covenant dispensation. The <u>ceremonial laws</u> pointed to Christ's substitutional sacrifice upon Calvary's Cross giving Him the right to mediate for the real forgiveness of our sins. In the conflict with Satan, Christ had triumphed over satanic forces through His sinless life qualifying Him as a perfect sacrifice to pay the penalty for the sins of this fallen world. It was <u>by His death</u> that "*the record of your debt" could be nailed* to Calvary's Cross. This action [Calvary's Cross] thereby "disarmed *the principalities and supernatural powers* <u>by making</u> a public spectacle of them through Christ's sinless life and His sacrifice upon Calvary's Cross. Therefore, **for whatever reason** "*you,*" which is grammatically linked by its mandatory case agreement to *the principalities and supernatural powers,* cannot pass judgment upon believers for not <u>eating</u> and <u>drinking</u> neither <u>by taking part</u> in festivals nor a new moon or the sabbaths because these were only **a shadow** of Christ's death, His subsequent mediation to forgive sins and His final work of mediation that's performed in preparation for the atonement, which is the blotting out of sins truly forgiven from the books at the conclusion of the investigative judgment.

The mainline Protestant and Evangelical Churches are as ignorant of the plan devised for our salvation as were the unbelieving

Jews who rejected and killed Christ for the blasphemy, that they themselves were committing. The bigoted Jews came to believe that the actual act of performing "the sacrifices and offerings," the keeping the new moon services, along with their strict observance of the six ceremonial Sabbaths, these outward observances earned them "the assurance of their salvation now and in the judgment." At the time of Christ's first advent, the Jews were not looking to be saved from their sins; they already considered themselves saved and forgiven simply by participating in the sacrificial services. Isaiah 1:11-21, Isaiah 28:14-18, Isaiah 29:9-21, Isaiah 30:1, and Isaiah 30:8-11. The statement made by the apostle in Colossians 2:16-17, "**for whatever reasons** *you* (the Greek word translated as "*you*") in Colossians 2:16-17 is welded by its mandatory case agreement to the Greek word translated as [*the principalities and supernatural powers*]; consequently, "*they*" cannot pass judgment upon those who have accepted Christ as their personal Savior and are not performing these outward observances, the food and drink offerings or keeping the new moon festivals or the six ceremonial Sabbaths. Their refusal to keep the ceremonial laws served as an indictment against the spiritual credibility of the unbelieving Jews at the time the Book of Colossians was written, which was after Christ's death upon Calvary's Cross.

These formal requirements, the ceremonial laws, were only **a shadow** of Christ's sacrifice, along with His subsequent mediation to forgive sins, and His final work of atonement, which is the blotting out of sins truly forgiven from the Books of Records at the conclusion of the investigative judgment. The misapplication of the apostle's reference to the six ceremonial Sabbaths as being a shadow of Christ's first advent and His subsequent daily and final work of mediation in the heavenly sanctuary is as great an impeachment of the spiritual credibility of the mainline Protestant and Evangelical Churches as was the rejection of Christ by the Jewish Sanhedrin, along with God's professed people during His first advent. The Jews refused to accept Christ as the Lamb of God who was to save His people "from" their sins. In Colossians 2:16-17, the point the Apostle Paul is making about *you* passing judgment upon believers for their rejection of the entire sacrificial system of the Old Covenant dispensation was these services only served as a shadow of Christ's sacrifice upon Calvary's Cross and His subsequent daily and final work of mediation in the antitypical heavenly sanctuary. Hebrews 10:1. The mainline Protestant and Evangelical Churches of this generation are as ignorant of the plan of salvation as were the unbelieving Jews during His first advent, who rejected and killed Christ for the blasphemy that they themselves were committing. The mainline Protestant and Evangelical Church theologians are as ignorant of the plan of salvation as were the religious leaders in the past dispensation. The plan of salvation is designed to give those born into this world through no fault of their own possessing a fallen nature, which has caused them to transgress God's holy law, the legal right to claim Christ's sacrifice upon Calvary's Cross-paid the penalty they rightfully deserve for their transgressions of God's Holy Ten Commandment Law; and as justified believers, they can come boldly to the throne of grace demanding from their all-powerful Mediator the real forgiveness of their sins in preparation for His final work of mediation, which is the investigative judgment.

There were six ceremonial Sabbaths, the first three were observed during the spring calendar year, the Passover, Unleavened Bread, and the Feast of Weeks, better known today as Pentecost. The last three were observed during the fall calendar, the Feast of Trumpets, the Day of Atonement, and the Feast of Tabernacles. The three ceremonial Sabbaths observed during the spring calendar year were symbolic of Christ's first advent, His unblemished sacrifice for sin, and the ripening of the harvest for the Lord's first advent. The Passover was the first ceremonial Sabbath of the spring calendar, which began at twilight on the fourteenth day of Nisan the first month in the Jewish calendar year. The Passover, the first ceremonial sabbath of the spring calendar year began on the 14th of Nisan and lasted for seven days. The slaying of the Passover lamb symbolized [foreshadowed] Christ's blood spilled upon Calvary's Cross for our transgressions of God's holy law. The Apostle says this action **disarmed** *the principalities and supernatural powers*, making a public example of them <u>by His sinless life and subsequent death upon</u> Calvary's Cross. Therefore, the Apostle Paul says, "Christ our Passover was sacrificed for us" (1 Corinthians 5:7), representing the first fruits of our salvation.

The second ceremonial Sabbath of the spring calendar year was the Feast of Unleavened Bread. The Feast of Unleavened Bread consisted of three individual ceremonial Sabbaths regardless of the day of the week they fell. The first ceremonial Sabbath, which took place during the Feast of Unleavened Bread, was the "first fruits" observed on the 15th day of the month of Nisan, where the sheaf offering was waved before the Lord at the time of the Passover celebration. The second ceremonial Sabbath, which took place during the Feast of Unleavened Bread, was Omar observed on the 16th of Nisan, representing the "first fruits" of the barley harvest, which was a shadow of the resurrection of Jesus Christ as the first fruit of those who have fallen asleep. 1 Corinthians 15:20. The Apostle Paul says, in speaking of the resurrection of the Lord and all His people, "Christ the first fruits; afterward, they that are Christ's at His second coming." 1 Corinthians 15:23. The last ceremonial Sabbath, which took place during the Feast of Unleavened Bread occurred on the 21st of Nisan. The "Feast of Weeks," better known today as "Pentecost" was the third and final ceremonial Sabbath of the spring calendar year. The Feast of Pentecost was observed 50 days after Omer, the second of the three ceremonial Sabbaths observed during the Feast of Unleavened Bread, symbolizing the first fruits of the resurrection of life. The spring calendar symbolically represented Christ's first advent, His sacrifice upon Calvary's Cross, and the outpouring of the Holy Spirit during the early rain, representing the beginning of the New Covenant proclamation that Christ has physically come for the salvation of all who would be saved "from" "that which causes sin' in their lives. Matthew 1:21.

The three ceremonial Sabbaths observed during the fall calendar were symbolic of the impending judgment and Christ's final work of mediation for the deliverance of God's people. The entire sacrificial system was a shadow of Christ's **triumph over** *the principalities and* *supernatural powers, **making a public spectacle over them*** by His sinless life, His willingness to die upon Calvary's Cross to save fallen humanity from "that which causes sin" in their lives, and through the two phases of His High Priesthood in the antitypical heavenly sanctuary to determine who is worthy to receive eternal life. Romans 8:1-4, Hebrews 8:1-5, Hebrews 12:24, Hebrews 13:11-12.

The fourth in the line of ceremonial Sabbaths was the Feast of Trumpets, the first of the fall calendar year. The "Feast of Trumpets" commenced on the 1st of Tishri, announcing the impending judgment, symbolic of the threefold warning message in Revelation the 14th chapter. Revelation 14:6-11. The Feast of Trumpets, the first of the fall calendar year, was symbolic of the message for this time; consequently, it was followed by the Day of Atonement, the fifth in the line of the ceremonial Sabbaths. The fifth in the line of ceremonial Sabbaths was "the Day of Atonement," specifically designed for "the cleansing of sins transferred to the typical earthly sanctuary during the year," which was the last service performed by the high priest in his yearly ministration. Leviticus 16:1-34. This service was symbolic of Christ's closing work of mediation, to make atonement for His people by "the cleansing of sins truly forgiven from the heavenly sanctuary" after the conclusion of the investigative judgment. Daniel 8:14, Revelation 14:6-7.

In the sacrifices offered by the Israelites during the year, Christ was represented not only as the Lamb of God who takes away sins but also as our great High Priest who mediates for the real forgiveness of our sins and makes atonement for truly forgiven transgressions at the conclusion of the sacrificial system. Leviticus 16:30-34. The sacrifices performed during the year pointed to Christ's better and more perfect sacrifice upon Calvary's Cross. Consequently, Christ was not only symbolically foreshadowed as the Lamb of God who was to provide a perfect sacrifice for sin but also as our great High Priest who will atone for the sins truly forgiven after the completion of His final work of mediation, which is the investigative judgment. The typical earthly sanctuary service, the sacrifices and offerings performed during the year, the new moon festivals, along with the six ceremonial Sabbaths were all symbolic of Christ's death, subsequent resurrection, and His daily work of mediation" to forgive our sins. In addition, the typical earthly sanctuary was symbolic of Christ's final work of atonement, which is the blotting out of sins truly forgiven from the Book of Records at the conclusion of the investigative judgment; this service was specifically performed in preparation for the final deliverance of God's people.

The sixth in the line of ceremonial Sabbaths was the Feast of Tabernacles. There were three annual feasts that required all of Israel to appear before the Lord at Jerusalem, the Passover, the Day of Pentecost, and the Feast of Tabernacles. The Feast of Tabernacles was the conclusion of the sacrificial service for the yearly cycle. This ceremonial sabbath was specifically designed to close the yearly calendar so the people could reflect upon God's goodness and merciful generosity in providing them with all the necessities of life and protection from their enemies during the calendar year. However, this feast was not only for thanksgiving and to serve as a memorial of God's protecting care over Israel while they wandered in the wilderness after their deliverance from Egypt, representing the land of their bondage. It was during the Feast of Tabernacles that the Israelites would dwell in booths or tabernacles of green huts in commemoration of their temporary stay here on earth while they spiritually prepared for their heavenly home after the Day of Atonement was completed. John 14:1-3. Therefore, just a little before the Feast of Tabernacles was the Day of Atonement, when, after confessing their sins, the people were declared to be at peace with Heaven in preparation for their permanent heavenly residences.

The entire sacrificial system along with the six ceremonial Sabbaths were symbolic. The typical earthly sanctuary along with its services served as a parable of Christ's sacrifice for sin, His daily and final work of mediation in the antitypical heavenly sanctuary. These services pointed to Christ's complete **triumph over** *the principalities* and *supernatural powers. However, satanic forces have* continually tried to persuade the sin-loving multitudes to adopt false doctrines that remove Christ as their only mediator and judge. Daniel 8:11-12. In

Jesus Christ stands the very essence and foundation of the ceremonial law. The apostle says Christ occupies the center of the entire sacrificial system. The plan devised for our salvation is symbolically outlined through the typical earthly sanctuary and its services. The parable of the typical earthly sanctuary and its services emphasizes the importance of accessing Christ's daily mediation to obtain the real forgiveness of sins in preparation for His final work of atonement, which is the blotting out of sins truly forgiven from the Book of Records at the conclusion of the investigative judgment. Hebrews 8:1-5, Hebrews 9:6-12.

In Colossians 5:17, for reasons already established, the Greek words translated as "eating and by drinking neither by a festival or a new moon or the Sabbaths" are all grammatically linked by case agreement. This fact establishes these services are **only a shadow** of the **physical coming** of Christ, His sacrifice upon Calvary's Cross, His daily mediation to forgive sins along with His final work of atonement in the heavenly sanctuary, which is the blotting out of sins truly forgiven from the Books of Records at the conclusion of the investigative judgment. Hebrews 8:5, Hebrews 10:1, Daniel 8:14, Revelation 14:6-7. Therefore, this is why these ceremonial laws were referred to as a shadow, and were all done away with after Calvary's Cross, God's Holy Ten Commandment Law including His Seventh Day Sabbath has nothing to do with the ceremonial laws; the Seventh Day Sabbath is the 4th commandment in God's Holy Ten Commandment Law, which the apostle says will be the standard of righteousness used by Christ to evaluate our characters during His final work of mediation, which is the investigative judgment.

The three ceremonial Sabbaths observed during the fall calendar were symbolic of the threefold warning message given to the guilty inhabitants of the earth by God's seventh religious movement just before Christ's Second Advent. Daniel 12:12. The first angel's message of Revelation the fourteenth chapter, points directly to Christ's final work of mediation, which is the investigative judgment. Daniel 7:9-10.

The Bible expressly states that God's holy law will be the standard of righteousness used by Christ to evaluate our characters during His final work of mediation, which is the investigative judgment. Consequently, for the Protestant and Evangelical Churches to use Colossians 2:14 to claim God's holy law is no longer binding upon believers today, they must completely disregard the case agreement of the words appearing in these Bible verses. Colossians 2:12-17. Likewise, to establish the Seventh Day Sabbath is no longer binding upon believers today, they must prove that God's Holy Ten Commandment law is part of the ceremonial law, which is not supported by the scriptures. Exodus 20:1-18. The Bible teaches that the Ten Commandments are separate and distinct from the ceremonial laws. Deuteronomy 31:24-26, Deuteronomy 10:1-5. The ceremonial laws stood as a witness against sinners and were placed on the side of the Ark of the Covenant which contained God's Holy Ten Commandment Law. The Ark of the Covenant containing God's Holy Ten Commandments demands the observance of the Seventh Day Sabbath as a memorial of God's creative work while acknowledging Him as the lawgiver. There is no biblical evidence in Colossians 2:12-17 establishing that God's Ten Commandment Law, along with the Seventh Day Sabbath, was nailed to Calvary's Cross. The apostle is clear on this point; after claiming justification by faith, it's the record of your debt created by your transgressions of God's holy law that's been nailed to Calvary's Cross. Therefore, the Ten Commandments, including the fourth commandment, the Seventh-day Sabbath are not part of the ceremonial law; consequently, its observance is still binding upon believers today.

12

THE PROTESTANT AND EVANGELICAL CHURCHES CLAIM – GOD'S HOLY LAW HAS BEEN ABOLISHED

The mainline Protestant and Evangelical Churches claim Christ's death abolished God's Holy Ten Commandment Law. They use poorly translated Bible verses like Ephesians 2:11-15 to support their false and malignant doctrines. In the New International Version (NIV), Ephesians 2:11-15 reads like this; Verse 11, "Therefore, remember that formerly you who are Gentiles by birth and called uncircumcised by those who call themselves the circumcised (that done in the body by the hands of men) Verse 12, remember that at that time you were separate from Christ, excluded from citizenship in Israel and foreigners to the covenants of the promise, without hope and without God in the world. Verse 13, but now in Christ Jesus, you who were once far away have been brought near through the blood of Christ. Verse 14, for he himself is our peace, who has made the two one and has destroyed the barrier, the dividing wall of hostility, Verse 15, by abolishing in his flesh the law with its commandments and regulations. His purpose was to create in himself one new man out of the two, thus making peace." The mainline Protestant and Evangelical Churches use poorly translated Bible verses like **Ephesians 2:11-15 to support their false and malignant** doctrines, claiming Christ, by His death upon Calvary's Cross, "abolished the law with its commandments and regulations."

In all honesty, it's very hard to imagine how someone could claim "justification by faith," while believing at the same time, that the law defining their [transgressions] has been abolished by the very act of claiming Christ's death paid the penalty they rightfully deserve for their [transgressions] of a law that doesn't even exist; particularly when the apostle says our faith establishes the existence of God's holy law, which defines sin in our lives. Romans 3:19-20, Romans 3:31, Romans 7:7, Galatians 2:17-18. Therefore, it will be clearly established in this chapter that the apostle in Ephesians 2:11-15 is not stating Christ's death abolished God's holy law as advanced by the mainline Protestant and Evangelical Churches of this dispensation.

If Ephesians 2:11-18 were retranslated from the original language with the **subject** appearing in **bold** letters, the *direct object* appearing in *italics,* and the <u>indirect object underlined</u>, the retranslation of the Bible verses would read like this; remember, the only way to understand what the apostle is trying to communicate is by following the case agreement of the words appearing in the retranslated Bible verse[s]. After Ephesians 2:11-18 has been retranslated from the original language, with the definitions of the words properly represented and the moods & tenses attached to the words correctly amplified, and case agreement respected, it will become obvious what was abolished by Calvary's Cross was not God's holy law but "the legal demands of the law," requiring the death of the transgressor after justification by faith is claimed. Romans 5:1-2, Romans 8:1-4.

In the retranslation of Ephesians 2:11-18, please remember <u>the indirect object receives the benefits or the consequences of the action described</u> in the Bible verse. Verse 11, Therefore, you must remember that **you were formerly unbelievers** <u>by the flesh</u> **being called uncircumcised** by those declaring themselves circumcised, made with human hands, <u>by the flesh</u>. Verse 12, You were continually <u>then at that time</u> without Christ **having been made alienated** from the citizenship of Israel and **strangers** of the covenant of promise **having** no *hope* and **without God** <u>in the world</u>. Verse 13, But now <u>because of Christ</u> **those being** formerly far off they can at some point in time be made near <u>by the blood</u> of Christ. Verses 14-15, for **He** is our **peace** and **has made** *us* **at the same time** *all one* **having at that time abolished** <u>by</u> His <u>body</u> *the dividing wall* of separation **having rendered ineffective** *the hostility created by the law* of those commandments <u>through their legal decrees</u> so that *these two* He might create <u>by Himself</u> *one new reborn human being for the purpose* **of making** *peace*. Verse 16, And accordingly He created at the same time the possibility for *all those* being reconciled <u>to God by one body</u> through Calvary's Cross **having at the appropriate time abolished** <u>by Himself</u> *the hostility*. Verse 17 and having at the time of His arrival, He preached peace <u>to you, those</u> far off, and *peace* <u>to those who are</u> near Verse 18, because through Him we have **all been given** *this access* <u>by one Spirit</u> to the Father.

The mainline Protestant and Evangelical Churches claim **God's holy law has been abolished by Christ's death upon Calvary's Cross. These blind guides use Ephesians 2:11-15 to support this false doctrine, which is partially due to its poor translation.** In Ephesians 2:15, the Greek word δόγμασιν is incorrectly translated by the (NIV) New International Version as commandments and "regulations." However, the same Greek word δόγμασιν is incorrectly translated by the Revised Standard Version (RSV) as the law of commandments and "ordinances." The King James Version (KJV) erroneously translated the same Greek word δόγμασιν, as commandments contained in "ordinances." The New English Bible (NEB), mistakenly translates the same Greek word δόγμασιν, as he annulled the law with its rules and "regulations." The Phillips Paraphrase Bible (PPB) is the worst, inaccurately translates the same Greek word δόγμασιν in this way, by His sacrifice He removed the hostility of the law with all its commandments and "rules." However, the Catholic Study Bible (CSB) is marginally better, translating the same Greek word δόγμασιν in this way; through His flesh abolishing the law with its commandments and "legal claims."

In the New Testament, the Greek word δόγμασιν appears two times in its exact form; Ephesians 2:15 and Colossians 2:14. The

Strong's call number for the Greek word δόγμασιν is 1378, which represents a legal decree. The three other times the same Greek word δόγμασιν appears in the New Testament is Luke 2:1, Acts 16:4, and Acts 17:7. In Luke 2:1, it's translated as a "decree" issued by Caesar." In Acts 16:4, its translated as the "decrees" of the apostles, and in Acts 17:7 it's translated as Christ's followers violating the "decrees of Caesar." There is no defense for translating the Greek word δόγμασιν any other way than "legal decree." The Bible teaches "that the wages of sin demands the death of the transgressor," which is <u>*a legal decree*</u>. Romans 6:23. Notwithstanding the reasons why all have transgressed God's holy law, (Romans 5:12-14) the apostle says (Galatians 4:4), when the time had fully come, (Mark 1:14-15) God sent forth His Son, born of a woman, born under the law, to redeem those under the law; and this was accomplished by clearly establishing that man as God created him could keep the law; consequently, Christ's dying for our transgressions, gives Him the legal right to mediate for the forgiveness of our sins so that in the judgment He could condemn sin <u>by the flesh</u> representing the moving agent causing all of fallen humanity to transgress God's holy law. Romans 8:1-4. Therefore, the death of the spotless Son of God confirmed, for all time, the justice of the <u>*legal decree*</u> of the law, irrevocably declaring to the unfallen universe that "the wages of sin" rightly demands the death of the transgressor, regardless of the circumstances associated with transgressions.

In Ephesians 2:15, the Greek word νόμον, translated as the "law" is welded by its case agreement to the Greek word ἔχθραν, translated as "hostility" in Ephesians 2:14. Consequently, the "hostility" referred to in the Bible verse was created by <u>*the legal decrees*</u> of the law. As a result, the law must exist, because <u>*the legal decree*</u> creates the "hostility" referenced in the Bible verse. Galatians 2:17-18, Romans 4:15. This is why claiming Christ's substitutional sacrifice paid the penalty sinners rightfully deserve for their transgressions establishes the existence of God's holy law. Romans 3:31. In Ephesians 2:15, the apostle is simply stating <u>*the legal decree*</u> of the law created the "hostility" that's been abolished after believers claim Christ's death upon Calvary's Cross paid the penalty they rightfully deserve for their transgressions of God's holy law. This is called justification by faith. Romans 5:1-2. As a result, those claiming justification by faith are commanded to access Christ's [daily mediation] and form sanctified characters in harmony with the law, thereby creating peace between the parties in preparation for the judgment. Romans 6:20-22.

Ask yourself this one very simple question, why would the apostle say, "Do we then make void the law by our faith, God forbid yea we establish the law" (Romans 3:31) if God's holy law has been abolished by our faith how could the Apostle Paul make this statement? Ephesians 2:17-18. In direct opposition to what the mainline Protestant and Evangelical Churches of this generation are erroneously claiming the apostle emphatically says our faith does not abolish the law, which is also confirmed by Christ's own testimony, "Think not that I have come to abolish the law." Matthew 5:17. However, the mainline Protestant and Evangelical Churches of this generation are erroneously claiming otherwise, which clearly establishes their complete ignorance of the everlasting gospel.

In Ephesians 2:11, the apostle commands the Gentiles to remember that they were formerly unbelievers and called uncircumcised by the legalistic Jews who were controlled by the flesh while claiming to be God's particular people, having been previously circumcised, but only by human hands. Romans 2:25-29. In Ephesians 2:12, the apostle says the Gentiles were controlled by the flesh, strangers to God, and without hope in the world due to their transgressions creating hostility resulting from the legal decrees of the law. In Colossians 2:13, the apostle goes on the say because of Christ's death peace could be created between the parties where there was previously only hostility. The hostility was caused by transgressions requiring the death of the sinner due to the legal decree of the law. Romans 6:23. As a result of Calvary's Cross, those who were formerly hostile to God, meaning they were controlled by the flesh, may claim "justification by faith" obtain free access to Christ's daily mediation and form "sanctified" characters in harmony with God's holy law in preparation for the investigative judgment. This justification is made possible because Christ's death paid the penalty sinners rightfully deserve for their transgressions of the law, allowing justified believers to make peace with their Creator by accessing Christ's "daily mediation" to receive the real forgiveness of their sins. Therefore, the sacrifice provided for our transgressions is designed to abolish the hostility created by our transgressions of the law, which is a legal decree, thereby opening a lifeline of support for fallen humanity due to Christ's death upon Calvary's Cross providing free access to His daily mediation to forgive sins in hope of receiving a positive verdict in the judgment.

The everlasting gospel proffered fallen humanity reconciliation with the government of heaven in both dispensations due to Christ's sacrifice and His subsequent mediation to forgive all our transgressions. In the past dispensation, the promise of Christ's death would abolish the dividing wall of hostility that caused the separation between the parties. However, the legal decree of the law still demands the death of the transgressor in this dispensation. Romans 6:23. The everlasting gospel declares Christ paid the penalty sinners rightfully deserve for their transgressions of the law in both dispensations; however, this declaration does not [make void] the legal decree of the law. Romans 3:19-21, Romans 3:31. When believers claim "justification by faith" this represents an admission of guilt, Galatians 2:17-18, which gives Christ the legal right to forgive the sins of all those willing to access His "daily mediation" with the intent of forming sanctified characters in preparation for His final work of mediation, which is the investigative judgment.

The everlasting gospel was introduced because the legal decree of the law demands the death of the transgressor regardless of the circumstances associated with fallen humanity's transgressions. The apostle goes on to state, that the justifying power of Calvary's Cross was provided, so that, at some point in time, justification by faith could be claimed making it possible to reconcile everyone to God by abolishing the hostility that's created by the transgressions of God's holy law. The hostility, created by the transgressions of God's holy law still demands the death of the transgressor in this dispensation, which is a legal decree, however, the everlasting gospel provides a payment for transgressions and the possibility of forming sanctified characters by accessing Christ's daily mediation to receive the real forgiveness of sins resulting in a positive verdict in the judgment. Therefore, the everlasting gospel was designed to satisfy the legal decrees of the law, which demands the death of the transgressor, not to make void the law that defines sin and requires the death of the transgressor, which is a legal decree grammatically linked to the hostility between the parties. Romans 3:31, Ephesians 2:15.

In the controversy with Satan, to proffer the everlasting gospel to fallen humanity Christ condescended to assume humanity not just to provide a perfect sacrifice for sin but to establish for all time that man as God created him could keep the law. In harmony with this line of thinking it's important to understand that Christ came to condemn sin <u>by the flesh</u> as the moving agent in fallen humanity. Romans 8:1-4. The everlasting gospel still demands that the legal decree of the law be enforced sometime after human probation closes, when Satan, his evil angels along with fallen humanity, who have joined Satan in his rebellion against the authority of heaven, are destroyed in the lake of fire, which is the second death. Consequently, it's obvious the government of Heaven feels it's essential that the second death is condoned by the fallen and unfallen worlds regardless of the circumstances surrounding humanity's transgressions. Ephesians 2:16, Romans 5:12-14, Romans 8:1-4. It was during His first advent, that Christ preached peace to both the Jews and Gentiles by declaring that through His sacrifice, justified believers can have free access to His "daily mediation" so that by the Holy Spirit the born-again believer can receive the real forgiveness of their sins and a positive verdict in the judgment. Therefore, the keys to the kingdom of heaven represent the believers' understanding that the daily mediation of Christ to forgive sins is as essential to the plan devised for our salvation as was His death upon Calvary's Cross, because, by His death, He gained the right to mediate for the real forgiveness of our sins and determine in the judgment who is worthy to receive eternal life.

Closing Thoughts

The conditions of eternal life are the same today as they were in the Garden of Eden before the fall of our first parents, strict obedience to God's holy law. If eternal life was established upon any other principle, then the stability of the universe would be in question. If sinners, meaning professed believers, were allowed to enter heaven as unsanctified transgressors of the law, the death and destruction witnessed here on earth would be seen in heaven. "As the sacrifice on our behalf was complete, so our restoration from the defilement of sin is to be complete." The Faith I Live By, Page 89, by E.G. White. In the judgment, the claims made upon Christ's righteousness will not cover one cherished sin. Hebrews 10:26-27.

The True Witness says, "To him that overcomes will I grant to sit with me in my throne even as I also overcame and am set down with my Father in His throne." Revelation 3:21. How did Christ overcome sin and Satan's temptations? He was born, "born again," He was conceived by the Holy Spirit, "full of grace and truth." Consequently, at His birth, He was born with absolutely no propensity to transgress God's holy law. Romans 1:4, Romans 5:12-14, Hebrews 1:3, Hebrews 7:15, Luke 1:35. The scriptures clearly teach Christ was born into this world possessing an unfallen human nature, (Hebrews 1:3) entering this world with the same unfallen nature Adam possessed before his first transgression. Romans 5:12-14. Therefore, "Christ came to the earth, taking humanity, and standing as man's representative, _**to show**_ in the controversy with Satan that man, _**as God created him**_, connected with the Father and the Son, could obey every divine requirement." The Signs of the Times, June 9, 1898, by E.G. White.

In the controversy created by Satan's rebellion, Christ "vanquished Satan in the same nature over which in Eden Satan obtained the victory. The enemy was overcome by Christ in His human nature. The power of the Savior's Godhead was hidden. He overcame in human nature, relying upon God for power. The Youth's Instructor, April 25, 1901. E.G. White. The scriptures are clear, only those who overcome "that which causes sin" in their lives will receive eternal life. However, this principle is not being proclaimed from the pulpits of Christendom today. The majority of pastors are simply blind guides. As a result, their "abominations," (false doctrines) are making a "host" of believers spiritually "desolate," while after claiming justification by faith the misguided multitudes feel saved, forgiven, and "assured of their salvation now and in the judgment."

The sin-loving multitudes of this generation are taught that a mere profession of faith in Christ's atoning blood qualifies them as overcomers. Matthew 7:21. The Apostle Paul says, in Philippians 3:9-15, that the perfection of character is a prerequisite for receiving eternal life. In Romans 6:20-22, he confirms this point, by stating that sanctification and its end is eternal life. In Galatians 5:16, the apostle commands believers to walk by the Spirit and says if they do, he denies the idea of the possibility of the fact existing that a born-again believer would even consider transgressing any of God's holy requirements. 1 John 3:9, and 1 John 5:18. The conditions of eternal life have not changed simply because Adam elected to transgress God's holy law and the "Most High" felt compelled to offer his descendants an opportunity to form sanctified characters in harmony with His holy law so they could avoid suffering the second death in the lake of fire originally prepared for the devil and his evil angels.

When the rich young ruler asked Christ, "What must I do to be saved" (Luke 18:18) Christ's response was; "If thou would enter life, keep the commandments." In Matthew 19:17-19, Christ said, "I have not come to abolish the law but to fulfill the law and the prophecies. For it would be easier for heaven and earth to pass away than for one dot in the law to be _**changed**_. If preachers were asked the same question today, their answer would be, "believe, believe, only believe Christ's death paid the penalty you rightfully deserve for your transgressions," and obedience to God's holy law, as originally proclaimed amid the thunders of Mt. Sinai, is not required. The popular Churches of this generation claim God's holy law has been either _**changed**_, (Catholicism) _**made void by our faith**_ (mainline Protestantism), _**and/or is a yoke of bondage**_," Evangelicalism. Conversely, the command given by Christ to believers is made very clear; "if you love me keep my commandments." John 14:15.

In this dispensation we are admonished not to be deceived by the false doctrines abounding in Christendom today, stating God's holy law has been changed, *abrogated*, and/or is a yoke of bondage. Matthew 5:17-19, Matthew 15:3-9. The counsel found in the scripture states, "In vain do they worship me teaching as doctrine the commandments and precepts of men." Matthew 15:9. The Bible says, it is not the hearers of the law who are *__righteous__* before God, but the doers of the law will be justified. The apostle specifically says, that after claiming "justification by faith" we must form sanctified characters in harmony with the law or we will be destroyed with the Devil and his evil angels in the lake of fire, which is the second death. Romans 2:2-16. If Christ were here today, He would answer the question asked by the rich young ruler in the same way, "If you would see life keep the commandments." Matthew 19:16-22, John 14:15. When answering the question, "What must I do to be saved," (Luke 18:18) Christ has been extremely consistent, if we are to receive eternal life, we must be "born again" (John 3:7) and the Bible says that a "born again" believer would rather die than knowingly transgress even one of God's holy requirements. 1 John 3:9, John 14:15.

In this dispensation, after claiming "justification by faith," believers can rejoice in the hope of receiving the new covenant promise of salvation. Hebrews 10:16-18. Those who receive the New Covenant promise of salvation will be seen "keeping the commandments of God" as naturally as Adam did before his first transgression. 1 John 5:3, Revelation 14:12, 1 John 2:3-4. The reason why believers should rejoice in the hope of receiving the New Covenant promise of salvation is the Bible emphatically declares that the wages of sin is still death, which is a legal decree still existing in this dispensation, with sin being just as clearly defined in the Bible as the transgressions of the law. Therefore, if you want to receive eternal life, it can be confidently stated that the scriptures teach you must form sanctified characters in harmony with God's Holy Ten Commandment Law because the same will be the standard of *__righteousness__* used by Christ to evaluate our characters during His final work of mediation, which is the investigative judgment. James 2:8-12, Romans 2:12-16, Revelation 14:6-7.

After the fall of our first parents, God's great mercy was graciously introduced (Romans 3:25-26), while His justice was confirmed when it was established that Christ would pay the penalty sinners rightfully deserve for their transgressions so that He could mediate for the forgiveness of our sins. The everlasting gospel (the good news) was not an afterthought. The plan devised for our salvation was created before the foundation of the universe. Revelation 13:8. Therefore, the plan of salvation is said to be: **"The mystery hidden for ages."** (Ephesians 3:3-6, Colossians 1:21-27, Ephesians 3:9-12) which the apostle calls the good news, translated as the everlasting gospel in our modern Bibles. The result of God offering the good news to fallen humanity established several things about the character of God and the immutability of His holy law. The law demands the death of the transgressor, which is a legal decree. Through Satan's sophistries, the angels in heaven, along with the unfallen worlds, were made to question why one transgression should require the death of the transgressor. The unfallen worlds didn't have full knowledge of the malignant nature of transgression. Satan took advantage of this ignorance, knowing if he was immediately destroyed for his rebellion, the unfallen worlds would serve God out of fear instead of an intellectual understanding of the malignant nature of transgression. Therefore, in order to clear up the controversy regarding Satan's rebellion, Christ said if anyone transgresses the law, they become a slave to sin, and a slave to sin cannot inherit eternal life.

As established in earlier chapters, the born-again believers clearly understand transgression must be avoided at all costs. The reason for this is very simple, the born-again believer understands that the transgressor develops a fallen nature, which has also been defined in earlier chapters as "that which causes sin" in our lives. As a result of Satan's sophistries, one-third of the angelic hosts rebelled against God's authority, eventually requiring their expulsion from heaven, (Revelation 12:7-9) with the promise of their eventual destruction in the lake of fire, which is the second death. Revelation 20:11-15. To permanently prolong his existence, Satan caused the fall of our first parents. After their transgression, Satan subsequently declared that they, along with their enslaved sinful offspring, were declared just as deserving of death as himself and his sympathizers because of their transgressions. As a result of Adam's one transgression, all of Adam's descendants would be born into this world, without their consent, possessing an overpowering propensity to transgress; and Satan knew by personal experience that all of Adam's descendants would inevitably transgress God's laws. Since all would transgress the legal decree of the law would demand they receive the same punishment as Satan and his evil angels rightfully deserve. Therefore, this argument seems conclusive to the unfallen worlds but unfair because all of Adam's descendants have transgressed the law having been born, without their consent, with a fallen defective nature.

To protect the integrity of the law, someone equal to the law must pay the penalty sinners rightfully deserve for their transgressions, while being capable of mediating for the real forgiveness of their sins along with presiding in the judgment. The Bible is clear, that several loyal angels offered their lives to save fallen humanity; however, they were limited in their ability to save fallen humanity from their sins, primarily because they could not mediate for the real forgiveness of sins or preside in the judgment. Only One equal with the law and capable of mediating for the real forgiveness of sins while presiding in the judgment could offer the everlasting gospel to fallen humanity. Offering the everlasting gospel to fallen humanity required the death of God's only Son; and by doing so "the Most High" established the immutability of His holy law, while at the same time, giving Christ, the legal right to mediate for the real forgiveness of our sins and as the "True Witness" preside in the judgment. Therefore, Christ's death upon Calvary's Cross established for all time that the wages of sin must be death, with sin being just as clearly defined in the Bible as the transgressions of God's Holy Ten Commandment Law.

The everlasting gospel established forever God's great mercy while confirming His justice in demanding the death of the transgressor. Through the sacrifice provided for our transgressions, the "Most High" obtained the legal right to offer eternal life to any of Adam's descendants willing to comply with the conditions of eternal life while legitimizing the destruction of those refusing to repent. The penalty sinners rightfully deserve for their transgressions has been stayed, creating the opportunity for all to resist sin and Satan's temptations simply by accessing Christ's "daily mediation" to receive the real forgiveness of sins. The great deceiver tried to subliminally justify open rebellion against the mandates of heaven by undermining the authority of God to enforce the dictates of His holy law, that governs the behavior of all His created beings.

The prince of evil has accomplished the same thing here on earth by subliminally incorporating doctrines that undermine the authority of God to enforce the edicts of His holy law. The same question artfully presented in heaven is being asked by the Christian world today; is God's law an evil or a good? The mainline Protestant and Evangelical Churches claim God's holy law is evil, calling it void because it can't be kept, consequently, any gospel demanding strict obedience to the same it's "a yoke of bondage." Conversely, the Apostle Paul says God's "law is holy, just and good," Romans 7:12 and a transcript of Christ's character. Therefore, since every government has laws demanding the death penalty, consequently, so does the Government of Heaven, and the born-again believer along with the unfallen worlds now agree with God's justice in demanding the death of the transgressor, concluding that it must also be good, legitimate, and righteous, (Romans 6:23) to ensure the stability of the universe.

The everlasting gospel upholds the justice of the law. The fallen sons of Adam are being offered eternal life if they acknowledge the authority of the law by claiming "justification by faith" so they can access Christ's daily mediation and put to death "that which causes sin" in their lives. The good news of the Bible is made very clear; all who desire can be delivered from "that which causes sin" in their lives. In both dispensations, all may receive eternal life if they claim by faith Christ's death paid the penalty they rightfully deserve for their transgressions of the law and subsequently access Christ's "daily mediation" to receive the real forgiveness of their sins in preparation for Christ's final work of mediation, which is the investigative judgment.

In the Bible, the process of receiving the real *"let-go-ness"* of your sins is called sanctification, which is God's predetermined plan to receive eternal life. 2 Thessalonians 2:13. After the fall of our first parents, God's great mercy was revealed by offering a stay of execution from the dictates of the legal decree of His holy law. This stay of execution is good news for sinful humanity translated as the everlasting gospel. The everlasting gospel revealed that God's only Son would provide an acceptable sacrifice for our transgressions and subsequently mediate for the real forgiveness of our sins. John 17:3, Ephesians 4:15-16, 1 John 1:9, 1 John 3:9, 1 John 5:18-20. Therefore, the introduction of the everlasting gospel, spearheaded by the great theme of salvation, *"justification by faith,"* does not make void God's holy law, on the contrary, it establishes forever that justice and mercy stand at the foundation of the law and the government of heaven.

13

THE PARABLE OF THE WEDDING FEAST

The next seven chapters are designed to establish there will be an investigation into the character and lives of all those who have claimed Christ died for their transgressions of God's Holy Ten Commandment Law to determine if they are worthy to receive eternal life. The reader needs to understand the daily mediation of Christ to forgive sins is as essential to the plan of salvation as was His death upon Calvary's Cross because by His death He gained the right to mediate for the forgiveness of sins and as the "True Witness" preside in the judgment. In Matthew the 22nd chapter, Christ uses a parable to introduce the idea that "the everlasting gospel" includes a judgment when the character and lives of all those who have ever claimed "justification by faith" will come up in review before the "Most High" to determine if they have complied with the specific conditions of eternal life. Revelation 14:6-7, Daniel 7:9-10, 2 Corinthians 5:10.

In the parable of the wedding feast, God's professed people are seen ignoring the invitation of salvation. Even though all efforts were exhausted to extend the gospel invitation to His professed people, after a period of time, the King (Christ) commanded the offer be extended to all those willing to attend the wedding feast. The disciples were instructed to gather "All whom they found" willing to attend the wedding, so the "hall may be filled." Matthew 22:10. While the invitation was extended to all, the King still required an inspection of those who had accepted the invitation to determine if they had complied with the conditions of the wedding invitation. Therefore, only those who had accepted and complied with the King's requirements, evidenced by them putting on the wedding garment, "which is the <u>**righteousness**</u> of the saints," were allowed to remain after the investigation was completed. Revelation 19:8-11.

When the King came into the wedding feast and found there a man not attired in a *"wedding garment,"* the King questioned him, **"Why are you here? How did you get in without the wedding garment?"** The man was speechless! The King immediately told His servants to take the man and throw him outside into outer darkness, bound *"hand and foot."* Christ's words should speak volumes about the message for this time. Those living in this dispensation who feel assured of their salvation now and in the judgment, immediately after claiming justification by faith while refusing to clothe themselves with sanctified characters in preparation for the investigative judgment, will perish in the lake of fire, which is the second death. Therefore, the parable of the wedding feast introduces the idea that "the everlasting gospel" concludes with "the investigative judgment" when the character and lives of all those who have ever claimed "justification by faith" will be investigated to determine if they have complied with the conditions of eternal life.

The parable of the wedding feast establishes that a spiritual work of preparation must be performed before those who have accepted the gospel invitation can be awarded eternal life. This <u>*determination*</u> takes place at the conclusion of the investigative judgment. The parable makes the message for this time very clear, those who neglect the spiritual preparation necessary to stand in the presence of God without a mediator after human probation closes will be cast into outer darkness sometime after the conclusion of the investigative judgment. Revelation 14:6-7, Malachi 3:2. The parable teaches the gospel invitation was extended to all, and obviously those who accepted attended the wedding feast. Notwithstanding this fact, the King Himself performed an individual investigation of those who had accepted the invitation to determine if they had made the proper spiritual preparation necessary to qualify as guests at the wedding feast. Therefore, the proper spiritual preparation necessary to qualify as guests at the wedding feast is the sanctification of our characters, which has been established as a prerequisite for receiving eternal life. Revelation 22:11, Romans 6:20-22.

The parable of the wedding feast teaches that an individual investigation will be conducted into the character and lives of all those who have claimed "justification by faith" to determine if they have formed sanctified characters in this life and are therefore worthy to receive eternal life. The scriptures clearly teach that sanctified believers will be seen obeying God's holy law as naturally as Adam did before his first transgression. 1 John 5:3, Hebrews 10:16-18. The everlasting gospel was designed to "bring about the obedience of our faith" in God's holy law (Romans 16:25-26), and for this to take place, we must by the Spirit put to death "that which causes sin" in our lives. Romans 8:12-13. The sanctification of our characters can only occur by accessing Christ's daily mediation to receive the real forgiveness of our sins. Revelation 20:12. Therefore, "the parable of the wedding feast" plainly teaches that the everlasting gospel includes an investigative judgment when the character and lives of all those who have claimed justification by faith will be investigated to determine if they have formed sanctified characters in harmony with God's holy law and are worthy to receive eternal life. John 3:36.

In the parable of the wedding feast, the gospel invitation was first offered to God's professed people; however, when the invitation was ignored, Christ's disciples were commanded to invite everyone to attend the wedding feast. This symbolized the Jew's rejection of the gospel, resulting in their rejection of Christ as the Messiah during His first advent. The parable reveals there was a horrific spiritual blindness existing among God's professed people at the time of Christ's first advent. As a result of this bigoted blindness, the invitation was extended to the Gentile nations. In the parable, all were required to put on the wedding garment to qualify as guests at the wedding feast. The same is true in our generation! The gospel invitation has been freely offered to all; however, few alleged believers feel any inclination to form sanctified characters in harmony with God's holy law in preparation for Christ's final work of mediation, which is the investigative judgment. Therefore, in harmony with the parable, notwithstanding your claims made upon justification, unless you comply with the specific conditions of eternal life, Christ will, at the conclusion of the investigative judgment, command His holy angels to "cast [you out] into outer darkness where there will be weeping and gnashing of teeth."

It was well before Christ's crucifixion He explained to His disciples that He would be put to death as a sin offering and raised again as an all-powerful Mediator capable of delivering justified believers from "that which causes sin" in their lives. However, His disciples were not looking for deliverance from their sins; they were taught from childhood that the Messiah would deliver Israel from the Roman occupation of their country. It was far beyond their comprehension that the Messiah would offer Himself as a substitutional sacrifice for their transgressions so He could mediate for the real forgiveness of their sins. The disciples were completely ignorant of these truths, so when trials came, their faith failed, resulting from their distorted understanding of the gospel invitation. As a result, Christ's death fully destroyed their hopes as if they had never been previously forewarned.

The same ignorance exists in Christendom today. This ignorance has produced a satanic indifference toward the spiritual preparation necessary to stand the brightness of Christ's second coming. In our dispensation, the sin-loving multitudes have the same distorted understanding of the gospel that prevailed in the past dispensation. The sin-loving multitudes are not looking to be saved from their sins. As a result, they have rejected the prophecies pointing to the spiritual preparation necessary to stand in the presence of God without a mediator after the close of human probation. Revelation 7:1-17. Revelation 14:6-7. The threefold warning message of Revelation 14:6-11 commands all to spiritually prepare to stand in the presence of God without a mediator after Christ concludes His final work of mediation. The message for this time points to Christ's final work of mediation, performed in preparation for the atonement, which is the blotting out of sins truly forgiven from the Book of Records at the conclusion of the investigative judgment. Malachi 3:1-5, Revelation 15:5-8. The parable of the wedding feast illustrates all must put to death "that which causes sin" in their lives before the gospel invitation closes or "their names will be blotted out of the Book of Life" and they will be destroyed with the Devil and his evil angels in the lake of fire, which is the second death.

In harmony with the parable of the wedding feast, the threefold warning message of Revelation the 14th chapter states that the hour of the investigative judgment has come. Revelation 14:6-7. As it was in the parable of the wedding feast, the threefold warning message is ignored by the sin-loving multitudes of this generation. Daniel 8:14, Revelation 11:18-19, Hebrews 9:23-24. The judgment message points to the final withdrawal of the gospel invitation (Revelation 7:4, Revelation 10:7) and the spiritual preparation necessary to stand in the presence of the "Most High" without a mediator after human probation closes. Malachi 3:1-5.

The spiritual preparation required to stand in the presence of God without a mediator after the gospel invitation closes goes unheeded by this generation for the same reasons the Jews misinterpreted the prophecies identifying Christ as the Messiah during His first advent. Daniel 9:24-27. As clearly established in the preceding chapters, the spiritual preparation necessary to stand in the presence of God without a mediator when Christ ceases His final work of mediation in the heavenly sanctuary is the sanctification of our characters. Romans 6:20-22. Therefore, the sin-loving multitudes of this generation have no more understanding of these important truths than if they had never been revealed in the scriptures.

Satan distorts every truth that would make us wise unto salvation. The prophecies clearly reveal the closing events of Earth's history will find this generation <u>*unready*</u>; despite this fact, "a peace and safety message" is being presented from the pulpits of Christendom today. Matthew 24:44. Those who would receive the benefits of Christ's final work of mediation should permit nothing to interfere with their duty to perfect holiness in fear of God now while human probation lingers. Hebrews 12:14. The peace and safety message presented from the pulpits of Christendom today has removed Christ as the believers' only mediator and judge; this "***abomination***" creates the illusion of salvation now and in the judgment simply by making a profession of faith in Christ atoning blood, which has left professed believers spiritually "***desolated***" throughout the ages. Daniel 8:11-12, Daniel 9:27, Daniel 11:31-32, Daniel 12:11, and Matthew 24:15.

In the book of Revelation, the Apostle John says, "The dead were judged by what was written in the books according to their works," and ***not by what they profess to believe***. Revelation 20:12. To awaken the sleeping multitudes, the threefold warning message of Revelation the 14th chapter is being given to the guilty inhabitants of the Earth by God's seventh religious movement proclaiming that "the hour of His judgment has come" and that Babylon has fallen. The parable of "the wedding feast" is the message for this time, declaring that professed believers must form sanctified characters in harmony with God's holy law now before human probation closes. The message for this time represents that all must form sanctified characters in harmony with God's holy law before human probation closes or they will perish in the lake of fire, which is the second death. Therefore, Satan distorts every truth that would make us wise unto salvation; the Bible is extremely clear on this subject, the law proclaimed amid the thunders of Mt. Sinai will be the standard of ***righteousness*** used to evaluate our characters during Christ's final work of mediation, which is the "***investigative judgment***." Romans 2:12-16, Revelation 14:6-7.

The majority of Christians today do not study their Bible for themselves; consequently, they become confused by "every wind of doctrine" advanced by their religious leaders. As a result, the confused multitudes call Satan's counterfeit gospel "good" while they call God's true gospel "evil" because it requires them to form sanctified characters in harmony with God's holy law before human probation closes or suffer the second death in the lake of fire with the Devil and his evil angels. If they studied the Bible as someone looking for hidden treasure, the principles of redemption would have a positive influence on their lives. The very foundation of the "everlasting gospel" contains important truths concerning salvation that, if properly understood, would motivate believers to immediately access Christ's "daily mediation" and overcome sin while human probation lingers. Hebrews 10:16-18. However, this concept has been completely disregarded by the religious leaders of this generation. Romans 6:20-22.

The principles relevant to our salvation; *justification* (Romans 5:1-20) *sanctification*, (Acts 26:18), **the real forgiveness of your sins** (Luke 1:77) **the atonement**, (Hebrews 9:23-24, the investigative judgment (Daniel 7:9-10), **the starting date for the cleansing of the new covenant heavenly sanctuary**, (Daniel 8:14, Revelation 11:18-19) *pardon*, (Colossians 2:14) *repentance*, (Mark 4:12) *belief*, (John 16:9) *faith*, (Romans 3:21-22) **the relationship between the old and new covenants**, (Hebrews 8:10, Jeremiah 31:31-34) **and that the gospel is to bring about the obedience of our faith.** Romans 3:24. All these concepts have been completely misconstrued, if not entirely rejected, by the leading churches of this generation, which is the reason why the second angel's message is being proclaimed to the world in the last days of Earth's history. Throughout the ages, our religious leaders have distorted the great truths of salvation into a license to sin to gain popularity with the sin-loving multitudes. These blind guides have completely misrepresented the plan devised for our salvation to gain riches and fame. The reason they have gotten away with this "abomination" is the sin-loving multitudes are repulsed by the idea of forsaking and putting away their sins, which makes them spiritually desolate. As a result, they feel any gospel that requires separation from sin is "evil" and have been conditioned by their church leaders to feel Satan's false cheap grace gospel that tolerates continued transgressions, which leaves them spiritually desolate, is "good." Isaiah 30:8-10.

The unsuspecting multitudes desire smooth things spoken to them concerning their salvation. Consequently, they chase after false teachers promising them eternal life simply by making a profession of faith in Christ's atoning blood. 2 Thessalonians 2:1-10. In Galatians 5:16, the apostle commands us to walk by the Spirit and emphatically states if we do we will not commit the deeds of the flesh. As established in past chapters, in Galatians 5:16, the apostle employs a double negative with a subjunctive kicker to categorically deny the fact, of the possibility existing that a born-again believer would transgress God's holy law. Notwithstanding this powerful admonition, the unsuspecting multitudes remain ignorant that if they walk by the Spirit, they will not commit the deeds of the flesh; consequently, the sin-loving multitudes of this generation remain as ignorant of the everlasting gospel today as were the unbelieving Jews during Christ's first advent. Therefore, because the majority do not walk by the Spirit, "strong delusion comes upon them," and they shall believe a lie and perish in the lake of fire with the Devil and his evil angels because they believe God's plan of salvation is "evil" and that Satan's false cheap grace gospel is "good." Isaiah 5:20.

After Christ's "death" and resurrection, He immediately received approval from His Father to commence with His daily work of mediation to forgive the sins of those willing to access Him in the antitypical heavenly sanctuary to receive the deliverance from "that which causes sin" in their lives. Subsequently, the Holy Spirit was dispatched to the Earth to convict the world of **sin**, which is the transgressions of the law, to convict the world of **righteousness**, which is defined as obedience to God's holy law, and to convict the world that God's holy law will be the standard of **righteousness** used by Christ to evaluate our characters during His final work of mediation, which is the investigative **judgment**, John 16:8. Therefore, the commencement of Christ's final work of mediation, which is the investigative judgment, dictating the soon close of human probation, along with the confusion existing in Christendom regarding the everlasting gospel and the perpetuity of God's Holy Ten Commandment Law is the message for this time.

14

SPIRITUAL INFLATION – THE ILLUSION OF SALVATION, NOW AND IN THE JUDGMENT

When I was a child, between the ages of eight and thirteen, I sold newspapers on the beaches of Wildwood, New Jersey, and during that time, I made between three hundred and seven hundred dollars per week. However, due to the accelerated inflation witnessed in this country resulting from the fractional lending practices of the European Central Banks being established here in the United States, the money I made while on the shores of Wildwood, New Jersey, approximately forty years ago, would equate to about $6,000 per-week today. Shortly after 1913, when Woodrow Wilson sold the financial freedom of the United States citizens to the European Central Banks to buy the presidency, inflation in this country has been out of control. This runaway inflation has been caused by the debt-laden "fiat" currency issued by the privately owned Federal Reserve Bank. The debt-laden "fiat" currency issued by the privately-owned Federal Reserve Bank has robbed everyone living in the United States of the value and economic stability of the debt-free gold-backed U.S. dollars existing in this country before 1913; meaning before Woodrow Wilson sold the financial freedom of the United States citizens to the European Central Banks to buy the presidency.

Today the worth of the U.S. "fiat" dollars issued by the privately-owned Federal Reserve Bank, compared to its value in 1913, stands at about 4½¢ and falling. Nothing is more debilitating to a nation's economy than giving control of its money supply to a few corrupt and ruthless central banksters. Therefore, Mayer Anselm Rothschild said, "Permit me to issue and control the money supply of a nation, and I care not who makes its laws." Once in control of the United States money supply, these corrupt central banksters flooded the U.S. marketplace with money during the latter stages of the Industrial Revolution (1913 to 1927). This created the same type of runaway inflation during the Roaring Twenties we are presently experiencing in this country. However, in 1927 when the privately owned Federal Reserve Bank abruptly cut off the money supply, this country was thrust into the Great Depression, 1929 to 1935. The same deceitful banking practices have caused the economic downturn we are presently experiencing in this country and will continue until these banksters obtain what they want, a one-world, cashless, fiat currency system where no man can buy or sell without government approval. Revelation 13:15-17.

In the year 1927, when the privately-owned Federal Reserve banksters intentionally dried up the money supply, this caused the inflationary wealth created during the Roaring Twenties to be destroyed in a moment when the stock market crashed in 1929, leading to the rapid decline of real estate prices and the Great Depression, which lasted for years. During the stock market crash, many took their own lives when they saw their inflationary wealth vanish in a moment. The spiritual application of this example should be very apparent. In Christendom today, there are untold multitudes who are essentially committing the same type of spiritual suicide because they have developed an overinflated opinion of their spiritual condition due to the deceitful doctrines advocated by their religious leaders.

With all the information covered in the proceeding chapters, it should be easy to recognize [understand] how Satan has been distorting the everlasting gospel into a license to sin throughout the ages. In direct opposition to the plainest statements found in the scriptures (Matthew 7:13-14), the sin-loving multitudes of this generation feel assured of their salvation now and in the judgment immediately after claiming "justification by faith" regardless of their unsanctified spiritual condition. Those arrogantly declaring themselves assured of their salvation now and in the judgment immediately after claiming "justification by faith" have developed an overinflated opinion of their spiritual condition due to their ignorance of the plan devised for their salvation. Therefore, the arrogant assumption of salvation existing in Christendom today is the direct result of a deceptive counterfeit gospel advocated by the leading churches of this generation.

The deceptive counterfeit gospel being advocated from the pulpits of Christendom today causes the deceived multitudes to arrogantly ignore the requirement for justified believers to form sanctified characters in harmony with God's holy law before eternal life can be awarded them in the judgment. The overinflated opinion of one's spiritual condition is caused by the false doctrines that create the illusion of salvation now and in the judgment simply by claiming Christ's death paid the penalty sinners rightfully deserve for their transgressions of the law. The false doctrines advocated by the Christian Churches of this generation reduce obedience to a mere optional requirement to obtain salvation. Conversely, the true gospel does not; (Romans 16:25-26); the answer to the rich young ruler's question, "What must I do to be saved" would be the same today as it was during Christ's first advent, "If you would enter life keep the commandments." John 3:36. Therefore, someone needs to remind the Catholic, mainline Protestant, and Evangelical Churches that the wages of sin [is] still death in this dispensation.

The rich young ruler represents a large class of professed believers who would be excellent Christians if there was no cross for them to bear and no sins to forsake. The rich young ruler represents the professed Christians of this generation who prefer to be saved [in] their sins. The misunderstanding of the plan devised for our salvation has prospered by reason of a counterfeit gospel that tolerates continued transgressions. This false gospel has caused the misguided multitudes to feel assured of their salvation now and in the judgment immediately after claiming "justification by faith" regardless of their unsanctified spiritual condition. As a result, the deceived multitudes of this generation have an overinflated opinion of their true spiritual condition. The "True Witness" addresses this over-inflated opinion of their spiritual condition by identifying the problem, the pastors have universally accepted false doctrines that remove Christ as the believers' only mediator and judge; consequently, the deceived multitudes feel (saved) "rich and increased with goods and in need of nothing, *not knowing*, they are actually wretched, pitiable, poor, blind and naked in God's sight." Revelation 3:15-17. Therefore, in direct opposition to the plainest statements found in the scriptures, the misguided multitudes of this generation *feel assured of their salvation now and in the judgment* immediately after claiming "justification by faith," *not knowing* their unsanctified spiritual condition is deplorable in God's sight.

In Christendom today, untold multitudes are pronouncing themselves saved and forgiven immediately after claiming Christ's death paid the penalty they rightfully deserve for their transgressions of the law, regardless of their unsanctified spiritual condition. This illusion of salvation exists because these alleged believers are taught by their pastoral staff that justification means, "Just as if I have never sinned." Romans 5:1-2. However, when properly investigated, our pleadings to obtain justification mean the exact opposite, just as if I have sinned and that I deserve to die because I am a transgressor of the law. Galatians 2:17-18. When believers plead, "justification by faith," they are accepting the plea-bargain agreement offered to fallen humanity by the government of heaven; consequently, they are admitting that Christ's death paid the penalty *they rightfully deserve* for their transgressions of the law. Romans 3:19-21. The sinners [plea] to accept the [agreement] offered to fallen humanity by the government of heaven confirms their understanding that anyone claiming justification by faith clearly understands that "the wages of sin is [still] death" in this dispensation and that once the stay of execution is lifted, at the close of human probation, anyone still found to be an unsanctified transgressor of the law will be destroyed in the lake of fire, with the Devil and his evil angels, which is the second death. Romans 3:31, Romans 6:23, Revelation 20:12-15.

In this dispensation, while human probation lingers believers can still plead Christ died for their transgressions of the law and consequently stand before God, justified by faith; however, in harmony with their justified status believers are commanded "to fight the good fight of faith" and are admonished to access Christ's "daily mediation" to receive the real forgiveness of their sins and form sanctified characters in this life if they expect to receive a positive verdict in the judgment. Philippians 3:9-16. The everlasting gospel clearly states that after pleading Christ's death paid the penalty sinners rightfully deserve for their transgressions of the law, this [*plea*] proffers a stay of execution of the death penalty sinners rightfully deserve for their transgressions of God's holy law; however, the [*agreement*] between the parties still demands that these justified believers come boldly to the throne of grace, accessing Christ's "daily mediation" to form sanctified characters in harmony with God's holy law in preparation for Christ's final work of mediation, which is the investigative judgment. Consequently, according to the everlasting gospel, the sinner's plea to accept the agreement proffering justification to anyone claiming Christ's death paid the penalty they rightfully deserve for their transgressions of God's holy law is specifically contingent upon them forming sanctified characters in harmony with God's holy law if they expect to receive a positive verdict in the judgment. Therefore, the arrogant assumption of salvation witnessed in Christendom today violates the [*plea agreement*] offered to fallen humanity by the government of Heaven, evidenced by the untold multitudes pronouncing themselves saved and forgiven immediately after *pleading* "justification by faith" because their unsanctified spiritual condition violates the requirements to receive eternal life, indigenous to the *agreement* offered to fallen humanity by the government of Heaven, so they can avoid the death penalty unsanctified believers rightfully deserve for their transgressions of God's holy law.

The everlasting gospel is not ambiguous; a positive verdict in the judgment can only be obtained by justified believers if they have been truly forgiven of their sins. This concept is specifically outlined in God's plan of salvation. Hebrews 10:16-31. According to the plainest statements found in the scriptures, the everlasting gospel demands that justified believers must comply with the specific terms of salvation to receive eternal life. The specific terms of salvation to receive eternal life are very simple; (John 5:36) justified believers are required to access Christ's "daily mediation" and, by the Spirit, put to death "that which causes sin" in their lives before the stay of execution has been lifted and human probation closes. Romans 8:12-13. The apostle makes it perfectly clear that justified believers must crucify their fallen nature if they expect to receive a positive verdict from Christ during His final work of mediation, which is the investigative judgment. Galatians 5:16-24, Ephesians 4:22-24. The everlasting gospel clearly states that the Government of Heaven has **_agreed_** to stay the execution of sinners giving fallen humanity sufficient time to accept the specific terms of eternal life indigenous to the everlasting gospel so that everyone **_pleading_** justification by faith will have free access to Christ's daily mediation to obtain the real forgiveness of their sins in preparation for the investigative judgment and the close of human probation. Therefore, the specific terms of eternal life indigenous to the everlasting gospel specifically state that after Christ concludes His final work of mediation, human probation closes; consequently, the stay of execution will be lifted, and the death sentence sinners rightfully deserve for their transgressions of the law will be universally enforced with the approval of the universe.

The legal right to offer this **_plea agreement_** to fallen humanity has been justified by the merits of Calvary's Cross, which is referred to in the Bible as the good news and translated as the everlasting gospel. The everlasting gospel universally proffers a stay of execution to all the fallen sons of Adam due to the circumstances associated with their transgressions of God's holy law. Romans 3:23. Notwithstanding a stay of execution has been universally implemented due to the merits of Calvary's Cross, those claiming "justification by faith" are instructed to form sanctified characters in harmony with God's law before human probation closes if they expect to receive eternal life. In the actual context of any ***plea bargain agreement***, the specific terms of salvation offered to fallen humanity by the government of Heaven through the everlasting gospel must be extremely clear and very specific; the plea bargain agreement offered to fallen humanity by the government of Heaven must make it perfectly clear that anyone claiming "justification by faith" understands why they have transgressed God's holy law (Romans 3:23) and that despite their compromised spiritual condition, there is absolutely no excuse for their continued transgressions! Romans 6:15-16, Galatians 5:16-18. This means the parties to the plea agreement both clearly understand that Christ came to condemn sin by the flesh, (Romans 8:4) meaning it's the carnal nature possessed by fallen humanity that's the moving agent in the sinner's life that has caused all of Adam's descendants to transgress God's holy requirements, consequently, the everlasting gospel demands that the fallen nature must be put to death if justified believers are to receive a positive verdict in the judgment. Romans 8:1-4, Romans 8:12-13.

In the context of the arrogance existing in Christendom today, when sinners claim Christ's death paid the penalty they rightfully deserve for their transgressions of the law, they are actually admitting that God's law exists (Romans 3:31) while acknowledging their fallen nature is "that which causes sin" in their lives and that the penalties associated with any future transgressions of the law still demands the death of the transgressor, specifically when the stay of execution is lifted and human probation has closed. Consequently, for these reasons, the specific terms of eternal life are made very clear by Jesus Christ, you must be born-again, John 3:7, and the reasons for this specific requirement are made very clear by the Apostle John; because a born-again believer would rather die than knowingly transgress any of God's laws. 1 John 3:9, 1 John 5:18-20.

Accordingly, the untold multitudes who feel assured of their salvation now and in the judgment simply because they have claimed justification by faith are being completely deceived by their church leaders. In harmony with the plainest statements found in the scriptures, the believer's plea to accept justification by faith essentially means, just as if I have sinned and that I deserve to die because I am a transgressor of the law. Therefore, in harmony with the everlasting gospel, as justified believers, Romans 5:1-2, you are required to access Christ's "daily mediation" for the specific purposes of forming sanctified characters in harmony with God's holy law in preparation for His final work of mediation, which is the investigative judgment, (James 2:8-12), and this specific requirement of the everlasting gospel [is] "the message for this time," (Revelation 14:6-13) and [not] the peace and safety message presently being sounded from the pulpits of Christendom today!

One of the **most** obvious principles established in the scriptures is that the everlasting gospel was designed to save fallen humanity "from" their sins, (Matthew 1:21) and the reasons for this requirement should be extremely clear; since the wages of sin is death, after the stay of execution is lifted, sinners will be destroyed in the lake of fire with the Devil and his evil angels, which is the second death. In spite of the fact that believers can stand before God *"justified by faith,"* after pleading Christ's death. paid the penalty they rightfully deserve for their transgressions of the law. Thus, they must still comply with the specific terms and conditions of salvation, indigenous to the everlasting gospel, if you expect to receive eternal life. The specific conditions to obtain eternal life, as defined in the everlasting gospel, demand that justified believers must form sanctified characters in harmony with God's holy law before human probation closes, (Hebrews 10:26-27), or they will suffer the second death in the lake of fire with the Devil and his evil angels. Revelation 20:12-15. Consequently, pleading *"justification by faith"* doesn't even remotely mean, *"just as if I have never sinned."* In all actuality, our claims made upon justification in fact mean is the exact opposite, just as if I have sinned and that I deserve to die because I am a transgressor of the law. Galatians 2:17-19.

To reiterate, the reader needs to understand that Christ came to condemn sin by the flesh, meaning the fallen nature all of humanity has received at birth [without their consent] from their earthly parents must be put to death because it's now no longer an excuse for the continued transgressions of God's holy law. The apostle emphatically says the fallen nature must be put to death if we are to receive eternal life. Romans 8:12-13. In order to receive a positive verdict in the judgment the everlasting gospel demands justified believers put to death their fallen defective human nature, evidenced by justified believers forming a sanctified character in this life. The biblical evidence is overpowering, the sanctification of our character is the predetermined way all are to receive eternal life, (2 Thessalonians 2:13), and sanctification is evidenced by the justified believer's obedience to God's laws. John 17:3. Therefore, Christ says to know God is eternal life, and this "life" will be evidenced by the justified believer's continual obedience to His commandments, (John 14:15), consequently, if you claim to have the assurance of salvation now and in the judgment immediately after pleading justification by faith while you are transgressing any of God's commandments, Christ and the apostles collectively declare that you are an adulterer and a liar, and that you shall not inherit eternal life. Romans 7:1-6, 1 John 2:3-6, and John 8:34-35.

In Romans 6:20-22, the Apostle Paul emphatically confirms obedience is the natural by-product of true sanctification; and in Romans 6:14, after stating that **sin** in the future will have no more dominion over you because as justified believers, you are not under the law, you are now presently *under the grace of Christ;* in order to make this point even clearer, in Romans 6:15-16, the apostle asks the following rhetorical question, "therefore *then* after claiming justification by faith *may* we possibly continue to sin because we are not *under the law but under grace*; the reader needs to understand that grammatically speaking [his response categorically confirms that you should not be found at any time wishing for this], by emphatically stating, "for you already know that the power you are presently yielding *yourselves to as obedient slaves* you are **slaves** to that power you are presently obeying, either of sin, *which leads to death* or obedience *that leads to righteousness.*" It's important to keep in mind that in Romans 6:14, (the Greek words translated as *"under the law"* are grammatically linked by their case agreement to your *fallen nature*). Consequently, in these Bible verses, Romans 6:15-16, we have the same two contrasting powers identified in the previous three Bible verses (Romans 6:12-14) [the *law* of **sin**] that leads to death and [the *justifying grace* of Christ], which is designed to save His people "from" their sins. Matthew 1:21, Romans 5:1-2. Therefore, one of the **most** obvious principles developed in the scriptures is that the everlasting gospel was designed to save fallen humanity "from" their sins, (Matthew 1:21) and the reasons for this should be extremely clear; after human probation closes the stay of execution will be permanently lifted, and since the wages of sin still demand the death of the transgressor, unsanctified sinners will be eternally destroyed in the lake of fire, with the Devil and his evil angels, which is the second death.

The question that must be repeatedly asked the blind guides pastoring the mainline Protestant and Evangelical churches of this dispensation [is this], do we then make void God's holy law after believers plead justification by faith? To make his point as clear as possible, the apostle employs a Greek grammatical nuance consisting of a negative with an optative kicker, in order to deny the idea of the possibility of the fact existing that the believer's faith makes void God's holy law. In Romans 3:31, the apostle employs a negative with an optative kicker to establish that God's holy law has not been made void by the believer's faith, conversely, when believers plead justification by faith this action confirms their understanding that God's holy law exists and that it specifically defines sin in their lives.

In addition, as justified believers, they are admonished to access Christ's "daily mediation" for the expressed purpose of putting to death, by the Spirit, "that which causes sin" in their lives. The believer's claim to be justified by faith acknowledges their understanding that unless they become sanctified by the truth, in preparation for Christ's final work of mediation, which is the investigative judgment, they cannot receive eternal life. Romans 3:31, Galatians 2:17-19, Romans 8:12-13 and Romans 6:20-22. Consequently, the evidence is overpowering, the apostle makes it perfectly clear that the wages of sin [is] still death in this dispensation, and that sin is specifically defined in the scriptures as the transgressions of God's holy law. In order to eliminate any ambiguity on "what must I do to be saved," the apostle explicitly declares that through the law comes knowledge of sin, Romans 3:19-20, Romans 7:7, while the Apostle James emphatically states that God's holy law, which the Apostle Paul says defines sin in our lives, will be the standard of righteousness used by Christ to evaluate our characters during His final work of mediation, which is the investigative judgment. James 2:8-12, Revelation 14:6-7.

It's important to remember that Christ said after His departure the Holy Spirit would be dispatched to convict the world of **sin**, which is defined as the transgressions of **God's holy law**, and to convict the world of **righteousness**, which is defined as obedience to **God's holy law,** and to convict the world of the coming **judgment,** and the apostle specifically says that **God's holy law** will be the standard of **righteousness** used to evaluate our characters during Christ's final work of mediation, which is **the investigative judgment.** Daniel 7:9-10. Consequently, the only way to obtain a positive verdict in the judgment is that you must by the Spirit put to death your fallen nature, (Galatians 5:24) with your fallen nature representing your unnatural propensity to transgress **God's holy law,** which the entirety of fallen humanity received at birth, without their consent, from their earthly parents.

The sin problem indigenous to fallen humanity is why the apostle says Christ came to condemn sin by the flesh; meaning sin as the moving agent, this was done in order to establish [for all time] that man as God created him could keep the law and that the wages of sin justly requires the death of the transgressor. Romans 8:1-4, Romans 6:23. Therefore, if you expect to receive a positive verdict in the judgment, after _**pleading**_ Christ's death paid the penalty you rightfully deserve for your transgressions of the law, according to the everlasting gospel [proffering the _**agreement**_ to fallen humanity], so that all could receive eternal life, justified believers are admonished to "fight the good fight of faith," and by the Spirit, form sanctified characters in this life before the stay of execution is lifted when human probation closes and the dictates of the law will be strictly enforced upon transgressors, which will take place with the unanimous and unconditional approval of the fallen and unfallen worlds because they are now perfectly convinced, that justice and mercy stand at the foundation of the law and the Government of Heaven. Romans 8:12-13, Revelation 22:11, Romans 6:20-22, Revelation 14:6-7.

15

FIGHT THE GOOD FIGHT OF FAITH

In Revelation 7:9-13, the Greek word translated as "clothed" appears in the middle voice and has a stem attached in the participle, perfect. In Greek grammar, the middle voice represents a work someone is performing upon themselves, while the perfect tense means this work of clothing has already been accomplished in the past and has a specific application to the present. Consequently, in Revelation 7:9, the Greek word translated as "clothed" means the sealed have already clothed themselves with white robes while human probation lingers. Revelation 7:1-4. The sealed have followed Christ's instructions in the parable of the wedding feast and clothed themselves with the wedding garment in preparation for the investigative judgment and the soon close of human probation. Revelation 14:6-7, Revelation 14:12-13. The angel says, the white robes, [the sealed have clothed themselves with] in preparation for the investigative judgment and the soon close of human probation, is the righteous character of the saints. Revelation 19:8. The sealed have developed a righteous character by accessing Christ's daily mediation to put their sinful nature yielding sinful propensities to death.

This _**work**_ of clothing themselves in white robes has made the sealed secure against Satan's temptations, which they have performed [past tense] in preparation for the investigative judgment and the soon close of human probation. John 14:15-26. In [agreement] with the everlasting gospel, the "sealed" have, after [pleading] the merits of Calvary's Cross, accessed Christ's "daily mediation" with the expressed intention of forming sanctified characters in harmony with the law knowing when the gospel invitation closes the stay of execution will be lifted and all must stand in the presence of God without a mediator in the heavenly sanctuary pleading for the real forgiveness of their sins. Revelation 22:11. Through their claims made upon justification, they have received the fulfillment of the new covenant promise of salvation (Revelation 14:12), which the leading churches of this generation have rejected as legalism. Hebrews 10:16-18. Therefore, the sealed can stand before the Most High without a mediator after human probation closes because they "have fought the good fight" of faith while human probation lingers and have by the Spirit put to death "that which causes sin" in their lives. Romans 8:12-13.

In Revelation 7:1-8, the Greek word translated as "sealed" is grammatically linked by its case agreement to the Greek words translated as "the great multitude," which no man can number except for Christ during His final work of mediation, which is the investigative judgment. Revelation 7:9-13. In Revelation 7:9, the prophet specifically states that the sealed are "the great multitude" who have heeded the threefold-warning message of Revelation 14:6-11 and have previously "clothed themselves in white robes" while human probation lingers. Consequently, the white robes represent the righteous character of the sealed, (Revelation 19:8) "who have died in the Lord henceforth," (Revelation 14:13) starting from the commencement of the investigative judgment, (Revelation 14:6-7) to the close of human probation. Revelation 7:4, Revelation 15:5-8, Revelation 22:11. In harmony with the parable of the wedding feast, the angel says, "their deeds will follow them" into the judgment because they are worthy to receive eternal life. Therefore, while the gospel invitation lingers, the sealed represent those who have "fought the good fight of faith," by accessing Christ's "daily mediation," and by the Spirit [they have already] "clothed themselves in white robes" in preparation for the time when they must stand in the presents of God without a mediator after Christ concludes His final work of mediation, which is the investigative judgment. Revelation 22:11, Revelation 14:1-5 and Revelation 14:6-13.

"The strongest evidence of man's fall from a higher state is the fact that it costs so much to return. The way of return can be gained only by hard fighting, inch by inch, hour by hour." Ministry of Healing, Page 308-309, by E.G. White. "Character building is the _work_, not of a day, nor of a year, but of a lifetime. The struggle for conquest over self, for holiness and heaven, is a lifelong struggle. Without continual effort and constant activity, there can be no advancement in the divine life, no attainment of the victor's crown." Ministry of Healing, Page 452, by E.G. White. In Romans 8:12-13, the Apostle Paul articulates these same ideas; using specific "stems," meaning Greek word endings, the apostle is communicating the exact same principles. However, because the translators do not amplify the "stems" attached to the Greek words, the force of the apostle's statements, regarding our involvement [_work_] in obtaining salvation, is somewhat lost in translation. When looked at closely, the Apostle Paul's statements become very clear regarding our involvement in being redeemed from "that which causes sin" in our lives. Therefore, this personal involvement is essential if we are to obtain eternal life.

In Romans 8:12-13, the "stems" attached to the Greek words employed by the Apostle Paul appear in the middle voice. The same is true in Ephesians 4:16 and Ephesians 4:22-24 and are also employed by the Prophet John in Revelation 7:9 and Revelation 7:13, which specifically describes the sealed and their involvement [_work_] in clothing themselves in white robes. Those who engage in this warfare are _working_ out their salvation with fear and trembling. The Bible clearly teaches that "the **work** of gaining salvation is one of co-partnership, it is a joint operation. There is to be cooperation between God and repentant sinners. This is necessary for the formation of the right principles in the character. The justified believer is to make earnest efforts to overcome that which hinders them from attaining the perfection of character. However, they are wholly dependent upon God for success. Human effort by itself is not sufficient. Without the aid of divine power, it avails nothing, God works, and the believer _works_. The resistance of temptation must come from the believer, who must draw their power from God." See also Acts of the Apostles Page 482, by E.G. White. After claiming justification by faith, the Apostle Paul commands believers to access Christ's "daily mediation" and by the Spirit put to death "that which causes sin" in their lives, therefore, this represents the _work_ that must be completed by believers through the power of the Holy Spirit while human probation lingers. Revelation 22:11, Revelation 7:4.

The Bible is clear on this point, *"No one will be borne upward without stern, persevering effort on his own behalf. All must engage in this warfare for themselves; no one else can fight our battles. Individually we are responsible for the issues of the struggle."* Ministry of Healing, Page 309, E.G. White. "There is a science of Christianity to be mastered, a science that is much deeper, broader, and bigger than any human science as the heavens are higher than the earth. The mind is to be disciplined, educated, and trained, for we are to do service for God in ways that are not in harmony with inborn inclinations. "<u>Hereditary and cultivated tendencies to do evil must be overcome</u>." Ministry of Healing, Page 454, by E.G. White. "It will cost us an effort to secure eternal life. It is only by long and reverberance, effort, sore discipline, and stern conflict that we shall be overcomers. But if we patiently and determinedly wait, in the name of the Conqueror who overcame for _us_ in the wilderness temptation, and overcome as He overcame, we shall have the eternal reward. Our efforts, our self-denial, and our perseverance must be proportionate to the infinite value of the object of which we are in pursuit. Third Testimonies, Pages 324-325, by E.G. White. "Often, He [Christ] met those who had drifted under Satan's control, and who had no power to break from his snare. To such a one, discouraged, sick, tempted, and fallen, Jesus would speak words of tenderest pity, words that were needed and could be understood. Others He met who were fighting a hand-to-hand battle with the adversary of souls. These He encouraged to persevere, assuring them that they would win; for angels of God were on their side, and would give them the victory." The Desire of Ages, Page, 91 by E. G. White.

"If we [are to] obtain the victor's crown we must stretch every nerve and exercise every power. We can never be saved in inactivity." Fourth Testimonies, Page 537, by E.G. White. "But Christ has given us no assurance that to attain the **<u>perfection of character</u>** is an easy matter. A noble, all-around character is not inherited. It does not come to us by accident. A noble character is earned by individual effort through the merits and grace of Christ. God gives the talents, and the power of the mind; **<u>we form the character</u>**. It is formed by hard, stern battles with self. Conflict after conflict must be waged against hereditary tendencies. We shall have to criticize ourselves closely and allow not one unfavorable trait to remain uncorrected." Christ's Object Lessons, Page 331, by E.G. White. This is why in the book of Revelation, "the True Witness" (Christ) condemns those who flippantly claim to have "the assurance of salvation now and in the judgment" simply because they believe Christ's substitutional sacrifice paid the penalty they rightfully deserve for their transgressions of the law. Revelation 3:14-22. Satan and his evil angels acknowledge the same! Therefore, no one can be saved without stern and persevering effort on their own behalf, all must engage in the warfare of putting to death "that which causes sin" in their lives, no one else can fight this battle for another; individually, we are responsible for the issues in the struggle of overcoming sin and Satan's temptations.

The counterfeit gospel advocated by the popular churches of this generation is designed to create <u>only</u> the illusion of salvation. Conversely, the message for this time is to fear God and give glory to Him who made the heavens and the earth for the hour of His judgment has come. Revelation 14:6-7. The significance of this message clearly states that the holy law of God will be the standard of character used in the judgment. Revelation 14:6-7, Daniel 7:9-10, James 2:10-12. In direct opposition to this message, the sin-loving multitudes of this generation are not admonished by the pulpits of Christendom to form sanctified characters in harmony with God's holy law. The dispensational churches teach this is a failed dispensation and that it's God's design to replace it with a new dispensation wherein dwells righteousness. The dispensational churches believe demanding strict obedience to God's holy law is legalistic by its very nature. This deception is founded upon the false doctrine that a gospel requiring obedience to God's holy law is a yoke of bondage because it cannot be kept; consequently, it's legalistic to demand obedience to God's holy law in this failed dispensation.

The dispensational churches teach that a gospel demanding strict obedience to God's holy law represents a yoke of bondage because it confines believers under constant condemnation. Those given over to this deception feel the requirement for rendering strict obedience to God's law has been made void by their faith (Galatians 3:23-24); however, according to the Apostle Paul, nothing could be further from the truth. Romans 3:31, Romans 6:15-16. The apostle clearly states that our faith does not make void the believer's responsibility of rendering strict obedience to God's Holy Ten Commandment Law. Galatians 2:17-18. In addition, after introducing "justification by faith" (Romans 5:1-2), the apostle emphatically states, "What shall we say then are we to continue in sin that grace may abound," his response is, "By no means, how can we who have died to sin still live in it," with sin being clearly defined in the scriptures as the transgressions of the law. 1 John 3:4, Romans 7:7, Romans 3:19-20. The good news of the Bible is to bring about the obedience of our faith, not the exact opposite (Romans 16:25-26), and Christ specifically said anyone who sins is a slave to sin, and a slave shall not inherit eternal life. John 8:34, and Romans 6:12-16.

The very idea of claiming Christ died for your transgressions confirms your understanding that God's holy law exists while at the same time acknowledging your understanding that the wages of sin still require the death of the transgressor in this dispensation. Aside from the fact that your pleadings of "justification" confirm your understanding that the agreement between the parties acknowledges the punishment linked to your transgression[s] has been stayed until human probation closes, your pleadings that Christ died for your transgressions condones that at some time after human probation closes, unrepentant sinners will be justly destroyed in the lake of fire with the Devil and his evil angels, which is the second death. Therefore, if the requirement for obeying God's holy law has been made void by our faith, then the punishment linked to our transgressions must have also been made void; because the apostle is very clear on this point, where there is no law, there is no transgression. Romans 4:15.

Since the requirement to claim Jesus Christ died for our transgressions of God's holy law, is still obligatory in this dispensation, then God's holy law must also be binding upon justified believers in this dispensation. If the wages of sin no longer require the death of the transgressor in this dispensation, what rationalization is there to destroy sinners in the lake of fire with the Devil and his evil angels, and what is the standard employed in the judgment? Revelation 14:5-6, Revelation 20:11-15. In addition, if our faith has relieved everyone from their responsibility to obey God's holy law, why is the new covenant promise of salvation designed to write God's holy law upon the hearts and minds of believers in this dispensation? (Hebrews 8:10) Therefore, contrary to the counterfeit gospel advocated by the dispensational churches, the everlasting gospel emphatically states that (sanctification) is a specific requirement for receiving eternal life, which represents natural obedience to God's holy law, Romans 1:5, and since God's holy Ten Commandment law will be the standard of righteousness used by Christ to evaluate our characters during His final work of mediation, which is the investigative judgment, (James 2:8-12, Hebrews 10:16-18, Philippians 3:10-12 and 1 John 5:3) how can the mainline Protestant and Evangelical churches possibly claim God's holy law is no longer binding upon believers living in this dispensation.

The counsel given by Christ to His disciples while on the Mount of Olives was, "Do not let anyone deceive you" (Matthew 24:4); the same council is applicable today. The following facts have already been established. The scriptures teach that God has predestined all of humanity to be saved through the sanctification of their characters. The promise of eternal life offered to fallen humanity required the death of God's only Son, confirming Christ's legal right to mediate for the real forgiveness of our sins. The ongoing theme of this series of books is to represent that the mediation of Christ to forgive sins is as essential to our salvation as was His death upon Calvary's Cross. Our assurance of salvation is established upon the fact that a payment has been made for our transgressions of the law, thereby giving "justified" believers the legal right to come boldly to the throne of grace, accessing Christ's "daily mediation" demanding to receive the real forgiveness of their sins in preparation for Christ's final work of mediation, which is the investigative judgment. Therefore, if you expect to receive eternal life, you must be saved *from* your sins, which can only take place by a faith that works (James 2:17-24); consequently, if you expect to receive a positive verdict in the judgment, *your "**hereditary and cultivated tendencies to do evil must be put to death**,"* before the stay of execution has been lifted when human probation closes. James 2:14-24, Revelation 14:6-7, Daniel 7:9-10.

The Bible clearly states believers must by the Spirit put to death the deeds of the flesh (Romans 8:12-13), or the holy angels will destroy them at the Lord's second coming. Matthew 13:41. The apostle says, "For God has done what the law weakened by the flesh could not do; sending His own Son in the likeness of sinful flesh and for sin, He condemned sin in the flesh, ***in order that the just requirements of the law might be fulfilled in us who walk not according to the flesh but according to the spirit***." Romans 8:3-4. The apostle says, "To set the mind on the flesh [the fallen nature] is death" (Romans 8:5), because "the mind that is set on the flesh is hostile to God; it does not submit to God's law; indeed it cannot, and those who are in the flesh [meaning still controlled by their fallen nature] cannot please God, (Romans 8:6-7) because they are under the law of sin working death in their lives. Romans 6:16, Galatians 5:18.

The plan devised for our salvation addresses the root cause of the sin problem; (Galatians 5:16-24); the fallen nature that causes the deeds of the flesh must be put to death if we are to receive eternal life. Romans 7:4-6, Romans 7:21-25. There is no question our works do not save us; however, we are definitely judged by what we say and do in this life. Romans 2:12-13, 2 Corinthians 5:10, Revelation 20:12-15. After claiming Christ's blood paid the penalty you rightfully deserve for your transgressions of the law, **_by this testimony_**, you are admitting (Matthew 12:36) that the wages of sin still requires the death of the transgressor in this dispensation, while accepting the biblical definition of sin, which is the transgression of the law. Galatians 2:17-18. It's obvious there can be no transgressions if there were no laws. Romans 4:15. Consequently, claiming Christ died for your transgressions of the law does not abolish the law that caused you to claim, "justification by faith" (Romans 3:31); therefore, claiming "justification by faith" confirms your understanding that the law exists (Galatians 2:17-19) and that "the wages of sin is [still] death" in this dispensation. Romans 3:19-21, and Romans 6:23.

The Bible teaches those who claim justification by faith have entered into a plea agreement with the government of heaven, and Jesus Christ [the True Witness] is the prosecutor, who will enforce the specific terms of the plea agreement after human probation closes. John 5:22-24. The Apostle Paul says those who have claimed "justification by faith" must form sanctified characters in harmony with the law, or Jesus Christ [the True Witness] will condemn them to their eternal destruction during His final work of mediation, which is the investigative judgment. Romans 8:33-34. The same faith that claims Christ died for the transgressions of the law will lead believers to pursue the glory of God (Romans 5:1-2), which is the sanctification of their character. 2 Corinthians 3:17-18. The Apostle Paul continually emphasizes that true faith will gradually transform those claiming justification into Christ's likeness; consequently, by cooperating with the Holy Spirit the fallen nature you inherited at birth from your earthly parents will be put to death, and by doing so you are *"fighting the good fight of faith,*" changed into the likeness of your Creator in preparation for the investigative judgment. 2 Corinthians 7:1.

This transformation of character is called Bible sanctification, and the apostle says the end of this "good fight of faith" is eternal life. Romans 6:20-22. The Apostle Paul says that God has predestined all of humanity to be saved through the sanctification of their characters. The Apostle John refrains from using these terms or employing complex arguments, he simply confirms what Christ told Nicodemus "That we must be born again if we are to receive eternal life." However, Christ's command, "that we must be born again if we are to receive eternal life," must be understood in its correct context, that a born-again believer would rather die than knowingly transgress God's holy law. John 3:7, 1 John 3:9, 1 John 5:18-20. Therefore, because "the wages of sin is [still] death" in this dispensation and since "sin" is clearly defined in the Bible as "the transgression of the law," when convicted by the "Holy Spirit" as a transgressor of the law believers will claim "justification," thereby creating the hope of receiving eternal life if they "fight the good fight of faith" and <u>by the Spirit</u> put to death "that which causes sin" in their lives before the stay of execution is lifted and human probation closes.

16

LEGALISM IS MANMADE SALVATION

The Webster's English Dictionary defines legalism as "strict, literal or excessive conformity to the law or a religious, moral code." This chapter will establish Webster's definition does not even remotely represent the correct biblical meaning of legalism. It is not faith that claims salvation without complying with the conditions upon which eternal life can be granted. The "everlasting gospel" is extremely clear on this subject, "eternal life" is awarded to the "born-again" believer who understands that Christ died for their transgressions leading them to access His daily mediation for the ongoing "sanctification" of their character with the end of this maturation process producing a positive verdict in the judgment.

Consequently, in the overall context of the everlasting gospel, the arrogant assumption of salvation resulting from simply claiming justification by faith is legalism. It is just as legalistic to say you can be saved in your sins as it is to say you can be saved by "excessive conformity to the law or some set of religious, moral codes." The conservative or the liberal may seem righteous and spiritual by all outward appearances. However, when their faith fails to prevent their continued transgressions of God's holy law evidenced by no change in nature while at the same time maintaining they have "the assurance of salvation now and in the judgment" simply because they have performed some religious duty or made a profession of faith in Christ's atoning blood, they are essentially legalists. Isaiah 1:12-18, Hebrews 10:1-6. Therefore, the truth is legalism can be manifested in the lives of both conservative and liberal believers.

The Webster English dictionary defines legalism "as strict, literal or excessive conformity to the law or some set of religious, or moral code;" conversely, the Bible does not; the apostle says, "What does it profit my brethren if a man says he has faith but has not works of the law? Can his faith save him? James 2:14-17. The answer is obvious, the scriptures teach that no one is saved who is a transgressor of God's law in this life or the next; the counsel given by Christ and His prophets is very clear, do not be deceived by every wind of doctrine; (John 14:15, 1 John 5:3) do not believe those who claim strict obedience to God's holy law is legalism. When your religious leaders claim strict obedience to God's holy law is legalistic, tell them Christ must have been the biggest legalist that has ever existed, for He kept the law perfectly and commands justified believers to do the same. Matthew 19:17, 1 John 2:3-6. Therefore, if the Holy Spirit dwells in your heart, the idea of performing the desires of the flesh cannot possibly exist. Galatians 5:16-24, 1 John 3:9, 1 John 5:18.

The Bible says Christ was filled with the Spirit and obeyed the Divine precepts perfectly. The apostle says all the fallen sons of Adam can do the same if they comply with the conditions of eternal life. John 14:15, Luke 6:46. The desire to keep God's holy law perfectly does not mean you are trying to save yourself by your works; it means you have experienced the new birth, and the Holy Spirit is giving you novel desires capable of permanently altering your nature so you can control your actions. As you demonstrate your love for Christ by "keeping His commandments" you are working out your salvation with fear and trembling. The presumption of salvation based upon one's self-serving interpretation of the everlasting gospel is legalism, for we are told the good news of the Bible is that Christ died for our transgressions thereby giving justified believers free access to His daily mediation so they can receive the real forgiveness of their sins bringing about the obedience of their faith resulting in a positive verdict in the judgment, and not the exact opposite. Romans 16:25-26. The English dictionaries define legalism "as strict, literal or excessive conformity to the law or a religious, or moral code." Conversely, this is not the biblical definition of legalism, for Christ kept the law perfectly and commanded justified believers to do the same; therefore, Christ is not commanding us to become legalists when He says if you love me, keep my commandments. John 14:15, Luke 6:46, and 1 John 2:4.

The facts are the professed believers, who arrogantly claim to have the assurance of salvation now and in the judgment immediately after maintaining Christ's death paid the penalty they rightfully deserve for their transgressions of the law, are just as legalistic as those trying to save themselves by their works. The scriptures make it clear; salvation is not obtained simply by making a profession of faith (Matthew 7:21-23); salvation *takes place through the new birth,* evidenced when the truth becomes the abiding principle in your life. When this change occurs, obeying God's commandments is no longer a burden, but a delight. John 14:15. The *"born again"* believer would rather die than knowingly transgress even one of God's known requirements. The desire to obey God's holy law can only take place if the fallen nature is put to death, and we are commanded to put to death our fallen nature, which is by no means legalistic. Christ says, "This is eternal life, that they *know* thee the only true God and Jesus Christ whom thou hast sent." John 17:3. In the same vein of thinking, the Apostle John declares, "he who says *'I know Him'* but disobeys His commandments is a liar, and the truth is not in him. By this we may be sure that we are in Him; he who says he abides in Him ought to walk in the same way He walked." 1 John 2:4-6. Therefore, if the Apostle John were alive today, the leading churches of this generation would call him a legalist for making these statements.

Legalism! Legalism!

The pastors of this generation are calling everyone legalists who feel obedience to God's requirements is essential if a positive verdict is to be received in the judgment. The born-again believer has, by the Spirit, put to death the fallen nature they inherited at birth [without their consent] from their earthly parents. The fallen nature creates the desires of the flesh, which the born-again believer hates. Transgressing God's holy law is repulsive to those who have experienced the new birth. The born-again experience represents character perfection, which will produce natural obedience to God's holy law while the ongoing sanctification of the character is progressive with its end being eternal life.

Conversely, the cry of legalism comes spewing out of the mouths of those claiming to have "the assurance of salvation now and in the judgment," while, at the same time, their sinful behavior denies they have obtained "the character perfection" God's word declares all must have obtained if they are to receive a positive verdict in the judgment. Romans 6:20-22, Romans 7:4-6, Romans 8:5-8, Galatians 5:16-21, Ephesians 4:20-24, 1 John 1:9, Romans 8:28-30. Therefore, when professed believers claim to have "the assurance of salvation now and in the judgment" immediately after claiming justification by faith, while they remain under the control of their fallen nature, they are "adulterers" [Romans 7:1-6] and the worst kind of legalists because they are trying to obtain salvation based upon their own man-made plan, which creates only the illusion of salvation.

If you ask the majority of pastors today what a legalist is, most will respond, "a legalist is someone who is trying to keep the law perfectly," or some similar variation of this response. As stated before, this definition makes Jesus Christ the biggest legalist that has ever lived. John 9:29, John 14:15. If you do not love the law (Psalms 119:127) and in your Christian experience you do not find yourself longing to be in harmony with the principles upon which the government of heaven has been established, then you do not understand the everlasting gospel was designed to bring about the obedience of our faith. Romans 2:17-27. The new covenant promise of salvation offers the fallen sons of Adam the wonderful possibility of having God's holy law written upon their hearts and minds (Hebrews 8:10), so rendering willing obedience to God's requirements is not a burden; it's a delight. 1 John 5:3. Ask yourself this question; do you believe God's law is good or evil? If this question seems odd or ridiculous, the sad fact is that almost 100% of the Christian Churches today teach that God's holy law is evil, because any gospel demanding obedience to the law is a yoke of bondage since the law keeps believers under continual condemnation.

The mainline Protestant and Evangelical Churches claim God's law yields unjust condemnation because no one can keep the law in this dispensation. However, the death sentence, the law demands, is not a problem with God's holy law. The problem exists with the transgressor. As stated many times, the unnatural propensity to transgress God's holy law, that humanity received at birth from their earthly parents, is "that which causes sin" in our lives. Romans 5:12-14, Romans 8:5-8. The Bible expressly says this character defect has caused all of humanity to transgress, which creates hostility between the parties. As a result, the everlasting gospel is proffering eternal life to the fallen sons of Adam if they claim justification and, by the Spirit, put to death their fallen nature and subsequently form sanctified characters in harmony with the law in preparation for Christ's final work of mediation, which is the investigative judgment. Therefore, the Apostle Paul says that "no human being will be justified in His [God's] sight by works of the law since through the law comes a knowledge of sin." Romans 3:19-20.

In Matthew 5:17, Christ says think not that I have come to destroy the law (Matthew 5:17) but to set believers free from its condemnation. The Bible teaches those who claim justification can access Christ's daily mediation and become empowered by the Holy Spirit to obey the law as naturally as Adam did before his first transgression. This type of obedience is made possible only by putting to death "that which causes sin" in our lives. According to the Apostle Paul, a gospel demanding strict obedience to God's law is not a yoke of bondage, for he states, "The law is holy, just, and good" (Romans 7:12) and the psalmist says it's a transcript of God's character, in fact, the Bible says where there is no law, there is no transgression[s]. Romans 4:15. Therefore, Christ's own words confirm those who desire to keep the law perfectly are His true believers and not legalists. John 14:15, Revelation 14:12.

The great truth of "justification by faith" has stood as a mighty beacon guiding thousands of sin-burdened souls to the true source of power so they can form sanctified characters in preparation for the investigative judgment. However, justified believers can only form sanctified characters in harmony with God's holy law by accessing Christ's daily mediation to obtain the real forgiveness of their sins. However, many professed believers have a distorted understanding of the everlasting gospel. They believe that once justified by faith, they are assured of their salvation now and in the judgment.

This misunderstanding causes these allegedly justified believers to violate the plea agreement offered to fallen humanity by the government of heaven, which requires justified believers to form sanctified characters in harmony with God's holy law in preparation for Christ's final work of mediation, which is the investigative judgment. The believers who feel "assured of their salvation now and in the judgment" immediately after claiming justification by faith fail to fight the good fight of faith and form sanctified characters in harmony with God's holy law in preparation for Christ's final work of mediation, which is the investigative judgment. The motivation to access Christ's "daily mediation," so they can by the Spirit put to death "that which causes sin" in their lives, [_ceases to exist_] when professed believers feel saved and forgiven immediately after claiming Christ died for their transgressions. Therefore, these misguided believers are legalists because they have removed Christ as their only mediator and judge; consequently, they have been given over to the abomination of desolation.

The vast majority of believers living in this dispensation believe in a false man-made gospel that creates only the illusion of salvation. These misguided souls are trying to save themselves by their works. The "works" they are performing represent the repeated claims they are making upon justification, which create the illusion of salvation. As a result, claiming "justification by faith" is actually what assures these alleged believers of their salvation now and in the judgment, not the born-again experience that creates the burning desire to obey God's holy law. Therefore, their legalistic understanding of the gospel is hereafter referred to as the "once saved [by claiming justification by faith] always saved if you stay saved" doctrine, and you stay saved by continually claiming Christ died for your transgressions of the law. Isaiah 1:12-18.

It's important to understand that the stay-saved part of this deception is created by continually claiming justification, with its Old Testament equivalent being, the continual sacrificing of animals. Hebrews 10:1-6. Satan has used the "once saved, always saved if you stay saved" doctrinal deception to deceive God's professed people throughout the ages. It's the abomination that makes professed believers spiritually desolate. The "once saved, always saved if you stay saved" deception is salvation by works. The "once saved, always saved if you stay saved" deception is nothing more than man-made salvation. Simply put, the unsuspecting multitudes of this dispensation are instructed (by their pastors) that they can have the assurance of salvation now and in the judgment simply by claiming "justification by faith," which is legalism because it's not what the Bible teaches. Romans 6:20-22, Ephesians 4:22-24. Therefore, the great theme of salvation, justification by faith, which has stood as a mighty beacon guiding thousands of sin-burdened souls to seek the true source of power that should motivate justified believers to form sanctified characters in preparation for the investigative judgment, has been distorted by the leading churches of this dispensation into a license to sin just like it was for the bigoted Jews in the past dispensation. Isaiah 1:12-18, Hebrews 10:1-6.

The "once saved, always saved if you stay saved" doctrine is legalism. This doctrine is an abomination unto the Lord because it distorts the gospel message into manmade salvation, which leaves its victims spiritually desolate. Isaiah 30:1. The abomination that makes desolate distorts God's predetermined plan of salvation into a license to sin for the following reasons. 2 Thessalonians 2:13. The Apostle Paul, with great clearness of mind, presents the doctrine of "justification by faith" as the grace providing believers free access to an all-powerful Mediator capable of truly forgiving their sins. Romans 5:1-2.

The justifying power of Calvary's Cross has provided believers access to Christ's "daily mediation" so they can form sanctified characters in harmony with God's holy law before the gospel invitation closes. However, the doctrine of justification by faith has been used to circumvent and undermine the good news of the Bible, which is to bring about the obedience of our faith in God's holy law, not the exact opposite. Romans 16:25-26. Therefore, in Christendom today, when professed believers claim justification by faith, they feel "assured of their salvation now and in the judgment," however, to maintain this illusion of salvation, they must continually repeat the same legalistic process, just like the bigoted Jews did in the past dispensation by constantly sacrificing animals, which produced the same bigoted egotistical assumption of salvation. Isaiah 30:1, Isaiah 1:12-18, Hebrews 10:1-6.

It's important to understand that ***the once saved, always saved if you stay saved deception*** has been created by the false doctrines that produce the assumption of salvation simply by claiming justification by faith, which is nothing more than legalism because it is manmade salvation. The Bible says no one is saved simply by claiming "justification by faith." Unless truly born-again these alleged justified believers will not form sanctified characters in harmony with God's holy law before probation closes, consequently, they will inevitably commit the unpardonable sin after human probation closes and be destroyed by the holy angels at the Lord's second coming. The plan of salvation is very clear on this specific point, we must be born again; consequently, after claiming Christ died for your transgressions of the law, the genuine born-again experience will naturally lead to the sanctification of the believer's character; as a result, they will not suffer the second death in the lake of fire, which was originally prepared for the Devil and his evil angels. This eternal determination, which was originally prepared for the Devil and his evil angels, will be declared in the judgment regardless of how many times a day these allegedly justified believers have claimed Christ's death paid the penalty they rightfully deserve for their transgressions of the law. Romans 2:12-15, Romans 6:20-22.

The great truths of the Bible have proffered salvation to the fallen sons of Adam throughout the ages. The central theme of salvation is spearheaded by "justification by faith," which has given believers the right to claim Christ's death paid the penalty sinners rightfully deserve for their transgressions of the law and subsequently come boldly to the throne of grace demanding from their all-powerful Mediator, the real forgiveness of sins, representing the sanctification of their characters in preparation for Christ's final work of mediation, which is the investigative judgment; anything contrary to this understanding of the everlasting gospel represents legalism.

There is nothing more intoxicating than a legalistic religion that saves believers in their sinful condition. When the illusion of salvation is created simply by continually claiming Christ's death paid the penalty you rightfully deserve for your transgressions of the law, the gospel is converted into a license to sin. The "once saved, always saved if you stay saved" deception defines salvation by works. It is a legalistic religion possessing no commitment from the believer to be cleansed from all unrighteousness. 1 John 1:9, Titus 2:11-14. The lost cannot recognize this deception. Revelation 17:8-9. They have accepted doctrines that remove Christ as their only mediator and judge. Daniel 8:11-12. The "once saved, always saved, if you stay saved" doctrine is the direct result of accepting false doctrines that sever the judgment message from the everlasting gospel, which is the abomination that makes believers spiritually desolate. Therefore, the "once saved, always saved, if you stay saved" doctrine converts the everlasting gospel into a license to sin.

The everlasting gospel became legalistic during the old covenant dispensation when the illusion of salvation was created simply by sacrificing animals. Isaiah 1:12-18, Hebrews 10:1-6. The animal sacrifices required in the past dispensation symbolized the death of Christ, the promised Redeemer, who would pay the price sinners rightfully deserve for their transgressions of the law. The animal sacrifices of the past dispensation represented the death of Christ upon Calvary's Cross, symbolizing, in this dispensation, the justification believers receive when they claim by faith Christ's death paid the penalty sinners rightfully deserve for their transgressions of the law.

The Jews, in the past dispensation, like the professed Christians of this dispensation, mistakenly believed the actual act of claiming "justification by faith" "assured them of their salvation now and in the judgment." This error is the New Testament equivalent of **_the once saved, always saved if you stay saved doctrine_** as described in this chapter. The poison indigenous to the "once saved, always saved if you stay saved" doctrine (Revelation 3:17-18) is the creation of the illusion of salvation now and in the judgment immediately after claiming Christ's death paid the penalty you rightfully deserve for your transgressions of the law, which converts the everlasting gospel into a license to sin. Therefore, nothing is more debilitating to the spiritual health of professed believers than a legalistic religion that saves sinners in their sinful condition; Christ is very clear on this point, if you are to receive eternal life you must be born again, and the Prophet John says that a born-again believer will not transgress God's holy law.

The Bible says Christ is the only one Who can mediate for the forgiveness of our sins and make the final determination of salvation in the judgment. The "once saved, always saved if you stay saved" deception subliminally removes Christ as the believers' only mediator and judge. According to the "True Witness," this deception is the "abomination" that will make a "host" of God's "very elect" spiritually "desolate" as we near the closing scenes of earth's history. Matthew 24:15, Revelation 3:17-18. The "once saved, always saved if you stay saved" deception is a false covenant our church leaders have made with death, which removes Christ as our only mediator and judge. It's the abomination that makes a host of believers spiritually desolate in both dispensations. Consequently, believers given over to the "once saved, always saved if you stay saved" deception are subliminally removing Christ as the believers' only mediator and judge in the same way the antichrist of Bible prophecy does through the deceptions of priestcraft. Daniel 8:11-12. This doctrine is contrary to God's plan of salvation (Isaiah 30:1), which is designed to write His holy law upon the hearts and minds of believers in both dispensations before salvation can be granted them in the judgment. Jeremiah 31:31-34, Hebrews 10:16-18.

The "once saved, always saved if you stay saved" doctrine freezes professed followers in their fallen, sinful condition. This abomination first removes Christ's daily mediation to forgive sins. Then after believers claim Christ's blood paid the penalty they rightfully deserve for their transgressions; they feel saved and forgiven. This abomination leaves believers spiritually desolate by removing Christ's final work of mediation that's performed in preparation for the atonement, which is the blotting out of sins truly forgiven from the Book of Records as the conclusion of the investigative judgment. The reason for this is straightforward; the "once saved, always saved if you stay saved" doctrine causes professed believers to feel saved and forgiven in their present sinful condition. Romans 7:21-25. The "once saved, always saved if you stay saved" doctrine assures believers of their salvation in their sins, which is, without question, not even remotely biblical; the Bible says Christ came to save His people "**from**" their sins. Matthew 1:21.

Conversely, the "once saved, always saved if you stay saved" doctrine produces arrogant comments like, "We do not keep the law to be saved; we are keeping the law because we are saved." The "True Witness" says those who are making these arrogant assumptions of salvation are completely ignorant of the gospel invitation. After these legalists claim, "justification by faith," obedience becomes optional because their profession [sacrifices] is what produces the illusion of salvation now and in the judgment. Hebrews 10:26, James 2:14-26. Therefore, suffice it to say that the "once saved, always saved if you stay saved" deception subliminally removes Christ as the believers' only mediator and judge, which is the abomination that's making a host of believers spiritually desolate spoken of by the Prophet Daniel in both dispensations. Daniel 8:12, Daniel 9:27, Daniel 11:31, Daniel 12:11, and Matthew 24:15.

The True Witness says the real issue with those who have been given over to "the once saved always saved if you stay saved" deception is they have been blinded by their own <u>*over-inflated opinion*</u> of their spiritual condition. Those blinded by their own <u>*over-inflated opinion*</u> of their spiritual condition feel rich and increased with goods and in need of nothing, <u>*not knowing*</u> sanctification is a <u>*prerequisite*</u> for receiving eternal life. Revelation 3:17-18, Revelation 22:11. In the last days, the prophecies declare, due to the pastors misrepresenting the everlasting gospel to the unsuspecting multitudes, those "whose names are not written in the Lamb's book of life" (Revelation 17:8-9) will be of "one mind together with the beast" and its image. Revelation 17:13. Just before the close of human probation, those who believe in the "once saved, always saved if you stay saved" doctrine will join the ranks of those oppressing "God's commandment-keeping people," which is done in the name of religion. Revelation 14:12, Revelation 13:13-17. The "once saved, always saved if you stay saved" doctrine is an "abomination" unto the Lord because it removes Christ as the believers' "only mediator and judge" and subsequently leaves a host of believers spiritually "desolate." The "once saved, always saved if you stay saved" deception subliminally removes Christ as the believers' only mediator and judge, in the same way, the antichrist of Bible prophecy does through the deceptions of priestcraft. Daniel 11:31. The "True Witness" says "the abomination of desolation" will mislead even a "host" of God's "very elect" during the closing scenes of earth's history. Matthew 24:15. The lost cannot recognize the "once saved, always saved if you stay saved" doctrine is subliminally removing Christ as their only mediator and judge. As a result, they are led to their eternal destruction by those promising the deceived multitudes the very gates of paradise. Revelation 17:8-9. Therefore, the True Witness says nothing is more debilitating to the spiritual health of God's professed people than a legalistic religion that saves professed believers in their sins.

The Lord said, *"Woe to the rebellious people who carry out a plan, but it's not my plan."* Isaiah 30:1. In the past dispensation, the prophet says the professed people of God believed in a plan, but it was not God's plan of salvation. See the context of the 28th 29th and 30th chapters of Isaiah. The prophet informs us that the Jewish Sanhedrin had manufactured a legalistic plan, creating only the illusion of salvation. The unbelieving Jews created a plan tolerating continued transgressions, *"adding sin to sin"* while feeling assured of their salvation now and in the judgment. Isaiah 30:1. In the Acts of the Apostles, Dr. Luke says most Jews believed sacrificing animals assured them of their salvation now and in the judgment. Acts 13:46. Therefore, any gospel that does not require justified believers to form sanctified characters in harmony with God's holy law before eternal life can be granted them in the judgment is legalism; because it is a manmade counterfeit gospel contrary to God's plan of salvation.

There is only one plan of salvation that can save humanity from the power of sin in their lives. Romans 6:12-23. The promise of eternal life is the same today as in the past dispensation. The old and the new covenants were designed to write God's holy law upon the hearts and minds of believers so they could obey God's holy law naturally, willfully, and perfectly in this life. Hebrews 10:16-18, 1 John 5:3. The biblical facts are "born again" Christians will obey God's Holy Ten Commandment Law as naturally as Adam did before his first transgression. This type of obedience is the result of the born-again experience. The born-again believer longs to develop a character in harmony with Christ's, who obeyed His Father's law perfectly while commanding others to do the same. John 14:15, 1 John 2:4. This is the covenant God has made with the fallen sons of Adam in both dispensations (Jeremiah 31:31-34, Hebrews 8:10), and any other gospel that contradicts this understanding of the born-again experience is simply not biblical. When our religious leaders fabricate a different gospel that prospers by tolerating continued transgressions (Galatians 1:8), it becomes legalism because it's a manmade "plan [a covenant they have made] with death," it is a "counterfeit" gospel that creates the illusion of salvation while believers continue to commit the same transgressions. Isaiah 28:14-18. Therefore, the True Witness condemns the rebellious hypocrisy of this generation consisting of alleged believers who have manufactured a legalistic plan that assures them of eternal life in their sins. John 8:34.

17

THE MYSTERY HIDDEN FOR AGES

The everlasting gospel is the mystery of salvation kept secret for ages. Ephesians 3:3-6. The idea God would offer eternal life to our sinful race at the cost of His dear Son (1 Corinthians 15:20-28) is a mystery even the angels of heaven have yet to completely comprehend. John 3:16, Ephesians 3:3-6, Ephesians 3:9-12. The introduction of the "everlasting gospel" caught Satan completely by surprise. All of heaven clearly understood the wages of sin must demand the death of the transgressor; however, no one ever transgressed, so the actual application of the legal demands of the law had never been imposed upon transgressors. Satan's rebellion called into question God's justice in demanding the death of the transgressor. The holy law of God required the death of the transgressor, and it could not be changed to accommodate any transgression, regardless of the circumstances. The "Most High" did not destroy Satan immediately after his rebellion for several reasons; however, when it became apparent the parties were at an impasse, it was determined that Satan along with his sympathizers should be expelled from heaven.

After his rebellion against the authority of heaven, to justify his existence, while living in open rebellion against God's authority,

Satan realized his eternal existence depended upon convincing others to join him in open rebellion against the authority of heaven. The reasoning behind this thinking is very simple and straightforward; in response to Satan's rebellion, if God destroyed everyone immediately after they transgressed, all of creation would serve God out of fear and not an intelligent appreciation of His wisdom and benevolence in demanding the death of the transgressor. In addition, after the fall of our first parents, the demand for the transgressor's death was proven far more complicated in its specific application for the following reasons. After inducing our first parents to transgress, Satan reasoned that Adam's one transgression would create a problem that would soon undermine the law's legal demands, thereby justifying his eternal existence as a transgressor of God's holy law. In the dark recesses of his disturbed mind, Satan was convinced the "Most High" would not be able to deal mercifully with Adam's one transgression while still protecting the legal decrees of the law thereby undermining the immutability of God's holy laws.

When plotting the overthrow of the government of heaven, Satan never anticipated God would send His own Son to provide an acceptable sin offering for humanity's transgressions. All who claim Christ's death paid the penalty they rightfully deserve for their transgressions of the law can accept the plea agreement offered to all of Adam's descendants by the government of heaven; as a result, they can stand justified by faith before God, and if they agree to comply with the conditions of the plan devised for their salvation, all could receive eternal life. The Bible says the plan of salvation was devised before the foundation of the universe; Christ would become human, taking Adam's place to demonstrate that man as God created him could keep the law. In addition, Christ would give His life to satisfy the legal demands of the law so that all of Adam's descendants may claim justification by faith and subsequently access Christ's "daily mediation" to receive the real forgiveness of their sins in preparation for Christ's final work of mediation, which is the investigative judgment. The Bible says the plan devised for our salvation was not an afterthought introduced by the "Most High" once rebellion erupted; therefore, the everlasting gospel is the mystery hidden for ages. 1 Corinthians 15:20-28.

The "Most High" could have destroyed Satan immediately after his rebellion. However, God, in His infinite wisdom, did not; rebellion was not to be overcome by force; this type of malignant behavior originated with Satan's sick and malicious personality. To protect the eternal security of the universe, the "Most High" allowed Satan time to develop the principles of his rebellion. After rebellion reared its ugly head, all would have an opportunity to witness the terrible results of rebellion so they would intelligently choose righteousness over sin and obedience instead of rebellion. The strict obedience to God's holy law stands at the very foundation of eternal life, and God desired that all His created beings would render willing obedience to the laws governing heaven. This allegiance to the law, which includes condoning its legal decree, is essential to the stability of the universe. Therefore, in order to justify the death of those who do not render perfect obedience to the laws governing heaven, the fallen and unfallen worlds must be convinced of God's wisdom in demanding the death of the transgressor.

The "Most High" introduced the plan of salvation to ensure the stability of the universe, so when Satan and his evil angels are finally destroyed in the lake of fire, everyone will agree that justice and mercy stand at the foundation of the law and the government of heaven. To best counteract Satan's rebellion, it was predetermined that the legal demands of the law would be temporarily postponed. In addition, seeing the unfairness of executing all of Adam's descendants, due to the circumstances directly related to the reasons for their transgressions, the Most High introduced the everlasting gospel proffering a stay of execution of the legal demands of the law being graciously offered to all of fallen humanity, consequently, anyone pleading Christ's death paid the penalty they rightfully deserve for the transgressions of the law are granted free access to an all-powerful mediator so they can put to death that which causes sin in their lives.

Consequently, justified believers are being put on probation to determine if they would comply with the conditions of eternal life. In this way, the unfallen worlds would be allowed to observe what the terrible results of transgression have done to Satan, his evil angels, and fallen humanity. This stay of execution would be implemented for the good of the universe so that all of God's created beings could understand the wisdom behind the legal demands of the law before the "Most High" would eternally execute transgressors in the lake of fire after the conclusion of the 1,000-year millennium. Revelation 20:7-15. Therefore, the "Most High" could have destroyed Satan immediately after his rebellion; however, infinite wisdom did not; the principles of Satan's rebellion must be given time to develop so that all could have an opportunity to witness the terrible results of sin and intelligently choose righteousness over transgression while condoning the eternal destruction of the wicked in the lake of fire, which is the second death.

After Satan's expulsion from heaven to secure eternal life in open rebellion against God's authority, he planned to induce Adam into open transgression. In addition, after Adam's one transgression, it was further argued by Satan that God's holy law was far too restrictive; it could not be obeyed by any of God's created beings, thereby ultimately condemning all of God's created beings to their eventual eternal **_destruction_**, in the lake of fire. Consequently, Satan argued God's holy law was a yoke of bondage because it could not be kept, essentially dooming all His created beings to their eternal destruction. In defense of Satan's accusation, that God's holy law could not be obeyed, it was quickly observed by the unfallen universe that for some unknown reason it was far easier to induce Adam's descendants into open transgression, which on the surface gave credence to Satan's accusations that God's holy law could not be eternally obeyed; however, when properly considered the propensity to transgress God's law indigenous to fallen humanity completely undermines Satan's rebellion.

In opposition to Satan's malignant accusations, the apostle gives the reasons why all of humanity has sinned, they have been born defective. Romans 3:23. In support of his statement, the apostle goes on to explain that the sins of Adam's descendants were not like Adam's first transgression in Eden, all of Adam's descendants were born into this world, ***without their consent***, possessing an overpowering sinful propensity to transgress God's requirements. Romans 5:12-14. Therefore, it was deceptively argued by Satan, to the unfallen worlds, that if Adam and his descendants were not immediately destroyed for their transgressions, how could God, "in justice," destroy Satan and his evil angels for their transgressions?

When Satan first rebelled against the authority of heaven the unfallen worlds did not completely understand the terrible results of sin, consequently, if Adam's descendants were not immediately destroyed for their transgressions, while Satan and his evil angels were, God's refusal to execute those born possessing a fallen defective human nature [without their consent] would certainly have caused God's justice to be questioned by the unfallen worlds.

The reasoning behind Satan's accusations is extremely sophisticated; all of Adam's descendants have transgressed the law having been born with a fallen defective nature, totally unlike Satan, his evil angels, and Adam's first transgression. Romans 5:12-14. Consequently, after rebellion erupted, Satan would be given time to further develop the foundation for his militant accusations of condemning the Divine decree "that the wages of sin should be death." Therefore, time was given Satan to develop his arguments so that all may choose to voluntarily obey God's holy law after witnessing the degradation of character observed in all those joining Satan in his open rebellion against the authority of heaven.

It was Christ's sacrifice that upheld the Divine decree "that the wages of sin should be death," while at the same time giving God the legal right to freely offer eternal life to the fallen sons of Adam if they agree to comply with the conditions of eternal life. The justice of the law, which demanded the death of the transgressor, was satisfied by Christ's death upon Calvary's Cross allowing the "Most High" the legal right to offer the fallen sons of Adam eternal life through the specific conditions indigenous to the everlasting gospel. Consequently, Calvary's Cross allowed the government of heaven to offer fallen humanity the everlasting gospel, paving the way for fallen humanity to accept a plea agreement and choose to obey the laws governing heaven and receive eternal life.

In an attempt to undermine the importance of rendering perfect obedience to God's holy law, which the Apostle Paul says is a prerequisite for receiving a positive verdict in the judgment, the professed ministers of this generation are trying to undermine obedience by saying "there is nothing that we can do to atone for our transgressions." Introducing "the Christ did it all doctrine!" This statement is technically correct; however, it's designed to deceive and mislead believers to accept a counterfeit gospel that tolerates continued transgressions. Daniel 8:12, Daniel 11:33-34. It is true; "there is nothing we can do to atone for our transgressions." In fact, there is nothing even the highest-ranking angel in heaven could do to atone for our transgressions. The life of the highest-ranking angel in heaven was not theirs to give as payment for our transgressions. In addition, the highest-ranking angel in heaven could not mediate for the forgiveness of our sins.

Only Christ, "the eternal one," who was equal with the law, could offer an acceptable payment for transgressions giving Him the right to mediate for the real forgiveness of our sins. In addition, Christ was the only one capable of making the final determination of salvation in the judgment. It is correct; "there is nothing we can do to atone for our transgressions." However, even though "there is nothing we can do to atone for our transgressions," this does not relieve those claiming "justification by faith" from their responsibility of rendering perfect obedience to God's holy law. It was Christ's sinless life that silenced Satan's accusation condemning the law as a yoke of bondage, establishing for all time, that man, as God created him, could obey every divine requirement[s]. Therefore, Christ's sacrifice, which includes more than just His death, (1 Corinthians 15:20-28), upheld the legal demands of the law while giving God the legal right to freely offer the everlasting gospel to fallen humanity.

The mystery hidden for ages, translated as the "everlasting

gospel," states that Christ's death upon Calvary's Cross paid the price for our transgressions, thereby making it possible for Christ to atone for the transgressions of those who have complied with the conditions of eternal life. **John 5:36.** Since all have sinned, [having been born with a defective fallen nature] God in His great mercy provided the life of His Son as a payment for transgressions. The good news of the Bible represents the hope of salvation created for those who have transgressed the law resulting from inheriting their parent's fallen defective nature. Romans 3:31, Romans 6:20-22. The good news of the Bible is the mystery hidden for ages, translated as the "everlasting gospel," which has been offered to all of Adam's descendants. The "everlasting gospel" is the mystery hidden for ages, which caught Satan completely by surprise. Therefore, when planning to overthrow the government of heaven, Satan never anticipated that God could provide fallen humanity with an acceptable sacrifice for their transgressions.

The everlasting gospel gave God the legal right to offer eternal life to those who have transgressed God's law yet elected to comply with the conditions established for their salvation. The great theme indigenous to the Bible is the fallen sons of Adam have received the good news, translated as the everlasting gospel, proffering "justification by faith," to those who simply acknowledge that Christ's death upon Calvary's Cross upheld God's justice in demanding the death of the transgressor. The legal demands of the law, the fallen sons of Adam rightfully deserve for their transgressions, have been nailed to Calvary's Cross; as a result, all those claiming, "justification by faith," can access Christ's "daily mediation" and by the Spirit put to death "that which causes sin" in their lives.

However, the reader needs to keep in mind that Christ came to condemn sin <u>by the flesh</u>, as the moving agent in the lives of fallen humanity. Romans 8:1-4. "The mystery [of salvation] kept secret for ages" confirmed for all time that God's holy law could be obeyed by unfallen humanity and that it's not a yoke of bondage, consequently, establishing that God is just in demanding the death of the transgressor regardless of the circumstances. Therefore, the mystery hidden for ages is the "everlasting gospel," which has proffered to fallen humanity a plea agreement giving justified believers the right to freely access Christ's "daily mediation" to obtain the real forgiveness of their sins with the intent of forming "sanctified" characters in preparation for Christ's "final work of mediation," which is the blotting out of sins truly forgiven from the Book of Records after the conclusion of the investigative judgment.

The Bible teaches we must be "ransomed from the futile ways inherited from our fathers, not with perishable things such as gold or silver, but with the precious blood of Christ, like that of a lamb without spot or blemish or any such thing." 1 Peter 1:17-19. In this Bible verse, a contrast is being established between our fallen defective human nature all have inherited at birth from our earthly parents, and Christ's unfallen human nature which is "without spot or blemish or any such thing." The "futile ways we inherited from our fathers" is the fallen defective nature humanity inherited at birth without their consent from their earthly parents. The apostle says the consequences of Adam's one transgression caused his nature to become fallen, representing our unnatural overpowering propensity to transgress God's holy law, and this defect has been passed on to all his descendants from generation to generation. Conversely, the apostle is contrasting "this great state of lawlessness," with Christ's unfallen nature, which was without "spot or blemish or any such thing." Therefore, the results of receiving a fallen defective nature, at birth, without our consent, the apostle says all have sinned, (Romans 3:23) consequently, we must be born again if we are to receive eternal life.

In almost all our modern Bibles, Romans 3:23 reads like this, "for all have sinned and fallen short of the glory of God." This is a terrible translation, what the apostle is actually trying to communicate is that "all have sinned having inherited their parent's fallen defective human nature." However, this idea is lost in translation due to Romans 3:23 being so poorly translated in every Bible investigated. If Romans 3:23 were translated correctly, the Bible verse would read like this, "For all have sinned having been made defective lacking in the glory of God." This translation clearly shows sin is the direct result of humanity inheriting a fallen defective human nature from their parents. The Apostle Peter says the fallen defective nature [humanity] received [at birth] is "the futile ways [we] inherited from [our] fathers." The apostle then contrasts the fallen defective nature all of humanity received at birth with Christ's unfallen human nature, which the apostle says was without spot or blemish of any kind. 1 Peter 1:17-19. In previous chapters, it was established that the unnatural propensity to transgress God's requirements is our fallen nature, defined as "that which causes sin" in our lives. The fallen nature produces our overpowering propensity to transgress God's holy law, which is welded by its case agreement to "the body of sin and death," the Apostle Paul says must be put to death if we expect to receive eternal life. Romans 7:4-6, Romans 8:12-13, Ephesians 4:22-24, Galatians 5:24. Therefore, if we expect to receive eternal life, we must be ransomed from the futile ways inherited from our earthly fathers, or we will be destroyed in the lake of fire originally prepared for the Devil and his evil angels.

In order to cure the sin problem in fallen humanity, Christ laid aside His royal robe, clothed His divinity with humanity, and stepped down from the highest position in the universe to provide a perfect sacrifice for sin so believers could access His daily mediation and by the Spirit put to death their unnatural propensity to transgress God's holy law. 1 Corinthians 15:20-28. "When Christ bowed His head and died, He bore the pillars of Satan's kingdom with Him to the earth. He vanquished Satan in the same nature over which in Eden Satan obtained the victory. Christ overcame the enemy in His [unfallen] human nature. The power of the Savior's Godhead was hidden. He overcame in human nature, relying upon God for power. This is the privilege of all. In proportion to our faith will be our victory." Youth Instructor, by E. G. White, April 25, 1901. In His unfallen human nature, Christ naturally chose to resist Satan's temptations, establishing forever that humanity, as originally created, could keep the law. As a result of Christ's victory, deliverance from the slavery of sin and Satan's temptations could be freely offered to our fallen race.

Therefore, it's been clearly established [past tense] that this slavery to sin and Satan's temptations resulted from the fallen defective nature humanity inherited at birth without their consent from their earthly parents.

The introduction of the everlasting gospel makes it possible for all of Adam's descendants to resist sin and Satan's temptations as naturally as Adam did before his first transgression in Eden. 1 John 3:9. The scriptures are clear, "To be redeemed means to cease from sin." Matthew 1:21, Romans 7:24-25, Romans 8:1-4, Ephesians 1:14, Philippians 3:12, Colossians 1:14. The plan of salvation was designed to forgive our sins, and redemption means complete separation from our unnatural propensity to transgress God's holy law. Galatians 5:24, 1 John 5:18. The apostle says, for where there is real forgiveness of sin, there no longer remains a need to claim Christ died for your transgressions. Hebrews 10:18. If believers do not understand that receiving the real forgiveness of sin[s] means complete separation from their propensity to transgress God's holy law, then they do not understand the plan devised for their salvation. Luke 1:77. Those familiar with God's plan of salvation understand the "born again" experience is the cure for the sin problem indigenous to fallen humanity. The apostle John emphatically states, "No one born again commits sin: for God's nature abides in him, and he cannot sin because he is born of God" 1 John 3:9, 1 John 5:18.

The same Greek word translated as "born again" in 1 John 3:9 and 1 John 5:18 is used by Christ in John 3:7 when commanding Nicodemus that we must be "born again" if we are to receive eternal life. In John 3:7, Christ specifically references the "born again" experience when commanding Nicodemus, "You must be ***born again*** if you are to receive eternal life." In these Bible verses, the apostle gives the reasons why the "born again" believer does not sin, "for God's nature abides in him and he cannot sin [better translated as he chooses not to sin] because he is born of God." 1 John 3:9. The reason Christ was successfully able to resist sin and Satan's temptations, from Bethlehem to Calvary's Cross, is made very clear; He was conceived (Luke 1:35) "by the Spirit of holiness" (Romans 1:3) bore into this world "without a carnal nature," (Hebrews 7:15-16) "full of grace and truth." John 1:14. Therefore, to provide fallen humanity with this "born again" experience (1 John 5:18), the Son of God elected to give up His royal position as the ruler of the universe, so He could redeem us from "that which causes sin" in our lives. 1 Corinthians 15:20-28.

If you ask Christians today why they need Jesus Christ, they will predictably answer, "because we are sinners;" however, they give this answer without thinking about what their response means. If Christ died to save His people "from" their sins, we are not saved until the sin problem has been fixed. (See explanations given on the Greek word translated as "from" in Matthew 1:21, in previous chapters of this book). The sin problem is fixed when, through the new birth, the truth becomes the abiding principle in your life. The "born again" experience makes believers eternally secure against committing known sins; consequently, they will naturally resist Satan's temptations. To fix the sin problem in fallen humanity, the nature must be changed (Ephesians 4:22-24) "that which causes sin" in our lives must be, by the Spirit, put to death (Romans 7:4-6); we must be born again, and according to Christ all must experience the new birth if they are to receive eternal life. John 3:3-9. Therefore, as stated before, the Apostle John gives the reason why a "born again" believer does not sin (1 John 5:18) because God's nature abides in him, and he chooses not to sin because he is born of God. 1 John 3:9.

The "True Witness" says, we are to overcome sin and Satan's temptations, in the same way, Christ overcame, (Revelation 3:21) and Christ overcame sin and Satan's temptations with an unfallen human nature. Hebrews 1:3. The Bible clearly says Christ was conceived by the Holy Spirit (Matthew 1:20); he was born into this world "born again," completely void of any sinful propensities. John 8:29-36, Hebrews 1:3, Romans 5:12-14, Hebrews 7:15-16. The fallen sons of Adam were not born holy, "full of grace and truth," completely void of any sinful propensities. This is why believers must, by the Spirit, put to death the fallen nature they inherited at birth from their earthly parents.

If we are to overcome sin and Satan's temptations, in the same way, Christ overcame sin and Satan's temptations, "we must be redeemed from the futile ways inherited from our earthly fathers." Revelation 3:21. If you ask Christians why they need Christ, they will predictably answer, "because we are sinners," without really thinking about what they are saying. If Christ died to save His people "from" their sins, then we are not saved until the sin problem has been fixed. Therefore, to communicate to Nicodemus how to fix the sin problem Christ said we must be "born again" because the sin problem is fixed through the new birth when the truth becomes the abiding principle in your life. Therefore, if Christ had a fallen nature when did He become born again, (John 3:7), and when did the truth become the abiding principle in his life, (1 John 3:9) when did Christ by the Spirit put to death "that which causes sin" in His life? Romans 8:12-13.

In Christendom today, untold multitudes are claiming to be "born again," while they, like Satan in heaven, are declaring God's holy law a yoke of bondage. The biblical facts are clear, Christ emphatically said to Nicodemus, "We must be born again" if we are to receive eternal life. John 3:3-9. In his outward appearance, Nicodemus seemed to be an honest sincere believer. However, Christ looked at his heart and clearly decerned hypocrisy and self-righteousness. In like manner, if believers would perform even a cursory examination of the Bible verses, they use to support their over-inflated opinions of their spiritual condition, they would quickly realize their arrogant assumption of salvation is based totally upon an incorrect understanding of the "born again" experience. If 1 John 5:18 and 1 John 3:4-10 were investigated and compared to the retranslated version of 1 John 5:1-5, provided in the next paragraph, the reader would quickly realize Christ did not need to be "born again." The Savior Himself said He was born into this sinful world with absolutely no propensity to transgress the law. John 14:30, Hebrews 1:3, Romans 5:12-14, 1 Peter 1:18-19, Colossians 1:15-19. When these Bible verses are properly understood (1 John 5:1, 1 John 5:18, and 1 John 3:9), it becomes extremely clear why Christ was able to lead a sinless life. Christ was born into this world "born again," possessing absolutely no propensity to transgress His Father's laws. See also The Faith I Live Page 49, by E. G. White.

In Christendom today, the confusion existing on Christ's nature is very problematic. Think about this for a moment. The Bible says all have sinned, having been born into this world with a fallen defective human nature producing unnatural and overpowering propensities to transgress. In earlier chapters of this book, it was established that the fallen defective human nature all of humanity received at birth, producing unnatural and overpowering propensities to transgress God's holy law, is defined as "that which causes sin" in our lives. The apostle commands us, on numerous occasions, to put to death "that which causes sin" in our lives. Ephesians 4:22-24, Romans 8:12-13, Galatians 5:16-24.

If Christ had a fallen nature, when did He put His fallen defective human nature to death? When did Christ become "born again," as required by Christ Himself and the scriptures? John 3:3-9. The apostle clearly states, "The mind that is set on the flesh [fallen nature] is hostile to God; it does not submit to God's law indeed, it cannot." Romans 8:7. "So then brethren we are debtors not to live according to the flesh" (Romans 8:12) [fallen nature] because "the mind that is set on the flesh, [meaning our evil propensity to transgress controls our actions] will die" (Romans 8:13) however, "if you by the Spirit have crucified the flesh" [representing the death of your fallen nature] "with its sinful desires" you will live. Galatians 5:24, Romans 7:4-6. Therefore, this is why Christ told Nicodemus, that "we must be born again" if we are to receive eternal life.

If Christ was born with a fallen nature, when did the truth become the abiding principle in His life? With this thought in mind, in these Bible verses, 1 John 3:9 and, 1 John 5:18, 1 John 5:1, the apostle makes statements concerning the "born again" experience, which confirms why Christ was able to lead a sinless life. This is how 1 John 5:1 would read if translated correctly: "Everyone believing that Jesus He is the Christ from God he has already been born again and everyone loving the process of being born again he also loves the idea of having been made born of God." The reverse is also true, which is confirmed by the fact that ever since the fall of Adam, all his descendants have transgressed the law. The reason they have transgressed the law is clear; they were born with a fallen defective nature controlled by their overpowering propensities to transgress God's holy law. Romans 3:23. This predisposition to transgress God's law is "that which causes sin" in our lives. Romans 5:12-14. The sheer numbers involved in the sin experiment dictate unless this fallen defective nature is put to death, none of Adam's descendants can receive a positive verdict in the judgment. Therefore, the reasons for this should be obvious, if your fallen nature is not put to death, you will inevitably commit "the unpardonable sin" sometime after human probation closes.

The vast majority of those professing belief in Jesus Christ claim to be "born again" simply because they have acknowledged Christ died for their transgressions of a law that they believe is no longer binding upon believers in this dispensation. However, if they were truly "born again," this experience would protect them from continued transgressions. The "born again" experience is realized when obeying God's holy law becomes the most important thing in your life. The "born again" believer would rather die than knowingly transgress God's holy law. The truth has become the abiding principle in their lives. As a result, rendering willing obedience to all of God's requirements is not burdensome, it's a delight. 1 John 5:1-3. For this reason, the thief on the cross was saved.

The truth had become the abiding principle in his life. After the "born again" experience, "justified believers" will naturally desire to become sanctified by the truth, which will remain an ongoing process, with the clear understanding that its end is eternal life. "Whoever is born of God overcomes the world, and this is the victory that overcomes the world, even our faith" in Christ's sacrifice and His "daily mediation" to forgive our sins. 1 John 5:4. When Christ said to Nicodemus, "You must be born again," <u>*this was not a suggestion*</u>; it was a command; consequently, if you expect to receive eternal life, you must be "born again," the truth must become the abiding principle in your life. The "born again" believer clearly understands the ramifications directly linked to transgressing God's holy requirements, which is slavery to Satan's temptations, and they would prefer death rather than experiencing the slavery linked to the transgressions of God's holy law. The real born-again believer clearly understands that death is a far better option than becoming a slave to Satan, who is the cruelest of tyrants. Therefore, this is why the Bible says a "born again" believer would rather die than transgress God's holy law. 1 John 3:9, 1 John 5:18.

The RSV translates 1 John 5:18 in this way, "We know that anyone born of God does not sin, but He who was born of God keeps him, and the evil one does not touch him." The KJV translates 1 John 5:18 in this way, "We know that whosoever is born of God sinneth not, but he that is begotten of God keepeth himself, and that wicked one toucheth him not." The NIV translates 1 John 5:18 in this way, "We know that anyone born of God does not continue to sin; the One who was born of God keeps them safe, and the evil one cannot harm them." These are especially bad translations. Here is how 1 John 5:18 should read if the exact definitions of the Greek words appearing in the Bible verse were employed while correctly amplifying the moods and tenses along with honoring the mandatory case agreement of the Greek words appearing in the Bible verse. "Now we already know this that all who have been made born of God he does not commit a sin, but he having been, at some point in time, made born of God this experience protects him, and the evil one cannot take hold of him." 1 John 5:18. The evil one (Satan) cannot overcome a "born again" believer because God's nature abides in them, and they choose not to sin under any set of circumstances.

The truth has become the abiding principle in their life. 1 John 3:9. Again, this is why Christ told Nicodemus, "He must be born again." John 3:7-8, John 2:12-13. The same Greek word translated as "born again" in John 3:7 is employed by the inspired writer in 1 John 5:18 and 1 John 3:9. These Bible verses clearly state that "born again" believers choose not to sin because death would be far more desirable than becoming a slave to Satan's temptations. Therefore, with this information in hand, what Christ was saying to Nicodemus becomes very clear, "we must be born again" because the "born again" experience would keep Nicodemus from desiring to transgress God's holy law.

In 1 John 5:18, the apostle says, "Now we already know this that all who have been made born of God he does not commit a sin, but he having been, at some point in time, made born of God, this experience protects him, and the evil one cannot take hold of him." In 1 John 5:18, when the apostle says, "We know," [this would be better translated as], *now we already know this*; consequently, when properly translated, what the Apostle John is actually saying is something that should be common knowledge to every believer. Why? Because the Greek words translated as "we know" appear in the indicative perfect active. This means that we should already know "that anyone born of God" chooses not to commit a sin. In 1 John 5:18, the Greek word translated as "born of God" appears in the participle perfect passive. The same "exact" form of the Greek word translated as "born of God" in 1 John 5:18, is also employed by Christ in John 3:7, referring to the spiritual experience Christ told Nicodemus that all must have if they are going to receive eternal life. When looking at the moods and tenses attached to the Greek words translated as "born again" in John 3:7, this experience represents an already completed action in the past, which has an ongoing spiritual application in the present with a predetermination that this experience will keep the believer from falling in the future.

The reason for this predetermination has already been established. After the born-again experience is realized, the truth has become the abiding principle in the life, which will protect the believer against continued transgressions now and in the future. In 1 John 5:18, the phrase "does not sin" appears in the indicative present, active, which means he who is **_presently_** "born again" chooses not to sin. Many translators insert the word "practice" before the Greek word translated as "sin" in an attempt to get around the emphatic statement made by the prophet that a "born again" believer **_presently_** chooses not to commit a known sin. Consequently, Greek grammar does not support inserting the word "practice" in the Bible verse. This information presents a real problem for all the so-called "born again" Christians of this generation who say God's law is no longer binding upon believers. The Bible clearly defines sin as the transgression of the law (1 John 3:4) and just as clearly states that a "born again" believer *presently* chooses not to sin [transgress the law] because God's nature abides in him, and he does not sin because he has been born of God. 1 John 5:18, and 1 John 3:9.

As stated before, the "born again" experience is realized when the truth becomes the abiding principle in life. 1 John 5:1-2. When believers are truly "born again," the most important thing in their lives is being transformed into the likeness of their Creator; this ongoing transformation represents Bible sanctification. 2 Corinthians 3:17-18, and 2 Corinthians 7:1. The apostle says, "no one born of God chooses to commit a sin: for God's nature abides in him, and he does not sin because he is born of God." 1 John 3:9. This same principle is being established by the Apostle Paul in Galatians 5:16; in this Bible verse, the apostle commands believers to walk by the Spirit, and unequivocally says you will not perform the deeds of the flesh. As established earlier the apostle is employing a double negative followed by a subjunctive kicker to establish that if you do walk by the Spirit he's denying the idea of the possibility of the fact existing that you will commit the deeds of the flesh. Therefore, if you are claiming to have "the assurance of salvation now and in the judgment," you must have already been "born again" (1 John 1:8); having previously put to death your evil desires you are not committing known sins. Galatians 5:24.

The scriptures teach when "justification by faith" is claimed, the Christian life has but just begun (Romans 5:1-2), and because the "born again" experience is confirmed by obedience to all of God's requirements, sanctification will be a naturally ongoing process, which leads to a positive verdict in the judgment. At the beginning of the Christian experience, believers will see themselves as transgressors of the law, hopelessly clad in the garments of unrighteousness. As a result, they will access Christ's "daily mediation" and, by the Spirit, put to death their sinful desires to transgress; this is done so they can _**presently**_ choose to obey and live. Romans 7:4-6. Since the wages of sin is death, whenever "born again" believers are convicted by the Spirit as transgressors of the law, they will immediately claim justification, "Just as if I have sinned," and stop transgressing because the truth has become the abiding principle in the life. Therefore, the born-again believer will obey the new truth as quickly as it is presented while "rejoicing in the hope of sharing the glory of God," which is the sanctification of their characters. Romans 5:1-2, 2 Corinthians 3:17-18, Romans 6:20-22.

Those who claim to have "the assurance of salvation now and in the judgment," have no hope of salvation, for the apostle says, "who hopes for something they have already obtained." Romans 8:24. After justification by faith is claimed, the real "born again" believer will move forward "unto perfection" (Philippians 3:9-15) "to grow up to the measure of the stature of the fullness of Christ" (Ephesians 4:13) this is done in the _**hope**_ of being found worthy to receive eternal life in the judgment. The genuine "born again" believer will, by the Spirit, crucify the fallen nature with its sinful desires. Galatians 5:24, Ephesians 4:22-24. The Bible teaches sanctification is a process; however, believers have experienced the new birth when the truth has become the abiding principle in the heart. After the "born again" experience, believers will crucify their fleshly desires and sinful passions. This represents the ongoing sanctification of their character, with its end leading to a positive verdict in the judgment. Romans 6:20-22.

After receiving new truths, the "born again" believer will give evidence of their relationship with Christ by immediately obeying all His requirements. 1 John 3:7-10. The scriptures clearly state that "born again" believers will rejoice in the hope of forming sanctified characters in this life. After the "born again" experience, everything in life is now looked at differently, because the truth has now become the abiding principle in life. The new birth is salvation; salvation is not the result of claiming justification by faith. 1 John 2:3-6. While claims made upon justification should be the result of the new birth, these claims will be authenticated by the ongoing sanctification of the believers' character, with its end eternal life. Romans 6:20-22. Therefore, those in Christendom who claim to have "the assurance of salvation now and in the judgment" must have already been "born again," having previously received the new birth they would rather die than knowingly transgress God's holy law, meaning His Holy Ten Commandment law, and His health laws. Romans 8:24, John 3:3-9, 1 John 3:3-9, 1 John 5:1, 1 John 5:18, 1 Corinthians 11:29, 1 Corinthians 3:16-17.

The real "born again" experience transforms the believer's desires. The things they once hated, they now love, and the things they once loved, they now despise. This attitude transformation results from the new birth, confirmed by the ongoing "letting go of" your sins. Through Christ's "daily mediation," the work of sanctification represents this continuing process, which leads to real forgiveness, meaning the power to actually "let go of" your sinful desires. When convicted by the "Holy Spirit" as a transgressor of the law, the "born again" believer will immediately stop whatever they are doing, which they now understand is out of harmony with the known will of their Creator. Conversely, unlike the alleged born-again believers of this generation, the Holy Spirit gives the true "born again" believer the desire to overcome their sins by imparting them the power to control their actions. The present-day alleged born-again experience does not accurately represent the spiritual condition of a real born-again believer, because the self-control referenced is lacking. As a result, these hypocrites will be found unworthy to receive eternal life during Christ's final work of mediation, which is the blotting out of sins truly forgiven from the Book of Records at the conclusion of the investigative judgment. Revelation 22:12-15, Matthew 7:21.

In the judgment, a mere profession of faith means nothing. Unless corresponding works back up your professions of faith, your claims to be born again are, in fact, false. James 2:17-23. The modern-day understanding of the born-again experience contradicts the "born-again" experience described in the scriptures. The born-again experience witnessed in Christendom today does not produce natural obedience to God's holy law; consequently, it's counterfeit and a complete deception. In Christendom today, millions of professed believers claim they have been born again while they continue to transgress God's holy law. According to the plainest statements found in the scriptures, the continued transgression of God's holy law by professed "born again" believers is simply impossible. Galatians 5:16-18. It is hypocrisy to claim to be born again if you cannot control your actions. Therefore, the born-again experience witnessed in Christendom today is a complete fraud because it does not comply with the biblical description of the "born-again" experience. 1 John 3:9, 1 John 5:18.

The command made by Christ to Nicodemus, <u>*if you are to see eternal life*</u>, "you must be born again," is still binding upon the believers of this generation. John 3:7-8. The unsuspecting multitudes of this generation are completely ignorant of the real "born again" experience described in the scriptures. The real "born again" experience produces natural obedience to God's holy law because the truth has become the abiding principle in your life. The actual "born again" believer serves the "Most High" with their whole heart and mind. Their desires have been transformed. Nicodemus did not understand Christ's words when He said, "That which is born of the flesh [the fallen nature] is flesh, and that which is born of the Spirit [the unfallen nature] is of the Spirit." John 3:6. The real "born again" believer, the things they once hated they now love, and the things they once loved they now hate.

Simply put, Nicodemus was as ignorant of the everlasting gospel as are the vast majority of professed believers today; consequently, regardless of your ignorance, the same command given to Nicodemus is given to all of fallen humanity, if you are to receive eternal life, "you must be born again," (John 3:36) the truth must become the abiding principle in the life. The Bible is extremely clear on this point, Christ told Nicodemus "If you are to receive eternal life, you must be born again," however, Nicodemus did not understand Christ's words because he didn't understand what Christ meant when stating, "That which is born of the flesh [the fallen nature] is flesh, and that which is born of the Spirit [the unfallen nature] is of the Spirit." John 3:6.

Therefore, the same command is applicable today, if you are going to receive eternal life you must be born again, and the Bible is emphatic on this point, that a born-again believer would rather die than knowingly transgress God's laws, both His Holy Ten Commandment Law and His mandatory health laws. John 3:7, 1 John 3:7-10 1 John 5:18-20, 1 Corinthians 3:16-17, 1 Corinthians 11:29, 1 Corinthians 10:31, 1 Corinthians 6:9-10 and Romans 12:1.

18

EVERY IDLE WORD MEN SHALL SPEAK – THEY SHALL GIVE ACCOUNT IN THE JUDGMENT

After making it through the first seventeen chapters of this book it should be clear by now that the proper understanding of the everlasting gospel involves accepting this very important fundamental doctrinal belief; that the daily mediation of Christ to forgive sins is as essential to the plan devised for humanity's salvation as was His death upon Calvary's Cross, because by His death He gained the right to mediate for the real forgiveness of our sins and as the True Witness preside in the judgment. This fundamental doctrinal belief explains why your claims made upon justification only temporarily postpone the death sentence sinners rightfully deserve for their transgressions of God's holy law.

The Bible teaches that the wages of sin still demands the death of the transgressor in this dispensation, with sin being just as clearly defined as the transgressions of God's holy law. In addition, the Bible emphatically states that God's holy law, contained in the Ark of the Covenant, which is located in the second apartment of the antitypical Heavenly Sanctuary, will be the standard of righteousness used by Christ to evaluate our characters during His final work of mediation, which is the investigative judgment. The everlasting gospel demands that justified believers form sanctified characters [in this life] that are *in harmony with God's holy law*, in preparation for Christ's final work of mediation, which is the investigative judgment. Therefore, if justified believers are not born again, evidenced by their willingness to keep all of God's holy requirements, representing the ongoing sanctification of their characters, these alleged born-again justified believers will not receive a positive verdict in the judgment.

The government of heaven declares any violation of God's holy law requires the death of the transgressor; however, notwithstanding the death sentence God's holy law demands, the government of heaven has proffered a *__plea agreement__* to the guilty inhabitants of the Earth, which is good news for Adam's descendants who have transgressed God's holy law due to the circumstances surrounding their birth, consequently, this good news is translated as the everlasting gospel. The everlasting gospel offers all of Adam's descendants eternal life based on certain conditions. The motivating factor for accepting the specific conditions to obtain salvation through the everlasting gospel takes place when the Holy Spirit convicts sinners that they deserve to die [eternally] because they are transgressors of God's holy law. Therefore, the conditions to receive eternal life specific to the everlasting gospel are by no means ambiguous; when believers *__plead__* guilty to transgressing God's Holy Ten Commandment Law, they are declared by the government of heaven to be "justified by faith" and are subsequently given free access to Christ's "daily mediation" to obtain the real forgiveness of their sins in preparation for His final work of mediation, which is to make atonement for transgressions at the conclusion of the investigative judgment.

According to the earthly sanctuary and its services, [the example and shadow of the heavenly sanctuary] the atonement is very specific, the atonement for sins can only take place during the antitypical Day of Atonement when the sins transferred to the heavenly sanctuary are cleansed from the heavenly sanctuary at the conclusion of Christ's final work of mediation, and since this service is directly related to Christ's final work of mediation in the Most Holy Place, the second apartment of the antitypical heavenly sanctuary, claiming justification by faith in this dispensation, which takes place in the outer court of the heavenly sanctuary, cannot be the atonement. Therefore, to establish the significance of this last statement, the Apostle Paul, in the book of Hebrews, has established that the daily and final work of mediation of the earthly high priest in the Typical Earthly Sanctuary, along with its specific services, is symbolic, representing a parable of Christ's daily and final work of mediation in the Antitypical Heavenly Sanctuary, (Hebrews 9:6-9) clearly establishing that it's impossible that continually sacrificing bulls, lambs and goats, which takes place in the outer court of the earthly sanctuary, could take away [meaning atone] for the sins of repentant believers in the past dispensation. Hebrews 10:1-4.

The parable of the Typical Earthly Sanctuary and its services teaches that the atonement takes place in the second apartment of the Typical Earthly Sanctuary, which is called the Most Holy Place, and this service takes place only on the Day of Atonement for the cleansing of sins transferred there by faith [that these innocent sacrifices] (the bulls, lambs, and goats) which were all sacrificed in the outer court, represented Christ's death upon Calvary's Cross as a substitutional sin offering for the death penalty sinners rightfully deserve for their transgressions of God's holy law in both dispensations. Consequently, the parable of the typical earthly sanctuary and its services teaches that the atonement is very specific, it represents the cleansing of sins transferred to the typical earthly sanctuary by faith that these sacrifices symbolically represented Christ's payment for their transgressions in hope of having their sins cleansed from the antitypical heavenly sanctuary during the antitypical Day of Atonement and eventually blotted out of the Book of Records at the conclusion of Christ's final work of mediation, which is the investigative judgment.

The everlasting gospel clearly teaches there will be an investigation into the lives of all those who have ever claimed Christ's death paid the penalty they rightfully deserve for their transgressions of the law either typically or antitypically. 2 Corinthians 5:10. This investigation into the lives of all those who have ever claimed Christ's death paid the penalty they rightfully deserve for their transgressions of the law is performed by Christ, (John 5:22, John 5:27, John 17:2, Matthew 25:31-32, Acts 10:42, Revelation 20:11-15 and 2 Timothy 4:1) and the Apostle Paul specifically says it's Christ, who is the justifier, (Romans 8:33-34) that will, as the True Witness, preside in the judgment, (Revelation 3:15-22) to determine, during His final work of mediation, which is the investigative judgment, if justified believers have formed sanctified characters in harmony with God's Holy Ten Commandment Law and are therefore worthy to receive eternal life. James 2:8-12, Daniel 7:9-10.

The Bible is emphatic on this point, that sin shall not arise a second time. In harmony with this understanding, the reader needs to fully comprehend that it was not only to provide a sacrifice for the sins of the world that Christ suffered and died for fallen humanity, it was to establish for all time that man as God created him could keep the law. However, it was not only to establish that man as God created him could keep the law, it was to establish for all time God's justice in requiring the death of the transgressor. The reason why sin shall not arise a second time is directly related to the born-again experience. In Romans 6:15-16, the Apostle Paul clearly articulates why a born-again believer would rather die than knowingly transgress God's holy law. In order to clarify what the apostle said in Romans 6:14 that "you are not under the law you are under grace," the apostle asks the following rhetorical question, "Therefore *then, may* we continue to sin because we are not *under the law but* under grace?" The Apostle Paul's response is, "Do not at any time wish for this, for you already know to whom you are presently yielding *yourselves* to as *obedient servants,* you are **slaves** to whom you obey; either of sin, which leads to death, or obedience, *which leads to righteousness."* The reason the Bible emphatically says that sin shall not arise a second time is the same reason why born-again believers would rather die than knowingly transgress God's holy law. Therefore, sin shall not arise a second time because the fallen and unfallen worlds have witnessed the terrible results of sin; and are now convinced of God's justice in dealing with Satan's rebellion.

In your understanding of the plan devised for your salvation, if you do not fully comprehend that claiming justification by faith only transfers your sins to the antitypical Heavenly Sanctuary, in preparation for Christ's final work of mediation, which takes place during the antitypical "Day of Atonement," when the characters and lives of all those who have ever claimed justification by faith are reviewed by Christ to determine if you are worthy to receive eternal life; you have been given over to the abomination of desolation, and Bible prophecy says you will go into perdition. Revelation 17:8-11. In the past dispensation, those given over to the abomination of desolation believed that the blood of lambs, bulls, and goats could take away their sins. Therefore, the Jews came to believe that the actual act of sacrificing animals along with their rigorous exactions to the ceremonial laws secured for themselves "the assurance of salvation now and in the judgment," which is categorically denied by the apostle in Hebrews 10:1-4 and specifically by the prophet in these Bible verses. Isaiah 1:10-17.

The parable of the typical earthly sanctuary and its services establishes that Christ's final work of mediation is performed during the antitypical Day of Atonement specifically for the cleansing of sins truly forgiven from the antitypical Heavenly Sanctuary which are subsequently blotted out from the Book of Records at the conclusion of the investigative judgment. The sealed, are grammatically linked by case agreement to the great multitude of believers who understand the "vision" of Daniel 8:14, consequently, they know why "the wages of sin must be death" (Romans 6:23); and why the introduction of the everlasting gospel, proffering a plea agreement to the fallen sons of Adam, only temporarily postpones the death penalty sinners rightfully deserve for their transgressions of God's holy law. Romans 3:19-26. Therefore, the apostle says: *"It's impossible for the blood of bulls and goats to take away sin."* Hebrews 10:1-4. Therefore, notwithstanding the death sentence sinners rightfully deserve for their transgressions has been graciously stayed, the Bible teaches that the legal demands of the law will be executed upon transgressors sometime after the conclusion of Christ's final work of mediation, which is the investigative judgment. Revelation 20:11-15.

There should be no confusion on this subject, the parties to the plea agreement have collectively acknowledged that during the investigative judgment, it will be determined by the True Witness if justified believers have put to death "that which causes sin" in their lives, which is the only criterion for receiving eternal life. If justified believers have been born-again, they have put to death "that which causes sin" in their lives, consequently, they will receive a positive verdict in the judgment. In like manner, if justified allegedly born-again believers have not complied with this specific condition to receive salvation indigenous to the everlasting gospel offered to fallen humanity by the government of heaven, they cannot receive eternal life. The everlasting gospel demands that we must be born again, unsanctified sinners will be eternally exterminated with the Devil and his evil angels in the lake of fire, which is the second death. The extermination of unsanctified sinners with the Devil and his evil angels in the lake of fire will be done by the Most High with the collective approval of the universe. John 5:35. Therefore, after human probation closes, to ensure the support of the fallen and unfallen worlds, the final eradication of Satan, his evil angels, along with fallen humanity who have joined him in his rebellion against the authority of heaven, will not occur until ***after*** the conclusion of the 1,000-year millennium; this is what the Bible teaches on the second death and the 1,000-year millennium, consequently there should be no confusion on this subject. Revelation 20:1-15.

There must be a clear understanding of the following doctrinal beliefs, that the earthly high priest's mediation in the typical earthly sanctuary along with its services represents a parable of Christ's daily and final work of mediation in the antitypical heavenly sanctuary, consequently, since claiming justification by faith takes place in the outer court of the antitypical heavenly sanctuary it's not the atonement for transgressions. The atonement is very specific, it's the blotting out of sins truly forgiven from the Books of Records at the conclusion of Christ's final work of mediation, which is the investigative judgment. Consequently, notwithstanding your claims made upon justification, the Bible teaches there will be an investigation into the lives of all those who have ever claimed Christ's death paid the penalty they rightfully deserve for their transgressions of the law. Therefore, understanding this point is essential to your salvation.

When believers claim justification by faith their sins are transferred to the antitypical heavenly sanctuary and are subsequently recorded in the Book of Records as a witness against these justified believers. If these justified believers overcome their sins, their sins will be cleansed from the antitypical heavenly sanctuary during the antitypical Day of Atonement and the record of their transgressions will be blotted out of the Book of Records at the conclusion of Christ's final work of mediation, which involves a work of judgment. Revelation 11:15-19. Consequently, Christ's final work of mediation involves an investigation into the lives of all those who have ever claimed justification by faith either typically or antitypically before final atonement can be made for transgressions.

This investigation into the lives of all those who have ever claimed Christ died for their transgressions of God's Holy Ten Commandment Law [and] (transferred their sins to the antitypical heavenly sanctuary) will determine your salvation, [and] _**not the sacrifices themselves**_ in the past dispensation [or] _**your numerous claims made upon justification**_ in this dispensation. The fundamental doctrinal beliefs essential to your salvation represent the understanding that claiming justification by faith takes place in the outer court of the antitypical heavenly sanctuary; therefore, claiming justification by faith either typically or antitypically is not the atonement for your transgressions, the atonement is very specific, it's the blotting out of sins truly forgiven from the Book of Records at the conclusion of Christ's final work of mediation, which is the investigative judgment.

The professed believers who fail to comprehend that the daily mediation of Christ to forgive sins is as essential to their salvation as was His death upon Calvary's Cross have been given over to the abomination of desolation. The Bible clearly teaches that the typical earthly sanctuary is a parable of the antitypical heavenly sanctuary, consequently, since claiming justification by faith takes place in the outer court of the antitypical heavenly sanctuary it cannot be the atonement for your transgressions. The atonement is very specific, it's the blotting out of sins truly forgiven from the Book of Records at the conclusion of Christ's final work of mediation, which is the investigative judgment. Consequently, if you do not understand that claiming justification by faith only transfers your sins to the antitypical Heavenly Sanctuary, in preparation for the time when Christ will evaluate your character to determine if you are worthy to receive eternal life, then you have been given over to the abomination of the intentional action of being made spiritually desolate by your distorted understanding of the plan devised for your salvation.

The parable of the earthly sanctuary and its services teaches that the atonement takes place in the second apartment of the typical earthly sanctuary, called the Most Holy Place, which the high priest entered only on the Day of Atonement specifically for the cleansing of sins transferred there by faith that the innocent sacrifices, (the bulls, lambs, and goats) represented Christ's death upon Calvary's Cross as a substitutional sacrifice for the death penalty sinners rightfully deserve for their transgressions of God's holy law. The parable of the earthly sanctuary and its services teaches that Christ's final work of mediation is for the cleansing of sins transferred to the heavenly sanctuary, which involves a work of judgment, when the characters and lives of all those who have ever claimed "justification by faith" either, typically or antitypically, will be evaluated to determine if they are worthy to receive eternal life. Therefore, the professed believers who arrogantly claim to have "the assurance of salvation now and in the judgment" immediately after claiming Christ's death paid the penalty they rightfully deserve for their transgressions of God's Holy Ten Commandment law, have been given over to the abomination of desolation.

While the gospel invitation lingers, the Savior says, "Every idle word that men speak, they shall give account thereof in the Day of Judgment." Matthew 12:36. Every line of scripture should be understood in its relationship to Calvary's Cross _**and the plan devised for our salvation**_. In Matthew 12:36, the Greek word ἀργὸν translated as "idle," is employed by the inspired writer several times to establish that the words believers speak in this life will be evaluated in the judgment. The Greek word ἀργὸν translated as "idle" in Matthew 12:36, appears in the New Testament an additional seven times. Matthew 20:3, Matthew 20:6, two times in 1 Timothy 5:13, James 2:20, Titus 1:12, and 2 Peter 1:8. The same Greek word ἀργὸν, translated as "idle" in Matthew 12:36, is used by Christ in Matthew 20:6 when He sees men "standing idle in the marketplace," He commands them to "go into the vineyard" and work. In 1 Timothy 5:13, the Greek word ἀργὸν, translated as "idle" in Matthew 12:36, appears two times and is translated as "idle" (KJV) and as "idlers" (RSV) and in the NIV, respectively "idle" and "idlers." In Titus 1:12, the Greek word ἀργὸν, translated as "idle" in Matthew 12:36, is translated as "lazy." However, in almost every modern Bible investigated, the Greek word ἀργὸν, translated as "idle" in Matthew 12:36, is left un-translated in James 2:20, which distorts the correct understanding of the Bible verse for the following reasons.

The following information is the reason why Christ says, "Every idle word that men shall speak they shall give account thereof in the Day of Judgment." This is how James 2:20 should read if retranslated correctly from the Greek, the original language of the New Testament. There is no attempt to make the re-translated Bible verse conform to English grammatical standards. "However, O vain man, you will at some point realize that faith with idle works is worthless." After claiming justification by faith, if your belief that Christ's death has paid the penalty you rightfully deserve for your transgressions of the law does not lead you to access Christ's "daily mediation" to obtain the real "let-go-ness" of your sins in preparation for His final work of mediation, which is the investigative judgment, biblically speaking your "faith is idle; consequently, it's worthless," because it doesn't exist. If those claiming "justification by faith" do not access Christ's "daily mediation" so they can, by the Spirit, form sanctified characters in harmony with God's holy law, then their faith is worthless. The result of having idle faith, Christ will, during His final work of mediation, find these slothful "lazy" servants just as deserving of eternal destruction in the lake of fire as the Devil and his evil angels. At the Lord's second coming, the holy angels will destroy all those who have a nonexistent faith (James 2:20), evidenced by them never putting to death "that which causes sin" in their lives while human probation lingers. Therefore, this is why Christ says in Matthew 12:36, "Every idle word that men shall speak they shall give account thereof in the Day of Judgment."

The Bible clearly states there will be an investigative judgment. Daniel 7:9-10, Revelation 14:6-7. The prophet says, "I saw the dead, the great and the small standing before the throne. And books were opened. And another book was opened, which is the book of life. And the dead were judged from the things having been written in the books, according to their works. And the sea gave up the dead in it, and death and Hades gave up the dead in them, and they were judged each one according to their works" and not by what they profess to believe. Revelation 20:12-13. In the judgment, the character and lives of all those who have ever claimed "justification by faith," either directly or indirectly, will come up in review before the Most High" to determine if they are worthy to receive eternal life. Romans 2:6-16. The claims that Christ's death paid the penalty you rightfully deserve for your transgressions of the law create a "*witness*" against you, which is recorded in the books of the heavenly sanctuary. Therefore, in the judgment, the names of those whose sins have been recorded in the Book of Records will be investigated by Christ during His final work of mediation, which is to atone for transgressions at the conclusion of the investigative judgment. Revelation 21:27.

The information contained in "the books of the heavenly sanctuary" will be used to determine the final destiny of all those whose names have been recorded in the Lamb's Book of Life. Those who have been found worthy to receive eternal life will have their names retained in the Lamb's Book of Life, and their sins will be blotted out of "the Book of Records" during the antitypical Day of Atonement at the conclusion of the investigative judgment. Those with unrepented sins remaining upon the books will be found unworthy of receiving eternal life, and their names will be blotted out of the Lamb's Book of Life. Exodus 32:32-33, Psalm 69:27-28. The information recorded in the

Book of Records will have an accurate account of your works, evidenced by the prophet's statement the dead were judged by what was written in the books according to their works. Christ, the "True Witness," says, "I know your works." In the judgment, every word you have ever spoken will be scrutinized; there is a value placed upon every deed you perform, which will be considered by Christ during the investigative judgment, for Christ says he that overcomes, as I have overcome, will receive a positive verdict in the judgment. The Bible clearly says there will be an investigation into the lives of all those who have ever claimed Christ's death paid the penalty they rightfully deserved for their transgressions of the law; this is called the investigative judgment. Daniel 7:9-10. Therefore, a correct understanding of the gospel message clearly dictates, that while we are not saved by our works, we are definitely judged by what we say and do in this life and not by what we profess to believe. 2 Corinthians 5:10, Revelation 20:12-13.

In Revelation 14:6-7, we are told that the hour of God's judgment has come. Acts 17:30-31. As established in previous chapters of this book, the threefold warning message of Revelation the fourteenth chapter is the message for this time; consequently, the question is asked, "Who can stand when He appears." Revelation 6:17. However, the unsuspecting multitudes are willingly ignorant of the fearful threefold warning message of Revelation 14:6-11, which has been revealed to the fallen sons of men "at the appointed time of the end," (Romans 16:25-26, Daniel 8:14, Revelation 10:6-7) specifically for bringing about the obedience of our faith before human probation closes.

The religious leaders of this generation are undermining the fearful nature of the proclamation regarding the start of the investigative judgment. The religious leaders of this generation are telling everyone they can "have the assurance of salvation now and in the judgment" simply by making a profession of faith in Christ's atoning blood. 1 John 5:12-13. As a result, the unsuspecting multitudes of this generation feel (saved) immediately after making a mere profession of faith in Christ's atoning blood. Their ignorance of the everlasting gospel makes it impossible for them to even remotely consider Christ might disagree with their over-inflated opinion of their spiritual condition.

In the judgment, Christ makes no mistake in His evaluation of character. When the lives of those who have claimed justification by faith come up in review before the "Most High," those who have not put to death "that which causes sin" in their lives will have their names blotted out of the Lamb's book of life. Matthew 7:21-23. In the judgment, the True Witness examines the characters of all those who have ever claimed His blood paid the penalty they rightfully deserve for their transgressions of the law to determine if their professions of faith correspond with their works. Hebrews 10:26. "The coming of Christ does not change our characters; it only fixes them forever beyond all change." The Faith I Live By, Page 169 by E. G. White. In the judgment, if it's determined you have an "idle" faith, meaning "a faith that doesn't _work_ reformation of the character," then this lack of genuine faith will stand as a "witness" against you during Christ's final work of mediation, which is the investigative judgment. As a result, Christ, the "True Witness," will declare your alleged "born again" experience a complete fraud. Consequently, during the anti-typical day of atonement, your names will be blotted out of the Lamb's Book of Life. Therefore, if your faith is "idle," producing no corresponding works of obedience to God's holy law, then, Christ will, during His final work of mediation, which is the investigative judgment, determine your faith doesn't exist and you will be destroyed in the lake of fire with the Devil and his evil angels which is the second death.

In the judgment, everyone who has ever claimed Christ's death paid the penalty they rightfully deserve for their transgressions of the law will be "weighed in the balances" to determine if they have formed sanctified characters in harmony with God's holy law. If there are found in the Book of Records unforgiven sins, your name will be blotted out of the Lamb's Book of Life. Romans 2:12-16, James 2:10-14, Matthew 22:11-14, Matthew 7:21-23. "When He [Christ] comes, He is not to cleanse us of our sins, to remove from us the defects in our characters, or to cure us of the infirmities of our tempers and dispositions. If wrought for us at all, this work will all be accomplished before that time. When the Lord comes, those who are holy will be holy still. Those who have preserved their bodies and spirits in holiness, sanctification, and honor, will then receive the finishing touches of immortality. But those who are unjust, unsanctified, and filthy will remain that way forever.

No work will then be done for them to remove their defects and give them holy characters. The Refiner does not then sit to pursue His refining process and remove their sins and their corruption. This is all to be done in these remaining hours of probation." See God's Amazing Grace, Page 243 by E. G. White. Those who feel saved, "rich, and increased with goods and in need of nothing" do so because they have accepted a counterfeit gospel that creates the illusion of salvation simply by making a profession of faith in Christ's atoning blood. Satan's counterfeit gospel is designed to make everyone feel "assured of their salvation now and in the judgment," __not knowing__ they are actually "wretched, pitiable, poor, blind, and naked" in God's sight. Revelation 3:17-18. Their faith lacks the corresponding works of "letting go of" their sins. Therefore, in the judgment (Revelation 14:6-7), when your names come up in review before the Most High, if your faith lacks the corresponding works of sanctification, your names will be blotted out of the Book of Life because you are still controlled by "that which causes sin" in your lives. Jeremiah 8:20.

The message for this time is made very clear, Revelation 14:6-7, those who have complied with the conditions of eternal life (Hebrews 10:16-18) will have their sins cleansed from the heavenly sanctuary during Christ's final work of mediation, which is the investigative judgment. Daniel 8:14, Revelation 20:12. The parable of the wedding feast dictates the final determination of salvation will not occur until after the cases of all those who have ever claimed justification by faith have been investigated. Daniel 7:9-10. Satan's deceptions are always founded upon the same principles, severing the judgment message, which pronounces death to transgressors, from the everlasting gospel, which promises life to those who comply with the conditions of eternal life. The deception that removes Christ as our only mediator and judge is the "abomination of desolation" referred to by Christ in Matthew 24:15 as spoken of by the Prophet Daniel in the following Bible verses. Daniel 9:27, the Jews, Daniel 11:31, the Catholics, and Daniel 12:11 the Protestant Reformation.

The True Witness expounds upon this deception in Revelation 3:14-22, and He specifically says this deception will deceive even the "very elect" during the closing days of Earth's history. Matthew 24:15. The everlasting gospel is distorted into a license to sin when Christ is removed as our only mediator (to forgive sins) and as our judge, which takes place when professed believers begin declaring themselves saved, sanctified, and forgiven of their sins. The everlasting gospel proffering a plea agreement to fallen humanity includes a judgment message condemning the transgressors of God's holy law to their eternal destruction while awarding the obedient with eternal life. The prophets declare the judgment message will be re-proclaimed to the world by God's "very elect" who still believe in the original advent message just before human probation closes, Revelation 14:6-11. However, when those appointed to proclaim the judgment message, "to every nation, tribe, tongue, and people," universally accepted, as one of their "fundamental beliefs," false doctrines that remove Christ as the believers' only mediator and judge, then look up for your redemption draws near and is even at the very door. Matthew 24:15, Matthew 24:34.

19

THE "TRUE WITNESS" SAYS "I KNOW YOUR WORKS"

In Christendom today, untold millions feel saved simply because they have asked Christ to forgive their sins. 1 John 1:9. The Bible says if you do not understand what it means to be truly forgiven of sin, you are completely ignorant of the everlasting gospel. Luke 1:77, Hebrews 10:16-18. The definition of forgiveness of sin means to "let-go-of" your propensity to commit that particular sin. This understanding will be established in the next book of this series of books titled "The Abomination of Desolation." As a result of the confusion existing in Christendom today on what it truly means to be forgiven of any specific sin, the gospel of Jesus Christ is saving very few "from" their propensity to sin[s]. Luke 13:23. The reason for this is very simple, which will be established in the next book of this series of books titled "The Abomination of Desolation." In Christendom today the unsuspecting multitudes believe pardon (Colossians 2:13) and forgiveness (1 John 1:9) have the same meaning. These terms may be synonyms in the English language; however, they are exact opposites in biblical Greek. Therefore, professed believers remain unforgiven of their sins while they arrogantly profess to have "the assurance of salvation now and in the judgment."

As established earlier, the "once saved, always saved if you stay saved" deception creates the illusion of salvation simply by claiming Christ died for your transgressions of the law regardless of your unsanctified spiritual condition. "What greater deception can come upon human minds than a confidence that they are right when they are all wrong? The message of the True Witness finds the people of God in a sad deception, yet honest in that deception. They know not that their condition is deplorable in the sight of God. While those addressed are flattering themselves that they are in an exalted spiritual condition, the message of the True Witness breaks their security by the startling denunciation of their true condition of spiritual blindness, poverty, and wretchedness." Third Testimonies for the Church, Page 253, by E.G., White. In Revelation 3:17-18, the "True Witness" condemns the arrogance that creates the illusion of salvation witnessed among His last-day remnant people.

The well-ordered sanctified lives of those who have a correct understanding of the everlasting gospel are a constant rebuke to those arrogantly professing to have the assurance of salvation now and in the judgment while they remain slaves to their sins. John 8:33-35. The "True Witness" directs His comments to the pastors of God's last-day remnant people who are seen advocating the same type of counterfeit gospel, creating the illusion of salvation that's in harmony with the arrogant assumption of salvation witnessed in apostate Christendom today. This breach of responsibility is now even causing God's "very elect" to remain "under the law," slaves to their sinful passions. Hebrews 10:26-27. Therefore, due to the misunderstanding of what it really means to be truly forgiven of a sin[s], there are untold millions existing in apostate Christendom today who have an overinflated opinion of their true spiritual condition caused by their self-imposed ignorance of the everlasting gospel. Luke 2:77, Hebrews 10:16-18, Matthew 1:21.

As it was in the past dispensation, the hypocritical self-styled professed Christians of this generation are deceived by a false gospel "covenant" their pastors have made with "death." Isaiah 28:14-22. The professed Christian Churches of this generation are deceiving the unsuspecting multitudes with "a covenant [they have made] with death" that creates the illusion of salvation immediately after claiming "justification by faith," while believers remain "under the law." Romans 6:12-14, Galatians 5:16-24. In an effort to counteract this deception, the "True Witness" is warning His "last day remnant people" that a discrepancy exists between their professions of salvation and their unsanctified lives, (Revelation 3:14-22) they claim to have faith, but it doesn't work to sanctify their characters. Despite this scathing warning, God's professed "last day remnant people" still feel assured of their salvation now and in the judgment immediately after claiming Christ's death paid the penalty they rightfully deserve for their transgressions of the law. Therefore, [Christ] the "True Witness" says their characters are completely out of harmony with His only standard of righteousness.

The Bible says God's only standard of righteousness is His Holy Ten Commandment law, which will be used to evaluate our characters during Christ's final work of mediation, which is the investigative judgment. Romans 2:12-16. The false doctrines creating the carnal security existing in Christendom today essentially "takes away" and/or removes the believer's need to access Christ's daily mediation to obtain the real forgiveness of their sins in preparation for His final work of mediation, which is the blotting out of sins truly forgiven from the "Book of Records," at the conclusion of the investigative judgment. Daniel 8:11-14. All those willingly ignorant of the importance of accessing Christ's "daily mediation" to have their sins truly forgiven have replaced His final work of mediation with their own self-serving understanding of their spiritual condition; consequently, they will naturally reject the message for this time. Revelation 14:6-13. The message for this time commands justified believers to truly "let go of" their sins in preparation for the time when they must stand in the presence of God without a mediator after the gospel invitation closes. Revelation 7:4, Revelation 15:5-8.

The True Witness says the pastors of His last-day remnant people have joined the unsuspecting multitudes of this generation with their arrogant assumption of salvation, which is satanically designed to "take away" (fundamentally removed by their false doctrinal beliefs)

Christ as their only mediator and judge. Daniel 8:11-12, Daniel 8:23-25, Daniel 11:31-32. The Prophet Daniel says removing Christ as our only mediator and judge is the "abomination" that makes a host of believers spiritually "desolate" by reason of a gospel that tolerates continued transgressions.

This is the same deception employed by the antichrist of Bible prophecy to deceive a host of Catholic believers through the deceptions of priestcraft, which Christ says will be used to deceive God's very elect in the last days of Earth's history. Matthew 24:15, Matthew 24:24. The "once saved, always saved if you stay saved" doctrine is the "abomination of desolation" spoken of by the Prophet Daniel, which has been accepted by the pastors of God's "last day remnant people" as one of their fundamental doctrinal beliefs. This apostasy is designed to "take away" the believers' need to access Christ's "daily mediation" to receive the real "let-go-ness" of sins before human probation closes. Therefore, this satanic fundamental doctrinal belief is specifically designed to cause a host of God's very elect to disregard Christ's final work of mediation that's performed in preparation for the atonement, which is the blotting out of sins truly forgiven from the "Book of Records" at the conclusion of the investigative judgment.

The fundamental doctrinal beliefs accepted by the pastors of God's last day remnant people are specifically designed to create the illusion of salvation now, and in the judgment, in the same way, the antichrist of Bible prophecy does through the deceptions of priestcraft. The "True Witness" is warning His very elect not to be deceived by the false doctrines presently being advanced by their pastors that are satanically designed to remove Christ as their only mediator and judge, which Christ says when universally accepted by God's last day remnant people is the "abomination of desolation" permanently standing in the holy place spoken of by the Prophet Daniel in Matthew 24:15. Therefore, in Revelation 3:14-22, Christ, the "True Witness," is warning His "last day remnant people" that they are being deceived by a counterfeit gospel, a "covenant their pastors have made with death," which is specifically designed to remove Christ as the believer's only mediator and judge, in the same way, the antichrist of Bible prophecy does through their fundamental doctrinal beliefs. Daniel 8:11-12, Daniel 8:23-25, Daniel 11:31-32.

In Daniel 8:11-13, the prophet describes the actions of the antichrist of Bible prophecy removing Christ's "daily mediation" to forgive sins while the truth concerning His final work of mediation is being "cast down to the ground and trampled underfoot." As referenced above, the false doctrines creating "the once saved always saved if you stay saved" *deception* removes Christ as our only mediator and judge, in the same way, the antichrist of Bible prophecy does through the deceptions of priestcraft. Through the deceptions of priestcraft, the impression sins are being forgiven is created by the priest in the confessional, while Christ's authority to make the final determination of salvation in the judgment has been given to the fallen sons of men. The goal of this satanic deception is to usurp Christ's power to forgive sins while His authority to make the final determination of salvation in the judgment is given to someone other than Christ, our only mediator and judge. Hebrews 9:15, and Hebrews 12:24. Therefore, the deceptions of priestcraft, creating the impression sins are being forgiven by the priest in the confessional while usurping Christ's authority to make the final determination of salvation in the judgment is the abomination that intentionally makes a host of believers spiritually desolate.

In the last days, when this "abomination" **referenced above** is universally set up in all of Christendom (Daniel 12:11), Christ will be removed as the believers' only mediator and judge, **which creates** the illusion of salvation and leaves a host of alleged believers spiritually desolate. As a result of this deception being universally established in all of Christendom at the time the first angel made his announcement, the second angel's message states that Protestantism was rejected by the "Most High" at the conclusion of the 1,290 years of Daniel 12:11 and God's last day remnant people were raised-up to proclaim "the message for this time" to a dying world. Revelation 14:6-11, Daniel 12:11-12. The false doctrine creating the illusion of salvation is "the once saved always saved if you stay saved" *deception*. Therefore, the "True Witness" is warning His "very elect" not to be deceived by "the once saved always saved if you stay saved" _deception_ established in apostate Protestantism today, which the prophet says is the abomination that makes those deceived spiritually "desolate" while they feel saved, sanctified, and forgiven of their sins. Revelation 3:17-18, Matthew 25:15.

The second angel's message was designed to alert the unsuspecting multitudes that the Protestant churches have accepted the same false doctrines that "remove" Christ as the believer's only mediator and judge presently employed by the antichrist of Bible prophecy. As a result, a "host" of Protestant believers are seen declaring their sins forgiven while asserting they have the assurance of salvation simply because they believe Christ's death paid the penalty, they rightfully deserve for their transgressions of God's holy law. This arrogance is caused by a counterfeit gospel established by their church leaders that creates the illusion of salvation "by reason of [a gospel that tolerates their continued] transgressions." Daniel 8:12, Isaiah 30:1. The Prophet Daniel says the antichrist of Bible prophecy has employed these same fundamental deceptions for years. Daniel 8:23-25. The key to thoroughly understanding this _deception_ is found in the correct understanding of Daniel 8:13; the Prophet specifically says believers are being deceived "by reason of [a gospel that tolerates their continued] transgressions." In Revelation 11:1-3, the Prophet John refers to the same _deception_ and warns those who cannot recognize how this deception operates, "Their names will not be found written in the Lamb's book of life." Revelation 17:8. This is why the Prophet Daniel says the antichrist of Bible prophecy shall prosper "by reason of [a gospel that tolerates continued] transgressions." In addition, he calls the removal of Christ's "daily mediation" to forgive sins while casting the truth, concerning His "final work of mediation," to the ground by giving it to the fallen sons of men, the abomination of desolation. Therefore, the model employed to create this _deception_ always _operates_ upon the same basic principles; Christ is removed as the believer's only mediator and judge, which creates the illusion of salvation.

It's important to understand what Christ is trying to communicate in Matthew 24:15, "when you see the abomination of desolation," spoken of by the Prophet Daniel standing in the holy place lookup for your redemption draws near and is even at the very door. In order to correctly comprehend what the prophets are trying to communicate, it's important to understand Satan's deceptions always _operate_ upon the same basic principles; Christ's "daily mediation" to forgive sins is removed in conjunction with His "final work of mediation" being cast down to the ground and given to the fallen sons of men. Daniel 8:11-12. Those given over to this deception feel saved, "rich and increased with goods and in need of nothing" simply because they have alleged Christ's death paid the penalty they rightfully deserve for their transgressions of the law. In Revelation 3:17-18, the "True Witness" communication is extremely clear; many who believe they are God's "very elect" have an over-inflated opinion of their true spiritual condition. The same message in Revelation 3:14-22 stands at the very foundation of what Christ is communicating in Matthew 24:15; that a "host" of God's "very elect" will be deceived by the same false doctrines employed by the antichrist of Bible prophecy to deceive a host of Catholic believers through the deceptions of priestcraft. Daniel 8:12-13. Therefore, the antichrist of Bible prophecy intentionally removing Christ as the Catholic's only mediator and judge, "by reason of [a gospel that tolerates their continued] transgressions," is the abomination that's making a host of unsuspecting believers spiritually desolate.

The Prophet says removing Christ as the Catholics' only mediator and judge is the abomination that makes a host of Catholic believers spiritually desolated; however, the real venom this deception creates is the illusion of salvation now and in the judgment. After confessing their sins to the priest in the confessional, the Catholic makes no effort to form sanctified characters in preparation for Christ's final work of mediation, which is the investigative judgment. The reason for this is very simple, those given over to the abomination of desolation feel assured of their salvation now and in the judgment immediately after confessing their sins to the priest and performing the penance assigned them in the confessional. In Matthew 24:15, Christ says, that in the last days, when the same "abomination" is universally established as a doctrinal belief among His "very elect," producing the same spiritually paralyzing effects the last days will come upon us with blazing speed. After claiming "justification by faith," those given over to this deception will make no effort to form sanctified characters in preparation for Christ's final work of mediation, which is the investigative judgment. The reason for this always remains the same, these alleged believers feel assured of their salvation now and in the judgment regardless of their unsanctified, spiritually "desolated" condition. The end will come quickly when God's "very elect" <u>**universally**</u>, accepts false doctrinal beliefs that remove Christ as their only mediator and judge. Matthew 24:34. Therefore, when you see the "abomination of desolation" spoken of by the Prophet Daniel permanently standing as a doctrinal belief universally accepted by God's "very elect," look up for your redemption draws near and is even at the very door.

PART II

A MESSAGE FOR THIS TIME!

20

THE SECOND WOE HAS PASSED –
BEHOLD THE THIRD WOE WILL COME QUICKLY

In the Last Days, after the fall of the Papacy, the prophet says the second woe has passed, behold the third woe is soon to come, (Revelation 11:14), chronologically speaking, the prophecies of Daniel and Revelation would be unsealed, primarily because the Bible [God's two witnesses] (Revelation 11:1-12) would now be in the hands of the common people who could study its saving truths without threats of death and/or imprisonment by the Papal authorities. As a result, its saving truths could be studied without restraint; consequently, the 144,000 would quickly realize that when Christ concludes His final work of mediation, which is the investigative judgment, human probation closes, (Daniel 12:1-2) which takes place when the king of the north, under the command of the one man antichrist, is destroyed during the alleged battle of Armageddon as advanced by the dispensational churches (Daniel 11:45) accordingly, all those who have ever claimed "justification by faith," from the first proclamation of the judgment message, in the year 1844 (Daniel 8:14), to the close of human probation, (Revelation 7:4) must stand in the presence of God without a mediator through the outpouring of the seven last plagues. Revelation 15:1-8, Revelation 16:1-20. This chapter is designed to establish that the message for this time is diametrically opposed to the peace and safety message sounding from the pulpits of the dispensational churches of this generation!

In Revelation 10:7, the close of human probation is specifically referenced, starting when the seventh angel sounds his trumpet. The prophecy says, when the seventh angel sounds his trumpet, "The mystery of God, as announced by His servants the prophets, will be finished," which can only take place, chronologically, after the year 1798, with the fall of the Papacy and passing of the second woe, (Revelation 11:14) when the prophecies referencing the commencement of Christ's final work of mediation would be unsealed, (Daniel 8:14) and proclaimed to every nation existing upon planet earth, by God's very elect, Revelation 14:6-11, who are specifically identified in Revelation 14:12, as those who are keeping the Ten Commandments as originally proclaimed by God Himself amid the thunders of Mt. Sinai, which includes the importance of observing the Seventh Day Sabbath, as a memorial of Jesus Christ creative power, while identifying Him as the lawgiver. In addition, the re-proclamation of the three angels' message of Revelation the 14th chapter will be accompanied by the importance of abiding by God's health laws; this dual proclamation will spearhead the final loud cry of **_the message for this time_**, specifically proclaimed by a small group of God's very elect who still believe in the original Advent Message and are diametrically opposed to the peace and safety message sounding from the pulpits of the dispensational churches of this generation! Revelation 14:6-11, 1 Corinthians 11:29, Revelation 18:23, and Revelation 18:1-4.

The small group of God's very elect who still believe in the original Advent Message clearly understand that when the prophecy says the seventh angel sounds his trumpet, Christ will commence His final work of mediation, which is the investigative judgment, as announced by the first angel of Revelation the 14th chapter. Revelation 10:7, Revelation 11:15-19, Revelation 14:6-7. It's essential to understand that the first angel's announcement, "that the hour of His judgment has come," is grammatically linked to the second angel's message announcing the fallen spiritual condition of the professed Christian churches at the time the seventh angel sounds his trumpet,

The Abomination of Desolation

which takes place chronologically after the passing of the second woe (Revelation 11:14); Therefore, this means that the announcement of the commencement of the investigative judgment, which started in the year 1844 at the conclusion of the 2,300 years of Daniel 8:14, must be proclaimed to the world by some other church organization whose doctrinal beliefs are diametrically opposed to dispensational theology as advanced by "the Churches of Babylon," the Catholic, mainline Protestant and Evangelical Churches of this generation.

The first angel's message [which the prophecy represents as a worldwide proclamation] takes place during the time when God's people could still possibly receive the seal of the living God upon their foreheads, (Revelation 7:1-3) representing the sealing time. The sealing time is grammatically linked to the third angel's message against receiving "the mark of the beast," particularly when it's being universally enforced by the Papacy's image. In addition, the sealing time is grammatically linked to the great tribulation dictating the soon close of human probation (Revelation 7:4) when the 144,000, (Revelation 14:1-5) representing that great multitude of believers who understand "the vision "of Daniel 8:14, (Revelation 7:9) have spiritually prepared themselves to stand in the presence of the living God without a mediator after human probation has closed, which takes place when Christ has concluded His final work of mediation, which is the investigative judgment. Revelation, 14:1-5, Revelation 11:14-19, Revelation 7:13-17, Revelation 13:11-17.

After the passing of the second woe, the prophet hears the sounding of the seven thunders, (Revelation 10:4) detailing the events transpiring during the third woe, which must take place chronologically between Revelation 6:13 (after the great Leonid Meteor shower of November 12th, 1833) and Revelation 6:14-17, (the second coming of Jesus Christ) [consequently, this specific time period] between Revelation 6:13 and Revelation 6:14-17, must be defined in Bible prophecy as the third woe, which includes the actions of Satan's sixth head/king, and Satan's seventh head/king of Revelation the seventeenth chapter, respectively identified as the Rothschild Banking Cartel, and the Papacy's image of Revelation the 13th chapter. In addition, the prophet says when the Papacy's image is completely formed in Protestant America it shall remain only a little while, Revelation 17:9-10 all of which occurs during the third woe, commencing with the sealing of the 144,000, which is grammatically linked to the start of the great tribulation and the proclamation of the threefold warning message of Revelation the 14th chapter. Consequently, the last days as defined in Bible prophecy (Revelation 13:15-17) shall be rapid ones. Therefore, when you see the signs which [it] (meaning the Papacy's image) is allowed to perform in the presence of the Papacy, [the first beast of Revelation the 13th chapter], (meaning with the Papacy's approval) human probation is about to close. Revelation 13:13-14, Revelation 19:19-20.

As referenced above when the seventh angel sounds his trumpet the prophecy says, the sealing of the 144,000 commenced, along with the great tribulation, (Revelation 7:14) during which time the Mystery of God will be finally withdrawn, Revelation 10:7. As stated earlier, the Mystery of God is finally withdrawn, when Christ ceases His final work of mediation (Daniel 12:1-2) which takes place specifically when "the mark of the beast" is scheduled to be strictly enforced worldwide by the civil authorities, (Revelation 13:15-17) which is the warning contained in the third angel's message of Revelation the 14th chapter and transpires simultaneously with the destruction of the king of the north (Daniel 11:45) during the **_alleged_** Battle of Armageddon, as advocated by the dispensational churches. Therefore, the reader needs to understand that Dispensational Theology, which the mainline Protestant and Evangelical Churches of this generation are presently teaching, is nothing more than Counter-Reformation Theology in disguise, the fulfillment of the same is being financed by Satan's sixth head/king of Revelation the seventeenth chapter, the Rothschild banking cartel, owners of the Federal Reserve Bank here in the United States.

The reader needs to understand that Counter-Reformation Theology was developed by the Papacy shortly after the Council of Trent (1545-1563) primarily because the early Protestant Reformers identified the Papacy as the antichrist of Bible prophecy, that blaspheming power who thinks themselves able to change God's times and the law, (Daniel 7:25); "the law" referred to by the prophet is God's Holy Ten Commandment Law and "the times" referred to in Daniel 7:25 are God's time prophecies, specifically "the seventy weeks of years" of Daniel 9: 24-27 and the "2,300 years" of Daniel 8:14, announcing the commencement of Christ's final work of mediation, which is the investigative judgment. The Papacy specifically claims to have the power to change God's Holy Ten Commandment law, which is the reason why Catholics worship on Sunday instead of Saturday, however, as predicted by the Angel Gabriel in the prophecy, the Papacy has also changed God's time prophecies, which is called Counter-Reformation Theology that's being presently disguised today by the Churches of Babylon as Dispensational Theology, which is extremely problematic for the following reasons.

In harmony with the correct understanding of Daniel 7:25, as advanced above; resulting from the great words of blasphemy the Papacy was speaking, the early Reformers were easily able to identify the Roman Catholic Church as the antichrist of Bible prophecy, who our historians have confirmed had been, at that time, persecuting God's people for more than 1,000 years causing them to flee into "the wilderness," Strong's call number (2028) representing [the new world in America] where they were protected from the Papacy's persecution for the entire one thousand two hundred and sixty years. Revelation 12:6. This time period, **_the Papacy's 1,260 years of persecution_**, is symbolically depicted in Bible prophecy as, (1) "one thousand and sixty days" (Revelation 12:6), and also **_in the same Bible prophecy_** as (2) "a time, and two times and half a time," (Revelation 12:14) and (3) as, "42 months" (Revelation 13:5) where the Papacy was specifically depicted by the early reformers as the first beast power of Revelation the 13th chapter that eventually received its deadly wound causing the world to wonder as to the real identity of the antichrist of Bible prophecy.

The Greek word translated as "wonder" RSV or "marvel" KJV, looks like this in the original language, θαυμάζω, and has a Strong's call number of 2296, its literal meaning is **"to wonder," meaning** causing speculation on the subject matter" as to the actual identity of the antichrist of Bible prophecy. In Revelation the 17th chapter, the prophet says he was carried away into "the same wilderness," Strong's 2028, again representing [the new world in America] where he saw [Satan] symbolized as a scarlet beast (Revelation 12:7) carrying the Papacy to power, symbolically depicted as the great harlot (Revelation 17:1-2) who is grammatically linked to the Mother of Harlots while also being depicted as "Mystery Babylon, the great," who has made all nations drunk with the wine of her abominations, which are the Papacy's false doctrines that have made the Earth's inhabitants spiritually desolate.

In Revelation 17:5, the prophet goes on to say that "the Mother of Harlots" had become drunk with the blood of the saints, so it's clear as defined above that "the Mother of Harlots" is a persecuting power. In Revelation the twelfth chapter the beast that carried "the Mother of Harlots" to power is specifically identified as Satan, having seven heads and ten horns, who the prophet later identifies as "the beast that arises from the bottomless pit" in Revelation the seventeenth chapter. Revelation 12:9-10 and Revelation 17:7-11. Shortly after the great Protestant Reformer, Martin Luther, nailed his ninety-five theses to the door of the All-Saints Church at Wittenberg, identifying the Roman Catholic Church as the antichrist of Bible prophecy, essentially starting the Protestant Reformation, almost immediately the Papal Church responded with Counter-Reformation Theology, which was developed by a Jesuit priest named Francisco Ribera. Indigenous to Counter-Reformation Theology was the Papacy's Gap Theory, which has now become the foundation for modern-day Dispensationalism, [that] combines Francisco Ribera's "Gap Theory" with Edward Irving's "Secret Rapture Theory."

Today millions of mainline Protestant and Evangelical believers can't recognize they are being deceived [as to the identity of the real antichrist of Bible prophecy] because they have accepted Dispensational Theology, which is [actually] Counter-Reformation Theology in disguise. The same beast (Satan) identified in Revelation the seventeenth chapter as, "the beast that arises from the bottomless pit," that carried the Papacy to power for 1,260 long and bloody years, is also symbolically represented as carrying Satan's sixth and seventh head/kings to power in the chronology depicted in Revelation the seventeenth chapter; previously identified respectively as the Rothschild banking cartel and the Papacy's image. It will be established in coming books that Satan's sixth head/king, the Rothschild banking cartel, is financing the birth of the Papacy's image, Apostate Protestantism, symbolically depicted as Satan's seventh head/king in the chronology outlined in Revelation the seventeenth chapter, that enforces "the mark of the beast" during the closing scenes of earth's history.

Today the Papacy is no longer recognized as [the antichrist of Bible prophecy] principally because the mainline Protestant and Evangelical Churches of this generation have accepted the Papacy's Counter-Reformation Theology, which "the Churches of Babylon" are collectively representing as Dispensationalism. The angel tells the prophet that the inability of the lost to recognize the identity of the real antichrist of Bible prophecy is principally due because Satan, "*was*" carrying the Papacy to power for 1,260 years, from 538 to 1798 and then "*was not*" carrying her to power after the Papacy received her deadly wound, however, [Satan] *was* still existing after the Papacy, Satan's fifth head/king in the chronology of Revelation the seventeenth chapter, received her deadly wound in the year 1798.

Consequently, after the Papacy received its deadly wound, Satan "*was*" still existing and immediately started carrying his sixth head/king of Revelation the seventeenth chapter to power. Once Satan's sixth head/king of Revelation the seventeenth chapter was firmly in power Satan started financing the direct fulfillment of Counter-Reformation Theology along with the formation of Satan's seventh head/king of Revelation the seventeenth chapter, the Papacy's image; therefore, notwithstanding, the collective distortion of the everlasting gospel into a license to sin by the Churches of Babylon, the reason why the mainline Protestant and Evangelical churches of this generation are being depicted in Bible prophecy as the Papacy's daughter harlots, who have become drunk by the wine of her fornicated doctrines, is they have accepted the Papacy's Counter-Reformation Theology and are collectively disguising the same today as Dispensational Theology, which is the subject of the second angel's message of Revelation the 14th chapter. Revelation 17:1-2, Revelation 17:6, and Revelation 17:8-9.

The mainline Protestant and Evangelical Churches have adopted the Papacy's Counter-Reformation Theology, which they are collectively representing today as Dispensationalism, consequently, Dispensational Theology is essentially nothing more than the Papacy's Counter-Reformation Theology in disguise. In harmony with Bible prophecy, the second angel's message is calling the unsuspecting multitudes out of Babylon because the Papacy's Counter-Reformation Theology is now being universally presented from the pulpits of Christendom today by the Catholic, mainline Protestant, and Evangelical Churches of this generation. As a result, millions of mainline Protestant and Evangelical believers are disregarding the second angel's message primarily because they no longer recognize the Roman Catholic Church as Satan's fifth head/king of Revelation the 17th chapter, the antichrist of Bible prophecy. However, notwithstanding this ignorance, the prophecy clearly identifies the Papacy as "the Mother of Harlots" in Revelation the seventeenth chapter primarily because she has daughters, depicted as the mainline Protestant and Evangelical Churches of this generation. The Papacy's daughter harlots are the mainline Protestant and Evangelical Churches who no longer recognize their mother as "the Woman Babylon" because they have become drunk with the wine of the Papacy's fornicated doctrines, Revelation 17:2, which according to the prophecy are the earth's abominations representing the false doctrines making the unsuspecting multitudes spiritually desolate. Therefore, the golden cup, "the Woman Babylon" is holding in her hands represents the earth's abominations, which are making a host of unsuspecting believers spiritually desolate because they can't recognize they are being deceived as to the real identity of the antichrist of Bible prophecy by their church leaders, the Papacy's daughters, who have accepted the Papacy's Counter-Reformation

Theology, which they are collectively representing today as Dispensationalism.

After the fall of the Papacy, the third woe includes all the events leading up to the close of human probation, resulting from the complete fall of the Protestant Reformation, culminating with their persecution of anyone not adhering to their satanic doctrines. This outright persecution of dissenters is made possible because Satan has successfully incorporated his open rebellion against God's authority into the faith of the mainline Protestant churches of this generation. Consequently, the second angel's message announcing the fall of Babylon points to God's rejection of the mainline Protestant churches in the year 1828, after the conclusion of the 1,290 years of Daniel 12:11.

The reader is required to investigate the explanations provided in Revelation, the 17th chapter. The prophet says the Papacy has written upon her forehead "mystery; Babylon the great the mother of harlots" who holds in her hands a golden cup full of the "earth's **_abominations_**," which are the false doctrines she employs to [intentionally] make the Earth's inhabitants spiritually **_desolate_**. The prophet says the Papacy is the "Woman Babylon," while further characterizing her as the "Mother of Harlots," obviously because she has daughters who are legitimately represented by the second angel as the mainline Protestant Churches of this generation. The reason the mainline Protestant Churches are being characterized as harlots has already been explained: they have prostituted themselves, **_in the same way_**, their mother has, to gain popularity with the sin-loving multitudes of this generation.

In Revelation 17:5, the Greek word μυστήριον, translated as "mystery," has a Strongs call number 3466 and is defined "as hiding the great truths of salvation." In the same Bible verse, the Greek word ΒΑΒΥΛΩΝ, translated as "Babylon," has a Strongs call number 997; its first literal definition is confusion. The Greek word translated as Babylon was derived from the Greek word Ἀψινθος, translated as wormwood in Revelation 8:11, having a Strongs call number 894, which means poisoning someone to death. Therefore, in harmony with the previously established understanding of the above-referenced Bible verses, the prophet is saying the Papacy is withholding the great truths of salvation from the unsuspecting multitudes by her confusing doctrines that tolerate continued transgressions and are poisoning alleged believers to death while creating the illusion of salvation now and in the judgment.

The correct interpretation of the seven trumpets introducing the three woes must be in harmony with the chronology specifically outlined in the prophecies of Daniel and Revelation. In the following Bible verses, Revelation 9:11, Revelation 11:7, and Revelation 17:8, the prophet specifically references the three woes, Revelation 8:13, and clearly states the fallen angel trying to destroy God's people is Abaddon and Apollyon respectively appearing in Hebrew and Greek, having a Strongs call numbers of (3) and (623), which means destroyer. In Revelation 9:1, the prophet says this fallen angel has the keys to the bottomless pit as opposed to Christ who has the keys to the kingdom of heaven.

In Revelation the twelfth chapter, the prophet says when God's two witnesses [symbolized in the prophecy as the Old and the New Testament] were finishing their testimony, nearing the conclusion of the Papacy's 1,260-year reign of oppression, Satan, "the beast that ascends from the bottomless pit" shall make open war upon them and their bodies shall lie in the streets of that great city for three-and-one-half years, which took place during the French Revolution. After the conclusion of the Papacy's 1,260-year reign of persecution, oppression, and the suppression of the scriptures the prophet says the second woe has passed; behold, the third woe shall come quickly.

In Revelation, the twelfth chapter, the prophet specifically identifies Apollyon as Satan, the Great Red Dragon who tried to kill Christ immediately after His birth. In the same chapter, the prophet says Satan tried to destroy God's true church, identified as those keeping God's ten commandments. However, God's true church was hiding in the wilderness, where a place had been prepared for her during the Papacy's 1,260-year reign of blood and deception. The prophet says God's true church was hiding from Satan in the wilderness specifically during the Papacy's 1,260-year reign of blood and deception.

The geographical location of the wilderness referenced in this Bible verse will be clearly identified in this series of books titled "The Abomination of Desolation," as the United States of America, which was eventually founded upon the religious and political freedoms not afforded those living among the European nations.

As established earlier, in Revelation the seventeenth chapter, the prophet is carried away into the same wilderness where he sees Satan depicted as the great red dragon, symbolized as the "beast that ascends from the bottomless pit," who [*was*] carrying the Papacy to power for 1,260 long and bloody years. Revelation 17:8-9. This beast has been previously identified in Revelation the twelfth chapter, as Satan, having the same seven heads and ten horns as the beast that was carrying the Woman Babylon to power for 1,260 years. Consequently, the early reformers were easily able to identify the Papacy as the first beast of Revelation the thirteenth chapter, and the antichrist of Bible prophecy, depicting her as that "blaspheming power who thinks themselves able to change God's times [God's time prophecies] and the law, [God's Holy Ten Commandment Law]. Daniel 7:25. However, it's important to recognize that in Revelation 17:8-9 the angel explicitly explains to the prophet that the lost can't recognize the beast.

The reason why the lost can't recognize the beast is that "the beast that you saw **was**, [existing] (for 1,260 years) and **was not**, [existing] (after the Papacy received its deadly wound) and is to ascend from the bottomless pit and shall go to perdition; and the dwellers upon the earth whose names have not been written in the Lamb's book of life from the foundation of the world, [representing the lost] will [be made to] marvel, the Greek word (θαυμάζω) translated as marvel having a [Strongs call number 2296] and its meaning [is to reconsider and begin to speculate upon the subject matter, thereby making them incapable] **of beholding** the beast. The Greek word (κόσμος) translated as "**beholding**" has a [**Strongs call number 991**] and by applying the correct definition **of the Greek word translated as beholding** means (the lost will speculate as to the identification of the beast and subsequently make the wrong determination as to who) the beast is that was carrying the Papacy to power because it was [carrying the Papacy to power for 1,260 years) and then it was not (after the Papacy received her deadly wound) however (the same beast) was still existing and would come again in the future. The beast will come again in the future as Satan's sixth head/king, which is the Rothschild banking cartel owners of the Federal Reserve Bank here in the United States, that will finance the Papacy's Counter-Reformation Theology so the lost accept it as the correct interpretation of the closing scenes of Earth's history. This universal acceptance of Dispensational Theology will pave the way for the formation of Satan's seventh head/king in the chronological progression of Revelation the 17th chapter, representing the United States of America under the control of Apostate Protestantism, which when completely formed in Protestant America shall remain only a little while. Revelation 17:10.

In harmony with the information just communicated in these Bible verses, "those whose names are not written in the Lamb's book of life" (representing the lost) the reason why they *have been made* to wonder [speculating upon and reconsidering] who the antichrist of Bible prophecy is (because) the mainline Protestant churches of this generation have adopted the Papacy's Counter-Reformation Theology, which is being collectively disguised today by [the Churches of Babylon] as Dispensationalism, originated by Evangelicalism, which is Satan's religion, depicted as the beast that ascends from the bottomless pit. The mainline Protestant Churches of this generation have become Dispensationalists; consequently, those who have accepted Dispensational Theology are "the lost" because they no longer recognize the Papacy as the antichrist of Bible prophecy specifically because their church leaders have accepted the Papacy's Counter-Reformation Theology while incorporating Satan's spirit of open rebellion against God's authority into their religious faith evidenced by the Papacy's daughter harlots declaring that God's Holy Ten Commandment Law is void primarily because any gospel requiring obedience to God's laws is a yoke of bondage since the same can't be kept. Daniel 7:25, Revelation 14:12.

In Revelation 14:8, the second angel announces the fall of Babylon, which includes the Protestant Reformation, and this announcement has been expressly confirmed by the Prophet Daniel, predicting that the mainline Protestant Churches would be rejected by the "Most High" at the conclusion of the 1,290 years. The reader needs to understand that the reason given for God's rejection of the mainline Protestant Churches is made very clear: they have been given over to the abomination of desolation; Daniel 12:11; consequently, the reader must realize that the complete fall of Protestantism will be accomplished by using the same fundamental deceptions employed by Satan to deceive a "host" of Catholic believers.

The deceptions of priestcraft remove the daily mediation of Jesus Christ to forgive sins, while the truth concerning His final work of mediation in the heavenly sanctuary is replaced by the false doctrines that create the illusion of salvation now and in the judgment immediately after confessing their sins to the priest and performing the penance assigned them in the confessional. This deception [the removal of Christ's daily and final work of mediation in the heavenly sanctuary] has been and will be more clearly established by the author of this book as "the abomination of desolation." Daniel 9:27, Daniel 11:31, Daniel 12:11, and Matthew 24:15.

The deceptions employed by Satan, depicted as "the beast that ascends from the bottomless pit," are honestly not that difficult to comprehend; however, believers have been deceived by their religious leaders and given over to a false gospel that tolerates their continued transgressions throughout the ages. The false doctrines tolerating continued transgressions are the earth's abominations that are making a host of believers spiritually desolate. The phrase the abomination of desolation appears in Daniel 9:27 and represents the Jewish Sanhedrin intentionally deceiving the children of Israel with the idea that constantly sacrificing animals assured them of their salvation now and in the judgment, causing them to reject Christ's daily and final work of mediation in the heavenly sanctuary.

The phrase also appears in Daniel 11:31 representing the Papal leaders intentionally misleading a host of Catholic believers with the deceptions of priestcraft; the phrase the abomination of desolation also appears in Daniel 12:11, representing Apostate Protestantism deceiving a host of mainline Protestant believers with the illusion of salvation simply by making a profession of faith in Christ's atoning blood, and the phrase is employed by Jesus Christ in Mathew 24:15, representing the pastors of God's last day remnant church deceiving God's very elect with the false doctrines that create the illusion of salvation now and in the judgment immediately after claiming justification by faith, which "the True Witness" specifically says to the angels [pastors] of the Church of Laodicea is not even remotely accurate. Revelation 3:14-22. The Bible is clear, the Sanhedrin, Apostate Protestantism, and the pastors of the Church of Laodicea have distorted the everlasting gospel into a license to sin *in the same way* the Papacy has through the deceptions of priestcraft. Therefore, the third woe represents the results of Satan's efforts to bring about the complete fall of the Protestant Reformation, which could only be made possible if Satan successfully incorporated his open rebellion against God's authority into the faith of the mainline Protestant churches of this generation evidenced by their persecution of anyone not adhering to their satanic doctrines.

In the year 538 A.D., at the commencement of the second woe, Justinian declared the Pope the temporal and spiritual ruler of the world and enforced that decree by order of the state; in that year, the Papacy was born, a church whose doctrines were enforced by order of the state. The prophecies explicitly state that Papal Rome would receive its deadly wound in the year 1798, after the conclusion of the Papacy's 1,260 years of oppression. After the 1,260 years concluded, the prophecy says the second woe has passed, representing the entirety of the Papacy's 1,260-year reign of blood, deception, and oppression, when she, through the power of the state, forced all nations to drink the wine of her fornicated doctrines under pain of death for over 1,000 years. When contemplating "the third woe," it's important to understand that the prophecy says it was during the Papacy's 1,260-year reign that she would "kill with the sword and with the flames of the stake by captivity and by plunder for some [1,000] years" all those who did not adhere to her satanic doctrines. Daniel 11:33. Consequently, the second woe represents the Papacy's entire 1,260-year reign of oppression, death, and the suppression of the scriptures.

After the fall of the Papacy, the prophet says the second woe has passed; behold, the third woe will come quickly. In this Bible verse, the phrase "*will come quickly*," represents the English translation of the Greek word ταχύ, defined in every Greek lexicon as "without unnecessary delay," having a Strong's call number 5035. As a result, the third woe represents more than just the actions of the Papacy's image during the closing scenes of Earth's history. After describing the events leading up to the fall of the Papacy in the year 1798, (Revelation 11:1-13), when God's two witnesses were finishing their testimony prophesying clothed in the Papacy's despotic oppression, the prophet says, "the second woe has passed; behold, the third woe *will come quickly*; therefore, the third woe represents the entirety of the events leading up to the formation of (the Papacy's image) in Protestant America, when, during the closing scenes of Earth's history, the Papacy's image would enforce the "mark of the beast" under pain of death, which the servant of the Lord says will come upon us with blazing speed. Revelation 11:14, Revelation 13:11-17.

To completely understand *the message for this time* the information contained in several other prophecies must be clearly understood, (Daniel 12:5-13) specifically the events taking place in Revelation 13:11-17, along with the correct chronological application of the two time periods referenced in Daniel 12:11-12, and the significance of the information contained in Revelation 11:14-19 with its specific relationship to the correct chronological application of Revelation 14:13 to *the message for this time*. The correct chronological application of Revelation 14:13 must be understood in harmony with "the Ark of the Covenant" being seen in heaven, which takes place when the seventh angel sounds his trumpet. The prophets clearly announce that when the seventh angel sounds his trumpet, the time had come for the dead to be judged by what was written in the books according to their works. Revelation 11:15-19. Therefore, the correct understanding of these prophecies identified in this chapter is essential for the following reasons.

The prophet says when "the Ark of the Covenant" was seen in heaven, the seventh angel had [past tense] sounded his trumpet, consequently, "the Mystery of God" as announced by His servants the prophets would soon be permanently withdrawn. Accordingly, the sounding of the seventh angel's trumpet means the second woe has passed and the third woe has commenced, along with the great tribulation, which is directly linked to the sealing of the 144,000 and the soon close of human probation. The close of human probation takes place at the conclusion of Christ's final work of mediation, which is the investigative judgment. Revelation14:6-7. The commencement of the third woe defined as the great tribulation takes place during the sealing of the 144,000 who are [grammatically linked by case agreement to "the great multitude of believers," who understand that no man is capable of numbering them with the saved except for Christ during His final work of mediation, which is the investigative judgment. Consequently, the answer to the question "who are these that have clothed themselves in white robes, and where did they come from" has already been grammatically answered, they are the 144,000 (who have spiritually prepared during the great tribulation) and can stand (past tense) in the presence of God without a mediator in the heavenly sanctuary, after the close of human probation. Therefore, _**the message for this time**_ includes the understanding that the great multitude of believers, who understand the "vision" of Daniel 8:14, represents all those who have died in the faith of the three angels' message, which takes place during the third woe, specifically commencing _**from the first proclamation of the judgment message to the close of human probation**_. Revelation 7:4, Revelation 14:9-11, Revelation 14:13.

To completely comprehend _**the message for this time**_ the correct understanding of the chronological application of Satan's sixth and seventh heads/kings of Revelation the seventeenth chapter must be obtained; the consequences associated with failure to recognize Satan's sixth and seventh heads/kings of Revelation the seventeenth chapter will absolutely cost millions of alleged believers their salvation. Revelation 17:8-9. The reader also needs to understand *the message for this time* clearly states that "the seven thunders" (Revelation 10:4) detail the events taking place during the third woe specifically when the third angel is making his announcement, resulting in there only being two groups of people living upon the earth when Christ returns, Revelation 6:17, those who have received "the mark of the beast" upon their foreheads [meaning it will be accepted willingly] or upon their right hand [meaning it will be forcefully accepted] this collective group is being contrasted with those who have received the seal of the living God [willingly] upon their foreheads. Revelation 14:1-5 and Revelation 14:9-11.

Therefore, it's important to understand while *the message for this time* includes the announcement "that the hour of His judgment has come" (Revelation 14:6-7) the reader needs to recognize that the first angel's message is grammatically linked to the second angel's message, announcing the fall of Babylon, specifically referencing the fallen spiritual condition of the Catholic Church, depicted as the Mother of Harlots in Revelation the seventeenth chapter, who has given birth to her daughter harlots, the mainline Protestant churches, and these designations are specifically applicable to the time when the first angel made his announcement; dictating that the third woe has commenced when the 144,000 are being sealed during the great tribulation. Revelation 7:14, Revelation 14:1-5, and Revelation 14:13.

As stated earlier, the specific evidence the second angel's message includes the explicit condemnation of the mainline Protestant churches is confirmed by the Prophet Daniel stating that at the conclusion of the 1,290 years of Daniel 12:11 (in the year 1828), the abomination that makes a host of believers spiritually desolate had been again universally re-established in all of Christendom confirmed by the fact that the same flattering gospel, advanced by the Papacy, (Daniel 11:31-33) had been permanently re-established as a doctrinal belief in all of the mainline Protestant churches, (Daniel 12:11) *and* that the abomination of desolation had been universally accepted by almost the entire protestant community. Therefore, the following is an **_important note to God's very elect_**, the protestant community had been previously for-warned years before that they were developing a name for being alive when they were actually spiritually dead in God's sight, **_Revelation 3:1_**, which is standard policy for the True Witness, **_Revelation 3:15-17_**, hence the Laodicean message is simply a repeat of the same warning given earlier to the early reformers.

As established earlier, the satanic plan of distorting the everlasting gospel into a license to sin is without question diabolical and is designed to be specifically accomplished by [subliminally] removing Christ as the believer's only mediator and judge; consequently, this "abomination" creates the illusion of salvation now and in the judgment and embodies the very foundation of the spiritual chicanery meticulously designed to make a host of believers spiritually "desolate." Therefore, the abomination that makes desolate represents the false doctrines employed by the Churches of Babylon that remove Christ as the believer's only mediator and judge, which is designed to create the illusion of salvation now and in the judgment simply by claiming justification by faith, which has been witnessed in every religious movement throughout the ages.

After receiving the explanation of the vision of Daniel 8:14, [in Daniel 9:24-27], the prophet says he understood that the "vision" of the 2,300-year prophecy of Daniel 8:14 pointed to the commencement of Christ's final work of mediation in the heavenly sanctuary; and that in the last days, a great multitude of believers would also understand the "vision" of Daniel 8:14 and make the proper spiritual preparation necessary to stand in the presence of God without a mediator after human probation closes. After making this statement in Daniel 10:1, the prophet permanently alters the phrase to represent that a host of unsuspecting believers [are being] (or) have been already given over to the abomination that makes them spiritually desolate throughout the ages, Daniel 9:27, Daniel 11:31, Daniel 12:11, Matthew 24:15-16, and Mark 13:14.

However, it's interesting to note that in Daniel 8:12, Daniel 9:27 and Daniel 11:31, the prophet assigns a grammatical nuance to the phrase depicting that the giving over of a host of believers to the Abomination of Desolation is the direct result of their religious leaders [intentionally] distorting the everlasting gospel into a license to sin. It's also important to understand that the second angel is specifically declaring that it's not only the "little horn" [power] that's performing the intentional act of giving a host of unsuspecting believers over to "the abomination of desolation," this spiritual chicanery is now being advanced by the mainline Protestant Churches at the time when the seventh angel sounds his trumpet; consequently, the reader needs to understand that the second angel is specifically addressing the fallen spiritual condition of the Catholic [*and*] the mainline Protestant Churches at the time the first angel makes his announcement.

It's important to understand the action of giving a host of believers over to the abomination of desolation is accomplished by removing "the daily" [mediation] of Christ to forgive sins while casting the truth concerning His final work of mediation to the ground by giving it to the fallen sons of men, the combination of which is what creates "the illusion of salvation now and in the judgment," that's always predicated upon the believer performing some outward legalistic action, like the sacrificing of animals, or confessing sins to a priest or simply by claiming justification by faith, and that this specific abomination "prospers by reason of a gospel that tolerates continued transgressions." Therefore, it's important to understand that ***the message for this time*** specifically states that when this "abomination" has been firmly re-established in all of Christendom thereby leaving a host of [alleged] believers, of all denominations, spiritually "desolate," the end will come quickly. Daniel 9:27, Jews, Daniel 11:31, Catholics, Daniel 12:11, mainline Protestants, and Mathew 24:15, Seventh-day Adventists.

The information just revealed is why the first angel's message is grammatically linked to the second angel's message announcing the fallen spiritual condition of the professed Christian churches at the time the seventh angel sounds his trumpet. Revelation 11:15. It's essential to understand why the first and the second angel's messages are grammatically linked to the third angel's message, which is yet to be completely fulfilled during the third woe. The third angel is proclaiming the most fearful warning message ever addressed to mortals, (Revelation 14:9-11) the condemnation against worshiping the beast and its image while receiving its mark upon your forehead or your right hand during the closing scenes of Earth's history. Consequently, to get the clearest understanding of "***the message for this time***" the combined information contained in several other prophecies must be clearly understood, revealing the reasons why Protestantism was rejected (Daniel 12:11) along with the specific way Christ is being removed as the believer's only mediator and judge by the false doctrines advanced by the pastors' of God's very elect, thereby creating the illusion of salvation while tolerating continued transgressions; all this information must be clearly understood because when Christ concludes His final work of mediation, which is the investigative judgment, human probation closes (Daniel 7:9-10) and all those who have ever claimed justification by faith from the first proclamation of the judgment message to the close of human probation must stand in the presence of God without a mediator through the outpouring of the seven last plagues.

Therefore, ***the message for this time*** reveals the events taking place during the seven thunders, which is significantly more than just announcing (the start of Christ's final work of mediation) Revelation 14:6-7 and exposing the obvious fallen spiritual condition of the professed Christian churches of this generation Revelation 14:8, ***the message for this time*** commands that the alleged believers of this generation must spiritually prepare for the time when church and state shall again unite, to force, "all, both small and great, both rich and poor, both free and slave," to worship the beast and its image, or be killed, which takes place during the closing scenes of Earth's history. Revelation 14:9-11.

The message for this time specifically addresses the events taking place during "the great tribulation," (Revelation 7:14) representing the time period of the third woe, when the image of the Papal beast [is being] formed in Protestant America [*and*] when it's been completely formed, the ten horns of Revelation the 17th chapter will give their authority over to Satan, the eighth beast, for one hour to war against the Lamb and His commandment-keeping people. Revelation 17:12-13. In Revelation 14:1-5, the prophet references the one hundred and forty-four thousand, having their Father's name written upon their forehead; and the angel says it is these who have not defiled themselves with women, (representing the false doctrines advanced by the Churches of Babylon) previously identified as the Catholic and the mainline Protestant Churches of this generation, which is the subject of the second angel's message. Therefore, because the 144,000 have heeded the second angel's message no lie is found in their mouths regarding the everlasting gospel; as a result, they have not been given over to the abomination of desolation by their respective church leaders, the Catholic priests, and the mainline Protestant pastors who have amalgamated into demon-possessed Satan worshipers evidenced by them babbling in unknown tongues and accepting Edward Irving's Evangelical dispensational theology.

The 144,000 are "the sealed," representing the great multitude of believers that understand the "vision" of Daniel 8:14; primarily because they have followed the Lamb wherever He goes in His final work of mediation, which is the investigative judgment, accordingly, they have developed spotless characters in this life making them capable of standing in the presence of God without a mediator during the outpouring of the seven last plagues. Revelation 7:9, Revelation 14:4-5. In Revelation the seventh chapter, the prophet specifically says the 144,000 are "the sealed," (Revelation 7:4) who are grammatically linked by case agreement to the great multitude of believers in Revelation 7:9 who are capable of standing in the presence of God without a mediator in the antitypical Heavenly Sanctuary after human probation closes. The great multitude of believers understand the "vision" of Daniel 8:14, points directly to the start of Christ's final work of mediation, specifically for "the cleansing of sins truly forgiven from the heavenly sanctuary," commencing at the conclusion of the 2,300 years of Daniel 8:14; therefore, since they have not defiled themselves with the dispensational theology, advanced by the harlots of the earth, they clearly understand that no man is capable of numbering them with the 144,000 except for Christ during His final work of mediation, which is the investigative judgment.

In Revelation the seventh chapter, the command is given not to hurt *the earth or any tree* until *the servants* of God have been possibly sealed upon their foreheads. Revelation 7:1-3. In Revelation 7:1-3, the Greek word σφραγίσωμεν, translated as sealed, appears in the subjunctive, which is the mood of possibility, meaning the individual sealing of God's professed people may or may not be successful during the great tribulation. However, after making this command the prophet says he heard the number sealed to be **144,000**; Revelation 7:4 and the Greek word ἐσφραγισμένων, translated as sealed appears as a masculine plural participle and as a verb in the perfect, passive tense in the genitive case, which dictates that the sealing of God's people has already been completed, [past tense]. Consequently, since the sealing of God's people has been completed, human probation has closed, evidenced by the fact that the prophet sees a great multitude of believers (Revelation 7:9), who are grammatically welded by case agreement to the sealed, standing before the throne and the Lamb clothed in white robes, holding palm branches in their hands.

This conclusion referenced above is further evidenced by the facts that in Revelation 7:9 the Greek words Μετὰ, and ταῦτα, translated respectively in the Bible verse, as "after this," appear respectively in the original language as, "a prepositional phrase in the *accusative case*" and as "a neutered demonstrative pronoun in the *accusative case*." As a result, the best possible translation of the Greek words Μετὰ, and ταῦτα, translated respectively [in] 100% of the Bibles investigated, as "after this," should actually be translated into the English language as, "in the middle of this," consequently, in Revelation 7:9, what the prophet is actually saying is that in "the midst of" the sealing of the 144,000, (Revelation 7:1-8), he sees a great multitude of believers who have already received the seal of the living God upon their foreheads [past tense] (Revelation 7:4); accordingly, they have been made capable of standing in the presence of God without a mediator after human probation closes.

In Revelation 7:9, the Greek word ἐστῶτες, translated as "**standing**," appears as "a masculine plural active verb, in the **nominative** case with a stem attached in the participle perfect active." In Revelation 7:9; the Greek word περιβεβλημένους, translated as "*clothed*" in the Bible verse appears in "the *accusative case* as a masculine plural active verb, with a stem attached in the participle perfect middle voice." This means in Revelation 7:9, the great multitude of believers have personally fought the good fight of faith and put to death "that which causes sin" in their lives while human probation lingered. Revelation 7:1-3. The 144,000 have by the Spirit personally clothed themselves in white robes and are therefore capable of standing in the presence of God without a mediator after human probation has closed. Revelation 7:4. In Revelation 7:9, the Greek word φοίνικες, translated as "**palm branches**" appears as "a masculine plural noun in **the nominative case**." In Revelation 7:9, the Greek words, ἐν, ταῖς, χερσὶν, αὐτῶν, translated as "in their hands" appear respectively "as a preposition in the dative case," then as "a plural feminine definite article in the dative case," then as "a feminine plural noun in the dative case" and finally as "a masculine plural personal noun in the genitive case."

After doing this brief investigation the best possible translation of Revelation 7:9 should read as follows; In the *midst of these things*, [meaning in the midst of the sealing of the 144,000 taking place in Revelation 7:1-3], the prophet beholds **a great multitude of believers** *which* to count *them* **not one** *of them* is capable of, made up of every nation and tribe and people and tongues, **they have been made capable of standing** before the throne and before the Lamb *having previously clothed themselves with white robes*; consequently, **they have palm branches** in their hands. After the prophet hears this information, the question is then asked who [are these] having clothed themselves in white robes, and what dispensation have they come from; the angel says these are they who have come out of the great tribulation; because they have previously washed their robes and made them white by the blood of the Lamb while human probation lingered. The great tribulation is grammatically linked to the sealing of the 144,000 in Revelation the seventh chapter, which takes place during the third woe when the third angel's message is being proclaimed to the world by God's very elect, therefore, chronologically speaking, the sealing of the 144,000 takes place between Revelation 6:13 and Revelation 6:14-16, when at the conclusion of the great tribulation the prophet says, "that the great day of God's wrath has come and who can stand before it," Revelation 6:17.

To completely understand, *the message for this time*, the question asked by the angel in Revelation 7:13-14, must be answered, "who are these that have previously clothed themselves in white robes and are capable of standing before the throne without a mediator in the heavenly sanctuary after human probation has closed." The answer specifically reveals what *the message for this time* actually is, they are the great multitude of believers, grammatically linked to the 144,000, who have received the seal of the living God upon their foreheads during the third woe, which is the great tribulation starting from the first proclamation of the judgment message to the close of human probation.

After revealing the answer to this question, it still might be unclear what the message for this time actually represents, consequently, it's important to note that the same 144,000 are referenced in Revelation 14:1-5, who are being [specifically depicted] as those who have not defiled themselves with women, representing the harlots of the earth, which is inclusive of the mainline Protestant and Evangelical Churches, whom the second angel of Revelation 14:8 is collectively condemning for deceiving the nations, in the same way, "the Mother of Harlots" has deceived the nations through (the deceptions of priestcraft). Daniel 8:23-25. Consequently, *the message for this time* specifically addresses how the antichrist of Bible prophecy is removing the daily mediation of Christ to forgive sins (Daniel 8:11-13), while casting the truth concerning His final work of mediation [for the cleansing of sins truly forgiven from the heavenly sanctuary], to the ground [specifically] by giving it to the fallen sons of men. Therefore, **the message for this time** is revealing that the results of the deceptions of priestcraft, along with the "flattering gospel" advanced by the Papacy's daughters' [is giving] a host of Catholic, mainline Protestant, and Evangelical believers over to the abomination of desolation resulting in the second angel's announcement to immediately separate yourselves from these apostate churches less you partake of their sins and receive the seven last plagues. Daniel 8:11-13, Daniel 11:31-33, Daniel 12:11, Revelation 14:8.

 After receiving the above explanation, it still might be unclear what the message for this time actually represents, consequently, the reader needs to recognize that the deceptions of priestcraft are particularly designed to create, "**the illusion of salvation now and in the judgment**" immediately after the Catholic confesses their sins to the priest and performs the penance assigned them in the confessional. **The message for this time** includes the second angel's warning alerting the unsuspecting multitudes not to be deceived by the same "flattering gospel" employed by the antichrist of Bible prophecy, who has "prospered by reason of a false gospel that tolerates continued transgressions." Daniel 8:11-12, Daniel 11:31-34. Accordingly, it's important to note that **the message for this time** reveals more than just (the start of Christ's final work of mediation), **it** depicts exactly how (the deceptions of priestcraft operate), which is the foundation of God's condemnation of Babylon and this condemnation includes the warning message to separate from the mainline Protestant and Evangelical Churches at the time the first angel makes his announcement. Revelation 14:8. In addition, **the third woe** is inclusive of all the actions taking place during the great tribulation (Revelation 10:4), meaning not just the formation of the Papacy's image in Protestant America during the closing scenes of earth's history, clearly establishing that the last days are coming upon us with blazing speed (Revelation 17:10) chronologically dictating that only God's people, who have previously received the seal of the living God upon their foreheads will be capable of standing in the presence of God without a mediator after human probation has closed, evidenced by the seven last plagues being poured out upon the worshipers of the beast and its image; therefore, establishing that ***the message for this time***, clearly dictates that the holiness of character possessed by the 144,000 is the holiness of character that all must possess if they expect to receive a positive verdict in the judgment. Revelation 14:4-5, Revelation 7:13-17.

The Bible is extremely clear on this point; in order to get the clearest understanding of ***the message for this time***, the antitypical heavenly sanctuary must be viewed as the very center of Christ's work on behalf of fallen humanity. To expound upon this understanding, the Bible specifically says the typical earthly sanctuary served as an example and shadow of Christ's daily and final work of mediation in the antitypical heavenly sanctuary. Hebrews 9:8-9. To clear up any ambiguity on this important subject, the Bible patently declares that the mediation of the earthly High Priest in the typical earthly sanctuary is a parable of Christ's daily and final work of mediation in the antitypical heavenly sanctuary. In the past dispensation, the mediation of the earthly high priest consisted of two separate and distinct divisions, the daily mediation, specifically for transferring sins to the typical earthly sanctuary through the animal sacrifices, and his final work of mediation, which was for "the cleansing of the sins transferred to the typical earthly sanctuary." The earthly high priest performed his final work of mediation once a year specifically for "the cleansing of the sins transferred to the typical earthly sanctuary," which took place only on "the day of atonement." Therefore, the earthly high priest's final work of mediation was symbolic of Christ's final work of mediation for the cleansing of sins transferred to the antitypical heavenly sanctuary, as announced by the prophet in Daniel 8:14, which is directly linked to the start of the investigative judgment in this dispensation; as announced by the prophets, Daniel 7:9-10, Malachi 3:1-5, and proclaimed by the first angel of Revelation the fourteenth chapter, Revelation 14:6-7, Revelation 11:15-19.

This chapter has established that after the second woe had passed (representing the termination of the Papacy's 1,260 years of oppression), Revelation 11:14, the prophet specifically states that in the days when the seventh angel was getting ready to sound his trumpet the mystery of God as announced by His servants the prophets, would be finished, representing human probation is about to close. In harmony with this understanding, it's important to recognize that simultaneously with the sounding of the seventh angel's trumpet (Revelation 11:15), "the Ark of the Covenant" was seen, Revelation 11:15-19, which is located in the second apartment of the antitypical heavenly sanctuary, clearly dictating that the antitypical "Day of Atonement" had commenced for "the cleansing of sins from the [heavenly] sanctuary" as announced by the prophet in Daniel 8:14, revealing the sobering fact that Christ has commenced with His final work of mediation, which is the investigative judgment. Revelation 10:5-7, Revelation 11:14-19, Revelation 14:6-7. Therefore the announcement in Revelation 11:15, that the seventh angel sounded his trumpet and the Ark of the Covenant was seen [in the temple of the tent of witnesses in heaven], clearly establishes that Christ had commenced His final work of mediation, [specifically] for the cleansing of sins truly forgiven from the heavenly sanctuary, which is directly linked to "the time when the dead are to be judged by those things written in the books according to their works" and not by what they profess to believe. Revelation 14:6-7, Daniel 7:9-10.

In the past dispensation, the first phase of the priest's work on behalf of sinners was "the daily mediation," which involved believers bringing their substitutional animal sacrifices to the outer court of the typical earthly sanctuary. These innocent [substitutional] animal sacrifices were symbolic of Christ's death upon Calvary's Cross, representing the innocent Lamb of God who was slain for our transgressions before the foundation of the universe. The animals slain in the outer court of the earthly sanctuary symbolically transferred the sins of repentant believers to the innocent sacrifices. After the sins of repentant believers were transferred to the innocent victim[s], which symbolically represents the justification believers receive in this dispensation when claiming Christ's substitutional sacrifice paid the penalty they rightfully deserve for their transgressions of the law; the officiating priest would then take the blood of the slain animals and sprinkle it seven times upon the curtain that separated the Holy Place from the Most Holy Place of the typical earthly sanctuary. The sprinkling of blood upon the curtain symbolically transferred the sins of the repentant believer to the mercy seat, which covered the Ark of the Covenant that was the depository for God's holy law, as originally proclaimed by the Most High Himself amid the thunder of Mt. Sinai. The Ark of the Covenant was located in the most holy place, the second apartment of the typical earthly sanctuary. The Bible says that God's holy law contained in the Ark of the Covenant will be the standard of righteousness used by Christ to evaluate our characters during His final work of mediation, which is the investigative judgment. The daily mediation of the earthly high priest continued [day] by [day] throughout the year; accordingly, the sins of repentant believers were transferred to the typical earthly sanctuary until the Day of Atonement, when the sins of repentant believers would be cleansed from the typical earthly sanctuary, which completed the sacrificial service of atoning for transgressions. Leviticus 16:1-34.

The second phase of the priestly ministration represents the High Priest's final work of mediation specifically for "the cleansing of sins from the earthly sanctuary." As established earlier, "the earthly sanctuary and its services" represents a parable of how the sins of repentant believers are transferred to the antitypical heavenly sanctuary and subsequently cleansed during the antitypical day of atonement. The mediation of the earthly high priest in both its phases where symbolic of Christ's daily mediation to forgive sins and His _final_ work of mediation for the cleansing of sins truly forgiven from the antitypical heavenly sanctuary. Hebrews 9:8-9. According to the typical earthly sanctuary, "the example and shadow of the antitypical heavenly sanctuary," (Hebrews 8:5-7) the cleansing of the antitypical heavenly sanctuary could take place only on the antitypical Day of Atonement, when Christ, our Great High Priest would enter the Most Holy Place, the second apartment of the antitypical heavenly sanctuary, specifically for the cleansing of the sins truly forgiven from the antitypical heavenly sanctuary.

As stated earlier, the Most Holy Place was the depository for the Ark of the Covenant, which contained God's Holy Ten Commandment Law that all of humanity has transgressed. The scriptures are extremely clear on this point, that God's holy law contained in the Ark of the Covenant, which is located in the most holy place, the second apartment of the antitypical heavenly sanctuary, will be the standard of righteousness used by Christ to evaluate our characters during His final work of mediation, which is the investigative judgment. Revelation 14:6-7, Daniel 7:9-10. In Revelation 11:15-19, the prophet says the investigative judgment started when the Ark of the Covenant was seen in the temple of the tent of witnesses in heaven. Therefore, according to the parable of the heavenly sanctuary, the declaration contained in Revelation 11:15-19 clearly dictates that when the seventh angel sounds his trumpet the antitypical Day of Atonement had commenced, specifically for "the cleansing of the sins truly forgiven from the antitypical heavenly sanctuary," representing that Christ had commenced with His final work of mediation, which is the investigative judgment.

When the prophet says then shall the sanctuary be cleansed (Daniel 8:14) this announcement establishes that Christ has commenced with His final work of mediation, for the cleansing of sins transferred to the heavenly sanctuary during the antitypical Day of Atonement, which the prophecy says is directly linked to the start of the investigative judgment. Consequently, in Revelation 11:15-19, the prophet's statement that the Ark of the Covenant was seen [in the temple of the tent of witnesses in heaven] gives clear evidence that Christ has commenced with His final work of mediation clearly dictating "that the time had come for the dead to be judged by what was written in the books according to their works. Revelation 11:18. Therefore, according to the prophets, Christ's final work of mediation unequivocally involves investigating the information recorded in the books, resulting in a work of judgment, when [respectively] the characters and lives of all those who have ever claimed "justification by faith" will be evaluated [by the True Witness] to determine if they have complied with the conditions of eternal life, by forming sanctified characters in harmony with God's holy law.

The scriptures are clear, if you have complied with the specific conditions of eternal life, by forming sanctified characters in harmony with God's holy law, your sins will be atoned for and subsequently blotted out of the Book of Records after the conclusion of the investigative judgment; accordingly, your names will be retained in the Lamb's book of life. It's important to keep in mind that the Holy Law of God, contained in "the Ark of the Covenant," located in the Most Holy Place, the second apartment of the antitypical heavenly sanctuary, will be the standard of righteousness used by Christ to evaluate our characters during His final work of mediation, which is the investigative judgment. Therefore, the cleansing of the heavenly sanctuary of the sins transferred there by faith represents Christ's final work of mediation, which is the investigative judgment, and according to the Prophet Daniel, Christ's final work of mediation commenced in the year 1844 (Daniel 8:14) immediately after the seventh angel sounded his trumpet evidenced by the Ark of the Covenant being seen by the prophet in heaven signaling to the wise that the sealing of God's people had commenced, which takes place during the great tribulation commencing with the start of the third woe detailing the events taking place during the seventh thunders as revealed in these Bible verses. Revelation 13:11-18, Revelation 14:1-13, Revelation 17:1-18, Daniel 11:40-45 and Daniel 12:1-13.

The correct understanding of the message for this time can only be realized when the significance of Christ moving from the Holy Place to the Most Holy Place is completely understood. The significance of Christ moving from the Holy Place of the heavenly sanctuary to the Most Holy Place of the heavenly sanctuary was to commence with His final work of mediation, specifically "for the cleansing of sins truly forgiven from the heavenly sanctuary" at the conclusion of the investigative judgment. It's essential to understand that Christ's final work of mediation for the cleansing of the heavenly sanctuary requires that an investigation be performed into the lives of all those who have ever claimed justification by faith, which takes place during the antitypical Day of Atonement and involves a work of judgment, Daniel 7:9-10, Revelation 11:15-19, Revelation 14:6-7 and according to the prophets, the investigative judgment started in the year 1844 at the conclusion of the 2,300 years of Daniel 8:14, as confirmed by the seventh angel sounding his trumpet. Revelation 11:15-19.

The Bible is very clear on this subject, the important truths concerning Christ's final work of mediation, which is the investigative judgment, are taught by the typical earthly sanctuary and its services. The believer's offering of the animal sacrifices represents a symbolic supplemental pleading acknowledging the believer's guilt for transgressing the law, however, [acknowledging the authority of the law] doesn't release the believer's obligation to render future obedience to God's holy law nor does it release them from the death penalty they rightfully deserve for originally transgressing God's holy law. According to the plea agreement the government of heaven is proffering fallen humanity, the admission of guilt doesn't represent a guarantee of a positive verdict in the judgment, and the Bible is very clear on the specific terms for receiving eternal life. The believer's acknowledgment of their guilt only transfers their sins to the antitypical heavenly sanctuary, the justified believer must subsequently access Christ's daily mediation for the specific purposes of putting to death "that which causes sin" in their lives before human probation closes if they expect to receive a positive verdict from Christ during His final work of mediation, which is the investigative judgment.

The important truths concerning Christ's final work of atoning for the sins of repentant believers, transferred to the heavenly sanctuary after claiming justification by faith, are taught by the earthly sanctuary and its services. In this dispensation the believer acknowledging their guilt for transgressing the law only transfers their sins to the heavenly sanctuary; the sins transferred to the antitypical heavenly sanctuary are recorded in the Book of Records and stand as a witness against the justified believer, which is the reason why the antitypical heavenly sanctuary is referred to as "the temple of the tent of witnesses in heaven." While it's essential to understand that Christ is our only mediator; it's just as important to fully comprehend that He is also our judge, Romans 8:33-34, who will condemn all those pleading "justification by faith" to their eternal destruction in the lake of fire if they fail to comply with the specific terms of salvation.

However, during the investigation, if it's determined your sins have been truly forgiven you will receive a positive verdict in the judgment, consequently, if truly forgiven, your sins will be atoned for and subsequently blotted out of the Book of Records at the conclusion of Christ's final work of mediation, which is the investigative judgment.

The earthly sanctuary and its services teach the important truths concerning the atonement; in the past dispensation, the sacrificing of animals acknowledged the sinners' guilt in transgression, while subsequently transferring their sins to the typical earthly sanctuary, where these sins would be cleansed from the earthly sanctuary on the Day of Atonement representing the conclusion of the high priest's final work of mediation in behalf of repentant believers. In like manner, in this dispensation, acknowledging your guilt in transgressing the law, only transfers your sins to the antitypical heavenly sanctuary, where they remain upon the books until the antitypical Day of Atonement, when your sins will be cleansed from the sanctuary during Christ's final work of mediation contingent upon you having put to death "that which causes sin" in your lives. Consequently, Christ's final work of mediation is to make atonement for the sins of repentant believers who have transferred their sins to the antitypical heavenly sanctuary after claiming justification by faith and have subsequently accessed His daily mediation in the hope of putting to death "that which causes sin" in their lives; accordingly, *the message for this time* clearly states (only the sins of repentant believers will be cleansed from the heavenly sanctuary at the conclusion of Christ's final work of mediation) and subsequently blotted out of the Book of Records at the conclusion of the investigative judgment.

The Apostle Paul specifically says that after Christ's death and resurrection, He commenced His "daily work of mediation" in the *holy place*, the first apartment of the new covenant heavenly sanctuary, to provide all those willing to access Him there with the real forgiveness of their sins in preparation for His final work of mediation, which is to make atonement for transgressions. It's essential to understand the important truths concerning the atonement are taught by the typical earthly sanctuary and its services, the biblical facts are overpowering, Christ will perform an investigation into the lives of all those who have ever claimed His death paid the penalty they rightfully deserve for their transgressions of God's holy law; and if it's determined that you have been truly forgiven of your sins, you will receive a positive verdict in the judgment, consequently, your sins will be atoned for and blotted out of the Book of Records at the conclusion of His final work of mediation, which is the investigative judgment. Therefore, the real forgiveness of sins *must* be obtained in preparation for Christ's final work of mediation, which is to make atonement for the sins truly forgiven at the conclusion of the investigative judgment.

The false doctrines employed by the antichrist of Bible prophecy are specifically designed to remove Christ as the believers' only mediator and judge, which according to the Prophet Daniel, is the abomination of desolation. If this term is correctly understood, [*by the author of this book*] what the Prophet Daniel is explaining in the following Bible verses should be extremely consistent, representing that a host of believers have been given over to the "abomination that makes them spiritually desolate" by their respective church leaders throughout the ages, [which is evidenced] by the phrase being consistently employed in several other Bible prophecies, Daniel 9:27, the Jews, Daniel 11:31, the Catholics, and Daniel 12:11 the mainline Protestant Churches. Consequently, when Christ employs the term in Matthew 24:15, what's specifically being communicated to God's very elect is that when you see the "abomination," which are **the false doctrines** removing Christ as the believers' only mediator and judge universally accepted by God's last day remnant people as a doctrinal belief, let the reader understand that human probation is about to close.

This prophecy is fulfilled when you see the [abomination], meaning false doctrines that remove Christ as our only mediator and judge that's specifically designed to make a host of His alleged last day remnant people spiritually [desolate], in the same way, the antichrist of Bible prophecy does through the deceptions of priestcraft, you can know for certain that human probation is about to close. Therefore, it's essential to understand the important truths concerning the atonement are taught by the typical earthly sanctuary and its services, an investigation will be performed into the lives of all those who have ever claimed "justification by faith" [thereby transferring their sins to the heavenly sanctuary where they are recorded in the books] and if it's determined that your sins have been truly forgiven, they will be atoned for, meaning blotted out of the Book of Records during Christ's final work of mediation, which is the investigative judgment; consequently, your names will be retained in the Lamb's book of life.

The prophecies of Daniel and Revelation are designed to alert the guilty inhabitants of the Earth that Christ's final work of mediation is being removed by the leading churches of this generation, Daniel 11:31, the Catholic Church, and Daniel 12:11, the mainline Protestant Churches. Accordingly, in Revelation 3:14-22, the "True Witness" is warning His last day remnant people their religious leaders have accepted the same fundamental doctrinal beliefs employed by the apostate churches of this generation, which creates only the illusion of salvation. The false doctrines that create "the illusion of salvation now and in the judgment" are being accepted by the pastors of God's last-day remnant people and will deceive, if possible, God's "very elect" during the closing scenes of Earth's history.

However, the 144,000 have not defiled themselves with these harlots, consequently, they are not deceived by the false doctrines advanced by the apostate churches of this dispensation (Revelation 14:4) [constituting Babylon as specifically condemned by the second angel], because the 144,000 follow the Lamb wherever He goes in His final work of mediation; as a result, they clearly understand that after Christ's death and subsequent resurrection, He commenced with His "daily work of mediation" in the *Holy Place*, the first apartment of the antitypical heavenly sanctuary to provide all those willing to access Him there with "the real forgiveness" of their sins. Therefore, because the 144,000 follow the Lamb wherever He goes in His final work of mediation, the 144,000 understand *the message for this time* clearly dictates that after believers claim "justification by faith," the real forgiveness of sins must be obtained in preparation for Christ's "final work of mediation," which is to atone for their transgressions by blotting them out of the Book of Records at the conclusion of the investigative judgment. Revelation 14:6-7, Daniel 7:9-10, 2 Corinthians 5:10.

<u>The message for this time</u> is spearheaded by the announcement that the investigative judgment has commenced, Revelation 14:6-7, which started in the year 1844, when Christ moved from the <u>Holy Place</u>, the first apartment of the heavenly sanctuary, to the <u>Most Holy Place</u>, the second apartment of the heavenly sanctuary. This change in Christ's ministration represents the commencement of His final work of mediation, "for the cleansing of sins truly forgiven from the antitypical heavenly sanctuary," which according to the prophets commenced in the year 1844 at the conclusion of the 2,300 years of Daniel 8:14, clearly establishing that the antitypical "Day of Atonement has commenced, "for the cleansing of sins truly forgiven from the heavenly sanctuary," representing Christ's final work of mediation, as announced by the first angel of Revelation the fourteenth chapter. Revelation 14:6-7.

The prophet <u>specifically</u> says when the Most Holy Place, the second apartment of "the temple of the tent of witnesses in heaven was opened," and the "Ark of the Covenant" was seen, "the time had come for the dead to be judged by what is <u>written</u> in the books according to their works" and not by what they profess to believe. It's clear, from this announcement, that the Bible teaches an accurate accounting of our deeds are being recorded in "the Book of Records," which is located in the antitypical heavenly sanctuary. Therefore, the opening of the second apartment of "the temple of the tent of witnesses in heaven," and the Ark of the Covenant was seen by the prophet, unquestionably points to the commencement of Christ's final work of mediation, when the sins of repentant believers will be cleansed from the heavenly sanctuary at the conclusion of Christ's final work of mediation and blotted out of the Book of Records at the conclusion of the investigative judgment. Daniel 8:14, Daniel 7:9-10.

The link between the cleansing of sins from the heavenly sanctuary, referred to in Daniel 8:14, and Christ's final work of mediation for the blotting out of sins truly forgiven from the Book of Records at the conclusion of the investigative judgment is absolutely undeniable. Revelation 11:15-19. The commencement of Christ's final work of mediation, which is the investigative judgment, started in the year 1844 at the conclusion of the 2,300 years of Daniel 8:14, which is gleaned from the prophecies of Daniel 7:9-10, Revelation 10:5-7, and Revelation 11:15-19 and constitutes *<u>the message for this time</u>*. Revelation 14:6-7. However, to get the clearest understanding of "*<u>the message for this time</u>*" the information contained in several other prophecies revealing the reasons why Protestantism was rejected (Daniel 12:11) along with the specific way Christ is being removed as the believer's only mediator and judge by the false doctrines advanced by the pastors' of God's last day remnant church, which creates the illusion of salvation now and in the judgment while subliminally tolerating continued transgressions; all of this information must be clearly understood because when Christ concludes His final work of mediation, human probation closes, (Daniel 7:9-10), and all those who have ever claimed justification by faith, from the first proclamation of the judgment message to the close of human probation, must be capable of standing in the presence of God without a mediator through the outpouring of the seven last plagues.

<u>The message for this time</u> reveals the events taking place during the seven thunders, which is the third woe and is significantly more than just announcing the start of Christ's final work of mediation while exposing the obvious spiritual confusion existing among the professed Christian churches of this generation. The <u>**underlining principles indigenous to the message for this time**</u> admonish believers to spiritually prepare for the time when church and state shall again unite, to force, "all, both small and great, both rich and poor, both free and slave," to worship the beast and its image or be slain, which the servant of the Lord says is coming upon us with blazing speed. The underlining principles indigenous to *<u>the message for this time</u>* admonish believers to spiritually prepare for the time when they must stand in the presence of God without a mediator when the

mark of the beast is scheduled to be strictly enforced by its image under pain of death; consequently, all those who have ever claimed "justification by faith," from the first proclamation of the judgment message to the close of human probation, must stand in the presence of God without a mediator during the outpouring of the seven last plagues. Therefore, the underlying principles indigenous to **_the message for this time_** make it clear that the holiness of character possessed by the 144,000 represents the holiness of character that all must have developed if they expect to receive a positive verdict in the judgment; and this understanding represents **_the real message for this time_** and not the peace and safety message sounding from the pulpits of the Catholic and the dispensational churches of this generation!

21

THIS IS OUR ASSURANCE – "THE LAODICEAN MESSAGE"

If someone goes by the literal application of the Greek word Λαοδικείᾳ, translated as Laodicea in Revelation 3:14, it represents the name of a city that existed along a trade route in Asia Minor during the early centuries. However, to understand the deeper morphological meaning of the Greek word Λαοδικείᾳ, translated as "Laodicea" in Revelation 3:14, and why Christ inspired its use in the context of Revelation 3:14-22, one must examine the origin of the Greek word Λαοδικείᾳ translated as "Laodicea" in Revelation 3:14-22. The Greek word translated as "Laodicea" is derived from two Greek words: λαός (meaning a "people") Strong's #2992, and δίκη (meaning a "principal decision") Strong's #1349. To give the literal interpretation of what Christ is saying in Revelation 3:17-18, the true meaning can be derived from the specific definitions of the two Greek words λαός (meaning a "people") Strong's #2992, and δίκη (meaning a "principal decision") Strong's #1349. The Laodiceans are people who trust in their ability to judge themselves. The Laodiceans decide spiritual matters for themselves at the exclusion of Christ, their alleged only mediator and judge. Therefore, they have removed and/or "taken away" Christ as their only mediator and judge, in the same way, the antichrist of Bible prophecy has through the deceptions of priestcraft. Daniel 8:11-12, Daniel 8:23-25, and Daniel 11:31.

In Revelation 3:17-18, Christ, the "True Witness," says the Laodiceans' self-serving opinion of their spiritual condition contradicts their actual spiritually desolated condition. The Laodiceans are people who feel assured of their salvation now and in the judgment simply because they find themselves in the unique position of acknowledging that Christ died for their transgressions of God's Holy Ten Commandment law, consequently, after making this legalistic bigoted determination they feel "rich and increased with goods and in need of nothing," **_not knowing_** their true spiritual condition is deplorable in God's sight. As a result of their confused understanding of reality, the "True Witness" introduces the solution to their problem. The relatively good news is that after stating their true spiritual condition is deplorable in God's sight, the True Witness goes on to say, "Behold, I stand at the door and knock" (Revelation 3:20), symbolizing Christ's willingness to work with anyone who humbly comes to Him for deliverance from the power of sin in their lives. The words of the "True Witness" are spoken directly to the pastors of the Church of Laodicea, addressing the over-inflated opinion they have of their spiritual condition. Therefore, if one goes by the literal application of the word Laodicea, it merely represents the name of a city that existed along a trade route in Asia Minor during the early centuries; however, the true spiritual morphology goes much deeper.

In Revelation 3:17-18, the counsel given to the pastors of the Church of Laodicea by the True Witness is that they are ignoring the message for this time. The Laodicean message states God's professed people think they are spiritually rich, "**_not knowing_**" they are spiritually impoverished, blind, and naked. The "True Witness" counsels them to purchase three things to fix their spiritually desolated condition. The first is gold refined by fire so they may be rich in faith. The second is white garments to clothe the shame of their nakedness. The third is eye salve so they can see the pastors promising them easy access to the gates of paradise are deceiving them with false doctrines creating the "illusion of salvation now and in the judgment." The mainline Protestant and Evangelical Churches of this generation are being condemned by the second angel for teaching that everyone can have "the assurance of salvation now and in the judgment" immediately after claiming Christ died for their transgressions of the law; conversely, the scriptures teach that no one is saved who is a transgressor of God's holy law, in this life, or the next. Romans 6:23, Hebrews 10:26-27, John 8:34-36.

Only through the precious blood of Christ, one equal with the law, could a perfect sacrifice for sin be provided. The good news of the Bible is Christ's death satisfied the legal demands of the law. As a result, believers can by faith plead that Christ's death paid the penalty they rightfully deserve for their transgressions of the law, and a hope of receiving eternal life is created predicated upon them complying with the specific conditions established before the foundation of the world for their redemption from "that which causes sin" in their lives. These conditions are by no means ambiguous as they are explicitly outlined in the scriptures. In Romans 5:1-2, the Apostle Paul says, "**Having been justified by faith**, we have peace *with God* through our Lord Jesus Christ, through Him we have obtained *access* by faith *to this grace* by which we stand, and we rejoice in the hope of sharing the glory of God." The Bible is clear on this subject, the glory of God is the sanctification of our characters (2 Corinthians 2:17-18), which is why the apostle says God has predestined all to be saved by the sanctification of our characters, (2 Thessalonians 2:13) and not simply by acknowledging Christ died for our transgressions of the law.

The foundation of the everlasting gospel is established upon Christ, one equal with the law, giving His life as a payment for our transgressions. However, this concept is repeated from the pulpits of Christendom more times than there are celestial bodies in the observable universe. Yet, liberals, as well as conservatives continue to transgress God's holy requirements because they have absolutely no idea why Christ felt compelled to provide fallen humanity with the opportunity to receive eternal life. To completely comprehend the true nature of the plan devised by the government of heaven for humanity's salvation, the extent of the sacrifice provided by the Most High to satisfy the legal demands of the law must be specifically quantified before a complete understanding of why the wages of sin **must** require the eternal eradication of the transgressor. Therefore, to properly establish the reasons why the wages of sin **must** require the eternal eradication of the transgressor becomes paramount before any intelligent speculation can be offered to define why the God of the universe would assume humanity, subject Himself to an ignominious death in order to provide a perfect sin offering, *__for the express purposes of establishing in the minds of all His created beings__* that **justice** and *mercy* stand at the foundation of the **law** and the government of heaven.

History is replete with incredible acts of heroism where people have given their lives to save others, however, the motive behind these acts of heroism is obvious, wars are fought to stop oppression, parents dying for their children, or someone diving in front of a car to save another. The motivation behind these acts of heroism is obvious and to a certain extent very easy to comprehend. The American Revolution was fought over taxation without representation while preventing the European central banksters from establishing a privately owned central bank in the United States controlling its banking system and subsequently issuing debt-laden U.S. currency, essentially reducing every U.S. citizen into slaves.

As a result, people were ready to give their lives to stop this type of satanic governmental oppression that existed in the old world. These examples, while obvious, don't even remotely apply to the magnitude linked to fallen humanity's specific situation; consequently, "when the time had fully come, God sent forth His son, born of woman, born under the law, to redeem those who are under the law so that they might receive adoption as sons" (Galatians 4:4-5). Accordingly, it was to provide eternal life to fallen humanity; however, understanding this concept must be all-encompassing considering the everlasting gospel does not negate the legal decree of God's holy law. To accomplish this all-encompassing consideration, the fallen and unfallen worlds must fully understand the malignant nature of rebellion and learn to abhor sin so that the terrible consequences associated with transgression can be voluntarily avoided for the stability of the universe. Therefore, this concept brings into question the specific reasons why the everlasting gospel has been proffered to fallen humanity, begging the question that must be asked, is the good news of the Bible, translated as the everlasting gospel, a license to sin?

The churches of Babylon believe the answer to this question is yes, consequently, their understanding of the plan devised for our salvation completely undermines God's plan of salvation, which is designed to free everyone claiming "justification by faith" from "that which causes sin" in their lives. Romans 8:12-13. Consequently, the good news of the Bible translated as the everlasting gospel, is not a license to sin. Romans 6:15-16. Therefore, to correctly answer this question, it's important to understand the malignant nature of sin, defined in the scriptures as the transgressions of the law, established that after Adam chose to transgress God's commands, his nature became fallen, and this fallen nature was passed on to his offspring from generation to generation, causing all of humanity to sin. Romans 3:23.

The Apostle Paul expounds upon the malignant nature of transgression in Romans 6:15-16; after establishing in Romans 6:12-14 that justified believers are not under the controlling power of their fallen nature if they are presently under the grace of Christ, he asks a rhetorical question in Romans 6:15, *"What then shall we, at some point in time, possibly continue to sin because we are not presently under the authority of the law, but rather fall under the authority of grace."* The apostle's response to this rhetorical question is extremely clear, *"You should not be found at any time wishing to rule out the consequences involved with that decision."* In Romans 6:16, he gives the reasons why he made such an emphatic determination, "You should already know that to whom you are yielding *yourselves as obedient* **slaves** you are **slaves** to that power you are obeying, either of sin which *leads to death* or obedience that leads *to life*. The consequences linked to even one transgression is slavery to your sinful propensities, consequently, you have become a slave to sin and cannot receive eternal life. John 8:34-35. Therefore, because the dispensational churches (Babylon) believe the everlasting gospel is a license to sin, they do not understand the plan devised for our salvation is designed to bring about the obedience of our faith, (Romans 1:5 and Romans 16:25-26) which requires believers put to death their fallen nature, defined as "that which causes sin" in our lives. See explanations already provided in Romans 6:1-4, Romans 6:14-23, Romans 7:1-6, Romans 7:13-20, Romans 7:21-25 and Romans 8:12-13.

The doctrinal beliefs of the Dispensational Church of this dispensation completely undermine the good news of the Bible, translated as the everlasting gospel; the biblical facts are obvious, no one can be saved who is a transgressor of God's holy law in this life or the next for the specific reasons already established in the first twenty chapters of this book. 1 John 2:3-4, and 1 John 3:9. The scriptures are clear on this very important subject, the everlasting gospel is by no means a license to sin. Romans 6:1-2 and Romans 6:12-14. To correctly understand the plan devised for our salvation, the everlasting gospel must be understood as the cure for the malignant effects of sin working death in our lives; specifically, when the legal decree of the law is strictly enforced after human probation closes and the stay of execution is lifted of the legal demands of God's holy law are strictly enforced. Therefore, it's important to understand that the wages of sin [still] require[s] the death of the transgressor in this dispensation. Romans 6:23, John 8:34-35.

The Bible says "When the time had fully come, God sent forth His son, born of woman, born under the law, to establish for all time that man as God created him could keep the law. However, it was not just to establish that God's law could be kept by all His created beings that the Most High set a moratorium on the legal decree of the law, it was to establish the malignant nature of sin turns humans into slaves of satanic agencies, capable of committing horrendous acts of evil, violence and sexual immorality. Therefore, in order to establish in the minds of the unfallen worlds, that the wages of sin **must** require the eternal eradication of transgressor[s], the Godhead determined, *for the good of the universe*, to allow the principles of Satan's rebellion to maturate in order to justify in the minds of all His created beings the legitimacy of the legal demands of the law.

The stay of execution of the legal decrees of the law is in place until human probation closes. The moratorium of the legal decree of the law has stayed the eradication of Satan's rebellion. The stay of the eradication of Satan's rebellion has allowed Christ to offer fallen humanity the right to come boldly to the throne of grace demanding deliverance from "that which causes sin" in their lives while human probation lingers. Consequently, the everlasting gospel provides a stay of execution of the legal decrees of the law. This stay of execution allows Christ the opportunity to condemn sin by the flesh. Romans 8:4. Therefore, after human probation closes Christ can destroy all those who have not put to death "that which causes sin" in their lives [along with the Devil and his evil angels in the lake of fire], which doesn't take place until after the 1,000-year millennium, thereby allowing all of God's created beings to investigate God's benevolence in how He has dealt with Satan's rebellion.

The result of Christ dying for our transgressions establishes for all time that the wages of sin must require the eternal death of the transgressor regardless of the circumstances surrounding fallen humanity's transgressions. At the final execution of Satan, his evil angels, and all those who have joined him in rebellion against the government of heaven, the fallen and unfallen worlds will be perfectly convinced that sin must be avoided at all costs because sin makes slaves of God's created beings causing them to commit horrendous acts of evil, violence and sexual immorality. These horrific acts are unpardonable after human probation closes. The good news of the Bible is that we no longer must be slaves of sin; Romans 7:25, after claiming "justification by faith" believers can access Christ's "daily mediation" and put to death "that which causes sin" in their lives. Consequently, they can become free moral agents before human probation closes. Romans 8:12-13. Therefore, the Catholic Church along with the mainline Protestant and Evangelical churches, are completely undermining the everlasting gospel by their false and satanic doctrines claiming that God's holy law can be changed or it's no longer binding upon believers today. Romans 6:1-2.

As stated, many times, "the daily mediation" of Christ to forgive sins is as essential to the plan for our salvation as was Christ's death upon Calvary's cross; because by His death, he gained the right to mediate for the real forgiveness of sins and determine in the judgment who is worthy to receive eternal life. The everlasting gospel gives Christ the right to condemn sin by the flesh, with the specific approval of the entire universe. The conditions to receive eternal life are by no means ambiguous, as they are explicitly outlined in the scriptures. In Romans 5:1-2, the Apostle Paul says, "Therefore, **having been justified by faith,** we have peace *with God* through our Lord Jesus Christ, through Him we have obtained *access* by faith *to this grace* by which we stand, and we rejoice in the hope of sharing the glory of God." The Bible is clear, the glory of God is the sanctification of our characters (2 Corinthians 2:17-18), which is why the apostle says God has predestined all to be saved through the sanctification of their characters, (2 Thessalonians 2:13) and not simply by acknowledging Christ died for their transgressions of the law.

The Bible specifically says salvation is conditional upon our sanctification, and if we comply with this condition, we will receive a positive verdict in the judgment. 1 Thessalonians 2:13 and John 3:36. However, in Revelation 3:15-17, there is revealed a complete discrepancy regarding the spirituality of God's very elect in the last days, and notwithstanding the malignant nature directly associated with transgression, the rejection of the Laodicean message by our religious leaders withholds from the unsuspecting multitudes of this generation "the keys to the kingdom of heaven." This "abomination," the conversion of the everlasting gospel into a license to sin, creates the carnal security witnessed in Christendom today, which causes professed believers to feel saved while they are actually spiritually "desolate" in God's sight. To break this carnal security, the True Witness pours forth the straight truth concerning "the true spiritual condition of His professed people." However, unlike the message given by the second angel to the dispensation churches of this dispensational, the "True Witness goes on to say to His professed people, "Behold, I stand at the door and knock, and if any man hears My voice and opens the door, I will come into him and sup with him and he with Me." Revelation 3:18-20.

The words spoken by the apostles and prophets demonstrate Christ's willingness to work with anyone willing to be delivered from the power of sin in their lives regardless of their denominational affiliation. However, the Laodicean message is extremely specific, it represents the present unholy spiritual condition of God's last-day remnant people, *as deplorable*; however, this *deplorable spiritual condition* is not their main problem. The **main problem** with God's last-day remnant people is they're **completely ignorant** that their true spiritual condition is deplorable in God's sight. The main reason for their confusion is that they trust in their ability to judge themselves at the exclusion of Christ, their alleged only mediator and judge. Therefore, if one goes by the literal application of the Greek word translated as Laodicean in Revelation 3:14, it merely represents the name of a city existing along a trade route in Asia Minor during the early centuries; however, its true spiritual meaning is much more profound; describing the deplorable spiritual conditions of those calling themselves God's last day remnant people.

Christ says, "Everyone who commits sin is a slave to sin." John 8:34. The servant of the Lord says "It is in this life that we are to separate sin from us, through faith in the atoning blood of Christ. Our precious Savior invites us to join ourselves to Him, to unite our weakness to His strength, our ignorance to His wisdom, and our unworthiness to His merits. God's providence is the school in which we are to learn the meekness and lowliness of Jesus. The Lord is ever setting before us, not the way we would choose, which seems easier and more pleasant to us, but the true aims of life. It rests with us to cooperate with the agencies that heaven employs in the work of conforming our characters to the divine model. None can neglect or defer this work but at the most fearful peril to their souls." The Great Controversy, Page 623, by, E.G., White. "There will be no future probation in which to prepare for eternity. It is in this life that we are to put on the robe of Christ's righteousness. This is our only opportunity to form characters for the home which Christ has made ready for those who obey His commandments." Christ's Object Lessons, Page 319, by E.G., White. There is no fence-sitting here; all are either "decided followers of Christ," or they are slaves of sin and "active servants of Satan." The Great Controversy, Page 508, by, E.G., White.

Today's church leaders are perverting the "new covenant promise of salvation" into a license to sin. The professed Christian Churches of this generation have made their own "covenant with death" while encouraging others to follow them into perdition. Revelation 17:8. The counterfeit gospel presented from the pulpits of Christendom today is an "abomination" to the Lord because it makes believers who are spiritually "desolate" feel rich and increased with goods and in need of nothing. Revelation 3:15-18. "Jesus died to save His people *from* their sins, and redemption in Christ means to cease the transgression of the law of God and to be free *from* every sin; no heart that is stirred with enmity against the law of God is in harmony with Christ, who suffered upon Calvary's Cross to vindicate and exalt the law before the universe." Faith and Works, Page 95, by, E.G., White. Therefore, "In order to receive help from Christ, we must realize our need. We must have a true knowledge of ourselves, [consequently], it is only he who knows himself to be a sinner that Christ can save." Eighth Testimonies for the Church, Page 316, by, E.G., White. Therefore, this last statement by E.G. White defines the problem with God's professed people, the real problem with God's people is not that they are wretched, pitiable, poor, blind, and naked in His sight, it's that they don't know their true spiritual condition is deplorable in God's sight, consequently, they last the motivation to correct the problem primarily because the pastors are deceiving them with false doctrines that create the illusion of salvation now and in the judgment simply by making a profession of faith in Christ's atoning blood.

The everlasting gospel clearly states Christ came to save His people *from* their sins; consequently, redemption in Christ means to cease "*from*" the transgressions of God's holy law. Matthew 1:21. Christ says, "Everyone who commits sin is a slave to sin," as a result, if we are to receive eternal life, "that which causes sin" in our lives must be put to death before the gospel invitation closes. In the message to the Laodiceans, the True Witness pours forth the straight truth concerning the real spiritual condition of His professed commandment-keeping people. The Laodiceans do not know their true spiritual condition is deplorable in God's sight. As a result, the "True Witness" is commanding the pastors of the Church of Laodicea, to "Write these things," because the people are ignorant their true spiritual condition is deplorable in His sight. Consequently, being completely ignorant of their true spiritual condition they declare themselves saved, and "assured of their salvation now and in the judgment," rich and increased with goods and in need of nothing, completely ignorant that they are actually "wretched, pitiable, poor, blind and naked" in God's sight.

As a result of accepting the false doctrines advanced by their pastors, the Laodiceans are ignorant of their true spiritual condition, and they are trusting in their ability to judge themselves apart from the law and at the exclusion of Christ, their alleged only mediator and judge. Revelation 3:17-18. The message for this time clearly states that Christ came to save His people *from* their sins; conversely, the Laodicean message states God's professed "commandment-keeping people" are ignorant of this sobering fact that redemption in Christ means to cease "*from*" the transgressions of God's holy law before human probation closes when the legal decree of the law is lifted and they must stand in the presence of God without a mediator in the Heavenly Sanctuary pleading for the forgiveness of their sins. Revelation 7:4, Revelation 7:9, Revelation 14:1-13. Therefore, if one goes by the literal application of the Greek word translated as Laodicea, it represents merely the name of a city that existed along a trade route in Asia Minor during the early centuries; however, its spiritual meaning goes much deeper as defined by the "True Witness" in Revelation 3:17-18.

22

THE HEALTH MESSAGE IS THE RIGHT ARM OF THE THREE ANGEL'S MESSAGE

The three angels' message of Revelation the fourteenth chapter, commands the guilty inhabitants of the earth to "*fear* God [meaning to be afraid] (Strong's call number 5399) and give *glory* to Him [meaning to render an opinion] (Strong's call number 1391) for the hour of His judgment has come and to worship Him who made the heavens and the earth and the sea and the fountains of water." Revelation 14:6-7. According to Thayer's Bible dictionary, the Greek word δόξαν translated as "**glory**" in Revelation 14:6-7 has a wide range of meanings; to render an opinion or give an estimation of the worth of something is the foundation of the meaning[s] of the Greek word δόξαν translated as "**glory**" in Revelation 14:7. The only way true worship can be given to our Creator is by obeying His laws, which includes His health laws. 1 Corinthians 3:16, 1 Corinthians 6:19-20, 1 Corinthians 9:27, 1 Corinthians 10:31, 1 Corinthians 11:29, and Revelation 14:12. Therefore, "obedience to the laws of health should be made a matter of earnest study, for willing ignorance on this subject is sin. Each one should feel a personal obligation to carry out the laws of healthful living." See The Great Controversy by E.G., White, Page 392.

The first angel commands the guilty inhabitants of the earth to fear God and give glory to Him, who made the heavens and the earth and worship Him, who made the sea and the fountains of water because the hour of His judgment has come. Consequently, we are commanded to properly investigate how we eat and drink since it's a form of the worship we are commanded to render Him who made the heavens and the earth. 1 Corinthians 11:29, Romans 12:1-2. Notwithstanding the command to worship God (Revelation 14:6-7), millions of allegedly "born again" believers are living in wanton disregard for the laws of health, which is considered a grievous transgression. 1 Corinthians 3:16-17. In addition, 1 Corinthians 11:29 commands us to research everything we eat and drink, or we will be condemned in the judgment. The Bible verse reads like this in the RSV; "For anyone who eats and drinks without discerning the body eats and drinks judgment upon himself." The Greek word διακρίνω translated as "discerning" in 1 Corinthians 11:29 (RSV) (Strong's call number 1252) means to investigate something.

This communication is extremely clear; as alleged followers of Jesus Christ, we are commanded to research the quality of food and drink we consume to keep our body and mind in top physical, mental, and spiritual condition. Consequently, we must be health reformers if we expect to receive a positive verdict in the judgment. However, only a small percentage of the professed followers of Jesus Christ are health reformers. As a result of the rejection of God's health laws, the ignorant multitudes of this generation are causing their physical, mental, and spiritual destruction while claiming to have "the assurance of salvation now and in the judgment" simply because they find themselves in the unique position of believing that a man named Jesus Christ died two thousand years ago for their transgressions of the law.

Despite the command to fear God and give Glory to Him who made the heavens and the earth because the hour of His judgment has come, an estimated 39 million people living in the United States (12% of the population) have been diagnosed with diabetes and about 95% have type 2 diabetes. The U.S. Center for Disease Control and

Prevention (CDC) has published several articles on the cause of type two diabetes; notwithstanding that 12% of the population has been diagnosed with diabetes, it's estimated that one in five people don't even know they have diabetes, which represents an additional 20% of the population. A report issued in 2005 by the (CDC) stated that type two diabetes has doubled since 1990, and if the present eating habits of Americans continue, they expect this trend to spiral upward at the same rate every ten years. Consequently, the (CDC) has now characterized type 2 diabetes as an epidemic. Therefore, this chapter is designed to establish that if you are experiencing health-related problems caused by your poor diet and are taking prescription medication to cure the problem rather than following God's original diet [plant-based], you're going to be destroyed in the lake of fire, which is the second death.

The information you receive from the United States regulatory agencies about the cause of type two diabetes is a total prevarication and a complete scam. The lies advanced by the healthcare industry are being collaborated by the misinformation coming from the (CDC), the U.S. Center for Disease Control and Prevention! This deadly and debilitating disease has traditionally been considered a disease occurring only in older adults; however, type 2 diabetes is rapidly increasing among middle-aged people and now even among children. In direct contradiction to the misinformation coming from the CDC, the dramatic increase in type 2 diabetes witnessed over the last 30 years has very little to do with the consumption of processed sugar. The sudden increase in type 2 diabetes is primarily due to the high intake of fatty bloody animal flesh and dairy products. In addition, the consumption of highly processed fatty "fast food" is one of the main culprits leading to the sudden rise in obesity resulting from poor dietary practices and the complete lack of exercise.

In North America, between 90–95% of all cases of diabetes are type 2, and those infected with this disease, called the "silent killer," are expected to triple over the next ten years. If left untreated, type 2 diabetes is a chronic, progressive condition that causes blindness, male impotence, loss of motor skills, loss of memory, and even results in the amputation of limbs, arms, legs, and other body parts. The pervasive effects this "silent killer" is having on our bodies are the direct result of a high-fat diet resulting in the lack of proper blood flow to all parts of the body, including our brains. This "silent killer" causes atherosclerosis, a disease affecting almost 75% of Americans, and is causing the premature death of millions. Atherosclerosis is a disease affecting the arterial walls of the body that become blocked due to the build-up of fatty materials called plaque, which is found in the blood system of those with high-fat diets rich in bloody fatty animal flesh and dairy products. Researchers have proven that environmental factors (almost certainly diet, weight, and lack of exercise) are the main culprits in the development of atherosclerosis, leading to type 2 diabetes. Therefore, despite the harmful physical effects this "silent killer" is having on the population, blindness, impotence, and the loss of limbs, the harmful spiritual effects poor dietary practices are having on the unsuspecting multitudes of this generation will be one of the main factors considered in the judgment, because its suicide. 1 Corinthians 11:29.

If the lack of proper blood flow to our eyes, the male penis, and our outer extremities (arms and legs) is causing these body parts to malfunction resulting in amputations and/or these body parts are rendered non-functional, what do you think these "silent killers" are doing to your brains. The frontal lobes of the brain (located just behind the forehead) contain the smallest blood vessels in the entire human capillary system. The capillaries taking blood to our eyes, and the male penis are the second and third smallest veins in the human body. However, they do not remotely compare to the smallness in size of the veins taking blood to the frontal lobes of the human brain. The veins carrying blood to the frontal lobes of the human brain are so small that only one red blood cell can pass through at a time.

The negative consequences linked to a high-fat diet [elevated in animal fats] result in high cholesterol, which causes atherosclerosis leading to type-2 diabetes. As a result, carnivores eventually develop erectile dysfunction of the brain. Why? Because these "silent killers" prohibit blood flow to the frontal lobes of the human brain. The lack of blood flow to the brain causes the premature spiritual death of a person far in advance of their actual physical death from alleged natural causes. If you don't have proper blood flow, you will certainly develop erectile dysfunction of the brain, and your spiritual life will die. However, human beings with erectile dysfunction of the brain can still function normally in society when performing their jobs, driving a car, hitting a baseball, or other less complex functions (eating) and/or even more complex functions, like brain surgery or programming a computer. Nevertheless, for all intents and purposes, those violating God's health laws become spiritually deceased far in advance of their actual physical death due to developing erectile dysfunction of their brains.

The Bible clearly states we are living in the sealing time, when God's people are receiving the seal of God upon their foreheads, meaning the frontal lobes of their brains. Revelation 7:1-13 and Revelation 14:1-5. It's important to understand what we eat, and drink is a form of the worship believers are commanded to render to the Creator of the universe. Revelation 14:6-7, Romans 12:1-2. According to the first angel's message, we are commanded to worship God; however, how can anyone claim to be worshiping God while they are violating God's health laws? 1 Corinthians 3:16-17, 1 Corinthians 6:19, Galatians 5:22. The Apostle Paul says those who are arrogantly violating the laws of health, eating, and drinking as they please, while they hypocritically "claim to have the assurance of salvation," will be condemned in the judgment. 1 Corinthians 11:29-30. The health message is infinitely more connected with our ability to worship God than the unsuspecting multitudes realize. The rejection of the health message by our religious leaders is the primary reason why millions have rejected the message for this time (Romans 12:1). Consequently, the clear facts are what affects the body is having a deleterious effect on our minds. Therefore, the sealed (Revelation 7:9) will be those "doing all to the glory of" God, which includes what they put into their bodies. 1 Corinthians 10:31.

The overpowering information found in the scriptures regarding health reform is extremely clear; if you are doing anything detrimental to your body and mind, you will be destroyed in the lake of fire, which is the second death. 1 Corinthians 3:16-17. In direct opposition to this understanding, it's estimated that 82% of the population is either overweight or obese. The CDC reports that 78% of those hospitalized for COVID-19 were either overweight or obese, so the immune-compromised are at risk, not the unvaccinated. If you eat and drink in harmony with God's original diet [plant-based], the promise is God will protect you from disease. Exodus 15:26 and Deuteronomy 7:15. Well, it's obvious that advice isn't being followed because 75% of the population is on some type of prescription medication due to their poor diets and a host of other extremely unhealthy lifestyle choices. At the same time, 200 million people just got the COVID-19 vaccine which is a DNA-altering untested mRNA message their brains didn't order. Overpowering information [case studies] exists in the alleged healthcare community establishes that the COVID-19 "death jab" causes antibody-dependent enhancement [ADE], which the CDC, the NIH, and DHHS all clearly understand is deadly. In addition, one in thirty-two children is now autistic, primarily because they have received 66 vaccinations by the time they are four years old. The facts are autism spiked 600% in every state of the union when the CDC increased the number of vaccines children are required to receive from (29) twenty-nine to (66) sixty-six. This information is why the use of drugs and vaccines to protect you from disease is expressly condemned by the Bible as "the works of the flesh," therefore, the apostle says those who do these things [take drugs and vaccines to protect themselves from diseases] shall not inherit eternal life. Galatians 5:19-21.

In Galatians 5:19-21, the apostle lists "the works of the flesh" which all of Adam's descendants are performing because they have received a fallen defective human nature __*which they inherited*__ [without their consent] (at birth) from their earthly parents. The apostle lists the works of the flesh, so there is no confusion about your spiritual condition. The apostle starts by condemning "sexual immorality." The

Greek word πορνεία has a Strong's call number 4202; the best possible translation is a promiscuous lifestyle which is extremely unhealthy. The facts are if a woman has had five sexual partners, she will develop Chlamydia which is one of the most common sexually transmitted diseases (STD) in the United States, with over 1.4 million new cases reported each year. Chlamydia causes a marked reduction in **tryptophan** which decreases serotonin (5-HT) in the brain resulting in depression, insomnia, and fits of rage. If a woman has had ten sexual partners, she is 100% more likely to develop cancer, infertility, and other health-destroying diseases. The reason for this is fascinating; every time you have sexual intercourse with someone, you are trading DNA which causes oxidative stress. Oxidative stress causes damage to the cells at the molecular level; this causes the release of free radicals. Simply put, free radicals are oxygen molecules that are made up of atoms with an uneven number of electrons. These atoms with an uneven number of electrons destabilize cells at the molecular level, which causes premature aging and cancer.

The apostle goes on to condemn the Greek word ἀκαθαρσία translated as "impurity," the Strong's call number is 167; the best possible translation is "uncleanness," which causes diseases, open sores like leprosy, caused by disregarding personal hygiene. The next in line is the apostle's denunciation of the Greek word ἀσέλγεια which is translated in a variety of different ways; the RSV translates it as licentiousness. The Strong's call number is 766; the best possible translation is unbridled control, reckless behavior, and outrageous conduct.

In today's society, licentious behavior would be defined as partying all night and all weekend, frequenting nightclubs regularly, having one-night stands, and having multiple sexual partners simultaneously. In Galatians 5:20, the apostle next lists the Greek word εἰδωλολατρία translated as "idolatry," the Strong's call number is 1495, and the best translation is "idolatry," meaning the worship of images. Therefore, it's essential to understand in Galatians 5:19-21, the apostle is listing "the works of the flesh" and says all of Adam's descendants are performing because they have received a fallen defective human nature *which they inherited* (at birth) [without their consent] from their earthly parents.

In Galatians 5:20, the apostle continues listing "the works of the flesh" and says if performed, *you shall not inherit the kingdom of heaven*. The apostle specifically condemns "sorcery," which is the Greek word φαρμακεία, and is translated as such 100% of the time in every Bible investigated. The Strong's call number is 5331, and the best possible translation of the word is pharmaceuticals, meaning prescription medications, and poisonous drugs. Even though the *first* definition of the Greek word φαρμακεία, is pharmaceuticals, "toxic poisonous drugs," [meaning prescription medications], *and*, according to Strong's concordance the translation of "sorcery" *represents the third* morphological meaning, consequently, the translation as "sorcery" is by no means grammatically justifiable *because* it is violating case agreement, [*regardless of these facts*] the translators employ the third morphological meaning of the Greek word φαρμακεία [pronounced as pharmakeia] as sorcery 100% of the time in every Bible investigated.

The first definition of any Greek word *must be employed* unless the case agreement justifies employing its second or third morphological meaning in the Bible verse. The Greek word φαρμακεία [pronounced pharmakeia] is also employed by the Prophet John in Revelation 18:23 and is irresponsibly translated as "sorcery," representing the third morphological meaning. Again, the first definition of any Greek word *must be employed* unless the case agreement justifies employing its second or third morphological meaning in the Bible verse. The context of Revelation 18:23 dictates that the unsuspecting multitudes are being deceived by the great men of the earth [who have become wealthy] through the sale of pharmaceuticals and government-mandated vaccines to the unsuspecting multitudes of this generation. The first definition of the Greek word φαρμακεία is pharmaceuticals, meaning prescription medications, "poisonous drugs," which are being deceptively sold to the unsuspecting multitudes by the healthcare industry; consequently, without case agreement justifying employing its second or third morphological meaning, the only possible translation of the Greek word φαρμακεία, appearing in Revelation 18:23, and Galatians 5:20 that's grammatically acceptable is pharmakeia, meaning drugs, prescription medications, and deadly vaccines. Therefore, it's important to understand in Galatians 5:19-21, the apostle lists "the works of the flesh" and says all of Adam's descendants are performing because they have received a fallen defective human nature **_which they inherited_** (at birth) [without their consent] from their earthly parents.

In Revelation 18:23, the first definition of the Greek word φαρμακεία is pharmaceuticals, "meaning prescription medication and vaccines." Consequently, the only possible justifiable translation of the Greek word φαρμακεία that's grammatically acceptable is [pharmakeia], meaning drugs, "pharmaceuticals," prescription medications, and DNA altering vaccines. The translation of the Greek word φαρμακεία as "sorcery" in Revelation 18:23 and Galatians 5:20 employs the third morphological meaning, which completely violates the case agreement of the Greek word φαρμακεία translated as "sorcery" 100% of the time in the above referenced Bible verses.

The facts are if you are getting vaccinated, you are being injected with genetic material that's man-made called [cDNA], which stands for "complementary DNA" (it's a man-made synthesized genetic material having a single-strand template because it's been reversed transcribed. This reverse transcription changes your [God-given genetic material, which has double-sided DNA templates]; this is extremely dangerous, and you are committing blasphemy for the following reasons. If you're taking prescription medication to cure diseases caused by your unhealthy eating habits, rather than changing your poor diet, you will be destroyed in the lake of fire, which is the second death. If you get vaccinated to protect yourself from disease [rather than following God's health laws], you are committing "the deeds of the flesh," and the apostle says you will be destroyed in the lake of fire, which is the second death. Therefore, the facts are clear; the apostle condemns the use of prescription medication and vaccines to cure and/or prevent diseases. This fact can only be ignored; it cannot be disagreed with because it's been proven 100% accurate in the following practical application[s].

The healthcare industry is doing a fantastic job of making the pharmaceutical companies astronomical profits. In the United States, 75% of those over 35 are on some type of prescription medication. This last comment must be understood, in light of the fact that prescription medications, only mask symptoms; they cure no one of diseases. In addition, all pharmaceuticals, meaning prescription medications, defined in Strong's as poisonous drugs, have toxic, harmful side effects, which require doctors to prescribe additional poisonous drugs to cure [mask] these symptoms. It's a never-ending, extremely toxic, and very profitable mad cycle; as a result, medical malpractice is now the third leading cause of death in the United States, while each year, almost two trillion dollars is spent on prescription medications and extremely expensive vaccines. These toxic drugs only mask symptoms while they cure no one of disease, and vaccines protect no one from disease; they actually cause cancer and a host of ancillary lethal side effects.

In addition to [the alleged great job] the healthcare industry is doing to fight disease and keep the population healthy, the latest statistics on heart disease state that 50% of all adults presently have some form of heart disease, while 40% will develop cancer at some point in their lifetime. An interesting point to consider is that treating cancer with expensive toxic drugs is a losing proposition evidenced by it producing a 97% mortality rate: conversely, it's extremely profitable, making the pharmaceutical companies and the healthcare industry almost one million dollars per cancer patient. It's obvious the healthcare industry is not in business to cure anyone of disease; they are in business to make the pharmaceutical companies INCREDIBLE profits, which they make by selling toxic drugs that often produce adverse side effects, rather than cure diseases. Therefore, the Bible expressly condemns prescription medications and vaccines, defined in the Strong's concordance as ingesting poisonous drugs to cure an overweight, obese population of disease and/or vaccinate the same to protect them from man-made deadly pathogens released into society by government-controlled agencies. Therefore, if you are taking drugs to cure yourself of a health-related problem caused by your poor eating habits, along with your irresponsible lifestyle choices and/or you're getting vaccinated to protect yourself from man-made pathogens, rather than changing your poor diet to plant-based and exercising regularly the apostle says you shall not inherit the kingdom of heaven. Galatians 5:21.

In Galatians 5:20, the apostle lists several other transgressions that are condemned as "the works of the flesh" and emphatically states if you do these things, you shall not inherit the kingdom of heaven. The Greek word ἔχθραι translated as "enmity," having a Strong's call number of 2189, with the best possible translation being enmity, hostility, and alienation. Addressing the same, it's essential to understand this enmity, hostility, and alienation is directed toward God since the root of the Greek word ἔχθραι is derived from the Greek adjective ἔχθρᾳ translated as enemies in Luke 23:12 and appears as the root of the Greek word ἔχθραν translated respectively as enmity and hostility in Ephesians 2:14-16. The next "works of the flesh" condemned by the apostle is defined as the Greek word ἔρις translated as "strife," having a Strong's call number of 2054, with the best possible translation being a readiness to quarrel (having a contentious spirit), affection for dispute.

The next transgression identified as "the works of the flesh," condemned by the apostle in Galatians 5:20, is the Greek word ζῆλος translated as "jealousy" having a Strong's call number of 2205 with the best possible translation being "burning emotions" which can be positive or negative. The negative connotation of the Greek word ζῆλος is obviously what's being condemned in Galatians 5:20 hence the translation of "jealousy" representing a kind of misguided zeal like the Jews had towards Christ, exemplified by their persecution of Christians. The next transgression classified by the apostle in Galatians 5:20 as "the works of the flesh" is the Greek word θυμοί translated as "anger," having a Strong's call number of 2372 with the best possible translation being "anger" in an evil way, not righteous indignation.

The next transgression specified by the apostle in Galatians 5:20 as "the works of the flesh" is the Greek word ἐριθεῖαι translated as "selfishness," having a Strong's call number of 2052, with the best possible translation being "the seeking of followers," which is very self-explanatory. Acts 20:30. The next transgression specified by the apostle in Galatians 5:20 as "the works of the flesh" is the Greek word διχοστασίαι translated as "dissension," having a Strong's call number of 1370 with the best possible translation being the use of opposing concepts that create divisions wrongly separating people into pointless factions. The next transgression identified by the apostle in Galatians 5:20 as "the works of the flesh" is the Greek word αἱρέσεις translated as "party spirits," having a Strong's call number of 139 with the best possible translation being a self-chosen opinion, creating a religious or philosophical sect that results in discord or contention concerning the truth about Christianity.

The next transgression specified by the apostle as "the works of the flesh" appears in Galatians 5:21 and is the Greek word φθόνοι translated as "envy," having a Strong's call number 5355 with the best possible translation being "displeasure at another's good fortune." The next transgression specified by the apostle in Galatians 5:21 as "the works of the flesh" is the Greek word μέθαι translated as "drunkenness," having a Strong's call number 3178 with the best possible translation being, "drinking alcohol," which is a total immune killer and carcinogen. The adverse effects of alcohol are too numerous to number; it causes high blood pressure, heart disease, stroke, liver disease, and severe digestive problems. Alcohol consumption causes breast, mouth, and throat cancer, esophagus, voice box, colon, and rectal cancer. It wreaks havoc on your immune system, dramatically increasing your odds of getting sick and causing learning disabilities and memory-loss problems. It also causes dementia, which, when diagnosed has proven to be a death sentence within a short period of time. Consequently, the Bible expressly condemns alcohol, and those who indulge in this pernicious sin shall not receive eternal life.

The next transgression specified by the apostle in Galatians 5:21 as "the works of the flesh" is the Greek word κῶμοι having a Strong's call number of 2970 with the best possible translation being a riotous party (drunken feast) which hosts unbridled sexual immorality. The apostle says those that do these things [identified as the desires of the flesh] shall not inherit the kingdom of heaven. Here the apostle is employing a double negative with a subjunctive kicker; this means he's denying the idea of the possibility of the fact existing that those that do these things [the deeds of the flesh] shall enter the kingdom of heaven. Therefore, if you are overweight or obese and/or doing drugs to cure a health-related problem caused by the consumption of dead animals, drinking alcohol, or eating other harmful products like processed food and drinks, eating candy, cakes, or ice cream rather than changing your poor eating habits, the apostle says you will be destroyed with the Devil and his evil angels in the lake of fire, which is the second death.

In Galatians 5:22, the apostle Paul lists the fruits of the spirit and says one is "self-control," translated as [temperance] by the KJV and many other modern Bibles. The Strong's call number is 1466, and the word looks like this ἐγκράτεια in the original language. The best translation would be "self-control" in all aspects of life. The health message doesn't only consist of controlling you're eating habits; it also requires believers to be temperate in all things, including sexual appetites, drugs, and alcohol, while condemning the lack of proper exercise. The apostle Peter admonishes us to "abstain from fleshly lusts that war against the soul" (1 Peter 2:11). However, in direct opposition to this righteous declaration, there are millions of professed believers who are enfeebling their minds and destroying their bodies by feasting upon the dead carcasses of animals, overeating, drinking alcohol, doing drugs legal or illegal, getting vaccinated while becoming couch potatoes.

The Bible is very explicit on this subject; your body is a gift from God, (1 Corinthians 6:19-20), it is "the temple of the Holy Spirit," and the born-again believer would rather die than destroy their bodies. At the same time, the idea of being enslaved by some pernicious habit is repulsive. If the consumption of dead flesh was ever safe, it's not now; the China Study has established that consumption of animal protein causes cancer and other health-related diseases. In addition, meat-eaters cannot maintain a proper ratio between omega six fatty acids and omega three fatty acids; the proper ratio is [2] two to [1] one; however, meat-eaters have a range around [17] seventeen to [1] one, which causes heart attacks and premature aging. If you do any research, 98% of the population is potassium deficient; the reason for this is that meat-eaters cannot consume enough potassium, which causes heart attacks and a host of other health-related problems. Therefore, with the overpowering information condemning the consumption of [bloody] [fatty] dead animal flesh, if you are consuming the same while refusing to exercise, the Bible makes it perfectly clear that you shall not inherit eternal life. 1 Corinthians 3:16-17, and 1 Corinthians 11:29.

Specifically addressing self-control, the majority of people eat three meals a day, eating highly processed foods and drinks, which produces an extremely overweight and obese population: in addition to causing cancer! The liver is the second most important organ in the body, performing almost 500 specific functions; one of them is detoxification. The brain orders the liver to start detoxifying your system after [12] twelve hours of fasting; this can't happen if you're eating [3] three meals a day; and if you're eating [5] five hours before going to sleep, this causes Alzheimer's and Dementia. If the liver is incapable of detoxifying your system, the brain orders your cells to absorb the toxins in your system, which causes molecular damage at the cellular level. This molecular damage eventually causes oxidative stress and the release of free radicals into the system. As stated before, these free radicals are molecules consisting of atoms lacking the correct number of electrons. When these free radicals come in contact with normal cells, they destabilize them at the molecular level, which causes oxidative stress and the production of additional free radicals into the system, causing cancer and premature aging.

The facts are everyone is only seven years old regardless of their chronological age; every cell in your body is no older than seven years. This is why a thirty-year-old woman looks beautiful and a ninety-year-old woman looks old, wrinkled, and ready to die. The reason for this is the consumption of highly processed foods and drinks along with the consumption of alcohol, the carnivorous diet, vaccinations, drugs, legal or illegal, and promiscuity, all of which cause oxidative stress, which releases free radicals into the system causing premature aging and cancer. With 99% of the population eating three meals a day, their systems are incapable of detoxifying themselves, which is why older people look terrible while younger people look significantly healthier. The consumption of highly processed foods and drinks along with refined sugar and simple carbohydrates is causing damage to your DNA which also causes oxidative stress.

There are over 100 foods and drinks [alleged products] that are sold in the United States but are banned in other countries. It's time to wake up; because you are commanded to do the research, and don't eat or drink anything processed; it's deadly. The apostle specifically addresses self-control in all matters in our lives. We are commanded to research everything we are eating and drinking; however, the majority of people are not; they are eating and drinking without researching what they are putting into their bodies. Therefore, if you are eating simple carbohydrates, and highly processed foods, if you are not exercising regularly, and if you are doing drugs, legal or illegal, you are destabilizing your cells are the molecular level that's causing oxidative stress resulting in the release of free radicals into the system causing premature aging and cancer, which the God of the universe will hold you accountable for in the judgment.

The facts are that 82% of the population is either overweight or obese, while 75% of the population is on some type of prescription medication. These drugs don't cure anyone of disease; they only mask symptoms. As a result, medical malpractice is the third leading cause of death in the United States, and when you include the adverse reactions linked to vaccinations, the two combined are killing more people than cancer and heart disease. The facts are when doctors go on strike, the mortality rates plummet. Obviously, drugs are dangerous, which is the reason they are expressly condemned by the Bible. Consequently, either God had no idea what He was doing when He created humanity, or the healthcare industry has been hijacked by pharmaceutical companies only interested in selling drugs that are not curing anyone of disease. Therefore, if you are taking medications to cure a health-related problem caused by your poor diet rather than changing what you are eating or if you're getting vaccinated to protect yourself from disease rather than following God's original diet [plant-based], the apostle says **you shall not** inherit the kingdom of heaven.

The cure for cancer and preventing premature aging is following God's health laws, which is considered illegal by the United States Government. There is plenty of research establishing there is a link between distorted PH levels and cancer patients. The facts are cancer cells thrive in an acidic [toxic] environment while they cannot survive in a normal, properly alkaline environment. The proper alkaline environment your body needs to sustain life is an extremely small range between 7.35 and 7.45; when these levels are not maintained, you will quickly become a cancer patient. The development of cancer cells makes your body even more acidic [toxic] as they produce large amounts of lactic acid. In addition, there is a lot of verifiable research concluding lactic acid is the primary energy source for cancerous tumors. Consequently, if you have cancer, your PH levels are lower than 7.35 to 7.45, meaning your body is too [toxic] acidic, resulting from your poor diets and terrible lifestyle choices. In addition, cancer and premature aging can be the result of your blood alkaline levels being too high, resulting from an overabundance of [base] in your system. This is caused by too much bicarbonate, lack of potassium, the consumption of alcohol, or poor lung function, resulting in a decrease of [acids] in the blood system like carbon dioxide caused by lack of exercise, smoking cigarettes or doing drugs like marijuana or crack cocaine.

The main organs responsible for maintaining proper PH levels are the liver, lungs, kidneys, and pancreas. At any time, if your PH level decreases below (<7.35), this is called acidosis; however, if your PH level increases above (>7.45), this is called alkalosis, which is directly linked to making the following poor lifestyle choices, eating large amounts of bloody flesh resulting in low potassium levels, poor lung function, resulting from lack of exercise, smoking, drinking, and doing drugs legal or illegal. The acidosis environment (less than <7.35 PH levels) is caused by these lifestyle choices, the carnivorous diet, eating meat, cheese, candy, cake, and processed foods loaded with refined sugar [the typical fast-food diet] and simple carbohydrates; this diet is directly linked to creating an acidosis environment, meaning PH levels lower than (<7.35), which causes oxidative stress resulting in the release of free radicals causing premature aging and the formation of cancer cells. In addition, foods loaded with refined sugar and simple carbohydrates are foods cancer cells love to eat; they need something to eat to survive, so the facts are foods loaded with refined sugar are what cancer cells eat to survive. Therefore, the God of the universe demands that our lifestyle choices should do nothing to interfere with the performance of the organs responsible for maintaining proper PH levels in the system.

The brain monitors your system to maintain your PH blood levels between 7.35 and 7.45 to sustain life and fight off deadly diseases; when these levels are not maintained, you will quickly become a cancer patient. The facts are, unless you're eating two meals a day, nothing between meals or five hours before going to bed, your liver will not be able to detoxify your system. As a result, the brain orders your cells to perform this function, which causes oxidative stress and the release of free radicals into the system resulting in premature aging. Unless you eat a healthy vegan diet loaded with fruits, nuts, grains, seeds, and vegetables, you're not ingesting enough antioxidants to neutralize these free radicals in your system. Consequently, your body will become way too acidic [toxic], which creates a very good environment for cancer cells to form, survive, and grow abnormally faster than your immune system can handle, causing premature aging, and cancer leading to early death. Too much acidity [toxic] is the underlying factor in creating oxidative stress, which causes cancer, premature advanced aging, and other degenerative diseases like type two diabetes, arthritis, fibromyalgia, and several other health-related disorders. The reason for these health-related disorders is oxidative stress which destabilizes the cells at the molecular level and subsequently floods the system with free radicals. Therefore, oxidative stress results from poor diets that cause your blood's PH levels to drop lower than 7.35 and 7.45, which is essential to sustaining life; otherwise, you will quickly become a cancer patient and look old, wrinkled, and unhealthy.

The basic health maxim to maintain health is to have a balanced bio-terrain [meaning proper PH blood levels]; it's important to work on this first, then everything else will return to normal. This balanced bio-terrain occurs when you eat or drink nothing even remotely questionable. For example, if you have an aquarium, and your fish are sick if you only treat the fish and do not fix the environment [that the fish are living in], you will wind up with a bunch of dead fish. It's the environment that matters in order to maintain your health, sustain life, and reversing premature aging. Consequently, the brain is continually monitoring your PH blood levels in order to sustain a healthy immune system so you can fight off deadly diseases and reverse premature aging; however, if your bio-terrain is unhealthy due to eating and drinking food[s] calculated to kill you then you will develop acidosis, your PH blood level decreases below the (<7.35) and oxidative stress will unquestionably result in the release of free radicals causing cancer, advanced premature aging, and other degenerative diseases like type two diabetes, arthritis, fibromyalgia, and several other health-related disorders.

Taking prescription medication to cure cancer or other diseases while your PH blood levels are highly acidic [toxic] is like washing dishes in a sink full of dirty water; even when you put in plenty of detergents, you can't get the dishes clean. If you're eating three meals a day, even if you're vegan, **sooner or later**, your blood will start to become acidic, and your brain will then order your cells to absorb the toxins that have built up in your system [acidic substances] to allow the blood to remain in a slightly alkaline environment. This buildup of toxic waste causes your cells to become more & more acidic and/or toxic, which results in their oxygen levels decreasing; this harms, [damages] the DNA of the cells along with their respiratory enzymes.

Over time these cells increase in acidity, and as a result, some die. These dead cells become acids and toxins floating around in your system that must be absorbed by your normal healthy cells in order to maintain the proper PH blood levels to sustain life. However, some of these acidified [toxic] cells don't die; they amalgamate to adapt to this new toxic environment created by your poor diet and lack of exercise. In other words, instead of dying [as normal cells do in this overly acid-toxic environment], these cells amalgamate to survive in this new toxic environment; consequently, they no longer respond to your brain's commands, and they begin feeding upon the organs designed to sustain life. Therefore, these abnormal cells disregard the indigenous DNA codes you received at birth from your Creator, and without orders from the brain, they start eating healthy organs, which is called cancer, causing advanced aging and leading to premature death.

The direct link between distorted PH blood levels and cancer is undeniable and is caused by lowering the oxygen levels in normal cells, which is directly linked to malfunctioning lungs and poor diets that cause oxidative stress and the release of free radicals into the system. The following information is extremely important to understand; the alkaline levels in your cells are dictated by the alkaline levels in your entire blood system. The alkaline levels in your entire blood system are directly related to the amount of oxygen in your system which is specifically linked to how often you exercise, enhancing the performance of your lungs which is aided by a healthy plant-based diet. The facts are toxic acidic blood holds very little oxygen. So, the more acidic [toxic] your system has become, the less oxygenated your cells are, which is the direct result of a toxic environment resulting from a lack of oxygen caused by your poor lifestyle choices resulting in oxidative stress and the release of free radicals into the system.

To make matters worse, lack of oxygen causes a fermentation process to take place in the actual cell itself, which creates lactic acid, further increasing acidity in the overall system and creating a toxic environment, thereby dramatically reducing the oxygen at the cellular levels, leading to oxidative stress and the eventual amalgamation of healthy cells into cancer cells causing advanced aging and premature death. The facts are the carnivorous diet, lack of exercise and poor lifestyle choices cause your blood to become too acidic, and unless your organs [the liver, lungs, kidneys, and pancreas] can detoxify your system immediately, your PH blood levels will be out of harmony with these levels, [7.35 to 7.45] and this will result in poorly oxygenated cells, resulting in oxidative stress and the release of free radicals in the system, which is an endocrine disruptor causing the formation of cancer cells and other deadly diseases.

In general, degenerative diseases result from acid waste [toxins] building up within our system, which are absorbed by our cells. When we are born, we have the highest alkaline mineral concentration in our system along with strong, healthy cells. It's from that point moving forward that the normal process of being bombarded by toxicants starts to rob us of our life, which takes place through acidifying our entire system resulting from oxidative stress which is an endocrine disruptor that causes premature aging and cancer, along with a host of other degenerative diseases. This toxic bombardment is why these degenerative diseases do not often occur in young people.

The reverse aging process requires two separate steps: physical and chemical, which can only occur if there is a spiritual reformation. The first step in reversing the aging process is to lower the acidity [toxins] in your blood system. Aging is the direct result of the brain ordering acidic toxic wastes to be absorbed by the cells because the liver has become too saturated due to the dietary infractions referenced in this section. The second step is to physically pull out old, stored waste [toxins] from the bloodstream so that it can be discharged from the body as waste, which can only be done through diet and exercise, not prescription medications. In order to accomplish this detoxification of the blood system, it's crucial to go vegan [plant-based] while exercising regularly and eating two meals a day, nothing between meals or five hours before going to bed. As stated before, after twelve hours, the liver starts detoxifying itself by releasing toxins into the system. If these toxins are **not** absorbed, it causes additional oxidative stress and the eventual release of more free radicals into the blood system, which can only be neutralized by antioxidants.

What are antioxidants? If you break down the word antioxidants, you get anti (against) oxidants (oxidation), meaning that antioxidants are substances that repair cell damage caused by oxidative stress at the molecular-cellular level. However, when certain types of damaged oxygen molecules are allowed to freely float around in your system for an extended period of time, they will eventually damage your cell's DNA which causes them to die or disregard the brain's commands due to oxidative stress. The absence of this cellular damage is why young people have the ability to fight oxidative stress more effectively. The result of this DNA cellular damage is what leads to cancer, advanced aging, and premature death.

Consequently, given the relationship between distorted PH blood levels resulting in oxidative stress and the production of free radicals causing cancer and other degenerative diseases, like Alzheimer's, Dementias, autoimmune disease, and inflammatory disorders, the very idea of curing cancer and other degenerative diseases can only be accomplished by alkalizing your blood system, which can only be accomplished [by] adopting a vegan diet, regular exercise, and avoiding processed foods. This is obviously the answer for reversing the aging process, which takes place through the oxidization of your cells, thereby stabilizing the mitochondria. Stabilizing the mitochondria is extremely important because it's the brain's original DNA programming. Therefore, maintaining proper PH blood levels is one of the basic strategies in battling cancer, and premature aging while improving your mental, physical, and spiritual health; it's not accomplished by taking toxic medications or getting vaccinated to protect you from disease.

The threefold warning message of Revelation the fourteenth chapter, commands the guilty inhabitants of the earth to fear God and give glory to Him for the hour of His judgment has come. Revelation 14:6-7. The second part of the three-fold warning message of

Revelation the 14th chapter announces the fall of Babylon (Revelation 14:8) which is repeated in Revelation the 18th chapter just before the final visitation of God's judgments are rained down upon those that have accepted the mark of the beast. Revelation 18:1-4. The third part of the three-fold warning message of Revelation the 14th chapter, promises God's unmingled wrath will be poured out upon anyone that receives the mark of the beast. With this command in mind, how can any believer expect to stand guiltless before the Lord during the final outpouring of God's unmingled wrath while they're eating foods condemned by the biblical standards of health reform? Romans 11:9-10.

The majority of Christendom consume animal flesh that's been declared biblically unclean, such as pork, shrimp, crabs, and lobsters, while almost every Christian eats meat with the animals' blood and fat remaining in its dead carcass. 1 Samuel 14:33-34, Leviticus 3:17, and Acts 15:19-20. Harmful stimulants such as coffee, tea, tobacco, and alcohol are ingested without solicitude for their health-destroying consequences. The consumption of intoxicants [such as beer, wine, and liquor] is consumed with wanton disregard for the health of the body and what these harmful products are doing to your brain. These intoxicants are killing the frontal lobes of the brain, which is the moral center making it almost impossible for those consuming these harmful products to receive the seal of the living God upon their foreheads. Revelation 7:1-4, Revelation 14:1-5, and Proverbs 20:1. These stimulants lessen physical strength, and whatever affects the body affects the mind, which lessens our ability to worship God as commanded by the threefold warning message of Revelation the fourteenth chapter.

When meat, dairy, highly processed fast food, candy, ice cream, soft drinks, beer, wine, and liquor are ingested, the immune system can no longer operate correctly to protect us from disease; consequently, the unsuspecting multitudes of this generation have turned to drugs [pharmaceuticals] and toxic vaccines to protect them from governmental planned-demic[s] releasing manmade pathogens into society. The United States Government is controlled by extremely sick individuals who have partnered with pharmaceutical companies, and they have collectively hijacked the healthcare industry. As a result of this unholy union, the healthcare industry is not in business to cure anyone of disease; they are in business to make profits for the pharmaceutical companies, which they do by selling toxic drugs that cure no one of disease. These toxic drugs administered by the healthcare industry only mask symptoms while causing more side effects. These side effects conjure into existence justification for prescribing more toxic drugs, which produce additional side effects. It's a mad, very profitable cycle of slavery that's controlling 75% of the population! Consequently, we have a malnourished, overweight, obese, drugged-out, sickly, prescription drug-taking stupefied population that's been successfully brainwashed into thinking that drugs and toxic vaccines are essential for their protection against these manmade diseases referred to above as planned-demic[s].

The conspiracy is so obvious that no time will be spent elaborating upon the profitability of the planned-demic[s] humanity has been forced to endure over the last few decades. The CDC owns the patents for the Coronavirus, and they have been involved in the GOFR [the gain of function research] for at least the last twenty [20] years. The GOFR is specifically designed to mutate animal viruses [that cannot infect humans] into deadly pathogens capable of infecting and killing millions of humans. Suffice it to say this information regarding the CDC and the GOFR, along with the biblical condemnation of vaccines and toxic drugs, should be extremely clear, yet millions are mindlessly taking drugs to cure themselves of self-inflicted diseases while they are foolishly complying with government vaccine mandates, for themselves and their children, which the Bible expressly condemns. Therefore, it's obvious they have become willingly ignorant of the apostle's warning that those who do these things shall not inherit the kingdom of heaven.

The Bible predicts during the closing events of earth's history that right-wing religious extremists will gain control of our legislative assemblies and mandate their own religious beliefs that expressly violate God's moral law, in the same way, governments are presently mandating universal vaccinations, which violate God's health laws. Revelation 13:11-17. Consequently, in like manner, the Bible predicts those that comply with the same type of unholy mandates shall receive "the mark of the beast" upon their forehead or their right hand; consequently, God's unmingled wrath will be poured out upon them without mercy. Conversely, those that remain loyal to the health laws as mandated by the Most High while obeying His moral law, which includes the seventh-day sabbath, shall receive the seal of the living God upon their foreheads. The majority of Christians eat and drink whatever they want, ignoring the fact that these unhealthy practices are completely out of harmony with the worship they are commanded to give their Creator as commanded in Revelation the 14th chapter; as a result, they will receive "the mark of the beast" upon their forehead or their right hand while those remaining loyal to their Creator's laws will receive the seal of the living God upon their foreheads.

The fearful threefold warning message of Revelation 14:6-11 commands the guilty inhabitants of the earth to worship God and give glory to Him for the hour of His judgment has come. It's important when considering this announcement that you are required to investigate everything you are eating and drinking, or you will be condemned in the judgment and destroyed by the holy angels at the Lord's second coming. In Matthew 13:41, the apostle says at the second coming, "the Son of man will send his angels, and they shall gather out of his kingdom all causes of sin and all evildoers." The Greek word σκάνδαλα translated as "all causes of sin" in Matthew 13:41, appears several times in the New Testament. In its exact form, the Greek word σκάνδαλα appears in the New Testament (4) four times, and with different stems, the Greek word σκάνδαλα appears an additional (11) eleven times. The best possible translation for the Greek word σκάνδαλα is "that which causes sin" in our lives, representing our fallen nature, the overpowering propensity to transgress God's holy law that humanity inherited at birth without their consent from our earthly parents. Those who have "_not_" put to death their propensity to transgress God's holy law (the Greek word σκάνδαλα translated as "all causes of sin" in Matthew 13:41) before the gospel invitation closes will be destroyed by the holy angels at the Lord's second coming. Romans 8:12-13.

The significance of the above-referenced information is the Greek word σκάνδαλα translated as "all causes of sin" in Matthew 13:41 (RSV), also appears in its singular form in Romans 11:9-10 and is translated as "pitfall" by the RSV and "stumbling block" by the KJV. In Romans 11:9-10, the Greek word σκάνδαλον translated as "pitfall" (RSV) or "stumbling block" (KJV) is without question referring to our fallen nature, producing [the desires of the flesh] representing the overpowering propensity to transgress God's health laws. When properly investigated, the message contained in Matthew 13:41 becomes obvious, at the Lord's second coming, the holy angels will destroy those who have been enlightened on the subject of health reform yet choose to ignore God's health laws at the expense of their own physical health and eternal salvation. Matthew 13:41, Romans 11:9-10. This proves that those who have not put to death their fallen nature, Romans 8:12-13 their God is their stomach, and they would rather forfeit eternal life rather than change their poor diets. Therefore, with the three angels' message in mind, how can anyone expect to stand guiltless before the Lord during the investigative judgment while they are eating and drinking anything condemned by the biblical standards of health reform? Romans 11:9-10, 1 Corinthians 11:29, 1 Corinthians 3:16-17.

The scriptures tell us our bodies are "God's temple" and if anyone destroys God's temple, God will destroy those that do the same during the final eradication of sin and sinners in the lake of fire, which is the second death. Revelation 20:12-14. The apostle says God's temple is holy, and that temple is you" (1 Corinthians 3:16-17). Consequently, in Revelation 14:6-7 because the prophet employs the same Greek word translated as worship in Romans 12:1, the health message is without question the right arm of the three angel's message of Revelation the fourteenth chapter. The reason for this should be apparent; the call to worship God includes how we are caring for our bodies and minds in preparation to stand when Christ appears. Revelation 14:6-7, Romans 12:1-2 and 1 Corinthians 11:29. It is impossible to truly worship God while we transgress His health laws, particularly when they dramatically affect our bodies and our minds. 1 Corinthians 3:16 and 1 Corinthians 6:19-20.

The spiritual preparation necessary to stand in the presence of the Lord at His second coming involves the perfection of Christian character, which is a process of putting to death our fallen nature, representing the character defect that causes sin in our lives. Romans 7:4-6. As established earlier, putting to death our fallen nature is clearly a prerequisite for receiving eternal life. Revelation 8:12-13, Galatians 5:16-24, 2 Thessalonians 2:13. Overcoming dietary infractions will be a natural byproduct for those who have been born again (Romans 11:9-10) because dietary infractions are caused by the fallen human nature we received at birth from our earthly parents. Galatians 5:19-21. If you are eating incorrectly, you are doing so because your nature is still out of harmony with your Creator's nature; consequently, you cannot worship God properly if you still possess "that which causes sin" in your life. Romans 12:1. The same Greek word σκάνδαλον translated as "that which causes sin" in our lives (Matthew 13:41) is the same Greek word σκάνδαλον translated respectively as "pitfall" (RSV) and stumbling-block (KJV) in Romans 11:9. Therefore, at the Lord's second coming, the holy angels will destroy those who still possess their fallen nature, representing the character defect that causes them to transgress God's laws, both His health laws and His moral law, which is the Ten Commandments. Matthew 13:41, John 14:15.

It's important to do a brief review in order to establish the next point; the Bible says, "The Son of man will send His angels, and they will gather out of His kingdom 'all causes of sin' and all evildoers." Matthew 13:41. As established earlier, the Greek word σκάνδαλον translated as "all causes of sin" in Matthew 13:41, is the same Greek word σκάνδαλον appearing in Romans 11:9, translated as "pitfall" by the Revised Standard Version and as "stumbling block" by the King James Version. As established earlier in this book, the Greek word σκάνδαλον translated as "all causes of sin" in Matthew 13:41, represents the fallen nature we inherited at birth from our earthly parents, which is the character defect "that causes sin" in our lives.

The Bible is very clear on this point, at the Lord's second coming the holy angels will destroy those who possess this character defect at the Lord's second coming. Matthew 13:41. In Romans 11:9, the Apostle Paul quotes the Psalmist, "Let their tables become a snare and a trap, and a 'pitfall' and a retribution for them; let their eyes be darkened so that they cannot see." The word table in this Bible verse obviously represents what is being eaten on the table, not the actual table itself. The prophet is very clear, those eating incorrectly do so because they are controlled by their fallen nature, defined as "that which causes sin" in their lives. Romans 3:23. The Apostle Paul says when you are eating or drinking, "do all to the glory of God" (1 Corinthians 10:31), and also says you should "present your bodies as a living sacrifice, holy and acceptable to God, <u>which is your spiritual worship</u>." Romans 12:1-2.

Without question then how and what you eat, and drink is a form of worship you are commanded to render to the Creator of the universe and is consequently salvational. When you eat correctly, you are rendering proper worship to the Lord; the call to health reform is an integral part of the third angel's message because the same word translated as worship in Revelation 14:6-11 is also employed by the apostle in Romans 12:1. All those who still possess "that which causes sin" in their lives, will eat incorrectly; because they will not be able to control their diets. The "everlasting gospel" proclaimed to the world by God's last day remnant people (Revelation 14:6-7) not only includes the judgment message, but it also includes a specific call to worship God in all manner of life, which includes what we put on our tables. Romans 11:9-10.

Despite the arguments just presented, it needs no prophet's eye to condemn the consumption of dead animals today and/or to abstain from the use of intoxicating liquor, tobacco, and the use of toxic drugs, legal or illegal, simple carbohydrates, and health-destroying harmful DNA-altering vaccines. These harmful products have proven to be a terrible curse to those living in our generation. See the movie

Food Inc. and/or go to www.earthlings.com. along with watching the videos titled Lethal Injection and The Game Changers. The professed believers of this generation, who have such a high and lofty opinion of their spiritual condition, should consider how they eat and drink before arrogantly claiming to have the assurance of salvation now and in the judgment. Revelation 3:17-19. After human probation closes, all those who still possess "that which causes sin" in their lives will be continually eating incorrectly while taking drugs to cure their health-related problems caused by their poor diets and getting vaccinated to protect themselves from man-made diseases; therefore, these apostates will subsequently be destroyed by the holy angels at the Lord's second coming.

The worship of God commanded by the three angels of Revelation 14:6-11 must affect every aspect of our lives. Those claiming to be ready to enjoy the companionship of holy angels should eat or drink nothing that's having a deleterious effect on their bodies and minds. There is now strong evidence to conclude that diet and exercise must go hand in hand to advance the Christian experience of worshiping the Creator of the heavens as commanded by the threefold warning message of Revelation the 14th chapter. The Apostle Paul communicated that those who neglected physical work would soon become enfeebled and more likely to be overcome by Satan's temptations. He desired to teach young ministers that by working with their hands, by exercising their muscles and ligaments they would become strong to endure the toils and deprivations awaiting them in the gospel field. The apostle realized that his own teachings would lack vitality and force if he did not keep all parts of his body properly exercised. 1 Corinthians 9:27, See also Acts of the Apostles Page 352 by E.G. White. Therefore, the true worship of God as commanded by the three angel's message of Revelation 14:6-11 must affect every aspect of our lives; consequently, this is why those who are born again will obey God's health laws and His moral law, which is the Ten Commandments.

Specifically addressing the subject of exercise and its relationship to the longevity of life [and the health of our body and mind] a group of scientists performed experimental research on laboratory rats. The scientists used one hundred laboratory rats all genetically modified to die within one year. The rats were separated into two groups; (50) fifty rats were forced to exercise (45) forty-five minutes per day while the other group of rats did not exercise. The rats that exercised forty-five minutes per day all lived longer than one year while the rats that did not exercise all died within six to eight months from the start of the experiment.

There was another study performed on people who needed stints due to poor diets resulting in atherosclerosis; a disease presently affecting almost 75% of Americans. As stated before, atherosclerosis is a disease where the artery wall becomes blocked due to the build-up of fatty materials referred to as cholesterol in the blood system. There were (100) one hundred people involved in the study. The one hundred people were divided into two groups. Those who received stents and those who did not, the (50) fifty people who received stents did not exercise. The (50) fifty people who did not receive stents all participated in a scheduled exercise program. The failure rate after one year among those who received the stent, but did not exercise, was (33%) thirty-three percent. The failure rate among those who did not receive the stent but participated in the scheduled exercise program was only (12%) twelve percent.

The worship of God must affect the mental, physical, and spiritual aspects of our lives. With this information at our disposal, it's clear that diet and exercise will enable professed Christians to worship their Creator properly as commanded by the third angel of Revelation the 14th chapter. In the judgment no value will be attributed to a mere profession of faith, we are not saved by our works, however, we are definitely judged by our works. Therefore, how can professed believers continue to eat or drink anything harmfully affecting their bodies and/or neglect the exercise necessary to sustain life arrogantly claim to have "the assurance of salvation now and in the judgment" simply because they believe Christ died for their transgression of the law?

The facts are that 90% of the minerals, nutrients, and vitamins have been depleted from our food supply due to monocropping. As a result, nutritional deficiencies exist at epidemic proportions among the unsuspecting multitudes of this generation. This deficiency is nondiscriminatory, affecting the rich, poor, black, white, or hispanic, resulting in 95% of the population suffering from at least one mineral and vitamin deficiency. This mineral and vitamin deficiency exists in the United States where 82% of the population is either overweight or obese; consequently, we have a population that's malnourished and overweight or obese at the same time. The reason for this deficiency is that 90% of the vitamins, minerals, and nutrition have been depleted from the soil due to monocropping, which is employed by almost 100% of farmers in the United States. Consequently, it's extremely important to research the nutritional value of the foods you are consuming in order to get the most nutritional value per caloric intake. The point is because 90% of the minerals, nutrients, and vitamins have been depleted from our food supply due to monocropping it's essential to do two things, start exercising regularly, this will enable you to consume more calories which means you're taking in more minerals, nutrients, and vitamins. The facts are muscle burns three to four times more calories than fat; as a result, those exercising will be healthier. The second thing is planting your gardens and fertilizing them with rock dust, which is something that I do, and the results are amazing. You can get the rock dust from any quarry[s]. This will return additional minerals, nutrients, and vitamins to the soil which has been depleted from the soil due to monocropping.

The United States Government is controlled by sick warmongering psychopaths who stay in power primarily because the unsuspecting multitudes have been dumbed down due to their dietary infractions, the consumption of alcohol, and drinking water spiked with fluoride and chlorine. It was during the Second World War that Hitler used fluoride to sedate and stupefy prisoners, and the United States Government is doing the same thing to its citizens; it's far easier to control unintelligent sedated dumbed-down people than it is an extremely intelligent awakened population. Therefore, because the God of the Universe has given us brains and requires us to employ the same to investigate the facts, and since there is no charge for using them, only those that are determined to obey God's laws, His health laws, and His moral law, which is the Ten Commandments, will be among those who will receive the seal of the living God upon their foreheads. Revelation 14:1-5.

23

LET THE READER UNDERSTAND

The title of this series of books is "The Abomination of Desolation," the phrase is employed several times in the book of Daniel and is also referenced by Christ in the gospels. Matthew 24:15-16, and Mark 13:14. The Hebrew word שִׁקּוּץ translated as "abomination," has a Strong's call number of 8251, and its definition is something horrific. The Hebrew word שָׁמֵם translated as "desolation," has a Strong's call number of 8074, and its definition is to destroy something and/or make it desolate (dead) as opposed to being spiritually alive. Revelation 3:1. The phrase is employed by the Prophet Daniel several times, and when considering the grammatical context when it's first employed by the prophet in Daniel 8:12-13, the correct (understanding of what's being communicated) should be translated as "the transgression that intentionally makes a host of believers spiritually "desolate." After receiving the explanation of the vision of Daniel the eighth and ninth chapters, the prophet says he understood the vision and that in the last days, a great multitude would also understand the vision of Daniel 8:14 (and after making this specific statement in Daniel 10:1), the same prophet permanently alters the phrase to represent that a host of unsuspecting believers [are being] (or) have been given over to the abomination that makes them spiritually desolate throughout the ages, Daniel 9:27, Daniel 11:31, Daniel 12:11, Matthew 24:15-16, and Mark 13:14.

However, it's also important to note that in these Bible verses, Daniel 8:12, Daniel 9:27 and Daniel 11:31, the prophet employs a grammatical nuance indicating that the giving over of a host of believers to the Abomination of Desolation is the direct result of their religious leaders [intentionally] distorting the everlasting gospel into a license to sin. It's also important to understand that it's not only the "little horn" [power] that's performing the intentional action of giving a host of unsuspecting believers over to "the abomination of desolation," this action has been taking place throughout the ages. In addition, it's also important to understand the action of giving a host of believers over to the abomination of desolation is accomplished by removing "the daily" [mediation] of Christ to forgive sins, while casting the truth concerning His final work of mediation to the ground by giving it to the fallen sons of men, the combination of which creates "the illusion of salvation now and in the judgment" once the believer performs some outward action, the sacrificing of animals, or confessing your sins to a priest or by claiming justification by faith, and that this specific abomination "prospers by reason of a gospel that tolerates continued transgressions," which leaves believers spiritually desolate. Daniel 8:11-13, Daniel 9:27, Daniel 11:31, Daniel 12:11 and Mathew 24:15.

The plan of distorting the everlasting gospel into a license to sin is without question diabolical and is designed to be specifically accomplished by [subliminally] removing Christ as the believer's only mediator and judge; consequently, this "abomination" creates the illusion of salvation now and in the judgment and embodies the very foundation of the spiritual chicanery meticulously designed to make a host of believers spiritually "desolate." The abomination that makes desolate represents the false doctrines employed by our church leaders that remove Christ as the believer's only mediator and judge; and is designed to create the illusion of salvation now and in the judgment simply by claiming justification by faith, which has been witnessed in every religious movement throughout the ages. In harmony with this conclusion, the correct understanding of the action taking place in Daniel 8:12 is referencing the little horn power magnifying itself against the Most High by removing the daily mediation of Christ to forgive sins while simultaneously usurping His final work of mediation by casting it to the ground thereby giving a host of unsuspecting believers over to "the transgression that makes them spiritually desolate."

In Daniel 8:12, the transgression that makes a host of believers spiritually desolate represents the deliberate action of the little horn power distorting the everlasting gospel into a license to sin by and through its church doctrines, which is specifically designed to create the illusion of salvation now and in the judgment, once some outward action is continually performed by professed believers. The direct application of this diabolical plan manifested itself in the past dispensation when the Jewish Sanhedrin were seen intentionally advancing false doctrines that subliminally incorporated the malignant idea that constantly sacrificing animals assured the Jews, participating in the sacrificial services, of their salvation; consequently, the action of sacrificing animals created for these misguided Jews "the illusion of salvation now and in the judgment," Isaiah 1:13.

However, the same fiendish deception has manifested itself in this dispensation, after the Catholic continually confess their sins to a priest and perform the penance assigned them in the confessional, this legalistic action creates for these misguided souls the illusion of salvation now and in the judgment, Daniel 11:31, while the same basic deception is deceiving a host of mainline Protestant and Evangelical believers, evidenced after repeatedly claiming justification by faith, the illusion of salvation now and in the judgment is created, Daniel 12:11. Consequently, the work of sanctification in all three of these specific applications ceases to exist, therefore, the True Witness says it's all salvation by works that will even deceive "if possible God's very elect" during the last days of Earth's history. Matthew 24:15-16 and Mathew 24:24.

Let the reader understand, that the same deception, the abomination that makes a host of misguided believers spiritually desolate

(Matthew 24:15-16) is now presently being advanced by the pastors of God's last-day remnant people, evidenced by the fact that after claiming justification by faith, these Laodicean believers, thinking they have complied with the conditions of salvation, feel saved and forgiven, consequently, the illusion of salvation now and in the judgment is created for God's very elect, "not knowing [meaning they are totally ignorant of the fact that] they are actually spiritually wretched, pitiable, poor, blind, and naked" in God's sight. Revelation 3:15-17.

As established earlier, Satan's diabolical plan, referred to as the "Abomination of Desolation," is designed to remove Christ as the believers' only mediator and judge, immediately after claiming "justification by faith," in either dispensation. In the last days of Earth's history, when you see "the abomination of desolation" permanently standing in the holy place of the New Covenant Heavenly Sanctuary thereby universally removing Christ as the Laodicean believer's only mediator and judge, in the same way the Jews did in the past dispensation, or the Catholic, mainline Protestant and Evangelical believers are doing in this dispensation, **let the reader understand**; this is a call for wisdom (Revelation 17:8-9) because it's always the same deception.

The prophecy says those stuck in Babylon cannot recognize this deception, primarily because the beast that carried the antichrist of Bible prophecy to power, is Satan, the eighth beast; consequently, they can't recognize they are being deceived by Satan, because "it," [the antichrist of Bible prophecy] "was" [existing] for 1,260 years, and then "it was not" existing, after it, [the antichrist of Bible prophecy] received its deadly wound (in the year 1798); however, even after Satan's fifth head/king of Revelation the 17th chapter, [the antichrist of Bible prophecy], received "its deadly wound," the prophet says [it still] "existed," and immediately transferred its wealth and power to Satan's sixth head/king of Revelation the 17th chapter, that would be capable of financing the direct fulfillment of Counter-Reformation Theology; however, it's all the same false theology previously employed by the antichrist of Bible prophecy, only it's now being disguised today as [Dispensational Theology], accordingly, it still removes Christ's daily mediation to forgive sins while usurping His final work of mediation, which is the investigative judgment, thereby creating the same illusion of salvation for a host of unsuspecting mainline Protestant and Evangelical believers, that's specifically designed to lead them to their eternal perdition.

Additionally, Christ says, after its again universally re-established in all of Christendom, [it] will deceive, "if possible, even God's very elect," meaning those attending the Church of Laodicea. Revelation 3:15-17. Therefore, when you see the "abomination of desolation," representing the false doctrines removing Christ as the Laodicean believer's only mediator and judge, which creates the illusion of salvation now and in the judgment, permanently standing in the most holy place of the new covenant heavenly sanctuary, meaning universally accepted by God's very elect as one of their doctrinal beliefs, "**let the reader understand**," that this generation shall not pass away until you see the Son of man coming in the clouds of heaven with power and great glory.

CONCLUSION
WILL THOSE WHO ARE SAVED BE MANY

When Christ was asked "Will those who are saved be many," His response was "Enter by the narrow gate, for the gate is wide and the way is easy that leads to destruction and those who enter by it are many; however, the gate is narrow, and the way is hard that leads to life and those who find it are few." Mathew 7:13. Speaking of the religious leaders of His day Christ said, "You can know them by their fruits." The false doctrines advanced by the dispensational churches create only the illusion of salvation now and in the judgment simply by making a profession of faith in Christ's atoning blood, this is not what the Bible teaches, because it does not pass the "fruit" test. The false doctrines creating the illusion of salvation now and in the judgment grants professed believers access to heaven against their will evidenced by them never forming sanctified characters in this life before human probation closes. If these allegedly saved believers would receive eternal life, the sanctification required to abide in the presence of the "Most High" must be forced upon them; therefore, if you think about it, Satan and his evil angels were cast out of heaven for refusing to obey the laws governing heaven; why then, are professed believers going to receive eternal life for refusing to abide by the same laws Satan and his evil angels were expelled from heaven for refusing to obey?

The very foundation of Satan's plan to distort the everlasting gospel into a license to sin requires the unsuspecting multitudes to accept two distinct and malignant principles; they must accept false doctrines that tolerate continued transgressions while exemplifying a perfect hatred towards the laws of the Government of Heaven, which includes God's health laws. Daniel 7:25, Daniel 8:13. Conversely, the everlasting gospel specifically states, "if we sin deliberately after receiving knowledge of the truth there no longer remains a sacrifice for sin but only a fearful prospect of judgment and the lake of fire that will consume the transgressor that was originally prepared for the Devil and his evil angels. Hebrews 10:26-27.

The deceptions circulating in Christendom today assure the sin-loving multitude of their eternal salvation while they continue to transgress God's holy law. Daniel 11:31-32. This series of books will establish that the pastors and priests who create this illusion of salvation are giving a "host" of believers over to the "abomination of desolation" spoken of by the Prophet Daniel in these Bible verses. Matthew 24:15, Daniel 9:27, Daniel 11:31-32, and Daniel 12:11. The "abomination" referred to by the Prophet Daniel represents the false doctrines that remove Christ as our only mediator and judge thereby creating the illusion of salvation now and in the judgment immediately after claiming Christ paid the penalty you rightfully deserve for your transgressions of the law, which leaves the deceived multitudes spiritually "desolate." Throughout the ages, this "abomination" has made a "host" of believers spiritually "desolate" while they feel "rich and increased with goods and in need of nothing" 1) simply by sacrificing animals, Isaiah 1:12-17. 2) confessing their sins to a priest, (Daniel 11:31-32) or 3) claiming Christ paid the penalty you rightfully deserve for your transgressions of the law. Daniel 12:11. The appetite professed believers have for following these false teachers is the reason why Christ said, "The gate is wide, and the way is easy, that leads to destruction" and those deceived by the false doctrines, "creating the illusion of salvation," will be many. Matthew 7:13.

Since Satan's expulsion from heaven, to obtain support for his rebellion it's been his plan to introduce false doctrines that distort the everlasting gospel into a license to sin. The distortion of the everlasting gospel into a license to sin has given a "host" of believers a false sense of carnal security, Daniel 9:27, the Jews, Daniel 11:31, the Catholics, Daniel 12:11, the Protestants, Matthew 24:15, and the Church of Laodicea. The True Witness explicitly warns His professed people, that the pastors of the Church of Laodicea are blind guides. These blind guides are promising God's professed people the very gates of paradise _**not knowing**_ their true spiritual condition is deplorable in God's sight. Revelation 3:17-18. Throughout the ages Satan's goal has always been to take out the watchmen on the walls of Zion [first] so that through their efforts, believers feel saved immediately after sacrificing animals, confessing their sins to a priest, or claiming Christ's death paid the penalty you rightfully deserve for your transgressions of the law. As a result of this deception, the unsuspecting multitudes make no _**individual effort**_ to attire themselves with the "wedding garment" (Revelation 19:8) consequently they are left spiritually desolate and are therefore incapable of standing in the presence of God without a mediator after human probation closes. Malachi 3:2.

The key to understanding the Laodicean message is that it's addressed to the pastors of God's last day remnant church. Consequently, it is essential to understand that the deceived multitudes are not being warned that their unsanctified spiritual condition is deplorable in God's sight. After the close of human probation, this fearful proclamation is made, those who have formed "sanctified" characters let them be "sanctified" still and those who are evil, (possessing unsanctified characters) let them remain unsanctified still. Revelation 22:11. Christ does not say those claiming justification by faith let them be saved still. All those having fought the good fight of faith have formed sanctified characters in harmony with God's holy law; consequently, they are naturally following His health laws. They have received the seal of the living God upon their foreheads before Christ ceases His final work of mediation in the heavenly sanctuary.

When Christ ceases His final work of mediation, mercy no longer pleads for the guilty inhabitants of the earth. Those who have accepted the false doctrines creating the illusion of salvation simply by confessing their sins to a priest or claiming justification by faith will receive "the mark of the beast" upon their forehead willingly; however, those who understand the real issues in the conflict yet chose to comply with the dictates of the state will receive the mark of the beast upon their right hand when the mark is enforced by its image during the closing scenes of earth's history. Revelation 13:11-18. It's important to understand that those who have received the mark of the beast upon their foreheads have been given over to the "abomination" that makes them spiritually "desolate." This group loves a religion that tolerates their continued transgressions of God's holy law. Matthew 24:15, Daniel 9:27, Daniel 11:31-32, Daniel 12:11. As a result of their unsanctified spiritual condition, they will not be able to stand the brightness of the Lord's second coming, because it will be to them a consuming fire.

The same basic deceptions employed by the antichrist of Bible prophecy to deceive the sin-loving multitudes of past generations (Daniel 7:8, Daniel 7:24-25, Daniel 8:11-13, Daniel 11:31-34, Revelation 13:1-10) will be employed to deceive God's "very elect" during the closing scenes of earth's history. Matthew 24:15, Revelation 3:17-18. Those whose names are not found written in the Lamb's Book of Life from the foundation of the world cannot recognize they are being deceived by the same legalistic gospel employed by the antichrist of Bible prophecy to deceive a "host" of unsuspecting Catholic believers. Through the deceptions of priestcraft, Christ is removed as the Catholic's only mediator and judge. Revelation 17:8-9. However, the deceptions of priestcraft, is nothing new, throughout the ages Satan's deceptions have remained the same; the illusion of salvation is created once some outward profession of faith is made in Christ's atoning blood while the authority to make the final determination of salvation in the judgment is transferred to someone other than Christ, our only mediator, and judge. The scriptures are clear, claims made upon justification must lead to the sanctification of your character or you cannot receive a positive verdict in the judgment. Romans 6:20-22, Matthew 13:41-42. Therefore, in order to deceive God's "very elect" Satan's plan has remained the same, a legalistic gospel is introduced specifically by the pastors of the Church of Laodicea that is specifically designed to remove Christ as the believers' only mediator and judge, which creates the illusion of salvation now and in the judgment once some outward profession of faith is made in His atoning sacrifice.

The scriptures plainly state Christ came to save His people *"from"* their sins; consequently, redemption means to cease "from" transgressing God's holy law. Matthew 1:21. The facts are if you are still a sinner you are not saved, 1 Corinthians 4:3-5, the Bible is clear, no one is saved who is a transgressor of God's holy law in this life or the next. Those who arrogantly claim to have "the assurance of salvation now and in the judgment" are usurping Christ's authority to make that determination during His final work of mediation, which is the investigative judgment. 1 Corinthians 10:12-13. At the last supper, Peter arrogantly stated if everyone betrayed Christ, he would remain loyal. However, Christ's response to him was all of His disciples, including Peter, would deny Him at His trial and subsequent crucifixion. In like manner, those who arrogantly claim they are saved, sanctified, and forgiven of their sins will deny Christ once adversity comes upon them if the truth has not become the abiding principle in their lives.

The reason Peter denied Christ was caused by his gradual separation from his dependency upon Christ, fashioned by the same arrogant assumption of salvation witnessed in the Christian world today. Accordingly, "Self-confidence led him [Peter] to the belief that he was saved, and step after step was taken in the downward path until he could deny his Master. Never can we safely put confidence in ourselves or feel this side of heaven, that we are secure against temptation. Those who accept the Savior, however sincere their conversion, should never be taught to say or to feel that they are saved. This is misleading. Everyone should be taught to cherish hope and faith; but even when we give ourselves to Christ and know that He accepts us, we are not beyond the reach of temptation. God's word declares that many shall be purified and made white and tried. Daniel 12:10. Only he who endures the trial will receive the crown of life. James 1:12. Those who accept Christ, and in their first confidence say I am saved, are in danger of trusting to themselves. They lose sight of their own weakness and their constant need for divine strength. They are unprepared for Satan's devices, and under temptation, many, like Peter, fall into the very depths of sin. We are admonished, "Let him that thinketh he stands take heed lest he fall." Christ's Object Lessons, by E. G. White, Page 155. Our only safety is in constant distrust of self and dependence upon Christ's help and mediation to forgive our sins. 1 Corinthians 10:12. Peter did not believe in once saved always saved. He, like many others today felt assured of his salvation now and in the judgment immediately after making a profession of faith in Christ's atoning blood; however, God's word declares we must be "born again" before eternal life can be granted anyone in the judgment; the truth must become the abiding principle in our lives.

The sad fact remains, during Christ's first advent He specifically warned that few will ultimately be saved having been deceived by their religious leaders. Considering Christ's statements, why do we see so many believers having such an over-inflated opinion of their spiritual condition simply because they have professed faith in Christ's atoning blood when Christ's testimony indicates most believers will be lost for refusing to form sanctified characters in this life before the gospel invitation closes. The second volume of this series of books will reveal the identity of the antichrist of Bible prophecy establishing how Satan's deceptions operate once established as doctrinal beliefs among God's professed people. Daniel 8:11-13. It will be established that the antichrist of Bible prophecy is a church organization that prospers by reason of a gospel that tolerates continued transgressions. Daniel 8:11-13. It's so easy to recognize. However, those who cannot recognize the foundation of Satan's deceptions will be lost. They will be lost because they have rejected the "keys to the kingdom of heaven." As a result of rejecting the "keys to the kingdom of heaven," they begin declaring their own sins forgiven and themselves assured of their salvation now and in the judgment immediately after claiming Christ paid the penalty they rightfully deserve for their transgressions of the law. They do this **_not knowing_** their unsanctified spiritual condition is deplorable in God's sight.

The reader is advised to enter by the narrow gate, for the gate is wide and the way is easy, which leads to destruction and those who enter by it are many. However, the gate is narrow, and the way is hard, which leads to eternal life, and those who find it will be but very few. Matthew 7:13-14. With Christ's advice having been received, why are all of God's professed people being told that they can have the assurance of salvation now and in the judgment immediately after claiming Christ died for their transgressions? The scriptures are clear, only those who by the Spirit put to death "that which causes sin" in their lives will be deemed worthy to receive eternal life. "True sanctification means perfect love, perfect obedience, perfect conformity to the will of God. We are to be sanctified to God through obedience to the truth. Our conscience must be purged from dead works to serve the living God. We are not yet perfect, but it is our privilege to cut away from the entanglements of self and sin and advance to perfection. Great possibilities, high and holy attainments, are placed within the reach of all." The Acts of the Apostles Page 565 by E.G. White.

This is our assurance of salvation; those claiming Christ paid the penalty they rightfully deserve for their transgressions make this claim [in the outer court of the heavenly sanctuary], consequently, justification, is not the atonement for our transgressions. The atonement is very specific; it's the blotting out of sins truly forgiven from the Book of Records at the conclusion of Christ's final work of mediation, which is the investigative judgment. In harmony with this understanding, the holiness of character possessed by the 144,000 is the holiness of character that all must possess if they expect to receive a positive verdict in the judgment.

The correct understanding of "**_the message for this time_**" includes comprehending that the following events will commence immediately after the seventh angel sounds his trumpet, which takes place during the third woe [representing the great tribulation] when the 144,000 will receive the seal of the living God upon their foreheads in preparation for the closing events of Earth's history and the soon close of human probation. Revelation 10:4. Therefore, the author of this series of seven books, titled "The Abomination of Desolation" will eventually establish the following facts.

(One) that dispensational theology is diametrically opposed to "*the message for this time*" as defined in the first volume of this series of seven Books titled "The Abomination of Desolation," and that the "Daily Mediation" of Christ to forgive sins is as essential to the plan devised for our salvation as was His death upon Calvary's cross because by His death He gained the right to mediate for the real forgiveness of sins and as the True Witness determine in the judgment who is worthy to receive eternal life.

(Two) in harmony with this understanding, that, the great multitude of believers in Revelation 7:9, understand the "vision" of Daniel 8:14, consequently, they will make the proper spiritual preparation necessary to stand in the presence of God without a mediator in the heavenly sanctuary after human probation closes. Therefore, the author will establish that dispensational theology is nothing more than Counter-Reformation Theology in disguise, consequently, it will be established that "the seventy weeks of years" of Daniel 9:24-27 represent a separate 490-year probation period specifically allocated for the Jewish Nation to spiritually prepare for Christ's first advent, which they failed to do and were rejected as God's special people by the Most High in the year 34 AD, therefore, as a result of their bankrupt spirituality, at the conclusion of the 490-years of Daniel 9:27, others were raised-up to proclaim the everlasting gospel to a dying world.

(Three) The great multitude of believers (Daniel 10:1) who understand the "vision" of Daniel 8:14, are the 144,000, who fully comprehend that "the seventy weeks of years" (Daniel 9:24-27) represent the first 490 years of the 2,300-year prophecy of Daniel 8:14, which terminates in the year 1844 when the prophet says, "then shall the sanctuary be cleansed." This understanding is [diametrically] opposed to Dispensationalism, which is nothing more than the Papacy's Counter-Reformation Theology in disguise. In this series of books titled "The Abomination of Desolation," there is a chapter titled "*The Systematic Dismantling of Dispensationalism.*" In this chapter, titled "The Systematic Dismantling of Dispensationalism," it will be established that the Dispensational Churches are promoting doctrines that only those not studying the Bible for themselves could believe. The author will use the exact Bible verses utilized by the Dispensational Churches to establish their false doctrines to Systematically Dismantle Dispensational Theology. The arguments contained in the chapter titled, "The Systematic Dismantling of Dispensationalism" will be so overpowering that anyone reading the information provided will immediately separate themselves from these harlots of the earth, identified as the Catholic, mainline Protestant, and the Evangelical Churches, who are referred to by the second angel as the Churches of Babylon. Revelation 14:8.

(Four) *The message for this time* also includes the identity of the king of the north, Daniel 11:40-45, who is destroyed during the [alleged] Battle of Armageddon as advanced by the dispensational churches, signaling to the 144,000 that human probation has closed. In this series of books titled "The Abomination of Desolation," there will appear a chapter titled "The Third Woe," which gives overpowering information specifically detailing the chronology of Revelation the seventeenth chapter, identifying Satan's Sixth head/king, as the Rothschild banking cartel, who is financing the direct fulfillment of "Counter-Reformation Theology" along with the formation of Satan's seventh head/king of Revelation the 17th chapter, representing the United States of America under the control of Apostate Protestantism, symbolized in Bible prophecy as the Papacy's image, that will when completely formed in Protestant America, will last only a short time.

(Five) In this series of books titled "The Abomination of Desolation," information will be provided that's in harmony with the second angel's message, dictating the reasons why the mainline Protestant Churches were officially rejected by the Most High in the year 1828 at the conclusion of the 1,290 years of Daniel 12:11. The reasons given for God's rejection of the mainline Protestant Churches in the year 1828, at the conclusion of the 1,290 prophetic days of Daniel 12:11, is the abomination of desolation had been again universally established in all of Protestantism!

(**Six**) It will be established in this series of books titled "The Abomination of Desolation," that God's last day remnant people is the Seventh-day Adventist Church that will become a worldwide religious movement proclaiming the threefold warning message of Revelation the 14th chapter to every nation, tribe, tongue and people starting after the conclusion of the 1,335 years of Daniel 12:12; therefore, it will be established that the Seventh-day Adventist Church is a movement of Bible prophecy.

(**Seven**) In this series of seven books titled "The Abomination of Desolation," it will be established that the sealing of God's people takes place during the great tribulation and that the sealed are grammatically linked by case agreement to the 144,000 who are grammatically linked by case agreement to the great multitude of believers who have clothed themselves in white robes during the great tribulation (Revelation 7:1-14); consequently, the spiritual description of the 144,000 (Revelation 14:1-5) applies to anyone deemed worthy to receive eternal life by Christ during His final work of mediation, which is the investigative judgment. Revelation 14:13.

(**Eight**) In this series of seven books titled "The Abomination of Desolation," it will be established that the prophecy says the 144,000 have been purchased from fallen humanity as the first fruits of God and the Lamb, and in their mouth, no lie was found regarding the everlasting gospel, consequently, they are spotless. In addition, a word-for-word study will be performed on Daniel the 11th chapter, which will clearly reveal who the king of the North [is] and how he comes to his end with no one to help him during the alleged Battle of Armageddon as advocated by the dispensational churches. Daniel 11:45. Therefore, the 144,000 who understand the prophecies have not defiled themselves with women, meaning the harlots of the earth, identified as the Churches of Babylon, consequently, they have rejected Dispensational Theology because they have a clear understanding of the closing events of earth's history.

(**Nine**) The specific time the second woe has passed will be established (Revelation 11:14) clearly dictating that we are now living during the great tribulation when God's people will receive the seal of the living God upon their foreheads and are made capable of standing in the presence of God without a mediator after human probation closes. (Revelation 7:9). The close of human probation takes place when the king of the north is destroyed during the alleged Battle of Armageddon as advocated by the dispensational churches. Therefore, in this series of books titled "The Abomination of Desolation," it will be established that "the sealed" are not only commandment keepers, (Revelation 14:12), but they have specifically rejected Dispensational Theology as advanced by the harlots of the earth, the Churches of Babylon, previously identified as the Catholic, mainline Protestant, and Evangelical Churches of this generation. Revelation 14:4-5.

(**Ten**) In this series of books titled "The Abomination of Desolation," the exact time for the commencement of the Third Woe and the Great Tribulation), will be established, Revelation 11:15-19 with an in-depth word-for-word study of Daniel chapters, seven, (7) eight, (8) and nine (9) will be conducted. It will be established that the Papacy is the antichrist of Bible prophecy that prospers by reason of a counterfeit gospel that tolerates continued transgressions. They accomplish this deception by removing Christ's "daily work of mediation" to forgive sins while casting the truth concerning Christ's final work of mediation, which is the investigative judgment, to the ground by giving it to the fallen sons of men. Daniel 8:11-14, Revelation 11:1-3.

(**Eleven**) The author will identify Satan's sixth head/king as the Rothschild Banking Cartel and that Satan's seventh head/king is the United States of America under the control of Apostate Protestantism that will when completely formed in Protestant America, represent an exact image of the Papal Church during the Dark Ages and will enforce "the Mark of the Beast" during the closing scenes of earth's history. Revelation 13:11-18. In addition, the author of this series of seven books titled "The Abomination of Desolation" will do a word-for-word in-depth study on the Papacy's claim to have the authority to forgive sins in the confessional, and using the same Bible verses the Papacy employs to establish this alleged authority, John 20:20-23 it will become clear that there is no biblical evidence giving the priest the authority or the ability to forgive anyone's sins. Consequently, after this in-depth study is performed the reader will become perfectly convinced that only Jesus Christ has the ability to forgive sins and the authority to determine in the judgment who is worthy to receive eternal life. Therefore, after the reader clearly understands that being truly forgiven of a specific sin means there no longer remains any propensity to commit that same sin ever again in the future; consequently, after this understanding becomes clear in the reader's mind, they will have "the keys to the kingdom of heaven."

(**Twelve**) Along with establishing that <u>*the message for this time*</u> is specifically designed to direct the minds of the unsuspecting multitudes to the commencement of Christ's final work of mediation, which is the investigative judgment, (Revelation 14:6-13) and that "the daily mediation" of Christ to forgive sins is as essential to the plan devised for our salvation as was His death upon Calvary's cross, the following volumes in this series of seven books titled "the Abomination of Desolation" will firmly establish that the real antichrist of Bible prophecy is the Roman Catholic Church "that blaspheming power that thinks themselves able to change God's times and the law," and that the "Mark of the Beast" is directly related to whose commandments you are keeping, the Papacy's altered Ten Commandments or God's Holy Ten Commandments, which includes the Seventh-day Sabbath, as a memorial of Jesus Christ creative power, while honoring Him as the Law-Giver.

In addition, the author of this series of seven books titled "The Abomination of Desolation" will clearly establish that there is a famine in the land, not of bread or water, but of hearing the words of the Lord being proclaimed from the pulpits of Christendom today. In addition, it will be clearly established that what you're eating and drinking is without question salvational. 1 Corinthians 11:29, and 1 Corinthians 3:16-17. The reader needs to understand that the healthcare industry is not in business to cure anyone of disease, they are in business to make a profit, which they do by selling drugs, and the drugs they sell cure no one of disease, prescription medications only mask symptoms. In addition, taking prescription medications is expressly condemned by the Bible, and if you are taking prescription medications to cure a disease caused by your poor diet or lifestyle choices you shall not receive eternal life.

(**Thirteen**) In this series of books titled "The Abomination of Desolation," it will be established that _**the message for this time**_ is designed to communicate that God's special people are not the Jews, they will be Christians and commandment keepers (meaning all ten of them, including the seventh-day sabbath) [Revelation 14:12] along with the importance of strictly obeying His health laws. 1 Corinthians 11:29. The very idea that the Jews are God's special people today is being palmed off upon the unsuspecting multitudes by the Churches of Babylon as Dispensational Theology, which is Counter-Reformation Theology in disguise.

(**Fourteen**) In this series of books titled "The Abomination of Desolation," it will be established that all those found worthy to receive eternal life from the start of the investigative judgment to the close of human probation will have, during the great tribulation, washed their robes and made them white by the blood of the Lamb [making them capable of standing] in the presence of God without a mediator after human probation closes. Revelation 14:12-13.

(**Fifteen**) It will be clearly established in the coming series of books that the reason why dispensational theology is diametrically opposed to _**the message for this time**_ is that it's identifying Satan's sixth head/king, Revelation 17:1-18, as the Rothschild Banking Cartel that's financing the direct fulfillment of dispensational theology, which as stated before is nothing more than Counter-Reformation Theology in disguise. In addition, it will be clearly established in the coming series of books that Satan's sixth head/king is financing the development of Satan's seventh head/king, the Papacy's image, which is Apostate Protestantism. Apostate Protestantism has accepted Edward Irving's Secret Rapture Theory. Edward Irving was a demon-possessed tongue-talking Presbyterian minister and all those presently talking in tongues the way it's being manifested today in the Catholic, mainline Protestant, and Evangelical Churches are without question just as demon-possessed as Edward Irving, the founder of Evangelical Theology, which is Satan's religion.

(**Sixteen**) It will be clearly established in the coming series of books that the Dispensational Churches hate God's laws, both His moral law and His health laws, and the revealing of the same is the engine that fuels the loud cry of Revelation 18:1-4 being proclaimed to the world by the 144,000, that includes the relationship of health reform to your own personal salvation which is expressly taught in the scriptures. 1 Corinthians 11:29, 1 Corinthians 3: 15-17, Romans 12:1, Galatians 5:20, and Revelation 18:23.

(**Seventeen**) In this series of books titled "The Abomination of Desolation," it will be established that the outpouring of the seven last plagues will last for one year, Revelation 18:8, and that,

(**Eighteen**) the loud cry will plainly identify the real antichrist of Bible prophecy as the Papacy, the first beast power of Revelation the thirteenth chapter, and not the one-man antichrist as advocated by the satanically controlled dispensational churches of this generation, Revelation 18:17, and that,

(**Nineteen**) Apostate Protestantism is fast developing into an image of the first beast of Revelation the thirteenth chapter that will enforce the worship of the Papal beast during the closing events of Earth's history, Revelation 14:11-14, consequently, they will be identified as the false prophet in Revelation 19:19-20 that worked the great signs that caused the unsuspecting multitudes to accept the mark of the beast upon their foreheads or their right hands.

(**Twenty**) The author of this series of books will specifically establish the correct interpretation of the 1,000-year millennium, revealing that the secret rapture and dispensational theology is a total deception (Revelation 20:1-15) and that it will be,

(**Twenty-One**) established in the minds of many that the loud cry (Revelation 18:1-4) is actually *the true message for this time*, as defined by the author of this book, and that the sealed,

(**Twenty-Two**) have made a firm commitment to health reform which is a motivating factor for a small remnant of God's very elect, who still believe in the original Advent Message, to declare that the great day of God's wrath is soon coming upon the guilty inhabitants of the Earth with blazing speed, resulting, in the question being asked who can stand before it, and

(**Twenty-Three**) with the answer to the question emphatically stating that only the sealed can stand the brightness of Christ's Second Coming and that they are,

(**Twenty-Four**) those who are grammatically linked by case agreement to the 144,000, representing "that great multitude of believers," (Revelation 7:9) [who understand the vision of Daniel 8:14] consequently they have spiritually prepared for the Second Coming, [specifically by washing their robes and making them white by the blood of the Lamb during the great tribulation], thereby making them capable of standing in the presence of God without a mediator after human probation closes, which is *the real message for this time*. Revelation 6:14-17. Therefore, the author of this series of seven books titled "The Abomination of Desolation," will establish *the real message for this time* is that the holiness of character possessed by the 144,000 is the holiness of character that all must possess if they expect to receive a positive verdict in the judgment. Revelation 14:4-5, Revelation 7:13-17.

In closing, it's essential to understand that if you are presently transgressing God's holy law you are a slave to sin, and Christ says that a slave shall not inherit eternal life. John 8:34-35. The Apostle Paul establishes the same point in Romans 6:14-16, by asking the following rhetorical question, "Therefore *then, may* we continue to sin since we are not *under the law* but *under grace*?" The apostle emphatically states not to wish for that, because you already know to whom you are presently yielding *yourselves* as *obedient servants,* you are **slaves** to whom you obey; either of sin, which leads to death, or obedience, *which leads to righteousness.*" It's important to remember that sin is defined in the Bible as the transgressions of God's holy law. Romans 3:19-20, Romans 7:7. So obviously, the apostle is not stating that God's holy law is no longer binding upon believers living in this dispensation, evidenced by declaring that the wages of sin "leads to slavery and death" (Romans 6:23) in the lake of fire, while the same apostle categorically denying that our faith in Jesus Christ makes void the law that defines sin in our lives! Romans 3:31.

The Bible says if we sin deliberately after receiving the knowledge of the truth there no longer remains a sacrifice for sin only the fearful prospect of judgment condemning the transgressor to their eternal destruction in the lake of fire, which is the second death. Hebrews 10:26-27. The Apostle James says that God's law, which defines sin, will be the standard of righteousness used by Christ to evaluate our character during His final work of mediation, which is the investigative judgment. James 2:8-12. In harmony with this understanding, Christ told Nicodemus that we must be born again if we are to receive eternal life, (John 3:7) and the same apostle says that a born-again believer would rather die than knowingly transgress God's holy law. 1 John 3:9. Therefore, the gospel has established that after claiming justification by faith you must form sanctified characters in harmony with God's holy law in preparation for the investigative judgment. Romans 5:1-2, and 2 Corinthians 3:17-18.

The message for this time is found in Revelation the 7th and 14th chapters. In Revelation the 7th chapter the sealed are grammatically linked to the 144,000 who receive the seal of the living God upon their foreheads during the great tribulation. Revelation 7:13-14. The sealed are grammatically linked to the great multitude of believers in Revelation 7:9, who have washed their robes and made them white by the blood of the Lamb in preparation for the investigative judgment. This last statement is evidenced by the information in the first angel's message in Revelation the 14th chapter. The sealed are those who have not defiled themselves with the false gospel advanced by the harlots of the earth, Revelation 14:4 at the time the first angel makes his announcement, and the sealed are grammatically linked to the great multitude of believers in Revelation 7:9 who understand the "vision" of Daniel 8:14 points directly to the start of the investigative judgment, Revelation 11:15-19, consequently, they are following the Lamb wherever He goes in His final work of mediation, which is the investigative judgment brought to light in Revelation the 14th chapter.

The prophecy specifically says the 144,000 are redeemed from the earth as first fruits because they understand that God's holy law is the standard of righteousness used by Christ to evaluate their characters during the investigative judgment. Revelation 14:5. In harmony with this understanding, Revelation the 14th chapter contrasts the 144,000, who have received the seal of the living God upon their forehead, with those who have received "the mark of the beast upon their forehead or their right hand," primarily because they have been deceived by the false gospel advanced by the harlots of the earth that tolerates continued transgressions. Consequently, the distinction between these two groups is made very clear, the keeping God's holy ten commandment law, which would include the seventh day Sabbath, Revelation 14:12 marks the distinction between those who receive the mark of the beast upon their foreheads and those who receive the seal of the living God upon their foreheads. Therefore, the message for this time is that the holiness of character possessed by the 144,000 is the holiness of character that all must possess if they expect to receive a positive verdict during Christ's final work of meditation, which is the investigative judgment. Revelation 14:6-7.

COMING SOON...
VOLUME II

In the Volume II of this series, the real antichrist of Bible prophecy will be revealed, along with explicitly defining exactly what the mark of the beast is. Throughout history, theologians have speculated as to the identity of the antichrist. In Volume #2 of this seven-book series, we will not speculate as to the identity of the antichrist, but rather discuss twelve points of identification, clearly establishing that the antichrist is a church organization that prospers by reason of a gospel that tolerates continued transgressions. In Volume #2 I will prove that the first beast of Revelation 13:1-10 is the antichrist, also depicted as the "little horn," power of Daniel, Chapter 7, who relentlessly persecuted God's people for almost 1,000 years. The antichrist is depicted as the "Woman Babylon" and the "Mother of Harlots." He is the originator of the earth's abominations, which have made a host of believers spiritually desolate from false gospel that tolerates open transgressions to God's law. The prophet says the beast carrying the "Mother of Harlots" to power is Satan, having "seven heads and ten horns." Revelation 12:3-7, Revelation 17:1-6. In Revelation Chapter 17, Satan is depicted as the scarlet-colored beast, having "seven heads and ten horns," who carried his fifth head/king to power for 1,260 years of prosperity by reason of a false gospel that tolerated continued transgressions. Consequently, the prophet says, "All those that dwell upon the earth will worship" the first beast of Revelation (Chapter 13), and "Everyone whose names have not been written in the Lamb's book of life." Revelation 13:8 and Revelation 17:8. Therefore, those who cannot recognize the antichrist and are part of a church that preaches a gospel that tolerates continued transgressions, will be led to their eternal perdition while thinking they are saved and forgiven of their sins!

Don't be one of them. Don't be fooled. Satan is crafty, evil, and after every soul! My intentions are to arm you with the knowledge you'll need to fight back the onslaught of evil that has besieged this world. We, us, the real church, are the only hope! Stay tuned for Volume II, coming soon.

Excerpt from Volume II

Throughout history, humanity has been plagued by various deadly diseases, including the black plague, malaria, smallpox, and "HIV" human immunodeficiency virus, the virus that causes AIDS. These are just a few deadly diseases humanity has been forced to encounter. The alleged deadly virus COVID-19 is the latest killer disease humanity has encountered, and according to the U.S. Center for Disease Control, COVID-19 has been declared a pandemic. The U.S. Center for Disease Control and Prevention (CDC) is a privately owned company masquerading as a government agency. The CDC first recognized COVID-19 as a pandemic on March 11th, 2020; however, the following information represents suspicious activity! "The 6.2 trillion-dollar stimulus package" [HR 748] was introduced to Congress in January 2019, almost one year before even one Covid-19 case was reported in the World. The "6.2 trillion-dollar stimulus package" was allegedly passed to offset the negative effects of 60 million people dying worldwide of COVID-19; however, our government gave the U.S. banks almost $5 trillion dollars of the $6.2 trillion dollar stimulus package. The real reason the $6.2 trillion dollar stimulus package was introduced to Congress was the U.S. Banks were bankrupt and the U.S. economy was going to crash, evidenced by the Repo rates spiking to 10% on 9-17-2019. However, prophetically speaking, it's obvious the pandemic was totally satanic and designed to serve as another 5 trillion-dollar government bailout of the U.S. banks, in addition to crashing the economy, killing the U.S. dollar, and replacing it with a one-world cashless fiat currency system thereby giving government[s] total control over who can buy or sell anything without the approval of the central banksters. Therefore, this sequence of events just described will give the governments total control over who can buy or sell anything without their approval, which is in harmony with Bible prophecy. Revelation 13:15-17.

Interesting Information

The CDC owns the patents to the coronavirus; (see Federal Case Number 120-CV-01384 LPS) consequently, it's a man-made pathogen; you can't patent something that occurs naturally in nature. In addition, the CDC has been involved in the "gain of function research" GOFR for at least the last 20 years. (see Federal Case Number 120-CV-01384 LPS). The GOFR is designed to mutate animal viruses [that cannot infect humans] into deadly pathogens capable of killing millions of people. Genetic research has indicated that COVID-19 was created in a laboratory, and (Federal Case Number 120-CV-01384 LPS) has provided overpowering information establishing that the CDC along with several other prominent U.S. universities, Harvard University and North Carolina Chapel Hill were involved in the GOFR, which is mutating animal viruses [that cannot infect humans] into deadly pathogens capable of killing millions of people, which is completely illegal. Consequently, in 2014-15 when world-renowned virologists started complaining about the CDC's involvement in the GOFR, the NIH [National Health Institute] was forced to cut the CDC's funding. After the NIH cut the CDC's funding, the GOFR was subcontracted to a company named Eco-Health Alliance, which the United States Government through the Obama and Trump administrations subsequently funded to continue with the GOFR, which represents criminal behavior. Interesting information, Peter Daszak is the president of Eco-Health Alliance and a board member of the WHO, the World Health Organization. When the same world-renowned virologists continued complaining about the United States funding the GOFR because it violates the Nuremberg Ten laws and treaties, the GOFR was moved to the Wuhan Institute of Virology (WIV), so they could finish mutating SARS Covid-2 into Covid-19 essentially creating a bio-weapon capable of killing millions of people.

The owners of the Federal Reserve Bank, here in the United States, hereafter the central banksters, subsequently instructed the WIV to release Covid-19 into society. Once this new killer disease (COVID-19) appeared in the United States, there was a mad rush to find a cure, so government mandates were issued to mass vaccinate the entire population allegedly to protect them from this man-made planned demic. The planned demic produced enormous profits for "the merchants and the great men of the earth" who are deceiving the unsuspecting multitudes with their sorcery. Revelation 18:23. The Greek word φαρμακεία, translated as "sorcery" in Revelation 18:23, is pronounced "pharmakeia," with its first definition being injecting poisons, toxic prescription medications into your system. When researching any killer disease, investigators first attempt to establish its origin. They try to come up with patient zero, the first person who contracted the killer disease. This discovery can be a long and laborious process. Therefore, notwithstanding that, after a cursory examination was performed establishing the CDC owns the patents to the coronavirus, and they have been involved in the GOFR for the last 20 years, (see Federal Case Number 120-CV-01384 LPS) humanity has encountered one killer disease that's far more onerous to implement its cure; however, we know the sin virus originated in Eden when Adam first transgressed God's holy requirements and its cure is not the Greek word φαρμακεία, translated as "sorcery" in Revelation 18:23, which is pronounced "pharmakeia," the cure for the sin virus is the everlasting gospel.

The Message For This Time: Part 1

It will be firmly established in this first book, spearheading a series of seven books, titled "The Abomination of Desolation" that the everlasting gospel was designed to "bring about the obedience of [our] faith" in all of God's holy requirements. Romans 1:5, Romans 16:25-26, 1 Corinthians 3:16, 1 Corinthians 11:29. With this thought in mind, these Bible verses (Hebrews 10:26-27, John 3:36) more clearly represent the message for this time (Revelation 14:6-13) than does the peace and safety message currently being presented from the pulpits of Christendom today. The Apostle Paul says if you sin deliberately after receiving the knowledge of the truth, there no longer remains a sacrifice for sin but only a fearful prospect of judgment pointing to the lake of fire that will consume the transgressors of God's holy law shortly after the conclusion of the investigative judgment. Hebrews 10:26-27, Daniel 7:9-10. In harmony with this understanding, the Apostle John says, "He who believes in the Son has life; however, he who does not obey the Son shall not see life, but the wrath of God rests upon him." John 3:36.

The scriptures do not recognize the idea that belief represents anything other than noncompromising obedience to all of God's holy requirements. James 2:19-26, John 14:15. The compromised state of existence, that all of humanity has been born into, required the introduction of the everlasting gospel to successfully counteract humanity naturally joining Satan in his rebellion against the authority of the government of Heaven. Romans 3:23, Romans 8:1-4. However, the introduction of the everlasting gospel doesn't make void our responsibility to obey God's holy requirements (Romans 3:31); on the contrary, it establishes our acknowledgment that the wages of sin should require the death of the transgressor and that man as God created him could obey all of God's holy requirements. In support of this understanding, the Bible emphatically states that after the gospel invitation closes, sinners will be destroyed in the lake of fire with the Devil and his evil angels, which is the second death, (Revelation 20:15) and this destruction of the Devil, his evil angels, in the lake of fire, along with all of humanity that have joined Satan's rebellion will be condoned by the fallen and unfallen worlds. Consequently, the Bible says sin shall not arise a second time.

The everlasting gospel was introduced to correct the sin problem in fallen humanity, not the exact opposite as subliminally advocated by the majority of the Christian churches today. In order to eliminate any confusion on this subject, the Bible clearly defines sin as the transgression of God's holy law (Romans 3:19-20, Romans 7:7-12) and specifically states that God's holy law will be the standard of righteousness used by Christ to evaluate our characters during His final work of mediation, which is the investigative judgment. James 2:8-12. Therefore, the message for this time points believers to the soon close of Christ's final work of mediation, which is the investigative judgment and the spiritual preparation necessary to "endure the day of His coming," for the prophet says, "Who can stand when He appears." Malachi 3:1-5, Revelation 14:6-7, Daniel 7:9-20.

www.ingramcontent.com/pod-product-compliance
Lightning Source LLC
Chambersburg PA
CBHW040744020526
44114CB00048B/2907